Personal Risk Management and Property-Casualty Insurance

Personal Risk Management and Property-Casualty Insurance

Edited by

Mary Ann Cook

Arthur L. Flitner

2nd Edition • 3rd Printing

The Institutes
720 Providence Road, Suite 100
Malvern, Pennsylvania 19355-3433

2nd Edition • 3rd Printing • November 2016

Library of Congress Control Number: 2013934319

ISBN 978-0-89463-663-9

Foreword

The Institutes are the trusted leader in delivering proven knowledge solutions that drive powerful business results for the risk management and property-casualty insurance industry. For more than 100 years, The Institutes have been meeting the industry's changing professional development needs with customer-driven products and services.

In conjunction with industry experts and members of the academic community, our Knowledge Resources Department develops our course and program content, including Institutes study materials. Practical and technical knowledge gained from Institutes courses enhances qualifications, improves performance, and contributes to professional growth—all of which drive results.

The Institutes' proven knowledge helps individuals and organizations achieve powerful results with a variety of flexible, customer-focused options:

Recognized Credentials—The Institutes offer an unmatched range of widely recognized and industry-respected specialty credentials. The Institutes' Chartered Property Casualty Underwriter (CPCU®) professional designation is designed to provide a broad understanding of the property-casualty insurance industry. Depending on professional needs, CPCU students may select either a commercial insurance focus or a personal risk management and insurance focus and may choose from a variety of electives.

In addition, The Institutes offer certificate or designation programs in a variety of disciplines, including these:

- Claims
- Commercial underwriting
- Fidelity and surety bonding
- General insurance
- Insurance accounting and finance
- Insurance information technology
- Insurance production and agency management
- Insurance regulation and compliance

- Management
- Marine insurance
- Personal insurance
- Premium auditing
- Quality insurance services
- Reinsurance
- Risk management
- Surplus lines

Ethics—Ethical behavior is crucial to preserving not only the trust on which insurance transactions are based, but also the public's trust in our industry as a whole. All Institutes designations now have an ethics requirement, which is delivered online and free of charge. The ethics requirement content is designed specifically for insurance practitioners and uses insurance-based case studies to outline an ethical framework. More information is available in the Programs section of our website, TheInstitutes.org.

Flexible Online Learning—The Institutes have an unmatched variety of technical insurance content covering topics from accounting to under-writing, which we now deliver through hundreds of online courses. These cost-effective self-study courses are a convenient way to fill gaps in technical knowledge in a matter of hours without ever leaving the office.

Continuing Education—A majority of The Institutes' courses are filed for CE credit in most states. We also deliver quality, affordable, online CE courses quickly and conveniently through CEU. Visit CEU.com to learn more. CEU is powered by The Institutes.

College Credits—Most Institutes courses carry college credit recommendations from the American Council on Education. A variety of courses also qualify for credits toward certain associate, bachelor's, and master's degrees at several prestigious colleges and universities. More information is available in the Student Services section of our website, TheInstitutes.org.

Custom Applications—The Institutes collaborate with corporate customers to use our trusted course content and flexible delivery options in developing customized solutions that help them achieve their unique organizational goals.

Insightful Analysis—Our Insurance Research Council (IRC) division conducts public policy research on important contemporary issues in property-casualty insurance and risk management. Visit www.insurance-research.org to learn more or purchase its most recent studies.

The Institutes look forward to serving the risk management and property-casualty insurance industry for another 100 years. We welcome comments from our students and course leaders; your feedback helps us continue to improve the quality of our study materials.

Peter L. Miller, CPCU
President and CEO
The Institutes

Preface

Personal Risk Management and Property-Casualty Insurance is the textbook for the course of the same name in the Personal Concentration track of The Institutes' Chartered Property Casualty Underwriter (CPCU) designation program.

Many insurance professionals deal with personal insurance and are required to help their customers manage their personal loss exposures. Accordingly, the textbook provides learners with the knowledge they need to understand their customers' personal loss exposures and apply the appropriate personal insurance coverages and other risk management techniques. Additionally, the course provides learners with the decision-making skills required to profitably price, underwrite, and manage a personal insurance portfolio in today's competitive insurance marketplace.

Highlights of this textbook include educational objectives that are directly linked to key content that will assist the learner in mastering relevant topics. Special exhibits link learning content to real life by using practical, current-event illustrations. Case studies based on business scenarios provide students with practical applications of the core content.

The Institutes would like to thank the individuals in the insurance and risk management community who have contributed to the development of this content, including CPCU Advisory Committee member F. Scott Addis, CPCU; Cheryl L. Ferguson, EdD, CPCU, AU; and Cathy Zielinski.

The Institutes are grateful to the many individuals who have contributed to previous editions of this textbook, including manuscript reviewers and CPCU Advisory Committee members.

For more information about The Institutes' programs, please call our Customer Service Department at (800) 644-2101, email us at CustomerSuccess@ TheInstitutes.org, or visit our website at TheInstitutes.org.

Mary Ann Cook

Arthur L. Flitner

Contributors

The Institutes acknowledge with deep appreciation the contributions made to the content of this text by the following persons:

Richard Berthelsen, JD, CPCU, AIC, ARM, AU, ARe, MBA

Pamela J. Brooks, MBA, CPCU, AAM, AIM, AIS

Kenneth R. Dauscher, PhD, CPCU, AIM

Cheryl Ferguson, EdD, CPCU, AU, API, AAI, AIM

Martin J. Frappolli, CPCU, FIDM, AIS

Nancy Germond, MA, ARM, AIC, ITP

Valerie Ullman Katz, CPCU, MBA, ARM, AIM

Melissa O. Leuck, ARM, CTP

Pamela Lyons, FCIP, CRM

Jacqueline McCloy Pell, FCIP

Ann Myhr, CPCU, ASLI, ARM

Karen Porter, JD, CPCU, ARP, AIS

Kathleen J. Robison, CPCU, ARM, AU, AIC, CPIW

Judith Vaughan, CPCU, AIC

Contents

Assignment 11

Personal Risk Management

Educational Objectives

After learning the content of this assignment, you should be able to:

▷ Describe the property loss exposures that individuals and families might face in terms of each of the following:

- The assets exposed to loss

- The causes of loss

- The financial consequences of loss

▷ Describe the liability loss exposures that individuals and families might face in terms of each of the following:

- The assets exposed to loss

- The causes of loss

- The financial consequences of loss

▷ Demonstrate how the six steps of the risk management process can guide individuals and families in their risk management decisions.

▷ Describe how risk control and risk financing techniques are used by individuals and families.

▷ Given a scenario regarding an individual or a family's property and liability loss exposures, evaluate the loss exposures and recommend an appropriate risk management technique for each.

Personal Risk Management

PROPERTY LOSS EXPOSURES

Virtually all individuals and families have property. Property used, stored, enjoyed, or displayed is property that may be exposed to loss. Such property may include a family's house, an individual's television, or a child's framed photograph. Losses to property can result in serious financial consequences to those who suffer the losses.

All property is subject to **property loss exposures**. Property may be destroyed, damaged, stolen, or lost, or may otherwise suffer a decrease in value because of a particular cause of loss (or peril).

Individuals and families face countless situations in their daily lives that present the possibility of a property loss that has financial consequences. For example, an individual's belongings could be destroyed by a flood, or a family's home and its contents could be destroyed by a tornado. These situations, and many more, are loss exposures that individuals and families might face.

Property loss exposures can be examined in terms of three loss exposure elements:

- Assets exposed to loss
- Causes of loss
- Financial consequences of loss

Property loss exposure
A condition that presents the possibility that a person or an organization will sustain a loss resulting from damage (including destruction, taking, or loss of use) to property in which that person or organization has a financial interest.

Assets Exposed to Loss

Assets exposed to loss are any items of property that have value. A common method of classifying property uses two broad categories— **real property** and **personal property**. Much like the term "real estate," real property includes land, buildings, attached structures, plants growing on the land, and anything embedded in the land, such as minerals. All other property, such as a bicycle or a sofa or a computer, is classified as personal property. Individuals and families can be faced with loss exposures by owning or having a legal interest in one or both of these types of property. See the exhibit "Examples of Assets (Property) Exposed to Loss."

Real property (realty)
Tangible property consisting of land, all structures permanently attached to the land, and whatever is growing on the land.

Personal property
All tangible or intangible property that is not real property.

Examples of Assets (Property) Exposed to Loss	
Real Property	Land, buildings, other structures attached to the land (swimming pool, storage shed, flagpole), whatever is growing on the land (trees, crops), and anything embedded in the land (foundations, underground pipes)
Personal Property	Dwelling contents, high-value articles (jewelry, silverware), rare or unique property (antiques, art work), business personal property, motor vehicles, trailers, watercraft, and aircraft

[DA00140]

Real Property

Individuals and families face property loss exposures that can arise from several types of owned real property. All real property is tangible property having a physical form that can be seen or touched.

For example, a single-family home purchased by an individual could pose a significant real property loss exposure. The land also indicates an additional real property loss exposure, as may any foundations or underground pipes. Any sheds attached to the land, or anything growing on it, such as trees, also could present real property loss exposures.

Personal Property

Listing all the specific kinds of personal property that individuals and families can own that are exposed to loss would be virtually impossible, when one considers the scope of the personal property definition. A general sampling of some personal property loss exposures includes those experienced by homeowners, renters, or condominium owners, who likely own furniture, televisions, and other electronic entertainment equipment. Additional household personal property can include computers, appliances, dishes, carpets, sports equipment, clothing, tools, books, jewelry, cameras, and digital recording devices. A homeowner could park a car in the driveway (the car is personal property) or have a boat at a vacation home (the boat is personal property). Additionally, personal property can include intangible property such as patents or copyrights (which are also often referred to as intellectual property). See the exhibit "Insuring and Pricing Personal Property Loss Exposures—Personal Property Categories."

Causes of Loss

Many causes of loss (or perils) can damage or destroy both real and personal property. In terms of real property, causes of loss faced by individuals and families include fire damage to a dwelling or storage shed, lightning damage

Insuring and Pricing Personal Property Loss Exposures— Personal Property Categories

For the purpose of identifying, insuring, and pricing personal property loss exposures, personal property can be divided into these categories:

Dwelling contents—the broadest category of personal property. A dwelling's contents may include furniture, appliances, draperies, electronics, kitchenware, groceries, clothing, sports equipment, tools, toys, and many other items common to the use of a dwelling as a home. Such items are generally insured as a group rather than individually.

High-value personal property—items of personal property worth considerable sums of money. Examples include jewelry, silverware, furs, and firearms. These items may be partially covered under the category of dwelling contents. However, they usually require a more specific type of insurance, because many property insurance policies limit the maximum amount of coverage available under specific loss conditions (for example, jewelry coverage is more limited for a theft loss under a homeowners policy than for a fire loss), for this category of personal property.

Rare or unusual property—items whose value comes from their unique characteristics. These items may often be one of a kind or one of a very few in existence in terms of like kind and quality and are not easily replaced. Examples of this type of property are antiques, works of art, coin or stamp collections, and other collectibles. Such items should be specifically listed for insurance purposes because most insurance policies limit the amount that an insurer will pay for this type of personal property.

Business personal property—personal property, such as office furniture and computer equipment, used for business purposes. Because most personal insurance policies limit or exclude coverage for business personal property, additional insurance coverage may be necessary.

Motor vehicles, trailers, watercraft, and aircraft—mobile property typically excluded (or covered only up to a certain limit) in policies covering dwellings and their contents. Because these items present unique loss exposures, they should be separately insured using the appropriate coverage form.

To keep the cost of personal insurance reasonable, personal insurance policies are designed to cover the loss exposures faced by the average person or family. If personal policies included unlimited coverage for all types of personal property, premiums needed to provide such coverage would be higher than most people could afford or would be willing to pay. For example, the cost to insure individual, expensive jewelry items against theft is not automatically included in homeowners policy premiums. Insurance professionals can help individuals and families understand the relationship between cost and coverage by explaining that, in order to keep insurance premiums reasonable for the average consumer, it is fair for those persons who own valuable or unusual items to pay an additional premium to insure them.

[DA00139]

to a tree, earthquake damage to a swimming pool, and wind damage to roof shingles. Personal property causes of loss can include theft of a car or damage to a car in an accident, disappearance of luggage and its contents while the owner is on vacation, and loss of a diamond that falls from its setting in a ring.

Even damage to a motorboat that collides with a dock is a personal property loss. Any loss that results from the countless possible causes of loss that can affect an individual's or a family's property has consequences in terms of asset value.

Financial Consequences of Loss

When property is damaged or destroyed, individuals and families sustain certain financial consequences. Financial consequences of loss can include one or more of these outcomes:

- Reduction in value of property—The difference between the value of the property before the loss (preloss value) and after the loss (post-loss value). For instance, if an individual severely damages the front bumper of an auto by colliding with a tree, the auto would be worth less after the accident than it was worth before the accident.

- Increased expenses—Expenses in addition to normal living expenses that are necessary because of the loss. For example, increased living expenses could include the expenses an individual incurs following a dwelling fire, such as the cost of renting a hotel room, while the dwelling is temporarily uninhabitable.

- Lost income—Loss of income that results if property is damaged. For example, if a hurricane damages a home rented to others, the owner might not be able to collect rent on the property until the house is repaired or replaced.

LIABILITY LOSS EXPOSURES

Individuals and families face a potential reduction in their assets from the possibility of being sued or being held responsible for someone else's injury.

Whether through owning property, driving a car, or entering into contracts with others, all individuals and families face personal **liability loss exposures**. Even if a liability claim is successfully defended, and therefore does not result in payment of **damages**, the party against whom the claim was made nonetheless incurs defense costs, other claim-related expenses, and potentially adverse publicity, all of which may produce a financial loss. The three elements of personal liability loss exposures are the assets exposed to loss, causes of loss, and financial consequences of loss.

Assets Exposed to Loss

The assets exposed to loss in a liability loss exposure are money or other financial assets. A liability loss can result from property ownership or from the actions of individuals or family members. For example, if an individual is at fault in an auto accident, he or she must pay damages for vehicle repairs or replacement, medical expenses, and other costs stemming from the accident.

Liability loss exposure
Any condition or situation that presents the possibility of a claim alleging legal responsibility of a person or business for injury or damage suffered by another party.

Damages
Money claimed by, or a monetary award to, a party who has suffered bodily injury or property damage for which another party is legally responsible.

As another example, if a renter breaches a lease, the landlord can sue for lost rental income and the asset that is exposed to loss is the renter's money or financial assets. If a house guest trips and breaks her leg on an unsafe sidewalk, the homeowner may be required to pay damages for her resulting medical expenses and perhaps the wages she loses while she recuperates.

Damages awarded in a liability judgment can take the form of general, special, and punitive damages. **General damages** are monetary awards to compensate victims for losses, such as pain and suffering, that do not involve specific measurable expenses. **Special damages** are a form of compensatory damages that compensate for specific, identifiable expenses associated with the injured person's loss, such as medical expenses or lost wages. **Punitive, or exemplary, damages** are awarded by a court to punish a defendant for a reckless, malicious, or deceitful act or to deter similar conduct; they need not bear any relationship to a party's actual damages. Punitive damages are generally awarded against companies, although they may be used against individuals.

Causes of Loss

The cause of loss associated with a liability loss exposure is the claim of liability or the filing of a lawsuit. The settlement of disputes between individuals and the indemnification for wrongs committed against individuals are within the scope of **civil law**. By contrast, criminal law deals with conduct that endangers the public welfare, such as the crimes of murder, rape, and fraud. Because such criminal acts are generally not the subject of insurance, civil law provides the legal foundation of insurance. Several types of claims fall under civil law, but the most common personal liability claims involve **tort** liability, contractual liability, and statutory liability.

These are examples of circumstances in which liability may be claimed or a suit filed:

* Breach of a legal duty, if that breach causes harm to another, such as injuries caused by an auto accident
* Breach of contract, such as a failure to pay rent on an agreed date
* Failure to adhere to requirements set out in statutes, regulations, or local ordinances, such as failing to provide a safe sidewalk at a residence

Tort Liability

An individual may face a claim for tort damages on the basis of any act of negligence, intentional torts, or absolute liability. See the exhibit "Sources of Tort Liability."

General damages

A monetary award to compensate a victim for losses, such as pain and suffering, that does not involve specific, measurable expenses.

Special damages

A form of compensatory damages that awards a sum of money for specific, identifiable expenses associated with the injured person's loss, such as medical expenses or lost wages.

Punitive damages (exemplary damages)

A payment awarded by a court to punish a defendant for a reckless, malicious, or deceitful act to deter similar conduct; the award need not bear any relation to a party's actual damages.

Civil law

A classification of law that applies to legal matters not governed by criminal law and that protects rights and provides remedies for breaches of duties owed to others.

Tort

A wrongful act or an omission, other than a crime or a breach of contract, that invades a legally protected right.

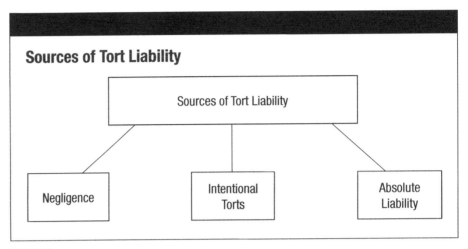

[DA00135]

Negligence

The failure to exercise the degree of care that a reasonable person in a similar situation would exercise to avoid harming others.

Negligence is the most common cause of liability losses. To prove that negligence has occurred, an injured party must prove that all four legal elements of negligence have occurred:

- A duty to act. (For example, a family has a duty to maintain its premises so as not to cause injury to a guest.)

- A breach of that duty. (For instance, if a family allows a child to leave a ball on the front entry steps of its home, it may have breached its duty to keep the premises safe.)

- An injury or damage occurs. (For example, a guest trips on the ball that was left on the steps and breaks his leg.)

- The breach of duty is the direct cause of the injury or damage in an unbroken chain of events. (In this example, the direct cause of the guest's broken leg is the ball that the child left on the steps.)

Regardless of whether the harm that results is intended, an intentional act can create liability. These are some examples of these acts, known as intentional torts:

- Libel is a written or printed untrue statement that damages a person's reputation. For example, if Ted prints an article in a local community newsletter falsely claiming that his neighbor, Paul, has been convicted of drunken driving, Ted may be guilty of libel.

- Slander is an oral untrue statement that damages a person's reputation. For instance, if, at a parent-teacher meeting, Susan publicly and falsely accuses a local pharmacist of selling illegal drugs to teenagers, she may be guilty of slander.

- Assault is the intentional and unlawful threat of bodily harm. For example, if Mary threatens to hit Betty, and Betty believes that Mary is ready and willing to carry out her threat, Mary has assaulted Betty.

- Battery is unlawful physical contact with another person. Continuing the previous example, if Mary hits Betty, she has committed battery. Betty may sue Mary for damages resulting from assault and battery.

- Trespass is the unauthorized possession or use of land. If Jacob parks his car in Chris's yard without Chris's permission, Jacob may be guilty of trespass.

- Nuisance is the violation of a person's right to enjoy use of property without disruption from outside sources. For instance, if a person persistently hosts noisy parties that last late into the night, the neighbors may seek an injunction against such activities under civil law.

Absolute liability is liability that does not involve proving negligence. For example, if a person keeps a pet alligator in a cage in his back yard and the alligator bites a neighbor, the owner of the alligator could be held liable regardless of whether negligence can be proved.

Contractual Liability

The possibility of contractual liability arises when an individual enters into a contract or an agreement. Leases for homes and apartments, as well as rental agreements for autos, power tools, and other equipment, typically contain provisions that transfer the financial consequences of liability losses from the owner of the property to the renter. For example, an apartment lease may require the tenant to assume liability for any injury or damage to others, even in instances in which the owner of the property is at fault.

Statutory Liability

Statutory liability exists because of the passage of a statute or law. Most important to individuals and families are the laws dealing with liability arising out of automobile accidents. These laws vary by state and change the legal basis of liability regarding negligence.

Financial Consequences of Loss

Because the asset exposed to loss in a liability loss exposure is money or other financial assets, the financial consequences of a liability loss can be serious. When a liability claim occurs, an individual or a family can suffer two major financial consequences:

- Costs of investigation and defense
- Money damages awarded if the defense is not successful or if the claim is settled out of court

Many liability claims are settled before they reach court. In such cases, parties to the claim negotiate the amount paid in damages, and the costs of investigation and defense generally are reduced. Because settling out of court usually is less expensive than a potentially long trial, insurance companies often try to reach out-of-court settlements. In theory, the financial consequences of a liability loss exposure are limitless. In practice, financial consequences are limited to the total wealth of the responsible party. Although some jurisdictions limit the amounts that can be taken in a claim, liability claims can result in the loss of most or all of a person's assets, as well as in a claim on future income.

RISK MANAGEMENT PROCESS

Individuals and families should use the risk management process to determine the best techniques for managing their loss exposures.

Often, significant, life-altering events such as marriage, having children, starting a new job, or making a major purchase (a home or car, for example) require individuals and families to evaluate the risks they face and the best ways to manage them. They may accomplish this by using the **risk management process**. Although this process was developed for organizations, individuals and families also can follow its steps to guide their risk management decisions. See the exhibit "The Risk Management Process."

Risk management process

The method of making, implementing, and monitoring decisions that minimize the adverse effects of risk on an organization.

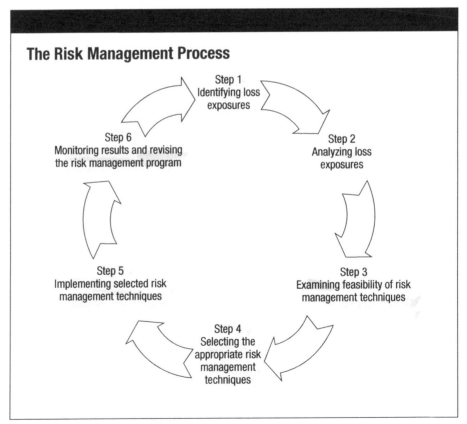

The Risk Management Process

Step 1
Identifying loss exposures

Step 2
Analyzing loss exposures

Step 3
Examining feasibility of risk management techniques

Step 4
Selecting the appropriate risk management techniques

Step 5
Implementing selected risk management techniques

Step 6
Monitoring results and revising the risk management program

[DA00095]

Step 1: Identifying Loss Exposures

Organizations use a wide variety of methods to identify their loss exposures. By contrast, individuals and families usually rely on friends, family members, and their insurance agent to help them identify their loss exposures. Friends and family members can help identify loss exposures by sharing their own loss histories and experience. The insurance agent may provide checklists that focus on common sources of loss exposures and use his or her own experience and training to help individuals and families determine areas that they may need to address with risk management techniques.

Two of the most common property and liability loss exposures that individuals and families must address are connected to home and automobile ownership. They are often also subject to a significant number of other liability loss exposures, such as an individual's liability stemming from a physical altercation at work.

Step 2: Analyzing Loss Exposures

Step two of the risk management process, analyzing loss exposures, entails estimating the likely significance of possible losses identified in step one. Together, these two steps constitute the process of assessing loss exposures, and they are therefore often considered the most important components of the risk management process.

When organizations analyze the loss exposures they have identified, they focus on four dimensions:

- Loss frequency—the number of losses (such as fires, auto accidents, or liability claims) within a specific time period
- Loss severity—the amount, in dollars, of a loss for a specific occurrence
- Total dollar losses—the total dollar amount of losses for all occurrences during a specific period
- Timing—when losses occur and when loss payments are made

Individuals and families may also use these components to guide their analysis. For example, a family could analyze its automobile loss exposures in this manner:

- Loss frequency—During the previous year, family members were responsible for two auto accidents and also filed a claim for a broken windshield.
- Loss severity—The loss severity for each of the auto claims was $11,500, $2,200, and $300, respectively.
- Total dollar losses—The total of the three losses for the policy year is $14,000.
- Timing—Generally, these kinds of property losses are settled in a matter of days or weeks. However, an automobile liability claim for hundreds of

thousands of dollars filed by a person injured in one of the accidents may require years to resolve.

Only a properly assessed loss exposure can be appropriately managed. Once a loss exposure has been assessed, the best ways to manage it may become immediately apparent. The remaining steps of the risk management process flow from this assessment.

Step 3: Examining the Feasibility of Risk Management Techniques

Risk control

A conscious act or decision not to act that reduces the frequency and/or severity of losses or makes losses more predictable.

Risk financing

A conscious act or decision not to act that generates the funds to pay for losses and risk control measures or to offset variability in cash flows.

Loss exposures can be addressed through **risk control** techniques and **risk financing** techniques. Risk control techniques minimize the frequency or severity of losses; for example, an individual can avoid automobile loss exposures by not purchasing or driving an auto. Risk financing techniques, such as insurance, generate funds to finance losses that risk control techniques cannot reduce or prevent. See the exhibit "Risk Management Techniques."

Risk Management Techniques

```
                                      ┌──────────────────────┐
                                      │  Risk financing      │
                                      │  techniques          │
                                      └──────────────────────┘
┌──────────────────────┐             │
│  Risk management     │─────────────┤
│  techniques          │             │
└──────────────────────┘             │
                                      ┌──────────────────────┐
                                      │  Risk control        │
                                      │  techniques          │
                                      └──────────────────────┘
```

[DA00096]

Risk management techniques are not usually used in isolation. Unless entirely avoiding a loss exposure, individuals should typically apply at least one risk control technique and one risk financing technique to each of their significant loss exposures. The risk control technique alters the estimated frequency and severity of loss, and the financing technique pays for losses that occur despite the controls.

This step of the risk management process entails determining the feasibility of risk management techniques. Individuals and families should examine all available risk control and risk financing techniques and determine which are feasible for them. After making this determination, they use the next step in the process to determine which of the feasible techniques is the most appropriate for each loss exposure.

Unlike organizations, most individuals and families have access to a limited number of feasible risk control and risk financing techniques, the most prevalent of which is the purchase of insurance. For some loss exposures, such as a fire exposure to a home, this method is mandated by the mortgage lender. In this case, the individual or family has a choice of buying suitable homeowners insurance or not buying the home.

Step 4: Selecting the Appropriate Risk Management Techniques

Once loss exposures have been identified and analyzed and possible risk management techniques considered, individuals and families can select the techniques that best prevent or reduce losses and that will adequately finance losses that occur. Selecting the most appropriate combination of risk management techniques is usually based on quantitative financial considerations as well as qualitative, nonfinancial considerations.

Most households choose risk management techniques by using financial criteria. That is, they choose the most effective techniques that will have the greatest positive (or least negative) effect on their assets. Households must compare the potential costs of completely untreated loss exposures with the costs of possible risk management techniques when considering whether a technique is economical.

A household's nonfinancial goals can constrain its financial goals, leading to the selection of risk management techniques that, although best for that family, might be inconsistent with its value maximization goal. For example, a family may install a home alarm system. The cost of the system's initial installation and associated monthly monitoring fees may exceed the resulting insurance premium savings. However, the additional nonfinancial benefit of the peace of mind the family experiences from feeling safer may outweigh the measure's financial costs.

Step 5: Implementing the Selected Risk Management Techniques

Implementing risk management techniques may involve any of these measures:

- Purchasing loss reduction devices, such as smoke alarms or flame-retardant roofing

- Contracting for loss prevention services, such as burglar alarm services

- Funding retention programs, such as maintaining a savings account to fund the loss exposures of small-value items that could be retained in a household operating budget

- Implementing and continually reinforcing loss control programs, such as keeping flammable materials away from heat sources
- Selecting agents or brokers, insurers, and other insurance providers who can suggest ways to deal with specific loss exposures (particularly out-of-the-ordinary loss exposures, such as coin collections and home entertainment centers)
- Requesting insurance policies and paying premiums for loss exposures that an individual does not want to retain (or is required to have by statute or by a lender), such as homeowners, automobile, and liability loss exposures
- Creating and updating a list of possessions that may be subject to loss

Implementing risk management techniques does not necessarily end with the initial implementation of a selected technique. For example, if a family purchases or builds a vacation home, it almost certainly will also decide to purchase property insurance. However, additional details, such as the exact placement of fire extinguishers, the terms and cost of insurance and noninsurance contract revisions, selection of an insurer, the timing of insurance premium payments, and the actual deposit of funds in a savings account for a retention program or to cover deductibles, must be addressed as the program is implemented.

Step 6: Monitoring Results and Revising the Risk Management Program

Individuals and families must monitor and periodically review their risk management program to ensure that it is achieving expected results. They also should adjust it to accommodate changes in loss exposures and in the availability or cost-effectiveness of alternative risk management techniques.

A risk management program should be adjusted as life-changing events occur. For example, if a family member acquires a driver's license, the family's auto loss exposures should be re-evaluated. Similarly, new dependents added to the family, or children leaving the home to attend college, can significantly alter a family's financial situation. Additionally, if individuals engage in new hobbies with significant loss exposures (such as coin collecting or the acquisition of expensive art), they should adopt additional risk management techniques to deal with these exposures. These techniques could include the use of safety deposit boxes or the purchase of insurance to safeguard these assets.

RISK MANAGEMENT TECHNIQUES

Individuals and families can manage the risks they face by using risk management techniques.

All risk management techniques fall into one of two categories: risk control or risk financing. Individuals and families may use both kinds of techniques to manage risks and ensure their well-being, financial stability, and security. See the exhibit "Risk Management Techniques."

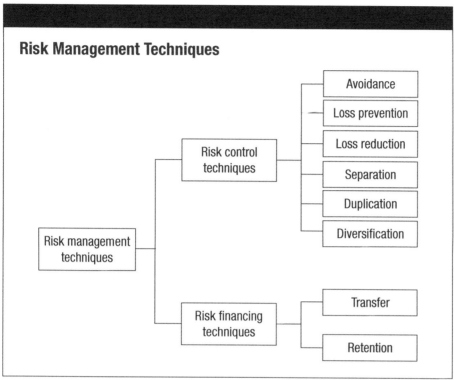

Risk Management Techniques

[DA00137]

Risk Control Techniques

Risk control techniques fall into one of six broad categories:

- Avoidance
- Loss prevention
- Loss reduction
- Separation
- Duplication
- Diversification

Each of these techniques aims to reduce either loss frequency or loss severity, or to make losses more predictable. Although some of these techniques, such as separation and duplication, are more appropriate for organizations, individuals and families can consider one or more of them as they review their specific loss exposures.

Avoidance

Avoidance

A risk control technique that involves ceasing or never undertaking an activity so that the possibility of a future loss occurring from that activity is eliminated.

The goal of **avoidance** is not simply to reduce loss frequency, but to eliminate any possibility of loss. For example, an individual living in a city may decide not to purchase a car in order to avoid automobile loss exposures. Additionally, if an individual is concerned about dying in an airplane crash, he or she can choose not to travel by air. However, by avoiding air travel, the individual increases the loss exposure to injury or death from the other means of transport chosen in its place. In some cases, avoidance is at least impractical, if not impossible. For instance, while automobile loss exposures may be avoided by not driving a car, most individuals and families require a car for daily activities.

Loss Prevention

Loss prevention

A risk control technique that reduces the frequency of a particular loss.

Generally, a **loss prevention** measure is implemented to break the sequence of events that leads to the loss. Determining effective loss prevention measures usually requires carefully studying how particular losses are caused.

As is the case with avoidance, a loss prevention measure may reduce the frequency of losses from one loss exposure but increase the frequency or severity of losses from other loss exposures. For example, a family living in a high-crime area may reduce the probability of theft by installing security devices in its home. Those security devices, however, might make it impossible for firefighters to enter the home or could trap a family member inside the home if a fire occurred.

Loss Reduction

Loss reduction

A risk control technique that reduces the severity of a particular loss.

An individual or family may also use **loss reduction** techniques. For example, by installing fire-resistant shingles, a family could expect reduced losses from a fire compared to the fire losses it could experience with standard shingles. Some loss reduction measures can prevent losses as well as reduce them. For example, using a burglar alarm in a home is generally considered a loss reduction measure because the alarm is activated only when a burglary occurs. However, because burglar alarms also act as a deterrent, they can prevent loss as well as reduce it.

Separation

Separation

A risk control technique that isolates loss exposures from one another to minimize the adverse effect of a single loss.

Separation is appropriate if a family can operate with only a portion of its assets left intact. For example, a family may store some of its jewelry in a safe at its home and store the remainder in a bank's safety deposit box. The intent of separation is to reduce the severity of an individual loss at a single location. However, by creating multiple locations, separation may increase loss frequency.

Duplication

Examples of **duplication** include maintaining a second set of records (such as copies of wills placed in a safety deposit box); spare parts for autos, household appliances, or yard machinery; and copies of keys.

Diversification

Diversification closely resembles duplication and separation. Families use diversification when they allocate their assets among a mix of stocks and bonds from companies in different industry sectors. A family might diversify investments by purchasing stock in a bank and stock in a pharmaceutical manufacturer and other unrelated industries. Because these are unrelated industries, any losses from one stock may be more than offset by profits in the other industries.

As with separation and duplication, diversification can increase loss frequency. However, by spreading risk, diversification reduces loss severity and can make losses more predictable.

Risk Financing Techniques

Risk financing can help individuals and families recover from loss or damage that might otherwise cause them significant financial impairment. Traditionally, risk financing measures generally have been categorized as either retention techniques or transfer techniques.

Retention

Usually, a family deliberately uses **retention** only to treat loss exposures that are within its financial means, such as when it selects a $1,000 deductible on collision insurance for its vehicles. For instance, although most individuals and families are offered insurance by retailers for the repair or replacement of new appliances (stoves, dishwashers, washers, dryers, and so forth), many choose instead to retain these risks, because the loss of an appliance would not be catastrophic and the repair or replacement cost is relatively minimal. If individuals and families do not plan to treat loss exposures or are unaware of them, they retain them by default. Retention is the default risk financing technique that results if an individual or family fails to identify or transfer a risk.

Most families and individuals do not retain losses on a pre-planned, structured basis. They generally pay for retained losses with reserve savings or may change budgeting priorities to pay for them. Retention can be planned or unplanned; complete or partial; or funded or unfunded.

Planned retention is a deliberate assumption of loss that has been identified and analyzed and may be chosen because it is the most cost effective or convenient technique, or because no other alternatives are available.

Duplication
A risk control technique that uses backups, spares, or copies of critical property, information, or capabilities and keeps them in reserve.

Diversification
A risk control technique that spreads loss exposures over numerous projects, products, markets, or regions.

Retention
A risk financing technique by which losses are retained by generating funds within the organization to pay for the losses.

Unplanned retention is the inadvertent, unplanned assumption of a loss exposure that has not been identified or accurately analyzed. For example, many individuals and families inadvertently retain flood losses because they do not anticipate that rain associated with the remnants of a hurricane will endanger their property. An individual or a family also may inadvertently retain losses if they select inadequate insurance policy limits. For example, if an insured with an auto liability limit of $100,000 is at fault in an auto accident that seriously injures another party, the insured may be liable for more than $100,000 in damages and may be required to pay the amount in excess of that figure. The excess amount, therefore, represents an unplanned retention.

Retention is complete if a loss exposure is entirely retained. Partial retention entails retaining a portion of a loss exposure and transferring the unretained portion through insurance or another risk financing technique. With insurance, the deductible represents the portion of the loss that the insured retains.

Funded retention is a pre-loss arrangement intended to ensure that funding is available to pay for losses that do occur. Unfunded retention is the lack of advance funding for losses.

Transfer

Insurance is the most prevalent form of risk **transfer**. The insurance buyer substitutes a small, certain financial cost, the insurance premium, for the possibility of a large, uncertain financial loss, which is paid by the insurer. Although insurance is only one approach to risk transfer, it is frequently the only method of risk transfer available to individuals and families.

Some risk transfer techniques, however, do not involve insurance. An example of such a noninsurance risk transfer is a hold-harmless agreement, which is a noninsurance contractual provision that obligates one of the parties to the contract to assume the legal liability of another party to the contract. A hold-harmless agreement may be included in an apartment lease, for instance.

Hedging is a noninsurance risk transfer technique in which one asset (money) is paid to offset the risk associated with another asset. For example, if a family agrees to pay a particular price for all of its home fuel oil in advance of the heating season, it is "hedging" against the possibility that fuel costs will increase during the season. See the exhibit "Examples of Risk Management Techniques Used by Individuals and Families."

Insurance

A risk management technique that transfers the potential financial consequences of certain specified loss exposures from the insured to the insurer.

Transfer

In the context of risk management, a risk financing technique by which the financial responsibility for losses and variability in cash flows is shifted to another party.

Examples of Risk Management Techniques Used by Individuals and Families

Risk Management Technique	Loss Exposure	Treatment
Risk Control Techniques		
• Avoidance	Death by airline accident	Drive instead
	Fire damage to home	Do not purchase home
	Theft of automobile	Do not purchase auto
	Storm damage to watercraft	Do not purchase speedboat
• Loss Prevention	Liability suit caused by injury on slippery floors	Install rugs
	Liability suit caused by fall on steep stairways	Install handrails
• Loss Reduction	Home fire	Install fire-resistant shingles and fire extinguishers
	Home burglary	Install burglar alarm
• Separation	Theft of valuables	Some valuables remain at home, others are stored in a safety deposit box
• Duplication	Loss of keys	Make duplicate set of keys
	Destruction by fire of valuable documents	Make additional copies
• Diversification	Steep reduction in value of a major family investment	Diversify investment into a variety of suitable assets
Risk Financing Techniques		
• Retention	Wear and tear on vehicles and clothing	Budget for acceptable loss exposures
• Transfer	Property damage due to fire or auto liability suit	Transfer risks to another individual or entity (often transferred by purchasing insurance)

[DA00136]

PERSONAL RISK MANAGEMENT CASE STUDY

The replacement or repair of assets could deplete one's savings and income. Although many individuals and families manage their risks of loss by observing what others do or by reading consumer advice articles, they can learn to apply to their own property and liability exposures the same risk management process used by organizations.

The risk management process is a systematic approach to treating property and liability loss exposures:

1. Identify the loss exposures
2. Analyze the loss exposures
3. Examine the feasibility of risk management techniques
4. Select appropriate risk management
5. Implement the selected risk management techniques
6. Monitor the results and revise the risk management techniques

Case Facts

John and Shirley, two working professionals in their mid-thirties, have been married for less than a year. Shirley's father, her last living parent, recently died, and she inherited her family's homestead, a farmhouse with two working fireplaces on two acres with an unattached three-car garage that contains a rentable apartment. The homestead is surrounded by two housing developments.

Because both John and Shirley love old homes, they decide to live in the farmhouse. The three-car garage is a boon because John and Shirley each have a car and John has a boat that requires storage. The apartment is attractive both for the rent revenue it provides and because its residents can monitor the premises when John and Shirley are both away on business travel. John and Shirley realize their recent marriage and the move to owning a home are life-changing events and that they need to make a conscious attempt to evaluate and manage their potential property and liability loss exposures.

Case Analysis Tools and Information

As John and Shirley begin the process of identifying their loss exposures, they should consider that they have different types of assets that are exposed to potential loss—real property and personal property.

Next, John and Shirley need to understand the common causes of property loss. The most common are fire, wind, lightning, and theft. Depending on the area, there may be other potential causes of loss such as earthquakes, tornadoes, or floods.

The couple must also understand that the financial consequences of property losses can be either reduction in value, costs to repair or replace property, increased expenses in addition to normal living expenses, or lost income.

In addition to their property loss exposures, John and Shirley must understand the potential for a liability loss exposure. Assets at risk in liability exposures are money and other financial assets. Liability loss exposures may result not only in financial damages, but also in costs related to investigation and defense if a liability claim is lodged. Although individuals and families rarely consider liability loss exposures, the typical causes of loss for liability purposes are these:

- Breach of a legal duty that causes harm to another (for example, an auto accident caused by careless driving).

- Breach of contract, such as failure to honor the terms of a contract (for example, paying rent by an agreed date).

- Failure to adhere to requirements established in statutes, regulations, or local ordinances (for example, failure to provide a safe sidewalk at a residence as required by local building codes).

Case Analysis Steps

As John and Shirley evaluate their property and liability loss exposures, they will follow the steps in the risk management process:

1. Identify the loss exposures, both property and liability.

2. Analyze the loss exposures, considering the potential causes of loss, loss frequency, loss severity, total dollar losses, and timing.

3. Examine the feasibility of risk management techniques, that is, actions they can take to reduce frequency or severity of losses, and ways they can finance the costs of loss.

4. Select appropriate risk management techniques for the identified property and liability exposures.

5. Implement the selected risk management techniques.

6. Monitor the results and revise the risk management techniques.

Although there are six steps in this process, it is possible to combine several as they are applied.

Identify and Analyze Property and Liability Loss Exposures

John and Shirley will begin by making a list of property loss exposures. Next, they will analyze them, assessing how frequently losses might occur, how much they might cost, the past total loss costs from such losses, and the timing of such losses:

- Land, farmhouse, and unattached garage—This property is mainly exposed to potential loss through fire, lightning, and windstorm. It is not in an area prone to earthquakes, tornadoes, and floods. However, the structures are relatively old and made of wood frame construction. Although there is no known past windstorm damage, the older construction suggests elements of its construction, such as the roofing shingles, may not be of the most recent design and attachment to resist wind damage. Although neither John nor Shirley have any history of incurring property losses in their previous residence, both realize that the wood frame construction of the home could cause any fire to be catastrophic. Property losses of this type usually incur immediate financial costs and settlement can occur fairly rapidly.

- Personal property—Virtually all of the couple's personal possessions will be maintained in the buildings or on the grounds. They have a large amount of furniture. Among Shirley's possessions are jewelry she inherited from her mother and documents describing her family lineage dating back to the arrival of the Mayflower. John and Shirley believe they live in a relatively low-crime neighborhood, but the possibility of theft always exists. They have no history of loss of personal property. However, because some possessions, such as jewelry, are of considerable value and other possessions, such as family lineage documents, are almost irreplaceable, they want to consider possible safeguards. They know through acquaintances that such property losses occur and loss settlement payments are not usually drawn out.

- Apartment—If the apartment is rented at the time of the loss, the property loss would be compounded by a loss of rental income. John and Shirley have no idea on the timing of payment for such losses.

- Two cars—Both cars are relatively new and, if damaged, would cost a significant amount to replace, if not repair. Shirley has an accident-free driving record. John has experienced two minor mishaps but no accidents involving other vehicles. His out-of-pocket costs associated with these occurrences totaled $2,500, but John knows that more severe accidents would involve higher repair costs. Payments for such losses can be fairly prompt or drawn out.

- Boat—The ownership and operation of a boat is a risk of loss whether the boat is on land or water. The boat must be towed to lakes and rivers, and operating the boat around docks and landings can pose potential problems. John is an experienced boater and has had no boating mishaps to date. Although the boat is a valuable possession, he believes the chances of a loss are fairly remote. He also believes such claims would be handled relatively promptly.

John and Shirley identified and analyzed these liability exposures:

- Land, farmhouse, and unattached garage—John and Shirley have not encountered any liability claims in their ownership of their previous residence, take meticulous care of their property, and attend to any premises hazards as soon as noticed. Nonetheless, they entertain frequently and often have invited guests. Moreover, the close proximity of the two housing developments increases the chance of invited or uninvited people on their property. Although John and Shirley have had no experience with liability claims, their insurance agent and friends have told them of incidents in which litigation has been drawn out and involved substantial amounts of money.

- Apartment—Neither John nor Shirley has any experience as landlords and contracting with tenants. They want to make their experience as trouble-free as possible and minimize their risk of financial loss. Nonetheless, they know that the constant presence on their property of tenants and their personal property represents an additional exposure, and they know that liability claims can be lengthy and complicated.

- Two cars—John's driving experience is marred only by his having backed into one mailbox and having grazed another. However, both John and Shirley have friends who have been in serious car accidents and been sued for property damage and substantial medical expenses, and related expenses. Moreover, the regular reporting in the local news media reminds them that auto liability claims are a common occurrence and can result in high claims costs and sometimes lengthy settlement negotiations.

- Boat—To date, John has had no incidents with the boat, and he hopes his experience will keep him accident free. Shirley, however, is new to boating and will have to learn to operate the boat. Their general knowledge indicates that the chance of a claim is possible, but remote.

Examine Feasible Risk Management Techniques

After John and Shirley have identified their loss exposures and analyzed them, they will consider feasible risk management techniques they might apply to each. They can choose from among risk control techniques such as loss prevention, **loss control**, avoidance, and loss reduction, and risk financing techniques such as transfer (insurance) and retention. Because there are a variety of risk control and risk financing techniques and because property and liability exposures are often intertwined, John and Shirley can explore a number of feasible risk management alternatives.

Loss control
A risk management technique that attempts to decrease the frequency or severity of losses.

First, they consider the land, farmhouse, and unattached garage. They can minimize the risk of electrical fires by ensuring the electrical system in the home meets current municipality code standards. They can minimize the risk of fire from using the fireplaces by installing glass fireplace doors, and they can minimize potential fire damage by installing fire extinguishers at strategic locations around the home, garage, and apartment. Most importantly, they can install multiple smoke detectors.

Nonetheless, the risk of substantial financial loss remains. John and Shirley have sufficient general savings to finance relatively small losses. Major losses, however, would require them to have sufficient accumulated savings to replace the home or undertake extensive repairs or to transfer the responsibility of funding such losses by purchasing insurance. They would also have to either endure the loss of rental income or purchase insurance to compensate for it.

Regarding liability, because it is not likely that John and Shirley will want to avoid injury to others by never or rarely having guests at their home, they should consider maintaining their home and grounds well and providing insurance coverage in the event there is an injury to someone.

To manage the risk of loss to personal property, John and Shirley can install a fire and burglary alarm system on the buildings. The one-time installation charge and a monthly service charge may be partially offset by a reduction in their insurance premium and the peace-of-mind assurance that there is detection service when they are away.

Heirloom jewelry and old family documents can be kept in a locked fireproof safe on premises or stored off premises in a bank safety deposit box. Fire extinguishers and smoke detectors are sound loss prevention and loss reduction techniques for personal property as well. However, the sheer number of other household possessions that cannot be kept off-site would necessitate that the couple either retain the costs of loss themselves or transfer the funding of loss through the purchase of insurance.

Regarding the apartment, John and Shirley could be held liable for losses incurred by tenants unless they make arrangements to transfer the risk of such losses. They can make contractual agreements transferring responsibility for losses to the tenants, including a requirement that the tenants carry their own insurance. They would certainly want to institute any loss prevention/loss reduction techniques, such as fire extinguishers and smoke detectors, that can be implemented at reasonable cost. For any responsibilities they cannot transfer, they can consider insurance.

Considering the risks related to their two cars, John and Shirley determine that they cannot take public transportation to work, so giving up the cars to avoid auto exposures is not realistic. They could take defensive driving courses to improve their driving skills and to assist in avoiding accidents. Nonetheless, there are potentially high property and liability losses associated with auto accidents, and they know it is wise to have sufficient automobile insurance, regardless of the minimum amount required by state law.

Aware of the risks associated with owning and operating a boat, John has taken a United States Coast Guard boating course to ensure he knows how to outfit a boat with safety equipment and operate it safely. He periodically takes a refresher course to stay current on equipment, laws and codes, and safe operating principles.

Shirley could refrain from operating the boat and thus avoid any potential for causing boating-related damage or injury. However, she and John have concluded it is likely she will have to operate the boat at some time and should therefore learn how to operate it safely. The couple will also need insurance to transfer the funding of any incurred losses.

Select the Appropriate Risk Management Techniques

Having thought about the risk management techniques that might be applied to their exposures, John and Shirley must determine how they will handle each exposure. In doing so, they will consider the impact of potential claims on their income, savings, and other financial assets as well as other nonfinancial, peace-of-mind considerations.

In relation to the land, farmhouse, and unattached garage, John and Shirley decide that fire extinguishers and smoke detectors are easily affordable and installing them is a common-sense action they can take. Similarly, fireplace doors strike them as sensible improvements. John and Shirley are concerned about the home's dated electrical system but know that upgrading it would require a substantial investment. Because the home will undoubtedly need a series of renovations over time, they will inventory what they think they will need to do and prioritize that list. In the meantime, they will be careful about overloading circuits and using extension cords. Finally, John and Shirley pledge that when undertaking renovations, they will perform the work in accordance with local code standards, which have undoubtedly changed since the home's construction.

John and Shirley decide that the installation of a fire and burglary alarm system is worth the investment. Although their annual cost is greater than the insurance premium savings, Shirley feels safer with the system in place, both when she and John are away and when she is home alone.

The couple has sufficient general savings to finance relatively small property losses. But for major losses, they are more comfortable purchasing insurance, substituting the known cost of insurance premiums for the potential unknown future loss.

Because John and Shirley will want to continue entertaining friends in their home, they will maintain their home and grounds well and provide insurance coverage in the event there is an injury to someone.

John and Shirley have already decided that the fire and burglary alarm systems are worth the investment. The systems also provide some loss prevention for their personal property. To further protect their personal property, they will keep some of the heirloom jewelry and old family documents in a locked fire-proof safe on premises and store others in a bank safety deposit box. Fire extinguishers and smoke detectors are sound loss prevention and loss reduction techniques for personal property as well. However, the sheer number of other household possessions necessitate that John and Shirley transfer the funding of most losses through the purchase of insurance.

To handle the apartment loss exposures, John and Shirley decide they will transfer responsibility for property and liability exposures to their tenants. The rental agreement will require that the tenants be responsible for their own personal property and carry their own insurance to cover it. The rental contract can also include a **hold-harmless agreement**. Because the costs are

Hold-harmless agreement (or indemnity agreement)

A contractual provision that obligates one of the parties to assume the legal liability of another party.

reasonable, John and Shirley will provide fire extinguishers and smoke detectors on the rented premises. They will also comply with local municipal codes that cover landlords and rental properties. For any responsibilities they cannot transfer, they will purchase insurance.

In considering how to handle the exposures related to their two cars, John and Shirley decide to forego defensive driving courses. Therefore, they must fund potential losses through retention and insurance. They purchase auto insurance and decide to increase their deductible on the collision coverage on their own cars. They believe they can afford to retain a larger part of a collision loss in exchange for the insurance premium savings. However, they also believe that they would have more at risk in a liability loss and they decide to purchase liability limits higher than the state mandated minimum.

For the boat-related exposures, John will continue to take a periodic refresher course to stay current on equipment, laws and codes, and safe operating principles. Because Shirley is a newcomer to boating, John insists that she take the U.S. Coast Guard boating course and join him in the refresher courses. Although this training can assist in preventing boat-related losses or reducing their severity, there remains the possibility of a complete loss of the boat in a mishap or liability caused by injury to another person or their property. John and Shirley will purchase insurance to cover those property and liability exposures.

Implement the Risk Management Plans and Monitor the Results

After the couple determines the risk management techniques they will use for the various exposures, they must implement them. Some of the actions they will take are to install the various loss prevention and loss reduction equipment and furnishings, engage a lawyer to assist in drafting a rental contract with tenants, and select an agent and insurance company to purchase the required property and liability insurance.

The last step in applying the risk management process is to monitor the exposures and risk management techniques used and to make adjustments as requirements or situations change. This means reviewing risk management plans at normal intervals such as at insurance policy renewal dates or rental contract renewals as well as when there are other significant life-changing events. For example, John and Shirley might decide to make major renovations to the farmhouse, perhaps even adding attached or unattached structures. That would be an appropriate time to review risk management techniques, insurance policy coverage, and limits of liability, and to make adjustments as necessary. See the exhibit "Risk Management Techniques for Miscellaneous Vehicle Related Loss Exposures."

Risk Management Techniques for Miscellaneous Vehicle Related Loss Exposures

Vehicle Type Exposed to Loss	Liability Loss Exposure	Risk Control Techniques	Risk Financing Techniques	Property Loss Exposure	Risk Control Techniques	Risk Financing Techniques
Motor home	Increased collision frequency	Operator training	ISO Miscellaneous Type Vehicle Endorsement with Amendment (Motor Home) Specialty policy	Explosion and fire / Windstorm and flood	Maintenance of propane equipment / Placement in secure location	ISO Miscellaneous Type Vehicle Endorsement with Amendment (Motor Home) / Specialty policy
Travel trailer	Increased collision frequency	Operator Training	ISO Miscellaneous Type Vehicle Endorsement / Specialty policy	Explosion and fire / Windstorm and flood	Maintenance of propane equipment / Placement in secure location	ISO Miscellaneous Type Vehicle Endorsement with Trailer/Camper Body Coverage Endorsement / Specialty policy / Deductible Retention for camping trailers
Motorcycle	Increased risk of injury to passenger	Helmet use	ISO Miscellaneous Type Vehicle Endorsement / Specialty Policy	Increased risk of collision with larger vehicle	Experience / Caution	ISO Miscellaneous Type Vehicle Endorsement / Specialty policy
Other two-wheeled vehicles (moped, dirt bike)	Increased risk of injury to youthful operators and passengers	Helmet use / Adult supervision / Caution on off-road terrain	ISO Miscellaneous Type Vehicle Endorsement / Specialty policy	Increased risk of crash on off-road terrain	Adult supervision / Caution on off-road terrain	ISO Miscellaneous Type Vehicle Endorsement / Specialty policy / Deductible Retention
Snowmobile	Risk of injury to youthful operators and passengers	Protective personal safety equipment / Adult supervision	ISO Homeowners Owned Snowmobile Endorsement / ISO Snowmobile Endorsement to PAP / Specialty policy	Collision with tree or another snowmobile / Overturning of the snowmobile	Adult supervision / Caution	ISO Snowmobile Endorsement to PAP / Specialty policy / Retention
Golf Cart	Risk of bodily injury to passengers or those in other golf carts	Operator knowledge of facility or community rules	ISO Homeowners / ISO Miscellaneous Type Vehicle Endorsement / Specialty policy	Collision with larger vehicle or another golf cart	Operator knowledge of facility or community rules	ISO Homeowners Golf Cart Endorsement / ISO Miscellaneous Type Vehicle Endorsement / Specialty policy
Antique and classic automobiles	No unique liability risk	Operator Training	ISO PAP / Specialty policy	Value appreciates rather than depreciates; ACV not applicable	Caution	ISO PAP Coverage for Damage to Your Auto (Maximum Limit of Liability) endorsement / Specialty policy
Other recreational vehicles (ATV, dune buggy, go-cart, play car)	Risk of bodily injury, especially to children operators and passengers	Adult supervision / Caution on off-road terrain	ISO Homeowners Low Power Recreational Vehicle Endorsement / ISO Miscellaneous Type Vehicle Endorsement / Specialty policy	Overturning of vehicle on rough terrain / Collision	Adult supervision of children / Caution on off-road terrain	ISO Miscellaneous Type Vehicle Endorsement / Specialty policy / Retention / Deductible

[DA05752]

SUMMARY

Individuals and families face a number of loss exposures in terms of the assets exposed to loss, the causes of loss to which property is exposed, and the financial consequences of loss. Assets exposed to loss can include both real property and personal property. Many causes of loss exist, including fire, theft, and collision, and they result in various financial consequences to property. These financial consequences include a reduction in value of property, increased expenses, and lost income.

A liability loss occurs because of an injury to another person or property. When a person who has an asset exposed to loss commits a breach of legal duty or a breach of contract, or fails to adhere to statutes, he or she may be responsible for related damages. Financial consequences of personal liability loss exposures can include damages paid to the plaintiff, settlement costs, legal fees, and court costs.

The risk management process consists of six steps:

1. Identifying loss exposures
2. Analyzing loss exposures
3. Examining the feasibility of risk management techniques
4. Selecting the appropriate risk management techniques
5. Implementing the selected risk management techniques
6. Monitoring results and revising the risk management program

Individuals and families use risk control and risk financing techniques to manage their risks. Risk control techniques can be categorized as avoidance, loss prevention, loss reduction, separation, duplication, and diversification. Risk financing can be accomplished through retention or transfer. The most prevalent risk transfer technique is insurance.

Individuals and families face a variety of property and liability loss exposures that can threaten their financial assets. They can use the risk management process used by business organizations to identify, evaluate, and manage the property and liability exposures identified, using loss prevention, loss control, loss reduction, and risk financing techniques.

The Personal Automobile Insurance Environment

Educational Objectives

After learning the content of this assignment, you should be able to:

▷ Evaluate each of the following approaches to compensating automobile accident victims:

- Tort liability system

- Financial responsibility laws

- Compulsory insurance laws

- Uninsured motorists coverage

- Underinsured motorists coverage

- No-fault insurance

▷ Describe no-fault automobile laws in terms of each of the following:

- Types of no-fault laws

- Benefits required by no-fault laws

▷ Explain how high-risk drivers may obtain auto insurance.

▷ Describe automobile insurance rate regulation in terms of each of the following:

- Rating factors

- Matching price to exposure

- Competition

- Other regulatory issues

The Personal Automobile Insurance Environment

2

COMPENSATION OF AUTO ACCIDENT VICTIMS

Under the legal system in the United States, persons who are injured or who incur property damage losses as the result of auto accidents that are the fault of other drivers are entitled to compensation and damages.

Automobile insurers and state governments have designed these approaches to compensating auto accident victims:

- Tort liability system
- Financial responsibility laws
- Compulsory insurance laws
- Uninsured motorists coverage
- Underinsured motorists coverage
- No-fault insurance

Tort Liability System

The tort liability system, which is based on fault, is the traditional and most commonly used method of seeking compensation for injured auto accident victims in the U.S. Most tort liability cases arise out of negligence. If a driver operates an auto in a negligent manner that results in bodily injury to another person or in damage to another's property, the operator can be held legally liable for damages incurred by the injured person. To avoid legal liability, auto owners and operators must exercise a high degree of care to protect others from harm.

Under the tort liability system, injured auto accident victims must prove that another party was at fault before they can collect damages from that party. The amount of damages can be determined through negotiations between the two parties or through a lawsuit and court settlement.

The major advantage of the tort liability system is that it provides a remedy for victims of negligent or irresponsible drivers who cause accidents. Injured victims are compensated for their costs, and the costs are allocated to the responsible party. The tort liability system may also act as an incentive for drivers to act responsibly in order to avoid lawsuits.

The disadvantages of the tort liability system include these considerations:

- Substantial time delays in reaching a settlement either through negotiation or through the courts
- Significant legal and administrative costs related to settling lawsuits or pursuing a case to judgment
- Punitive damage awards by juries that may be considered excessive

Financial Responsibility Laws

Financial responsibility law

Law enacted to ensure that motorists have the financial ability to pay for any property damage or bodily injury they might cause as a result of driving or owning an auto.

Financial responsibility laws require motorists to provide proof of financial responsibility (such as liability insurance) under these circumstances:

- After an auto accident involving bodily injury or property damage exceeding a certain dollar amount
- After a conviction for certain serious offenses, such as drunk driving or reckless driving, or after losing a driver's license because of repeated violations
- Upon failure to pay a final judgment that results from an auto accident

Motorists who fail to provide the required proof of financial responsibility can face suspension of their driver's license and vehicle registration. Proof of financial responsibility can include an insurance policy, a certificate of deposit, a surety bond, or a certificate of self insurance, depending upon the jurisdiction.

Financial responsibility laws provide some protection to victims of auto accidents against irresponsible drivers. These laws work in conjunction with the tort liability system to ensure that at-fault drivers will not only be held liable for accidents they cause, but also that they have a mechanism in place to pay for the financial consequences of those accidents.

Some potential disadvantages of financial responsibility laws include these considerations:

- Most financial responsibility requirements become effective only after an accident, a conviction, or a judgment.
- Financial responsibility laws do not guarantee payment to all accident victims. Persons injured by uninsured drivers, hit-and-run drivers, or drivers of stolen cars might not be compensated.
- Injured persons might not be fully indemnified for their injuries even when injured by motorists who can prove financial responsibility. Most financial responsibility laws set minimum financial requirements, which may not fully compensate a victim.

Compulsory Auto Insurance Laws

Most states have enacted **compulsory auto insurance laws** that require auto liability insurance for all motorists to drive legally within the state. In lieu of auto insurance, a motorist can post a bond or deposit cash or securities to guarantee financial responsibility in the event of an auto accident. In addition, many states require the insurer to verify insurance coverage and/or to notify the state if a policy is canceled or is not renewed. Other states may require insurers to submit information regarding the automobile insurance policies they have issued within that jurisdiction.

One advantage of compulsory insurance laws, as compared to financial responsibility laws, is that motorists must provide proof of financial responsibility before an accident occurs. By requiring proof of financial responsibility prior to an accident, compulsory insurance laws go beyond financial responsibility laws by ensuring that accident victims are compensated for their losses. Compulsory insurance laws work in conjunction with the tort liability system to ensure compensation for victims of auto accidents that are the fault of other drivers.

These are frequently cited disadvantages of compulsory insurance:

- Compulsory insurance laws do not guarantee compensation to all accident victims. Accidents and resulting injuries can be caused by drivers who do not comply with the law, such as hit-and-run drivers, drivers whose insurance has lapsed, out-of-state drivers with no insurance, drivers of stolen cars, or drivers of fraudulently registered vehicles.

- Compulsory insurance laws provide incomplete protection. The required minimum amount of insurance may not meet the full needs of accident victims. In some states, the required minimum limit for bodily injury coverage is as low as $10,000 or $20,000 per person.

- Compulsory insurance laws may not reduce the number of uninsured motorists. Some drivers do not insure their vehicles because insurance is too costly. Others let coverage lapse after demonstrating proof of insurance to satisfy vehicle registration requirements.

- Insurers argue that compulsory laws restrict their freedom to select profitable insureds. In addition, insurers fear that state regulators might deny needed rate increases, resulting in underwriting losses.

- Consumer advocates argue that if insurers are allowed to increase rates to compensate for accepting all applicants for insurance, rates might become unfairly high for good drivers. In effect, good drivers could be subsidizing rates for the high-risk drivers that insurers are required to insure.

- Compulsory insurance laws do not prevent or reduce the number of automobile accidents. This argument expresses one of the most serious problems associated with automobile insurance.

Compulsory auto insurance law

Law that requires the owners or operators of automobiles to carry automobile liability insurance at least equal to certain minimum limits before the vehicle can be licensed or registered.

Several states have implemented measures intended to respond to the disadvantages of compulsory insurance. Such measures include low-cost policies; no pay, no play laws; and unsatisfied judgment funds.

Low-cost auto insurance is intended to decrease the number of uninsured drivers by making minimal liability coverage available at a reduced cost. In New Jersey, for example, a basic policy offers $15,000 in personal injury protection, up to $250,000 in medical benefits for catastrophic injuries, and $5,000 property damage liability. Uninsured motorists, underinsured motorists, and physical damage coverages are not available. In Colorado, a low-cost plan provides **first party** medical expense or personal injury protection coverage with a maximum benefit of $25,000. A program in California offers bodily injury liability coverage up to $10,000 per person and $20,000 per accident.[1] Low-cost insurance programs are intended to provide some level of protection at a reduced cost to assist lower-income drivers in purchasing the insurance coverage required to comply with compulsory auto insurance laws.

No pay, no play laws prohibit uninsured drivers from initiating lawsuits for noneconomic damages, such as pain and suffering.[2] Only a few states have such laws, and some of those laws apply not only to uninsured drivers, but also to those driving under the influence of alcohol or using a vehicle while committing a felony.

A few other states have established **unsatisfied judgment funds,** which have these characteristics:

- An injured person can receive compensation from the fund after having obtained a judgment against a negligent driver and proving that the judgment cannot be collected.

- The maximum amount paid is generally limited to the state's minimum compulsory insurance requirement. In addition, most funds reduce the amount paid by any amount the injured person has collected from other collateral sources of recovery, such as workers compensation benefits or insurance.

- The negligent driver is not relieved of legal liability when the unsatisfied judgment fund compensates the insured person. The negligent driver's license is revoked until the driver reimburses the fund.

Unsatisfied judgment funds offer the advantage of providing injured accident victims some protection against irresponsible motorists. In addition, states with such funds attempt to keep uninsured drivers off the road by suspending their driver's licenses until they reimburse the unsatisfied judgment fund.

Uninsured Motorists Coverage

Uninsured motorists (UM) coverage compensates an insured for bodily injury caused by an uninsured motorist, a hit-and-run driver, or a driver whose insurer is insolvent. UM insurance is mandatory in many states and optional

---

First party

The insured in an insurance contract.

Unsatisfied judgment fund

A fund designed to provide a source of recovery for victims of motor vehicle accidents when an at-fault motorist is unable to pay any judgment.

Uninsured motorists (UM) coverage

Coverage that provides a source of recovery for occupants of a covered auto or for qualifying pedestrians who are injured in an accident caused by an at-fault motorist who does not have the state minimum liability insurance or by a hit-and-run driver.

in the rest. Most states require that all automobile liability policies contain UM coverage unless the insured voluntarily waives the coverage in writing.

Because compulsory insurance laws have not substantially reduced the number of uninsured drivers, there is the potential for unreimbursed losses if a driver is involved in an auto accident with an uninsured at-fault driver. UM coverage is an approach to compensating such auto accident victims that can be used to provide some financial protection against uninsured drivers.

UM coverage, however, has several disadvantages:

- As with other compensation methods, an injured person may not be fully compensated for his or her economic loss. Unless the insured has purchased higher UM limits, the maximum paid for a bodily injury claim is limited to the state's financial responsibility or compulsory insurance law requirement.

- Before an injured person can collect under UM coverage, the uninsured motorist's legal responsibility for the accident must be established. This can be difficult to establish in some cases and may involve legal proceedings, adding to the expense.

- Property damage is excluded in many states. In such states, for example, if a negligent uninsured motorist fails to stop for a red light and damages another car, the owner of the damaged car would collect nothing under the UM coverage. In some states, UM property damage coverage can be added at the insured's option.

- The victim is paying for insurance to protect against the failure of others to act responsibly. In effect, UM insurance provides coverage similar to the liability insurance that the negligent party failed to buy.

Underinsured Motorists Coverage

Underinsured motorists (UIM) coverage provides additional limits of protection to the victim of an auto accident when the negligent driver's insurance limits are insufficient to pay for the damages. UIM coverage can be added by endorsement to an automobile insurance policy and in some states is included automatically.

Although underinsured motorists insurance is sometimes combined with uninsured motorists insurance, the two coverages should not be confused. They do not overlap or duplicate each other. An insured can collect under one coverage or the other, depending on the situation, but not both. UM coverage applies when bodily injury is caused by an uninsured motorist, a hit-and-run driver, or a driver whose insurer is insolvent. In contrast, UIM coverage applies only when the at-fault driver has liability insurance with lower liability limits than the limits provided by the injured person's UIM coverage. UIM coverage can be triggered based on whether the losses are greater than the at-fault driver's liability limits (a damages trigger) or when

Underinsured motorists (UIM) coverage

Coverage that applies when a negligent driver has liability insurance at the time of the accident but has limits lower than those of the injured person's coverage.

those liability limits are lower than the injured person's UIM coverage (a limits trigger).

As with UM coverage, underinsured motorists coverage assists in compensating auto accident victims who would not be fully compensated otherwise. In this way, UIM coverage addresses one of the disadvantages of compulsory auto insurance. While limits may still be insufficient, it does offer some level of increased protection.

A disadvantage is that even the underinsured coverage may be insufficient to cover all costs. Also, the victim is paying for insurance to protect against the failure of others to act responsibly and to carry sufficient liability limits.

No-Fault Automobile Insurance

No-fault automobile insurance

Insurance that covers automobile accident victims on a first-party basis, allowing them to collect damages from their own insurers regardless of who was at fault.

No-fault automobile insurance is another approach for compensating auto accident victims. Many states have no-fault auto insurance laws that restrict the filing of lawsuits against at-fault drivers. Other states allow some type of first-party automobile insurance but do not restrict lawsuits.

Under a no-fault system, an injured person does not need to establish fault and prove negligence in order to collect payment for damages. In addition, certain no-fault laws place some restrictions on an injured person's right to sue a negligent driver who causes an accident. In some states, when a claim is below a certain monetary threshold, the injured motorist collects for injuries under his or her own insurance policy.

No-fault laws were developed to avoid the costly and time-consuming process of determining legal liability for auto accidents under the tort liability system. By eliminating the need to prove fault, no-fault laws allow accident victims to receive benefits much sooner after an accident and, as a result, may allow for a quicker recovery from injuries. Because no-fault laws limit the number of lawsuits that result from auto accidents, the burden on the state's court system is reduced, as are overall costs.

No-fault laws were developed to correct what was perceived as serious defects in the tort liability system based on fault. Proponents of such laws cite these as advantages of no-fault laws:

- They eliminate the need to determine fault. Following an auto accident, determining who is at fault is often difficult, especially when more than one driver has contributed to the accident.
- They eliminate inequities in claim payments. Those who favor no-fault laws argue that the tort liability system results in claim payment inequities. Small claims may be overpaid, and claims involving serious injuries may be underpaid.
- They expand the limited scope of the tort system. Many persons injured in auto accidents or the beneficiaries of those killed in auto accidents do

not collect, or collect less than their full economic loss, under the current tort liability system.

- They decrease the proportion of premium dollars used for claim investigation and legal costs. Under the tort liability system, a large proportion of the liability coverage premium dollar is used to pay for attorneys, claim investigation expenses, and other costs of determining fault.

- They reduce delays in payments. Many claims take months or even years to settle under the tort liability system, which often involves lengthy court trials and delays in the legal system.

Supporters of the tort liability system, however, present various potential disadvantages of no-fault laws:

- Assertions of premium savings and expense reductions are overstated and unreliable. Auto insurance premiums have not decreased significantly and, in some cases, have increased in states that have implemented no-fault plans.

- No-fault insurance may penalize safe drivers. The rating system used for no-fault insurance may unfairly allocate accident costs to the drivers who are not responsible for the accidents, thus increasing premiums for good drivers.

- No-fault benefits do not include payment for pain and suffering. Attorneys representing injured auto accident victims argue that the dollar amount of medical expenses and lost wages does not always represent the true loss to the victim, because the amount does not include damages for pain and suffering.

- No-fault benefits may increase fraud. In states with stated monetary thresholds, some physicians, lawyers, and other professionals abuse the system by inflating fees charged for services or charging for unnecessary services and procedures so that the claim exceeds the threshold. These actions lead to higher auto insurance costs for all policyholders.[3]

NO-FAULT AUTOMOBILE LAWS

Roughly one-half of the states in the United States have auto no-fault laws, which allow auto accident victims to collect first-party benefits from their own insurers.

No-fault laws authorize or mandate auto no-fault insurance—often referred to as personal injury protection (PIP)—and they define the benefits that insurers can or must provide. Thus, insurers in no-fault states often avoid the costly and time-consuming process of determining legal responsibility for auto accidents and instead handle claims quickly so that injured persons can be compensated for their medical expenses and lost wages.

No-fault laws

State statutes that require motorists to purchase (or require insurers to make available) insurance that provides minimum first-party benefits to injured persons regardless of fault.

Types of No-Fault Laws

Early proponents of no-fault insurance anticipated a system using a pure no-fault law. Under this system, an injured person would not need to establish fault and prove negligence in order to collect payment for damages, regardless of the injury's severity. A pure no-fault system would abolish use of the tort liability system for bodily injuries resulting from auto accidents. Opponents of a pure no-fault system argue that it would unfairly eliminate the right to certain legal actions; consequently, no state has yet enacted a pure no-fault law. Instead, certain states have enacted differing versions of no-fault laws, which prescribe one of three basic types of no-fault plans:

- Modified no-fault plans
- Add-on plans
- Choice no-fault plans

Modified No-Fault Plans

About half of the states with no-fault laws have modified no-fault plans. In contrast to pure no-fault plans, modified no-fault plans place some restrictions on the right to sue an at-fault driver but do not entirely eliminate the right.

Under a modified no-fault plan, injured motorists collect economic losses (such as medical expenses and lost wages) from their own insurers through the PIP benefits mandated by the plan. After collecting economic losses through their no-fault coverage, injured persons can sue at-fault drivers for any economic losses that exceed the no-fault coverage limits. For example, in a state that has a modified no-fault plan, John carries the minimum PIP medical coverage limit of $10,000 set by the plan. He is injured by an at-fault driver and incurs $25,000 in medical expenses. Because John's economic losses exceed the $10,000 limit, he has the right to sue the at-fault driver for the $15,000 of medical expenses that exceed the PIP medical coverage limit.

Additionally, injured motorists can sue at-fault drivers for noneconomic losses (such as pain and suffering, emotional distress, and disfigurement) if their injuries exceed a threshold stated in the law. The threshold can be either a **monetary threshold** (also called a dollar threshold) or a **verbal threshold**.

Monetary threshold (dollar threshold)

In a no-fault system, a dollar limit in total medical expenses an injured victim must exceed before he or she is permitted to sue the other party.

Verbal threshold

In a no-fault system, the designated criteria that are verbally "set forth in the statute that limit the right to sue."

When a monetary threshold applies, an injured motorist (or his or her survivors) can sue for noneconomic losses if the economic losses exceed a stated dollar amount. For example, in a state that has a modified no-fault plan with a monetary threshold of $5,000, Sally is injured by an at-fault driver. She incurs $3,000 in medical expenses and loses $4,000 in wages. Because Sally's economic losses exceed the $5,000 threshold, she has the right to sue the at-fault driver for any noneconomic losses she might have suffered.

When a verbal threshold applies, an injured motorist (or his or her survivors) can sue for noneconomic losses if his or her injuries meet a verbal description of serious injuries. Examples of injuries commonly described in verbal thresholds include death, permanent disfigurement or scarring, significant and permanent loss of a bodily function, and significant and permanent injury. Verbal thresholds sometimes specify a minimum disability period (the number of days the injured person has been disabled because of the accident) before the injured person can sue for damages.

Add-On Plans

An **add-on plan** is appropriately named because it adds no-fault benefits to auto insurance policies, but it differs from a modified no-fault plan because it places no restrictions on the injured person's right to sue a negligent party for damages. An add-on plan offers the insured the option of collecting for economic losses through his or her own insurer. For example, one state's add-on plan allows optional first-party coverage for medical expenses and loss of income, but the insured retains the right to seek compensation from the negligent driver. Under this law, all insurers that sell auto insurance in that state must offer every auto policyholder this coverage, but policyholders are not obligated to purchase it. In some other states with add-on plans, no-fault benefits must be purchased by all insureds.

Add-on plan

In a no-fault system, a plan that provides certain personal injury protection (PIP)-type benefits such as medical payments and disability coverages to injured victims, without regard to fault.

Choice No-Fault Plans

Under a **choice no-fault plan**, when an auto insurance policy is purchased or renewed, the insured can choose whether to be covered on a modified no-fault basis or not. In most states with choice no-fault plans, insureds who choose not to be covered on a modified no-fault basis must purchase add-on no-fault coverages. The modified no-fault option provides premium reductions in return for limitations on the right to sue for damages for certain types of auto injuries. If modified no-fault coverage is not selected, the insured retains full rights to seek compensation from the negligent party, but the insurer charges a higher premium. See the exhibit "Right to Sue in No-Fault Plans."

Choice no-fault plan

In a no-fault system, a plan that gives the insured the option, at the time an auto insurance policy is purchased or renewed, of choosing whether to be covered on a no-fault basis.

Right to Sue in No-Fault Plans

Type of Plan	Restrictions on Right to Sue?
Modified No-Fault Plans	Yes
Add-On Plans	No
Choice No-Fault Plans	Only if modified no-fault is selected

[DA00589]

Benefits Required by No-Fault Laws

Benefits required by no-fault laws typically include these:

- Medical expenses—usually subject to a limit
- Rehabilitation expenses—usually paid in addition to medical expenses
- Loss of earnings—a proportion of the insured person's lost earnings (usually subject to a maximum amount and time limit)
- Expenses for essential services—benefits paid for expenses incurred in obtaining services for necessary household tasks the injured person normally performs but now cannot
- Funeral expenses—usually paid up to a certain limit (sometimes included in the medical expense limit)
- Survivors' loss benefits—periodic income payments that partially compensate certain survivors for the death of a covered auto accident victim

Personal injury protection (PIP) coverage

Coverage that pays benefits, regardless of fault, for medical expense, income loss, and other benefits, resulting from bodily injury to occupants of a covered auto.

Insurers provide no-fault benefits by adding an endorsement to an auto insurance policy, typically called a PIP endorsement (or, in some states, "basic reparations"). The coverage provided by no-fault insurance is called **personal injury protection (PIP) coverage**. PIP endorsements vary by state, and in some states the no-fault laws specify precise policy language to be used in the endorsement.

Nearly all no-fault laws specify coverage only for bodily injury. No-fault laws generally exclude property damage for several reasons: property damage amounts are relatively small and damages are usually confined to vehicles; the amount of damage to property can usually be determined without difficulty; and auto insurers can usually settle claims for damage to their insureds' property quickly. See the exhibit "Efforts to Combat PIP Fraud."

Efforts to Combat PIP Fraud

PIP coverage in some states has been exploited by fraud rings. Fictitious pain clinics and corrupt medical and legal professionals have collaborated to assist many insureds in filing fraudulent PIP claims. Legislatures in various states are exploring revisions to no-fault laws that will curtail such claims. Among changes being considered is one that would reduce time frames for reporting auto accidents (sometimes sixty days) to allow insurers to review treatment plans earlier and avoid unnecessary treatments. Some states impose precertification guidelines for treatment of certain injuries, particularly soft tissue damage. The use of verbal rather than monetary thresholds helps avoid driving up medical costs unnecessarily.

[DA05496]

Some states require that insurers offer (for an additional premium) optional benefits higher than the minimum prescribed by no-fault laws. Additionally, some states require insurers to provide optional deductibles, allowing insureds to reduce or eliminate certain no-fault benefits for a reduced premium.

No-fault laws typically allow the no-fault insurer to collect payment (through **subrogation**) from at-fault parties to the extent that no-fault benefits were paid. Often, the insurer can require reimbursement of benefits it has paid to the insured if the insured subsequently recovers from the responsible party through legal action. Provisions for recovery under a no-fault law are described in the law and vary among states.

AUTOMOBILE INSURANCE FOR HIGH-RISK DRIVERS

High-risk drivers include those who habitually violate traffic laws, those who have been responsible for an excessive number of traffic accidents, and those who have been convicted of certain serious offenses, such as reckless driving, driving with a suspended license, or driving under the influence of alcohol or drugs. Insuring these individuals is extremely difficult for private insurers because of the high probability of a high-risk driver seriously injuring or killing other persons and causing extensive property damage.

Private insurers willingly insure drivers with average and above average driving records. Increasingly, private insurers also willingly accept some drivers with below average driving records in specialized high-risk driver programs. For those drivers who cannot obtain insurance from private insurers in this voluntary market, states have created mechanisms to make insurance available in a **residual market** (also called the shared market).

Voluntary Market Programs

Some insurers in the voluntary market offer insurance programs for high-risk drivers (often called nonstandard insurance programs). In contrast to insurers in the residual market, these voluntary insurers accept their own applications, service their policies, pay their claims and expenses, and retain full responsibility for their own underwriting results.

Because high-risk drivers are more likely to have accidents than other drivers, insurers that offer high-risk driver programs in the voluntary market may impose special restrictions and take other measures to reduce the risk to an acceptable level. Consequently, insurance in high-risk driver programs generally has several common characteristics:

- In many cases, private insurers limit coverage amounts to those that comply with the state's financial responsibility or compulsory insurance requirement. In some cases, private insurers offer optional higher limits.
- Medical payments coverage may be limited.
- Collision insurance may be available only with a high deductible.
- Premiums are substantially higher than premiums charged for average and above-average drivers.

Subrogation

The process by which an insurer can, after it has paid a loss under the policy, recover the amount paid from any party (other than the insured) who caused the loss or is otherwise legally liable for the loss.

Residual market

The term referring collectively to insurers and other organizations that make insurance available through a shared risk mechanism to those who cannot obtain coverage in the admitted market.

Safe driver insurance plan (SDIP)

Plan that allows for lower basic premiums for accident-free driving records and a surcharge for accidents.

Many voluntary insurers offering high-risk driver programs encourage insureds to drive responsibly through **safe driver insurance plans (SDIPs)**. Under these plans, premium credits are given to insureds who have no auto accidents or traffic convictions within a specified time period; however, insureds who incur traffic convictions or have at-fault accidents must pay higher premiums.

Residual Market Programs

States have developed various programs for high-risk drivers in the residual market, including these:

- Automobile insurance plans
- Joint underwriting associations (JUAs)
- Other programs

Automobile Insurance Plans

Automobile insurance plan

Plan for insuring high-risk drivers in which all auto insurers doing business in the state are assigned their proportionate share of such drivers based on the total volume of auto insurance written in the state.

Most states offer an **automobile insurance plan**, often called an assigned risk plan, for high-risk drivers who cannot obtain auto insurance in the voluntary market. Under a state's automobile insurance plan, all auto insurers doing business in the state are assigned their proportionate share of high-risk drivers based on the total volume of auto insurance written in the state. For example, an insurer that writes 10 percent of all the auto insurance in a state would be assigned 10 percent of the state's high-risk drivers.

Although state automobile insurance plans vary, they usually have common characteristics:

- Applicants must show that they have been unable to obtain auto liability insurance within a certain number of days (usually sixty) of the application.
- The minimum limits of insurance offered are at least equal to the state's financial responsibility or compulsory insurance requirement. (Most plans offer optional higher limits, as well as medical payments and physical damage coverages.)
- Certain applicants may be ineligible for coverage, such as those who do not have a valid driver's license, those convicted of a felony within the preceding thirty-six months, and habitual violators of state and local laws.
- Premiums are generally higher than premiums in the voluntary market. High-risk drivers are rated on the basis of their driving records and are charged accordingly.

While states use the term "assigned risk" to describe automobile insurance plans, most insurers no longer use or recommend that term. Insurers prefer to avoid negative characterization of their high-risk drivers for marketing purposes. Such insureds' driving habits may improve over time, and insurers may want to retain this newly profitable business.

Joint Underwriting Associations (JUAs)

Instead of offering an automobile insurance plan, several states have established **joint underwriting associations (JUAs)** to make auto insurance available to high-risk drivers. A JUA sets the insurance rates and approves the policy forms to be used for high-risk drivers. Although JUAs vary by state, generally a limited number of insurers are designated as servicing insurers to handle high-risk business.

Agents and brokers submit applications of high-risk drivers to the JUA or to a designated servicing insurer. The servicing insurer usually receives applications, issues policies, collects premiums, settles claims, and provides other necessary services.

In a state that offers a JUA, all auto insurers pay a proportionate share of total underwriting losses and expenses based on each insurer's share of voluntary auto insurance written in the state, a portion of which can be used to compensate the servicing insurers. For example, an insurer that writes 12 percent of all of the voluntary auto insurance in a particular state must pay 12 percent of the underwriting losses experienced by the JUA and 12 percent of the expenses, even though it is not required to insure high-risk drivers.

Joint underwriting association (JUA)

Organization that designates servicing insurers to handle high-risk auto insurance business; all auto insurers in the state are assessed a proportionate share of the losses and expenses based on their percentage of the voluntary auto insurance premiums written in the state.

Other Programs

A few states have enacted laws to establish a special **reinsurance facility** for high-risk drivers. Under this pool arrangement, insurers accept all auto insurance applicants who have a valid driver's license; the insurers issue policies, collect premiums, and settle claims. However, if an applicant for auto insurance is considered a high-risk driver, the insurer has the option of assigning the driver's premiums and losses to the reinsurance facility while continuing to service the policy. All auto insurers doing business in the state share any underwriting losses and the expenses of the reinsurance facility in proportion to the total auto insurance that they write in that state.

One state (Maryland) has established a state fund mechanism that provides insurance to high-risk applicants. Under this program, the state owns the fund but requires all private insurers to subsidize any losses; the private insurers, in turn, can recover those losses by surcharging their own insureds.

Reinsurance facility

A state-wide reinsurance pool to which insurers can assign premiums and losses for high-risk drivers; original insurers service the policies, but all insurers in the pool share the losses and expenses of the facility in proportion to the total auto insurance they write in that state.

AUTOMOBILE INSURANCE RATE REGULATION

All of the states in the United States require drivers to comply with state compulsory auto insurance laws or financial responsibility laws in exchange for the privilege to legally operate an auto. For most drivers, purchasing auto insurance is the only practical way to meet those requirements; therefore, the public often perceives purchasing insurance as a right rather than a privilege. Auto insurers are in business to make a profit, and this goal of profitability can conflict with the public's perceived right to buy insurance. Government regulation of insurance rates helps resolve this conflict.

State rating laws vary, but they generally require insurers to use rates that are adequate to pay all claims and expenses, reasonable (not excessive) for the exposure presented, and not unfairly discriminatory. In requiring adequate and reasonable rates, regulators must balance the concerns of insurers and consumers. Unfair discrimination occurs when an insurer applies different standards or treatment to insureds that present objectively similar loss potential. An example of unfair discrimination in auto insurance rating would be charging higher-than-normal rates for an applicant based solely on the applicant's race, religion, or ethnic background.

In applying the preceding requirements, auto insurance rate regulation is concerned with several issues:

- Rating factors
- Matching price to exposure
- Competition
- Other regulatory issues

Rating Factors

Rating systems vary by state and also by insurer. The rating of personal auto insurance is often computerized, but insurers decide which rating factors will be automated. All rating factors and discounts and credits reflect a change in the frequency and/or severity of a loss or in some way affect the cost of providing insurance.

Primary Rating Factors

Primary rating factors are the major factors that most states and insurers use for determining the cost of personal auto insurance. Although these factors have been used for many years in rating auto insurance, several states no longer permit the use of some factors that they consider unfairly discriminatory, such as age and gender. Primary rating factors include these:

- Territory—Determined by where the auto is normally used and garaged (parked overnight), territory is usually defined by the location of the insured's residence. Rural territories often have lower rates than urban territories because loss frequency and claim expenses tend to be higher in cities. Road conditions, state safety laws, and the extent of traffic regulation are territorial factors that affect the frequency and severity of auto accidents.

- Use of the auto—Insurers normally classify each insured auto for its principal use. Typical "use" categories include pleasure, driving to work or school, business, and farm use. Rates are generally lowest for farm and highest for business use, reflecting typical accident statistics.

- Age—Young drivers have less driving experience and tend to be involved in accidents more frequently than older drivers. Therefore, rates for younger drivers are often higher than those for more experienced drivers.

- Gender—In the past, women have tended to have fewer accidents than men in the same age categories, particularly among youthful drivers, so rates are often lower for women than for men. However, this tendency is changing as women's driving habits change.

- Marital status—Young married men tend to have fewer accidents than young unmarried men, and rates often reflect this tendency for this category of insureds.

Other Rating Factors

In addition to primary rating factors, other factors also affect loss statistics. Typically, these factors are not essential in determining the rating classification. Other rating factors that personal auto insurers use include these:

- Driving record—Almost all insurers use an applicant's driving record to determine whether the individual presents an acceptable exposure and, if acceptable, at what rate. Many insurers have safe driver insurance plans (SDIPs) that base premiums on the insured's driving record.

- Driver education—A premium discount may be provided for young drivers who complete an approved driver education course, usually including road experience. Also, some insurers offer premium discounts to drivers age fifty-five and older who successfully complete defensive driver training courses. Driver training can help reduce the frequency and severity of auto losses.

- Good student—Students who maintain good grades may be offered premium discounts because, theoretically, they have fewer accidents than poor or average students.

- Multi-car policy—Most insurers give a multi-car discount when more than one auto is insured under the same policy. This discount is based on the assumption that two or more autos owned by the same insured will not be driven as often as a single auto. Additionally, it is less costly for the insurer to cover additional autos under the same contract, so savings may be passed to the insured.

- Years of driving experience—Generally, drivers with more years of experience make fewer mistakes and have fewer accidents.

- Credit-based insurance score—Some insurers consider an applicant's insurance score. This numerical ranking is similar to a credit score, but without income data, and is based on information from an individual's financial history. Actuarial research indicates that insureds with low insurance scores submit more claims than insureds with high insurance scores. Some states consider insurance scores unfairly discriminatory and do not allow them as a rating factor.

- Type of auto—The performance, age, and damageability of an auto can affect the rates for physical damage coverage on it. For example, a new sports car would cost more to insure for collision coverage and possibly for liability coverage than an older station wagon because the sports car would be more expensive to repair, might be damaged more easily, and is more likely to be operated in an unsafe manner.

- Deductibles—Insureds who choose higher deductibles for collision and other physical damage coverage on their autos can receive a credit, sometimes a significant one, because the insured retains a portion of covered losses.

- Liability limits—Rates are generally based on the minimum liability limits required by the state, and premiums increase if the insured chooses higher limits. (However, doubling liability limits does not mean doubling the premium, and higher limits are often a bargain compared to minimum limits.)

Other Discounts and Credits

Some insurers also give discounts or credits for certain automobile features or practices of the insured that reduce insurer costs:

- Anti-theft devices can reduce the frequency of theft losses.

- Passive restraints (airbags) can reduce the severity of injuries.

- Reduced auto use by a student who attends a school that is more than a specified distance from home and does not garage an insured auto at school can reduce the frequency of losses.

- Having more than one type of policy with the same insurer (called a multi-policy or multi-account discount) reduces administrative costs.

- Multiple years of continuous coverage with the insurer (called a renewal or anniversary discount) reduces acquisition costs.

Factors That Affect Auto Insurance Rates

Primary factors:

- Territory
- Use of auto
- Age
- Gender
- Marital status

Other factors:

- Driving record
- Driver education
- Good student
- Multi-car policy
- Years of driving experience
- Credit-based insurance score
- Type of auto
- Deductibles
- Liability limits

[DA05737]

Matching Price to Exposure

Insurers often divide auto insurance applicants into homogeneous classes, or rating categories, such as "preferred," "standard," and "nonstandard," that reflect different levels of exposure to loss. For example, applicants with good driving records and rating factors that suggest they present minimal loss exposure are categorized as preferred. By offering lower rates to this category of insureds, insurers hope to attract and retain good customers. Conversely, applicants with poor driving records or rating factors that suggest they present greater loss exposure are categorized as nonstandard and are charged higher rates. Usually insurers also have a standard rating category for drivers that fall between these two extremes and present an average loss exposure.

Regulators usually approve these rating categories because policyholders receive equitable treatment based on the loss exposures they present.

Competition

Competition for profitable automobile business is often intense among insurers. When insurers are making a profit, they often compete with each other by lowering rates. However, insurers cannot decrease rates to the point at which they can no longer cover the costs of claims and expenses. In times of high underwriting losses and low profits, insurers must raise rates, restrict the number and types of new applicants they will accept, or take other steps to become more profitable.

Because of this tendency of insurers to consider competitive cycles in pricing personal auto insurance, regulators monitor rates carefully to ensure adequacy and reasonableness. Insurance regulators monitor rates primarily through rate filings, which are the documentation that an insurer files with a state to request a change in existing rates. Insurers' rates must always meet the state requirements that rates must be adequate, reasonable, and not unfairly discriminatory.

Other Regulatory Issues

Many other regulatory issues, such as these, affect auto insurance coverages and rates:

- Rising healthcare costs
- Environmental issues
- Vehicle modifications

Rising Healthcare Costs

Increases in automobile insurance rates can often be linked to that portion of the premium linked to healthcare costs. One component of auto insurance coverage is personal injury protection (PIP), which pays the healthcare bills for individuals injured in auto accidents.

Each year, more than two million American motorists suffer personal injuries from auto accidents, with about 38,000 dying in auto accidents.[4] Costs for treating these accident victims are rising rapidly, translating into higher auto insurance premiums. Costs for treating an auto accident victim range from $6,000 to $9,000 and can total tens of thousands of dollars.[5]

The increasing cost of healthcare in the U.S. places great strains on all systems used to finance healthcare coverage, including auto insurance as well as private employer-sponsored and public health insurance coverage. To illustrate, healthcare costs in the United States in 2007 totaled more than three times the 1990 total and over eight times the 1980 costs.[6] These costs directly affect not only the medical payments/PIP side of premiums, but also liability payments and uninsured motorists coverage.

Environmental Issues

Environmental issues can affect auto insurance coverages and rates because automobiles are a primary source of pollution emissions. Most environmental laws affecting auto insurance are state regulations. State emissions regulations, for example, increase auto costs and result in higher claim payments for more expensive autos.

As another example of environmental issues affecting auto insurance costs, California's "pay-as-you-drive" regulation enables insurers to offer consumers rates that are based on actual instead of estimated miles driven. This program provides financial incentives for California motorists to drive less, leading to lower-cost auto insurance, less air pollution through lower auto exhaust emissions, and a reduced dependence on foreign oil.[7] Because of increased concern about the environmental effects of auto use, the future may hold more state-based environmental regulations that not only curb pollution but also affect auto insurance rates.

Vehicle Modifications

The growing vehicle modification business adds performance parts and styling features that can affect auto insurance rates. Whatever the reason for the modifications (which can range from personal styling preferences to handicap access equipment), features must conform to local or regional vehicle standard regulations. However, compliance for some modifications is not always easy to detect or enforce. Such modifications as a lowered or raised suspension, increased engine size, and tinted windows can increase risk and insurance premiums because modifications can put insureds at a greater risk of collision. A modified vehicle can become untrustworthy and affect safety as well as auto insurance rates.

Even modifications that would appear to create safer vehicles, like improved brake systems, can increase insurance costs for several reasons:

- Modifications can increase auto values and, as a result, insurers' claim payments.
- Modified autos can attract thieves, also increasing insurers' claim payments.
- Auto performance modifications improve auto performance, which can result in more severe accidents.

SUMMARY

Victims of auto accidents caused by the negligence of another party are entitled to compensation and damages. Some of the approaches to compensating auto accident victims include these:

- Tort liability system
- Financial responsibility laws
- Compulsory insurance laws
- Uninsured motorists coverage
- Underinsured motorists coverage
- No-fault insurance

Roughly one-half of the states in the U.S. have no-fault laws that authorize or mandate one of three types of auto no-fault insurance plans: modified no-fault plans, add-on plans, and choice no-fault plans. These plans define the benefits that insurers can or must provide and define any restrictions on the right to sue the at-fault party.

Some high-risk drivers can purchase auto insurance from private insurers in the voluntary market that offer high-risk driver insurance programs. Other high-risk drivers can usually purchase insurance in residual market programs, which include automobile insurance plans, joint underwriting associations (JUAs), reinsurance facilities, and state funds. These programs share many common characteristics, and all require higher premiums than standard auto insurance to offset potential underwriting losses and expenses.

State insurance regulators require auto insurers to develop rates that are adequate to pay all claims and expenses, reasonable (not excessive) for the exposure presented, and not unfairly discriminatory. Insurers develop rating factors that conform to these requirements, and state regulators ensure that insurers apply rating categories that match the price of auto insurance to the appropriate level of loss exposure. Because insurers consider competitive cycles in pricing personal auto insurance, regulators monitor rates carefully to ensure adequacy and reasonableness. Other regulator and rating issues include the effects of rising healthcare costs on auto insurance rates, environmental issues, and vehicle modifications.

ASSIGNMENT NOTES

1.   Insurance Information Institute, *Issues Updates*, November 2007, www.iii.org (accessed December 17, 2007).

2.   Insurance Information Institute, *Issues Updates*, November 2007, www.iii.org (accessed December 17, 2007).

3.   Insurance Information Institute, *No Fault Auto Insurance*, October 2007, www.iii. org (accessed January 28, 2008).

4.   National Highway Traffic Safety Administration, www-nrd.nhtsa.dot.gov/ Pubs/811162.PDF (accessed February 3, 2010).

5.   Insurance Information Institute, http://huetherinsurance.com/PDF%20Files/ Auto%20Rates%20on%20the%20Rise.pdf (accessed February 4, 2010).

6.   The Kaiser Family Foundation, www.kaiseredu.org/topics_im.asp?imID=1&paren tID=61&id=358 (accessed February 3, 2010).

7.   "California Issues Regulations for Pay-As-You-Drive," *Insurance Journal*, www. insurancejournal.com/news/west/2009/09/10/103600.htm (accessed February 3, 2010).

3

Personal Auto Insurance: Liability, Medical Payments, and UM

Educational Objectives

After learning the content of this assignment, you should be able to:

▷ Summarize the sections of the Personal Auto Policy.

▷ Explain how the words and phrases included in the Definitions section of the Personal Auto Policy are used to determine whether coverage applies and, if so, whether it is modified, excluded, or limited.

▷ Summarize each of the provisions in Part A—Liability Coverage of the Personal Auto Policy.

▷ Summarize each of the provisions in Part B—Medical Payments Coverage of the Personal Auto Policy.

▷ Summarize each of the provisions in Part C—Uninsured Motorists Coverage of the Personal Auto Policy.

▷ Describe underinsured motorists insurance in terms of:

- Its purpose

- The ways in which it can vary by state

▷ Given a case describing a claim involving an individual or a family with a Personal Auto Policy (PAP) that includes liability, medical payments, and uninsured motorists coverage, determine what is covered, excluded, or limited, and for what amounts.

Personal Auto Insurance: Liability, Medical Payments, and UM

3

OVERVIEW OF THE PERSONAL AUTO POLICY

Many auto owners in the United States use some form of the Insurance Services Office, Inc. (ISO) Personal Auto Policy (PAP) to insure their personal auto loss exposures.

The PAP is designed to insure private passenger autos—vehicles such as cars, vans, station wagons, and sport utility vehicles designed primarily for use on public roads—as well as pickup trucks and full-size vans.

The PAP consists of a Declarations page, an Agreement and Definitions page, and six separate sections. Almost all PAPs also include one or more endorsements to comply with state-specific requirements or to meet specific coverage needs of some insureds.

These are the six sections:

- Part A—Liability Coverage
- Part B—Medical Payments Coverage
- Part C—Uninsured Motorists Coverage
- Part D—Damage to Your Auto Coverage
- Part E—Insured Duties Following an Accident or Loss
- Part F—General Provisions

Declarations

The Declarations page includes general information, such as the name and mailing address of the insured. This page also provides the name of the insurer issuing the policy and the name and address of the producer, if applicable. Other information on the Declarations page includes the policy period, a description of the covered autos, limits of liability, premium and rating information, and any endorsements that may apply to the policy.

Agreement and Definitions

The Agreement and Definitions page of the PAP includes a general agreement stating that the insurer is providing the coverage subject to payment of premium and to the terms of the policy. The definitions section uses simple-to-understand language to define important words and phrases that are used throughout the policy.

Overview of Coverages

The PAP coverages may be summarized in this fashion:

- Part A—Liability Coverage protects the insured against claims or lawsuits for bodily injury or property damage arising out of the operation of an auto.

- Part B—Medical Payments Coverage compensates for reasonable and necessary medical and funeral expenses because of bodily injury to the insured caused by an auto accident.

- Part C—Uninsured Motorists Coverage pays damages if an insured is injured by an uninsured motorist, a hit-and-run driver, or a driver whose insurer is insolvent.

- Part D—Coverage for Damage to Your Auto compensates for physical damage to a covered auto and to certain nonowned autos. Also referred to as physical damage coverage, Part D includes other than collision and collision coverages. Some insureds elect not to include physical damage coverage on their policies.

- Part E—Duties After an Accident or Loss outlines the duties required of an insured after an accident or a loss, such as requirements for notifying the insurer of the details of any losses that happen.

- Part F—General Provisions contains information such as how changes to the policy can be made, provisions for cancellation and termination of the policy, and descriptions of the policy period and territory.

Endorsements

In addition to the PAP coverage form, the policy also includes state-specific endorsements. These endorsements are usually used to adapt the PAP to state-specific laws and regulations applying to auto insurance. Endorsements are also available to provide additional coverages that are desired by some policyholders but are not purchased by all policyholders. These endorsements are separate from the PAP coverage form but must be considered as part of the overall structure of a PAP. See the exhibit "Overview of the Personal Auto Policy."

Overview of the Personal Auto Policy

Insured Risk	Peril (Cause of Loss)	Consequences	Treatment
Personal Auto	Accident with another vehicle	Damage to the "Other" vehicle; Financial—cost of repairs	PAP—Part A: Liability Coverage
Personal Auto	Accident with another vehicle	Injury to driver and/or passengers; Financial—costs of medical	PAP—Part B: Medical Payments Coverage
Personal Auto	Accident with another vehicle	Injury from uninsured or underinsured motorist; Financial—costs of medical, loss of wages, pain and suffering	PAP—Part C: Uninsured Motorists Coverage
Personal Auto	Accident with another vehicle	Damage to "Your" vehicle; Financial—cost of repairs, loss of use	PAP—Part D: Damage to Your Auto Coverage
Personal Auto	Accident with another vehicle	Injury to passengers in "Your" vehicle; Financial—costs of medical, loss of wages, pain and suffering	PAP—Part A: Liability Coverage

Continued on next page

Insured Risk	Peril (Cause of Loss)	Consequences	Treatment
Personal Auto	Accident with another vehicle	Injury to driver and passengers of "Other" vehicle; Financial—costs of medical, loss of wages, pain and suffering	PAP—Part A: Liability Coverage
Personal Auto	Accident with another vehicle	Property of persons not in vehicles: Financial—cost of repairs, cost of loss of use	PAP—Part A: Liability Coverage
Personal Auto	Accident with another vehicle, theft	Personal property damaged/lost while in vehicle; Financial—cost of repairs	Homeowners policy
Personal Auto	Accident with pedestrian	Injury to pedestrian; Financial—costs of medical, loss of wages, pain and suffering	PAP—Part A: Liability Coverage
Personal Auto	Vandalism	Damage to "Your" vehicle; Financial—cost of repairs	PAP—Part D: Damage to Your Auto Coverage
Personal Auto	Theft	Damage to / Loss of "Your" vehicle; Financial—cost of repairs or cost of replacement	PAP—Part D: Damage to Your Auto Coverage
Personal Auto	Single car accident	Damage to "Your" vehicle; Financial—cost of repairs	PAP—Part D: Damage to Your Auto Coverage
Personal Auto	Collision with an object	Damage to "Your" vehicle; Financial—cost of repairs	PAP—Part D: Damage to Your Auto Coverage
Personal Auto	Collision with an object	Damage to property of others; Financial—cost of repairs	PAP—Part A: Liability Coverage

PERSONAL AUTO POLICY DEFINITIONS

Insurance policies contain definitions of words and phrases that must be understood to determine whether coverage applies or other policy provisions are applicable. Some claim lawsuits have centered on the policy definition of words or phrases; consequently a thorough review of the definitions section is crucial to determining coverage.

Definitions in the Personal Automobile Policy (PAP) must be analyzed to determine whether coverage or a given policy provision applies. Certain words and phrases used throughout the policy are defined in the policy's Definitions section. Some definitions describe a word or phrase, and other definitions clarify the times or circumstances under which the coverage or other policy provision applies, as associated with specific words and phrases. A review of the purpose of the PAP Definitions and an explanation of those definitions that are likely to affect coverage enables insurance personnel to determine whether coverage applies.

Purpose of PAP Definitions

Most insurance policies, including the PAP, have a separate definitions section that explains both common terms and less frequently used insurance-specific wording to assist policyholders in understanding the coverage they have purchased. Because the PAP is designed for individuals and families who might not be familiar with insurance policy terms, the Definitions section appears at the beginning of the PAP for easy reference. In contrast, most commercial policy forms include the definitions section at the end of the forms.

The Definitions section is written in simple language designed to be easily understood by individuals who may not be familiar with insurance terminology. Whenever a defined term appears in other sections of the policy, quotation marks around that term indicate that it is defined in the definitions section.

The definitions clarify to whom, to what, when, and under what circumstances coverage, exclusions, insuring agreements, and other policy provisions apply. Consequently, these definitions are crucial to understanding the policy provisions and, in some cases, coverage can be extended or excluded based on the details in these definitions.

Individual sections of the policy sometimes define terms as they are used in that section. In contrast the terms in the Definitions section are defined for use in every section of the policy, whenever they are used. See the exhibit "Personal Auto Policy Definitions Sample."

Personal Auto Policy Definitions Sample

PERSONAL AUTO
PP 00 01 01 05

PERSONAL AUTO POLICY

AGREEMENT

In return for payment of the premium and subject to all the terms of this policy, we agree with you as follows:

DEFINITIONS

A. Throughout this policy, "you" and "your" refer to:

1. The "named insured" shown in the Declarations; and

2. The spouse if a resident of the same household.

If the spouse ceases to be a resident of the same household during the policy period or prior to the inception of this policy, the spouse will be considered "you" and "your" under this policy but only until the earlier of:

1. The end of 90 days following the spouse's change of residency;

2. The effective date of another policy listing the spouse as a named insured; or

3. The end of the policy period.

B. "We", "us" and "our" refer to the Company providing this insurance.

C. For purposes of this policy, a private passenger type auto, pickup or van shall be deemed to be owned by a person if leased:

2. Pickup or van.

It also means a farm wagon or farm implement while towed by a vehicle listed in **1.** or **2.** above.

J. "Your covered auto" means:

1. Any vehicle shown in the Declarations.

2. A "newly acquired auto".

3. Any "trailer" you own.

4. Any auto or "trailer" you do not own while used as a temporary substitute for any other vehicle described in this definition which is out of normal use because of its:

a. Breakdown;

b. Repair;

c. Servicing;

d. Loss; or

e. Destruction.

This Provision (**J.4.**) does not apply to Coverage For Damage To Your Auto.

[DA05934]

Important PAP Definitions

Certain words and phrases defined in the PAP Definitions section are used repeatedly throughout the policy provisions, or they weigh heavily on whether or not coverage is provided. These words and phrases are most significant:

- You and your—The words "you" and "your" refer to the named insured shown on the Declarations page. "You" and "your" also include an unnamed spouse of the named insured—provided that he or she is a resident of the same household. When an unnamed spouse of the named insured moves out of the household but remains married to the insured, the spouse is considered "you" for another ninety days or until the policy expires—whichever comes first. Coverage ceases if the spouse is named on another policy.

- Family member—A family member is a person who is related to the named insured or spouse by blood, marriage, or adoption and who resides in the named insured's household. This definition also includes a ward or a foster child. This term is significant under the PAP, which is designed to provide coverage for the named insured and other family members.

- We, us, and our—The words "we," "us," and "our" refer to the insurer providing insurance under the contract, generally the insurer named in the Declarations page.

- Bodily injury—"Bodily injury" is bodily harm, sickness, or disease, including death. This phrase is referred to in Part A—Liability Coverage and in Part B—Medical Payments Coverage, as well as in Part C—Uninsured Motorists Coverage, and defines the coverage for which payment will be made under the policy.

- Occupying—"Occupying" is defined as in, upon, getting in, on, out, or off. This definition is used in connection with Part B—Medical Payments Coverage and Part C—Uninsured Motorists Coverage, and it clarifies the coverages provided. For example, if an insured's friend, Jake, was injured while leaning over an insured vehicle to check the battery connection, then Jake was occupying the auto.

- Property damage—"Property damage" is physical injury to, destruction of, or loss of use of tangible property. This phrase appears only in Part A—Liability Coverage and defines the coverage for which some payments will be made under the policy. For example, if Fred's negligent operation of his auto causes damage to Sue's auto, Fred's PAP will pay to repair or replace Sue's auto and will pay any sums that Fred is legally obligated to pay for obtaining substitute transportation for Sue until her auto is returned to service.

Another PAP definition, "your covered auto," is one of two words or phrases included in the definitions section that have more detailed definitions than the other defined terms. This important definition describes the vehicles that are covered under the PAP and includes these four classes of vehicles:

- Any vehicle shown in the Declarations—Your covered auto includes any vehicle listed in the declarations. Covered vehicles can include private passenger autos such as cars, minivans, station wagons, sport utility vehicles, or pickup trucks owned or leased by the named insured.

- A newly acquired auto—This auto is a private passenger auto, pickup, or van acquired by the named insured during the policy period and meeting the eligibility requirements. Except for physical damage coverage (Coverage for Damage to Your Auto), a newly acquired auto is covered equally to the broadest coverage available to any vehicle in the policy on the date the vehicle is acquired. For coverage to continue beyond a specified time period, the insured must request coverage. These time periods depend on whether the vehicle is a replacement for another insured vehicle or an additional vehicle; and time periods are specified for Collision coverage, Other Than Collision coverage, and all other coverages.

- Any trailer you own—A trailer owned by the named insured is also a covered auto. A trailer is a vehicle designed to be pulled by a private passenger auto, pickup, or van.

- A temporary substitute auto or trailer—A temporary, non-owned, auto or trailer that is used as a short-term substitute for another covered auto that is out of normal use because of breakdown, repair, servicing, loss, or destruction. A temporary substitute auto is covered under all PAP coverages except damage to your auto (physical damage). For physical damage coverage, temporary substitute vehicles are treated the same as other non-owned autos.

☑ Reality Check

Personal Auto Policy Case: Outcome Determined by Policy Definitions

A New Mexico appeals court affirmed the decision of a lower court based, in large part, on the definitions of "you" and "your" in a couple's Personal Auto Policy. In this case, the Reynolds' insurer denied payment of a liability claim brought by John and Joanne Sheldon against James Reynolds for damages after the Sheldons were injured in an auto accident with James Reynolds. James's wife, Sara, owned the vehicle James was driving and had insured it under a separate policy before the two were married. James Reynolds had a separate policy on a vehicle he owned, and the Sheldons sued for coverage under James's policy. The insurer contended that the vehicle Reynolds was driving (owned and insured by Sara) at the time of the accident was not covered by his policy.

The Sheldons brought suit against the insurer for breach of contract and violations of Unfair Claims Practices Act and Unfair Trade Practices Act (among others). They argued that James Reynolds' policy covered the accident because James was driving a vehicle owned by his wife and that, for liability purposes, the "you" and "your" language in the policy applies to any vehicle owned by the named insured and the insured's spouse. The insurer argued that the Owned Vehicle exclusion in James's policy eliminated coverage for Sara's vehicle as a vehicle "other than your covered auto, which is … [o]wned by you"; that is, "you" and "your" apply only to the named insured, not the spouse. The lower court granted summary judgment in favor of the insurer, ruling that "you" and "your" should not be construed to apply to both husband and wife. The state court of appeals agreed.[1]

[DA05912]

PART A—LIABILITY COVERAGE

Because the financial consequences of automobile liability loss are potentially far greater than any damage that could occur to an insured's auto, the Personal

Auto Policy's Part A—Liability Coverage offers particularly valuable protection for the insured.

The Personal Auto Policy (PAP), from Insurance Service Office, Inc. (ISO), consists of a Declarations page, Definitions, and six separate parts. Part A— Liability Coverage provides protection against an insured's legal liability arising out of the ownership, maintenance, or use of an auto.

This section discusses these provisions of Part A:

- Insuring Agreement
- Supplementary Payments
- Exclusions
- Limit of Liability
- Out of State Coverage
- Financial Responsibility
- Other Insurance

Insuring Agreement

The Part A Insuring Agreement states the insurer's duty to pay damages and defense costs and defines the persons and organizations insured under Part A.

Damages and Defense Costs Covered

In the Insuring Agreement, the insurer agrees to pay damages for bodily injury or property damage for which an insured is legally responsible because of an auto accident. Damages may include both **compensatory damages** and punitive, or exemplary, damages. The policy limit(s) applicable to this coverage can be expressed either on a **split-limits basis** or a **single-limits basis**.

The damages covered also include any **prejudgment interest** awarded against the insured. Many states' laws allow plaintiffs (injured persons who file suit) to receive interest on a judgment from the time an accident occurs, or a lawsuit is filed, to the time the judgment is handed down. Prejudgment interest is added to the amount recovered to put the claimant in the same position as if he or she had received payment for damages at the time of the accident or suit.

Because prejudgment interest is considered to be part of the award for damages, it is subject to the applicable limit of liability for Part A. For example, assume an insured who is legally liable for bodily injury in an auto accident has a PAP with a $100,000 limit of liability. If the insured is found legally liable for injuring one person and ordered to pay a $50,000 judgment, plus $5,000 in prejudgment interest, the insured's PAP insurer will pay the full $55,000. However, if the judgment is for $95,000, plus $10,000 in prejudgment interest, the insured's PAP will pay only up to the $100,000 limit of liability.

Compensatory damages
A payment awarded by a court to reimburse a victim for actual harm.

Split-limits basis
Separate coverage limits that allow one limit for bodily injury to each person; a second, usually higher, limit for bodily injury to all persons in each accident; and a third limit for all property damage in each accident.

Single-limits basis
One coverage limit that applies to all damages arising from bodily injury or property damage or both, resulting from a single accident.

Prejudgment interest
Interest that may accrue on damages before a judgment has been rendered.

In addition to agreeing to pay damages for which the insured is legally liable, subject to policy limits, the insurer also agrees to defend the insured and pay all legal costs the insured may incur in a liability suit—even if the combined costs exceed the limit of liability. In other words, the insurer is obligated to pay defense costs in addition to the policy limits. When a large claim is involved, the insurer cannot simply offer, or "tender," its policy limits and be relieved of any further duty to defend the insured. However, the insurer's duty to settle or defend ends when the limit of liability has been exhausted by the payment of judgments or settlements.

The insurer also has no obligation to defend any claim that is not covered under the policy. If, for example, a suit alleges only that the insured intentionally caused bodily injury, the insurer has no obligation to defend the insured because the PAP specifically excludes bodily injury (or property damage) intentionally caused by the insured. However, courts have often held that an insurer's duty to defend is broader than its duty to pay damages. Various rules of law define an insurer's duty to defend, but these rules are beyond the scope of this discussion.

Persons and Organizations Insured

As stated in its Insuring Agreement, Part A of the PAP provides liability coverage for four classes of persons or organizations: the named insured and family members, any person using the named insured's covered auto, any person or organization legally responsible for the acts of a covered person while using a covered auto, and any person or organization legally responsible for the named insured's or family member's use of any automobile or trailer.

The named insured and family members are covered for the ownership, maintenance, or use of any auto or trailer. The named insured, referred to as "you" in the PAP, also includes the named insured's spouse if the spouse is a resident of the same household. Family members are persons related to the named insured by blood, marriage, or adoption, as well as wards or foster children, who live in the named insured's household. In addition, children who are temporarily away from home, such as those attending college, are still covered under their parents' policy. These insureds are protected, not only while driving covered autos, but also when operating borrowed autos, rented vehicles (autos or trucks), or any other auto, subject to the policy exclusions.

Any person using the named insured's covered auto is also covered under Part A. Unless otherwise noted the phrase "covered auto" is used in this discussion to mean "your covered auto" as defined in the PAP. The PAP definition of "your covered auto" includes any vehicle shown in the declarations; a "newly acquired auto" (as defined in the PAP); any "trailer"(as defined in the PAP) that the named insured owns; or any auto or "trailer" that the named insured does not own while used as a temporary substitute for any other covered auto that is out of normal use because of its breakdown, repair, servicing, loss, or destruction.

Part A also covers any person or organization legally responsible for the acts of a covered person while using a covered auto. Assume that, while driving his car to the post office to pick up a package for his employer, Bob negligently injures another person. If the victim sues Bob's employer, the employer is also covered under his PAP (because Bob is a covered person while driving his car, and the employer is responsible for his actions as an employee).

Coverage further extends to any person or organization legally responsible for the named insured's or family member's use of any automobile or trailer. This provision applies only if the person or organization does not own or hire the auto or trailer. For example, Cheryl, the named insured, injures a pedestrian while driving a car loaned to her by a local business to run errands for a nursing home. Because neither Cheryl nor the nursing home owns or has hired the car, Cheryl's PAP will defend both her and the nursing home against any allegation of liability for the injury to the pedestrian. However, the local business that loaned Cheryl the car would not be covered under Cheryl's PAP and would seek liability coverage under its own policy.

Supplementary Payments

Part A of the PAP contains a provision for payment of certain expenses that are considered to be **supplementary payments**, which, if paid, will not reduce the limit of liability. There are five supplementary payments in Part A:

- Cost of bail bonds—The insurer agrees to pay up to $250 for the cost of bail bonds (bail bond premiums) required because of an accident that results in bodily injury or property damage covered by the policy.

- Premiums on appeal bonds and bonds to release attachments—An insured ordered to pay a court-awarded judgment can appeal that decision to a higher court. An appeal bond guarantees that, if the appeal is lost, the insured will pay the original judgment and the cost of the appeal. During legal proceedings, the plaintiff may place an **attachment** on the insured's property, such as a vehicle. A release of attachment bond guarantees that the insured will pay any judgment, thereby permitting a release of the attachment on the insured's property.

- Interest accruing after a judgment—Interest that accrues after a judgment (called **postjudgment interest**) is also paid as a supplementary payment. For example, if the insured appeals a lawsuit, any interest that accrues after the judgment becomes payable to the plaintiff by the insurer. The insurer will pay this amount on behalf of the insured separately from the liability judgment, and the amount paid will not reduce the limit of liability.

- Loss of earnings because of attendance at trials—The insurer also pays up to $200 per day for an insured's loss of earnings (but not of other income) for attending a hearing or trial at the insurer's request.

- Other reasonable expenses incurred at the insurer's request—For purposes of defending a lawsuit, an insurer may make requests of the insured that

Supplementary payments
Various expenses the insurer agrees to pay under a liability insurance policy (in addition to the liability limits) for items such as premiums on bail bonds and appeal bonds, loss of the insured's earnings because of attendance at trials, and other reasonable expenses incurred by the insured at the insurer's request.

Attachment
The act of seizing property to secure a judgment.

Postjudgment interest
Interest that may accrue on damages after a judgment has been entered in a court and before the money is paid.

result in expenditures. Any such reasonable expenses are also covered as supplementary payments. For example, an insured may incur travel and transportation expenses to testify at a trial at the insurer's request.

Exclusions

As with most insurance policies, the Part A—Insuring Agreement describes broad coverage that is narrowed by exclusions. PAP liability coverage is subject to several exclusions.

Intentional Injury

The PAP does not provide liability coverage for an insured who intentionally causes bodily injury or property damage. For example, if Sam becomes enraged when he is caught in a traffic jam and deliberately rams the vehicle in front of him, his responsibility for any intentional property damage to the other motorist's car would not be covered under his PAP.

Property Owned or Transported

Liability coverage does not apply to damage to property owned or being transported by an insured. For example, if Alice is transporting a friend's suitcase and clothing while she is driving on vacation and is at fault in an auto accident in which these items are damaged, the loss to the items is not covered under Alice's PAP.

Property Rented to, Used by, or in the Care of the Insured

Liability for property rented to, used by, or in the care of the insured is not covered under the PAP. For example, if Don rents glassware and china for a party and those items are later damaged in an accident involving his car, his liability for damage to the rented glassware and china is not covered. However, this exclusion does not apply to damage to a residence or private garage. Therefore, if Don accidentally backs his car into the side of a vacation house he is renting, his liability for the damage to the rented house would be covered.

Bodily Injury to an Employee of an Insured

The liability coverage also excludes bodily injury to an employee of an insured who is injured during the course of employment. Compensation for the employee's injury is usually provided under a workers compensation law. However, injury to a domestic employee injured in the course of employment is covered if workers compensation benefits are not required or are unavailable for that employee.

Public or Livery Conveyance

A **public or livery conveyance** is one that is indiscriminately offered to the public (usually to carry people or property for a fee), such as a taxi or a bus. Part A liability coverage does not apply to an insured's ownership or operation of a vehicle while it is being used as a public or livery conveyance. For example, if local taxicab drivers are on strike and Harry decides to capitalize on the situation by transporting persons in his car for a fee, Harry's PAP liability coverage does not apply to this activity. The exclusion does not apply to share-the-expense car pools.

Public or livery conveyance
In case law, a method of transportation that is indiscriminately offered to the general public, such as a taxi or public bus.

Garage Business Use

Liability insurance does not apply to any insured while employed or engaged in the business of selling, repairing, servicing, storing, or parking vehicles designed for use mainly on public highways. This exclusion also applies to road testing and delivery of vehicles. For example, if an auto mechanic has an accident while road testing a customer's car, the mechanic's PAP liability coverage does not apply. The intent is to exclude a loss exposure that should be covered by a commercial auto policy, such as a garage policy, purchased by the owner of the business.

The garage business exclusion does not apply to the insured's covered auto when it is being driven by the named insured; a family member; or any partner, agent, or employee of the named insured or a family member. For example, if a mechanic injures someone while driving his covered auto (rather than a customer's auto) to a parts shop to pick up a part for his employer, the mechanic's PAP liability insurance would cover the loss.

Other Business Use

Liability coverage does not apply to any vehicle other than a private passenger auto, a pickup, a van, or a trailer (while it is being used with a covered vehicle) that is maintained or used in any business other than farming or ranching. The intent is to exclude liability coverage for commercial vehicles and trucks used in a business.

For example, if an insured drives a city bus or operates a large commercial truck, the insured's PAP liability coverage does not apply. Coverage for such vehicles is available through business auto policies.

Vehicle Used Without Reasonable Belief of Being Entitled

If an insured uses a vehicle without reasonable belief that he or she is entitled to do so, the liability coverage does not apply. For example, if Jake notices that the keys have been left in a stranger's car at a mall, takes the car for a ride, and causes an accident, his PAP does not provide liability coverage.

This exclusion does not apply when another family member (as defined) uses the owned auto of a named insured. For insurance purposes, it is assumed that a family member has permission to use another family member's car.

Nuclear Energy Liability Losses

The PAP excludes coverage of liability for bodily injury or property damage caused by an insured who is also covered by a nuclear energy liability policy. Almost anyone can become an insured under a nuclear energy liability policy because some of these policies have broad definitions of who an insured is and may include a member of the public. For example, if an individual accidentally drives his vehicle into a nuclear energy facility, causing the release of harmful radiation, he could potentially be considered an insured under that facility's nuclear energy liability policy and be covered for damages claimed by other parties exposed to radiation.

Vehicles With Fewer Than Four Wheels or Designed for Off-Road Use

Liability arising out of the ownership, maintenance, or use of any vehicle that has fewer than four wheels is excluded. Also excluded is liability coverage for any vehicle that is designed mainly for use off public roads, other than a nonowned golf cart, a vehicle being used by an insured in a medical emergency, or a trailer.

For example, any liability Fred might incur while driving a golf cart owned by the country club where he is playing golf would be covered. Although this provision excludes coverage for motorcycles, mopeds, and motorscooters, those vehicles can be covered by adding an endorsement to the PAP.

Other Vehicles Owned by Insured or Available for Insured's Regular Use

Any vehicle, other than a covered auto, owned by the named insured or made available for the named insured's regular use is also excluded. An insured can drive another person's auto on an occasional, as opposed to a regular, basis and still have coverage under his or her own policy. If the nonowned auto is furnished for the insured's regular use, the insured's liability coverage does not apply.

The intent of this exclusion is to encourage customers to accurately disclose the number of vehicles they own or regularly operate. Otherwise, the insured could insure and pay premiums for only one vehicle even though the insured drives several cars on a regular basis, substantially increasing the insurer's exposure.

Vehicles Owned by or Available for Family Member's Regular Use

A similar exclusion applies to vehicles (other than covered autos) owned by any family member or furnished or made available for the regular use of any family member. However, the exclusion does not apply to the named insured and spouse while maintaining or occupying such a vehicle. Therefore, the liability insurance under Bill's PAP would cover him while he is using a car owned by his daughter, who lives with him, which he has borrowed. If the daughter has insured her car, Bill would be covered by her policy on a primary basis, as well as his own policy on an excess basis.

Racing

PAP liability coverage does not apply to any vehicle that is located inside a racing facility for the purpose of preparing for, practicing for, or competing in any organized racing or speed contest.

Limit of Liability

Most PAPs are written on a split-limits basis, with the three types of limits stated in this order:

- Bodily injury to each person
- Bodily injury to all persons in each accident
- Property damage in each accident

For example, split limits of $100/$300/$50 mean that the insured has bodily injury liability limits of $100,000 per person and $300,000 for each accident, and a limit of $50,000 for property damage liability per accident.

Some policies are written with a single limit that applies per accident to the total of both bodily injury and property damage liability. For example, a policy might have a single limit of $300,000 for bodily injury and property damage liability. The Single Liability Limit endorsement modifies the policy to provide coverage on a single-limit basis.

The PAP states that the limits of liability for the policy will not be increased, regardless of the number of insured persons, claims made, vehicles or premiums shown, or vehicles involved in an auto accident. The most any claimant can recover for one accident is the applicable limit(s) stated in the declarations. For example, if Betty causes an accident while running an errand for her employer in her personal auto, the injured claimant might sue both Betty and her employer, because Betty was acting on her employer's behalf. Betty's insurer would handle the claim and respond to a lawsuit on behalf of both Betty and her employer. However, Betty's insurer would not pay more than the limits of liability on her PAP, even though it is responding on behalf of two parties. (Her employer might also have its own coverage.)

The Limit of Liability provision also states that no one is entitled to receive duplicate payments for the same elements of loss under Part A—Liability Coverage, Part B—Medical Payments Coverage, Part C—Uninsured Motorists Coverage, or any underinsured motorists coverage provided by the policy. This provision prevents insureds from collecting twice for one loss under different parts of the same policy.

Out of State Coverage

The PAP contains an Out of State Coverage provision that applies when an auto accident occurs in a state other than the one in which the covered auto is principally garaged. If the accident occurs in a state that has a financial responsibility law or a similar law that requires higher liability limits than the limits shown in the declarations, the PAP automatically provides the higher required limits for that accident.

In addition, if a state has a compulsory insurance law or a similar law that requires nonresidents to maintain coverage whenever they use a vehicle in that state, the PAP provides the required minimum amounts and types of coverage. This provision protects insureds when they are driving in other states by providing the benefits required by any state in which an accident occurs. For example, a driver who is not required to have "no-fault" personal injury protection (PIP) coverage in his or her home state would have PIP coverage when driving in a state that requires it.

Financial Responsibility

Many states' laws require insureds to demonstrate proof of financial responsibility after an accident or traffic violation has occurred. Under these laws, the PAP can be used to demonstrate proof of financial responsibility to the extent required by the state where the accident or traffic violation has occurred. In addition, if a financial responsibility law is changed to require higher minimum limits of liability, the PAP automatically complies with the new law.

Other Insurance

The Other Insurance provision of Part A addresses situations in which more than one auto policy covers a liability claim.

If the insured has other applicable liability insurance on an owned vehicle, the insurer pays only its pro rata share of the loss. The insurer's share is the proportion of the loss that the limit of liability bears to the total of all applicable limits. For example, Joseph accidentally injures another motorist while driving his owned auto and must pay damages of $60,000. Assume Joseph has a PAP with a $100,000 limit of liability with Insurer A and also has a PAP with a $50,000 limit of liability with Insurer B. If two auto liability policies cover the same owned vehicle, each insurer pays its pro rata share. Each insurer pays according to this formula:

$$\text{Insurer's share of damages} = \left(\frac{\text{Limit of liability of that insurer's policy}}{\text{Total limits of liability of all applicable policies}} \right) \times \text{Amount of damages}$$

$$\text{Insurer A's share} = \left(\frac{\$100,000}{\$150,000} \right) \times \$60,000 = \$40,000$$

$$\text{Insurer B's share} = \left(\frac{\$50,000}{\$150,000} \right) \times \$60,000 = \$20,000$$

If other liability insurance is available on a nonowned vehicle, including any vehicle used as a temporary substitute for a covered auto, the PAP coverage is excess over any other collectible insurance. For example, Ken borrows a car owned by Patti with her permission. Ken has a PAP with $100/$300/$50 liability limits, and Patti has a PAP with $50/$100/$25 liability limits. Ken negligently injures another motorist and must pay a judgment of $60,000. Patti's insurance is primary and Ken's is excess. Each insurer pays these amounts:

- Patti's insurer (primary)—$50,000 (Patti's per person limit)
- Ken's insurer (excess)—$10,000 (the excess over Patti's limit)

PART B—MEDICAL PAYMENTS COVERAGE

Soon after an auto accident that involves bodily injury, medical bills become due. Establishing who is at fault and should pay those bills often takes time, sometimes years.

Part B—Medical Payments Coverage of the Personal Auto Policy (PAP) provides auto accident medical coverage up to a limited amount without requiring a determination of fault.

Part B includes these provisions:

- Insuring Agreement
- Exclusions
- Limit of Liability
- Other Insurance

Insuring Agreement

The Part B Insuring Agreement states the insurer's promise to pay reasonable and necessary medical and funeral expenses incurred by an insured because of bodily injury caused by an accident. The insurer agrees to pay only those expenses incurred for services rendered within three years from the date of the accident. The types of expenses payable include those for medical, surgical, x-ray, dental, and funeral services. Unless otherwise noted, the phrases "medical expenses" and "medical payments" as used in this discussion are meant to include all of these types of expenses.

Medical payments coverage applies without regard to fault; therefore, whether or not the insured is legally liable for the accident, medical payments benefits may be paid for both the insured and other injured occupants of the insured's covered auto. Two classes of insureds are covered under Part B:

- The named insured and "family members" (as defined in the PAP)— These individuals are covered for their medical expenses if they are injured while occupying a motor vehicle or as pedestrians when struck by a motor vehicle designed for use mainly on public roads. Examples of covered losses include injuries to the named insured in an auto accident, injury to a family member's hand when a neighbor's car door shuts on it, and injuries a family member suffers when struck by a car while crossing the street.

- Any other person while occupying a covered auto—Medical expenses of passengers in a covered auto are covered. For example, if Mary owns her car and is the named insured, all passengers in her car are covered for their medical expenses under her policy. However, if Mary is operating a vehicle she does not own, passengers in the car (other than family members) are not covered under her medical payments coverage. Passengers in the nonowned vehicle can seek protection under their own policies or under the medical payments coverage that applies to the nonowned vehicle.

Exclusions

Many of the exclusions under Part B—Medical Payments Coverage are similar to those under Part A—Liability Coverage. There are several medical payments exclusions.

Motorized Vehicles With Fewer Than Four Wheels

If the insured is injured while occupying a motorized vehicle with fewer than four wheels, medical payments coverage does not apply.

Public or Livery Conveyance

An insured who is injured while occupying a covered auto that is being used as a public or livery conveyance (such as a taxi or public bus) will not receive medical payments. The exclusion does not apply to share-the-expense car pools.

Vehicles Used as a Residence or Premises

Injuries that occur while the vehicle is located for use as a residence or premises are excluded. For example, after his apartment building burns down, Steve decides to live in a van covered by his PAP while he looks for a new apartment. If Steve burns himself while cooking on a small stove in the van, the medical payments coverage will not pay for treatment of his injury.

Injury During the Course of Employment

Injuries that occur during the course of employment are excluded from medical payments coverage if workers compensation benefits are required or available. For example, if Rosa is injured while driving her car on company business and her employer provides workers compensation benefits, those benefits, rather than PAP medical payments coverage, would apply.

Other Vehicles Owned by Insured or Available for Insured's Regular Use

Medical payments coverage does not apply to an injury sustained by an insured while occupying, or when struck by, any vehicle (other than a covered auto) that is owned by the named insured or is furnished or available for his or her regular use. The underlying intent of this provision is to exclude medical payments coverage on vehicles the named insured owns or uses regularly but does not insure under the policy.

Vehicles Owned by or Available for Family Member's Regular Use

Medical payments coverage does not apply to an injury sustained by an insured while occupying, or when struck by, any vehicle (other than a covered auto) that is owned by or is furnished or available for the regular use of any family member of the named insured. However, this exclusion has an important exception: it does not apply to the named insured and spouse. For example, assume that John, who lives with his parents, owns a car and insures it under a policy separate from the policy that insures his parents' vehicles. The parents are injured while riding in John's car. Their medical expenses are covered under their own PAP (as excess over any medical payments coverage in the son's policy).

Vehicle Occupied Without Reasonable Belief of Being Entitled

If an insured sustains an injury while using a vehicle without a reasonable belief that he or she is entitled to do so, medical payments coverage does not apply. For example, Harry works at a hotel and, without permission, takes a guest's car from the garage for use on a brief errand. If Harry swerves off the road and is injured, neither Harry's PAP nor the guest's PAP will pay his medical expenses. As with Part A—Liability Coverage, this medical payments exclusion does not apply when another family member (as defined) uses the owned auto of a named insured. For insurance purposes, it is assumed that one family member has permission to use another family member's car.

Vehicles Used in the Business of an Insured

Coverage is excluded for bodily injury sustained by an insured while occupying a vehicle used in the insured's business. However, this exclusion does not apply to a private passenger auto, a pickup or van, or a trailer used with these vehicles. The intent underlying this provision is to exclude coverage of vehicles that should be insured under a commercial auto policy.

Bodily Injury From Nuclear Weapons or War

Injury from the discharge of a nuclear weapon (even if accidental) or from war, insurrection, rebellion, or revolution is excluded from medical payments coverage.

Nuclear Radiation

Bodily injury caused by nuclear reaction, radiation, or radioactive contamination is also excluded. For example, if an insured drives a covered auto near a public utility plant when an accidental release of radiation occurs, injuries resulting from the radiation exposure would not be covered.

Racing

Excluded from medical payments coverage is bodily injury an insured sustains while occupying any vehicle that is located inside a racing facility for the purpose of preparing for, practicing for, or competing in any organized racing or speed contest.

Limit of Liability

The limit of insurance for medical payments coverage is stated in the declarations. This limit, typically between $1,000 and $10,000, is the maximum amount that will be paid to each injured person in a single accident, regardless of the number of insured persons, claims made, vehicles or premiums shown on the policy, or vehicles involved in the auto accident. The intent is to prevent an insured person from collecting more than the stated medical payments limit for any one accident.

In addition, the Limit of Liability provision specifically states that no one is entitled to receive duplicate payments for the same elements of loss under Part B—Medical Payments Coverage, Part A—Liability Coverage, Part C—Uninsured Motorists Coverage, or any underinsured motorists coverage provided by the policy. For example, assume Janice has a limit of $5,000 for medical payments coverage, and she is injured by an uninsured motorist. Janice's medical bills are $5,000. Without this provision, Janice might be able to collect $10,000—that is, $5,000 under the medical payments coverage and another $5,000 under the uninsured motorists coverage—for the same bills.

Other Insurance

If the medical payments coverage of more than one insurance policy applies to a claim, each insurer pays its pro rata share based on the proportion that its limit of liability bears to the total of applicable limits. For example, Jeff is injured when he accidentally drives his car into a tree. His medical expenses are $6,000. Assume Jeff has a PAP with a medical payments limit of $5,000 with Insurer A and also has a PAP with a medical payments limit of $10,000 with Insurer B. If two automobile policies cover the same owned vehicle, each insurer pays its pro rata share.

Insurer A's pro rata share is calculated by multiplying the total amount of covered medical expenses ($6,000) by that proportion that the medical payments limit in Insurer A's policy ($5,000) bears to the sum of the medical payments limits in both policies ($15,000). The calculation of Insurer A's share can be shown in formula as follows:

$$\$6,000 \times \left(\frac{\$5,000}{\$15,000}\right) = \$2,000$$

Insurer B's pro rata share is calculated by multiplying the total amount of covered medical expenses ($6,000) by that proportion that the medical payments limit in Insurer B's policy ($10,000) bears to the sum of the medical payments limits in both policies ($15,000). The calculation of Insurer B's share can be shown in formula as follows:

$$\$6,000 \times \left(\frac{\$10,000}{\$15,000}\right) = \$4,000$$

With respect to a nonowned vehicle or a vehicle while used as a temporary substitute for the insured's covered auto, medical payments coverage under a PAP is excess over any other collectible auto insurance that pays medical or funeral expenses. For example, assume that David is driving his own car and Pam is his passenger. From Pam's perspective, David's car is a nonowned vehicle. David's car skids on a patch of ice and hits a tree. David's PAP has a $5,000 limit on medical payments coverage, and Pam's PAP has a medical payments limit of $10,000. If Pam's medical expenses are $6,000, David's insurer pays $5,000 as primary insurance and Pam's insurer pays the remaining $1,000 as excess insurance.

PART C—UNINSURED MOTORISTS COVERAGE

It can be emotionally devastating when a family member is severely injured by another driver in an auto accident. It can also be financially devastating if the at-fault driver is uninsured.

Part C—Uninsured Motorists (UM) Coverage of the Personal Auto Policy (PAP) is intended to compensate an insured and the insured's family members for injuries caused by an at-fault uninsured motorist, a hit-and-run driver, or a driver whose insurer is insolvent. The UM provisions in the PAP are usually modified or completely replaced by state-specific endorsements because each state's UM law may require unique provisions. However, the basic PAP UM provisions, though seldom used without modification, provide a basic understanding of the usual elements of this coverage.

Part C includes these provisions:

- Insuring Agreement
- Exclusions
- Limit of Liability
- Other Insurance
- Arbitration

Insuring Agreement

In the Part C—Insuring Agreement, the insurer agrees to pay compensatory damages that the insured person is legally entitled to recover from the owner or operator of an uninsured motor vehicle because of bodily injury caused by an accident. Such compensatory damages could include medical expenses, rehabilitation expenses, lost wages, and other losses resulting from the insured's bodily injury. Because the insuring agreement limits coverage to compensatory damages, punitive, or exemplary, damages (which are meant to punish a driver for a reckless, malicious, or deceitful act) are not covered.

UM coverage compensates insureds for damages caused by uninsured motorists without their having to sue the uninsured driver. However, UM coverage applies only if the uninsured motorist is legally responsible for the accident.

Although the standard PAP provides UM coverage only for bodily injury claims, some states' UM coverage applies to property damage claims as well. In such states, the UM property damage coverage is subject to a deductible, such as $200 or $300.

Insured Persons

Three classes of persons are considered insureds under UM coverage:

- The named insured and family members—These individuals are covered if injured by an uninsured motor vehicle while occupying a covered auto or a vehicle that is not owned by the named insured or a family member. They are also covered as pedestrians.
- Any other person occupying a covered auto—Passengers in a covered auto have coverage for bodily injury caused by an uninsured motorist.
- Any person legally entitled to recover damages because of bodily injury to a person described in the preceding two paragraphs—For example, a surviving spouse of a person killed in an accident caused by an uninsured driver is covered.

Uninsured Motor Vehicles

Part C specifies the types of vehicles that are considered **uninsured motor vehicles**. An uninsured motor vehicle is a land motor vehicle or trailer of any type that meets any of these criteria:

- No bodily injury liability insurance or bond applies to the vehicle at the time of the accident.

- A bodily injury liability policy or bond is in force, but the limit for bodily injury liability is less than the minimum amount required by the financial responsibility law in the state where the named insured's covered auto is principally garaged.

- The vehicle is a hit-and-run vehicle, whose operator or owner cannot be identified, that hits (a) the named insured or any family member, (b) a vehicle that the named insured or any family member is occupying, or (c) the named insured's covered auto.

- A bodily injury liability policy or bond applies at the time of the accident, but the insurance or bonding company (a) denies coverage or (b) is or becomes insolvent. For example, if Tom has a valid claim against a negligent motorist whose liability insurer becomes insolvent before the claim is paid, Tom can collect for his bodily injury damages under the UM coverage of his PAP.

Part C also specifies certain vehicles that are not considered to be uninsured motor vehicles. If an insured is injured by one of these vehicles, UM coverage does not apply. As stated in Part C of the PAP, the definition of uninsured motor vehicle does not include any vehicle or equipment that meets any of these criteria:[2]

- It is owned by or furnished or available for the regular use of you or any "family member."

- It is owned or operated by a self-insurer under any applicable motor vehicle law, except a self-insurer which is or becomes insolvent.

- It is owned by any governmental unit or agency.

- It is operated on rails or crawler treads.

- It is designed mainly for use off public roads while not on public roads.

- It is located for use as a residence or premises.

Exclusions

As with most coverages, Part C is limited by exclusions. The UM coverage has seven exclusions.

Owned But Not Insured Vehicle

This exclusion eliminates UM coverage for bodily injury sustained by an insured while occupying, or when struck by, any motor vehicle that is owned

> **Uninsured motor vehicle**
>
> A land motor vehicle or trailer that is not insured for bodily injury liability, is insured for less than the financial responsibility limits, is a hit-and-run vehicle, or whose insurer denies coverage or becomes insolvent.

by that insured but not insured for UM under "this policy" (the PAP under which coverage is being sought). For example, if Madeline has not purchased UM coverage under "this policy" on a vehicle she owns, and if, while occupying it, she is struck by a vehicle driven by an uninsured, at-fault driver, Madeline's PAP would not provide any UM coverage for this accident. If Madeline has purchased UM coverage for this vehicle under another policy, the auto could be covered under that other policy.

Owned Vehicle With Primary UM Coverage in Other Policy

If a vehicle owned by the named insured of "this policy" has primary UM coverage in another policy, and a family member is injured by an uninsured motorist while occupying the vehicle, "this policy" would provide no UM coverage for the family member. For example, Susan insures a car she owns and uses in her business under a business auto policy that includes UM coverage. Susan's daughter would not have UM coverage under Susan's PAP while occupying that vehicle.

Claim Settlement That Prejudices Insurer's Right of Recovery

UM coverage does not apply to a claim that the insured settles without the insurer's consent if such a settlement prejudices the insurer's right to recover payment. In a legal context, "prejudice" means to injure or damage another party's right. The purpose of this exclusion is to protect the insurer's right to assert a subrogation action against the party who is legally responsible for the insured's injuries. For example, George, who has UM coverage on his vehicle, is involved in a serious auto accident. He agrees to accept a payment from the at-fault driver that is well below the driver's liability policy limits because he intends to make a UM claim against his own insurer for any additional damages. This exclusion allows George's insurer to deny his claim because by accepting the low payment from the at-fault driver, George prejudiced the insurer's right to recover full payment from the at-fault driver.

Public or Livery Conveyance

If a person is injured while occupying a covered auto when it is being used as a public or livery conveyance (such as a taxi or public bus), UM coverage does not apply. For example, if Paul decides to supplement the family income by providing a part-time taxi service from the airport to local hotels, he would not have UM coverage while doing so. Because this exclusion applies only to "your covered auto," the insured and family members would be covered for UM while occupying a public or livery conveyance that is not "your covered auto." In addition, the exclusion contains an exception clarifying that the exclusion does not apply to a share-the-expense car pool.

Vehicle Used Without Reasonable Belief of Being Entitled

UM coverage does not apply to any person who uses a vehicle without a reasonable belief that he or she is entitled to do so. The exclusion contains an exception that states that the exclusion does not apply to family members.

No Benefit to Workers Compensation or Disability Benefits Insurer

UM coverage cannot directly or indirectly benefit any insurer or self-insurer under a workers compensation law or disability benefits law. In some states, if an injured employee receives workers compensation benefits, the workers compensation insurer has a legal right to recover the amount of the benefits from a negligent third party through subrogation. If an employee receives workers compensation benefits for an injury involving an uninsured, at-fault driver, the workers compensation insurer could sue the driver or attempt to make a claim under the injured employee's uninsured motorists coverage. This exclusion prevents the workers compensation insurer from obtaining reimbursement under the injured worker's UM coverage.

Punitive Damages

As stated in the Part C insuring agreement, UM coverage applies only to compensatory damages, which do not include punitive damages. For example, Debbie is struck by an uninsured vehicle driven by an at-fault driver and suffers serious injuries. Debbie is dissatisfied with the amount offered by her own UM insurer and sues the driver. The case goes to court, and the jury awards her punitive damages in addition to her compensatory damages. Debbie's own insurer would not pay the punitive damages amount under UM coverage.

Limit of Liability

The minimum amount of UM coverage available under the PAP is set by the financial responsibility or compulsory insurance law of the state in which the insured auto is principally garaged. Higher limits can be purchased for an additional premium. The limit of liability for UM coverage is shown in the declarations. UM coverage is normally written on a split-limits basis, but coverage on a single-limit basis is available by endorsement.

The limits shown are the most that will be paid regardless of the number of insured persons, claims made, vehicles or premiums shown in the declarations, or vehicles involved in the accident. This provision is intended to prevent "stacking" of UM payments under a policy that covers more than one car owned by the named insured. Stacking refers to situations in which the insured maintains that, because the policy covers, and premiums have been paid for, two (or more) vehicles, he or she should collect up to the stated limit multiplied by the number of vehicles. For example, assume the insured owns three cars that are covered by a PAP with a UM limit of $25,000 per person.

If the insured is injured by an uninsured motorist, the most the insured can recover is $25,000, not $75,000.

The UM section specifically states that no person will receive duplicate payments for any loss under Part A—Liability Coverage, Part B—Medical Payments Coverage, or Part C—Uninsured Motorists Coverage, or under any UM coverage provided by the policy. For example, if Christine is injured by a hit-and-run driver and incurs $5,000 in medical expenses, she cannot collect $5,000 under her medical payments coverage and then collect an additional $5,000 for the same expenses under her UM coverage. (She can, however, attempt to collect any additional damages under her UM coverage as long as they do not duplicate the expenses for which the insurer has already paid under her medical payments coverage.)

Likewise, the insurer will not make duplicate payment under the UM coverage if payment has been made by the person or organization legally responsible for the accident or if the injured person is entitled to receive payment under a workers compensation or disability benefits law.

Other Insurance

If other applicable UM insurance is available under one or more policies, these provisions apply to the payment for damages:

- The total amount paid will be no more than the highest limit of any of the policies that provide coverage. For example, Susan has two policies that both provide her UM coverage. One policy has a per-person limit of $100,000 and the other policy has a per-person limit of $250,000. The most she will be paid, regardless of how high her damages are, will be $250,000.

- Coverage for an accident involving a vehicle the named insured does not own, including any vehicle while being used as a temporary substitute for a covered auto, is provided on an excess basis over any collectible insurance providing coverage on a primary basis.

- For example, assume that Louis has UM coverage with limits of $50,000/$100,000 under his PAP. (These limits indicate $50,000 per person and $100,000 per accident for bodily injury. No property damage limit is given because UM coverage usually does not include property damage.) He is injured by an uninsured motorist while riding in Gayle's car. Gayle has $25,000/$50,000 of UM coverage. If Louis is entitled to $35,000 for his bodily injuries, Gayle's insurer pays the first $25,000 as primary insurer of her owned vehicle, and Louis's insurer pays the remaining $10,000 as excess insurance (because Louis does not own the vehicle).

- If "this policy" and another policy (or policies) provide coverage on a primary basis, each policy will contribute proportionally to the insured's recovery. Each insurer's share is equal to the proportion its UM limit bears to the total amount available under all applicable coverages provided on a primary basis.

- For example, John has two policies that both provide him UM coverage on a primary basis. The policy with Insurer A has a per-person UM limit of $100,000, and the policy with Insurer B has a per-person UM limit of $50,000. While driving his own vehicle, John is injured by an uninsured motorist, and his damages are $60,000. If two automobile policies cover the same vehicle on a primary basis, each insurer pays its pro rata share. Each insurer pays according to the following formula:

Insurer A: ($100,000 ÷ $150,000) × $60,000 = $40,000

Insurer B: ($50,000 ÷ $150,000) × $60,000 = $20,000

- If "this policy" and another policy (or policies) provide coverage on an excess basis, each policy will contribute proportionally to the insured's recovery, based on the excess limits each policy provides.

Arbitration

If the insurer and insured cannot agree on whether the insured is entitled to recover damages from an uninsured motorist or on the amount of damages, the dispute can be settled by **arbitration**. However, arbitration does not include disputes involving coverage, such as whether the driver of the covered auto had a reasonable belief he was entitled to use the auto.

If the insurer and insured consent to arbitration, each party selects an arbitrator, and the two arbitrators select a third arbitrator. If the two arbitrators cannot agree on a third arbitrator within thirty days, either party can request that the selection be made by a judge of a court having jurisdiction. Each party pays the expenses it incurs, and both parties share the expenses of the third arbitrator.

A decision agreed to by two of the three arbitrators is binding as to whether the insured is legally entitled to recover damages and the amount of damages. However, this decision is binding only if the amount of damages does not exceed the minimum limit for bodily injury specified by the state's financial responsibility law. If the amount of damages exceeds that limit, either party can demand the right to a trial within sixty days of the arbitrators' decision. Otherwise, the arbitrators' decision is binding.

Arbitration

An alternative dispute resolution (ADR) method by which disputing parties use a neutral outside party to examine the issues and develop a settlement, which can be final and binding.

UM/UIM ENDORSEMENTS AND STATE VARIATIONS

In most states, it is possible to supplement uninsured motorists (UM) coverage with underinsured motorists (UIM) coverage to address shortcomings of UM.

UIM coverage is an outgrowth of UM coverage. UIM coverage goes beyond UM coverage. It is important in situations in which a negligent driver is insured for at least the minimum required financial responsibility limits but the policy's liability limits are insufficient to pay the insured's damages.

Purpose of Coverage

An increasing number of insureds who have UM coverage with high coverage limits are involved in accidents with at-fault motorists who are insured at or slightly above the minimum state-required limits. Because in such situations the at-fault motorists are insured for at least the minimum state-required limits, they are not considered uninsured motorists under UM coverage provisions. Although a person who has been injured or whose vehicle has been damaged can seek recovery from the negligent motorist, any amount recovered may represent far less than the injured person's full damages.

For example, a victim may receive a $75,000 judgment against an at-fault motorist who has insurance for only $25,000 (the minimum required by the state's financial responsibility law) and no other assets to make up the difference. Unless the victim has UIM coverage, the most she can recover is $25,000. UIM coverage always applies to damages for bodily injury and, in some states, also includes damages for property damage.

In some states, the Underinsured Motorists Coverage Endorsement (PP 03 11) of Insurance Services Office, Inc. (ISO) can be added to the Personal Auto Policy (PAP) to provide coverage as a supplement to the UM coverage in the PAP. In several states, however, insurers use either a state-specific UIM endorsement or a single, state-specific endorsement providing both UM and UIM coverages that replaces the UM coverage of the standard PAP.

State Variations

Regardless of the policy provisions used by an insurer, individual states' UM/UIM statutes govern who is protected and under what circumstances. Where the insured's vehicle is registered or principally garaged determines which state's laws apply. Insurance and risk management professionals must be familiar with the laws in their states regarding both UM and UIM coverage. However, they should generally avoid applying court decisions related to UM to UIM cases. Courts (even in the same jurisdiction) do not always come to the same conclusion, especially in states where UIM coverage is optional but UM coverage is mandated.

Mandatory or Optional Coverage

Some states mandate that UIM coverage be provided on all auto liability policies. Other states allow insureds to reject UIM coverage, but typically only if the named insured rejects the coverage in writing.

Mandatory or optional limits for UIM coverage also vary by state. Many states require that the UIM limit equal the UM coverage limit, which, for many states, must also equal the PAP's bodily injury liability limit. In some states, the UM limit can be reduced, but not below the state's minimum financial responsibility limit.

Limits Trigger or Damages Trigger

Some states' UIM endorsements contain a "limits trigger." Other states' endorsements contain a "damages trigger." In general, a trigger is something that must occur or exist in order for coverage to apply. In states that apply the limits trigger, the endorsement applies when the negligent driver carries liability limits below the limits provided by the UIM coverage of the injured party.

For example, suppose Tom has an auto liability policy with a $100,000 UIM limit and Lynn has an auto liability policy with a single limit of $50,000, both of which exceed the minimum financial responsibility limits in her state. The two are involved in an auto accident, and Lynn is liable for Tom's damages. If Tom's damages are $60,000, he will collect $50,000 from Lynn's insurer and $10,000 under his UIM coverage. His UIM protection applies even if the limits of Lynn's policy are greater than the minimum required by the state. The key criterion for UIM protection with a limits trigger is that the liability limits of the other party's policy are less than the insured's UIM limits.

In states that apply a damages trigger, the UIM endorsement applies when the negligent driver carries liability insurance limits that are lower than the injured party's actual damages.

For example, assume Anne has purchased UIM coverage with a $50,000 single limit. Randy has purchased auto liability coverage with a $100,000 single limit. Randy causes an accident in which Anne is injured. If Anne's damages are $150,000, her UIM coverage will be triggered because Randy's policy limit is less than Anne's damages. However, if Anne's damages are $75,000, her UIM coverage will not be triggered because her damages are less than Randy's limit. The key criterion for coverage to apply under UIM coverage with a damages trigger is that the liability limits of the other party's policy are less than the insured's damages.

Stacking

Another UIM variation among states relates to stacking, which is the application of two or more limits to a single auto accident. Stacking may involve two or more separate policies (interpolicy stacking). The UIM policy limit of one policy would be added to (stacked on) the UIM limit of the other policy.

For example, when a husband and wife have separate policies, both policies may apply when either or both of them are injured by an underinsured motorist. If the UIM limit of the husband's policy is $25,000 and the UIM limit of the wife's policy is $50,000, when the policies' limits are stacked, the insured will be able to collect up to $75,000.

Some states allow interpolicy stacking by endorsement. Other states do not.

Stacking can also occur within a single policy that covers more than one vehicle (intrapolicy stacking). Some states allow intrapolicy stacking by endorsement. In some states, the insured can choose between stacking or nonstacking but must pay a higher premium for a policy that allows stacking. Other states prohibit intrapolicy stacking. They require that the maximum to be paid for an accident is the single (unstacked) UIM limit shown on the Declarations page, regardless of the number of insureds, claims made, vehicles or premiums shown on the Declarations page, or vehicles involved.

PAP LIABILITY, MEDICAL PAYMENTS, AND UNINSURED MOTORISTS COVERAGE CASE STUDY

A claim representative's job requires strong analytic skills, combined with a thorough understanding of the insurance policy contract that may apply to an insured's loss. Accident fact patterns may be simple or complex, but the same analysis is performed for every loss.

There are two steps the claim representative should perform when adjusting a loss. The first step involves DICE (Declarations, Insuring agreement, Conditions, and Exclusions).

If the first step indicates that the policy covers the loss, the second step involves determining the amounts payable under the policy. See the exhibit "DICE Analysis."

Case Facts

Margaret's father, John, owned a convertible-top sports car. John allowed Margaret to use his car for a trip during spring break. Margaret and her friend Sally decided to drive the vehicle from their homes in Pittsburgh to Fort Lauderdale, Florida. While Margaret was driving the car out-of-state in Florida, a large van made an illegal "U" turn and broadsided the convertible. Margaret and Sally were injured and were taken to a local hospital. Margaret had a fractured pelvis; Sally had a fractured wrist and a broken tibia that required surgery. Fred, the driver of the van, suffered a concussion, but was not otherwise injured.

Sally sued John, the vehicle owner; Margaret; and Fred for her injuries. Margaret sued Fred for her injuries.

DICE Analysis

A DICE analysis is a logical method to approach a coverage determination for most types of loss. DICE is an acronym for these policy parts:

- Declarations
- Insuring agreements
- Conditions
- Exclusions

The claim representative reviews the policy language in a logical order to determine whether coverage applies and, if it does, what dollar limit amounts may apply.

DICE analysis involves four steps:

- Review the declarations page to determine whether it covers the person or the property at the time of loss.
- Review the insuring agreement to determine whether it covers the loss.
- Review the policy conditions to determine compliance.
- Review the policy exclusions to determine whether they preclude coverage of the loss.

By carefully performing the four steps described and reviewing policy terms and any other policy endorsements with the facts of the loss, the claim representative can determine what—if any—coverage may apply to a loss.

[DA05891]

In addition to three weeks in the hospital, Sally missed one semester of her university education. Her damages (medical bills and forfeited tuition) totaled $227,000. Sally also acquired a three-inch scar on her leg.

Margaret was hospitalized for ten days and stayed at a rehabilitation facility for two weeks. She was unable to return to the university for her last semester, and her graduation was postponed until the following year. Before the accident, Margaret had been offered—and had accepted—a job offer that was contingent on her graduation. Because Margaret did not graduate, the job offer was withdrawn. The salary for the job would have been $35,000. Margaret's medical bills and forfeited tuition for the semester totaled $175,000.

Fred was hospitalized for three days. His medical bill was $4,500.

John's Personal Auto Policy (PAP) had liability limits of $250,000 per person and $500,000 per accident and property damage limits of $100,000. The policy included medical payment coverage of $500 per person and uninsured motorists (UM) coverage in the same amounts as the liability limits.

Fred had no insurance on his vehicle and was therefore in violation of state financial responsibility laws. He owned no property and had no other assets.

Sally was insured under her mother's PAP. Her mother, Jean, has a policy with medical payments coverage up to a $1,000 limit. Jean rejected UM coverage on her policy. See the exhibit "John's Personal Auto Policy Declarations."

John's Personal Auto Policy Declarations

Personal Auto Policy Declarations

POLICYHOLDER:
(Named Insured)

John Insured
210 Brookside Drive
Anytown, USA 40000

POLICY NUMBER: 296 D 468300

POLICY PERIOD: **FROM:** June 1, 20XX
TO: Dec. 1, 20XX

But only If the required premium for this period has been paid, and for six-month renewal periods If renewal premiums are paid as required. Each period begins and ends at 12:01 A.M. standard time at the address of the policyholder.

**INSURED VEHICLES AND
SCHEDULE OF COVERAGES**

VEHICLE	COVERAGES	LIMITS OF INSURANCE	PREMIUM
1 20XX Ford Focus		VINXXX	
	Coverage A—Liability	$ 250,000 **Each Person**	
		$ 500,000 **Each Occurrence**	$ 203.00
	Coverage B—Medical Payments	$ 500 **Each Person**	$ 36.00
	Coverage C—Uninsured Motorists	$ 250,000 **Each Person**	
		$ 500,000 **Each Occurrence**	$ 61.80
	Coverage D—Other Than Collision	**Actual Cash Value Less** $100	$ 41.60
	—Collision	**Actual Cash Value Less** $250	$ 131.00
		TOTAL	$ 473.40

POLICY FORM AND ENDORSEMENTS: PP 00 01, PP 03 06

COUNTERSIGNATURE DATE: June 1, 20XX

AGENT: A. M. Abel

[DA05906]

Case Analysis Tools

The claim representative should review John's PAP for policy language and analyze it with the DICE method to determine whether liability, medical payments, and uninsured motorist coverages apply to the losses. The claim representative should also review Jean's policy to determine whether its medical payments coverage applies. The insurer of Jean's policy will normally share coverage information with John's insurer as part of the claim process, as they both potentially cover Sally.

Determination of Coverage

The first of the two steps the claim representative should perform when adjusting a loss involves applying DICE analysis to determine whether the policy covers the loss. The claim representative analyzes four policy parts.

The claim representative reviews the policy declarations to confirm that the vehicle was operated by an insured or by someone who has permission to use the vehicle, and that the vehicle is indeed the covered auto.

Under John's policy, the convertible is a covered vehicle, and Margaret, as a "family member," is considered an "insured" under the policy:

> Definitions of Family Member and Insured in Part A—Liability Coverage
>
> F. "Family member" means a person related to you by blood, marriage or adoption who is a resident of your household. This includes a ward or foster child.
>
> B. "Insured" as used in this Part means:
>
> 1. You or any "family member" for the ownership, maintenance or use of any auto or "trailer"[3]

During the review of the policy declarations pages, the claim representative should confirm the limits of coverage as well as the inception and expiration dates of the policy. PAP policies may be written for time frames of either six months or one year. The date of loss must fall between the policy inception and expiration dates.

The claim representative then reviews the PAP policies' insuring agreements to determine whether the auto accident triggered coverage under the agreements.

John's insurer agreed to pay damages for bodily injury and property damages for which the insured is legally liable due to an auto accident. The initiation of a lawsuit under the policy can trigger liability coverage:

> Insuring Agreement, Part A—Liability Coverage
>
> A. We will pay damages for "bodily injury" or "property damage" for which any "insured" becomes legally responsible because of an auto accident. Damages include prejudgment interest awarded against the "insured". We will settle or defend, as we consider appropriate, any claim or suit asking for these damages. In addition to our limit of liability, we will

pay all defense costs we incur. Our duty to settle or defend ends when our limit of liability for this coverage has been exhausted by payment of judgments or settlements. We have no duty to defend any suit or settle any claim for "bodily injury" or "property damage" not covered under this policy. [4]

Two additional coverages to the PAP should be carefully examined. The first is Part B—Medical Payments Coverage. This coverage provides for "reasonable expenses incurred for necessary medical and funeral services because of 'bodily injury.'" "Bodily injury" is a defined policy term that clearly applies to the injuries sustained in this loss.

John's policy will provide medical payment coverage for both Margaret and Sally:

PAP Insuring Agreement, Part B—Medical Payments Coverage

B. "Insured" as used in this Part means:

1. You or any "family member":

a. While "occupying"; or

b. As a pedestrian when struck by; a motor vehicle designed for use mainly on public roads or a trailer of any type.

2. Any other person while "occupying" "your covered auto[5]

John's policy will pay medical expenses incurred by Margaret and Sally up to its medical payments limit of $500. The $500 limit applies separately to each injured person; that is, John's policy will pay $500 for Margaret's medical expenses and $500 for Sally's medical expenses.

Jean's policy will also pay for medical expenses incurred by Sally up to its medical payments limit of $1,000. All additional medical expenses incurred would be paid by other sources, such as health insurance. The health insurance is normally excess over the medical expense coverage provided by the PAPs.

The claim representative should also apply the DICE method to Part C—Uninsured Motorists Coverage of the applicable polices. UM coverage is available to the insured when it is proven that an uninsured motorist is responsible for the accident. In this instance, Fred, who had no insurance on his vehicle, made an illegal turn and caused the accident.

John's PAP policy provides UM coverage. John's policy's insuring agreement provides for payment of compensatory damages arising out of a motor vehicle accident for which no liability insurance applies:

Insuring Agreement of Part C—Uninsured Motorists Coverage

A. We will pay compensatory damages which an "insured" is legally entitled to recover from the owner or operator of an "uninsured motor vehicle" because of "bodily injury":

1. Sustained by an "insured"; and

2. Caused by an accident.

The owner's or operator's liability for these damages must arise out of the ownership, maintenance or use of the "uninsured motor vehicle".

Any judgment for damages arising out of a suit brought without our written consent is not binding on us.

C. "Uninsured motor vehicle" means a land motor vehicle or trailer of any type:

1. To which no bodily injury liability bond or policy applies at the time of the accident.

2. To which a bodily injury liability bond or policy applies at the time of the accident. In this case its limit for bodily injury liability must be less than the minimum limit for bodily injury liability specified by the financial responsibility law of the state in which "your covered auto" is principally garaged.[6]

Margaret can recover her compensatory damages under her father's policy.

The claim representative reviews the policies' conditions to determine whether the insureds have complied with all policy conditions, for example, that Margaret and Sally authorized the insurer to obtain medical reports and submitted proofs of loss. Also, because two policies potentially apply, they should have notified both insurers of the accident. All other conditions for both policies were met.

The claim representative reviews the policies' exclusions to determine whether of them eliminate coverage for the loss. John's policy apparently has no exclusions that apply.

Because Margaret was operating the convertible outside of her home state, the claim representative should review each policy's Out of State Coverage section.

The liability limits on John's PAP automatically comply with the state's financial responsibility laws. In this case, the limits of liability on John's policy are greater than the minimum required in any of the fifty states.

Determination of Amounts Payable

In the second of two steps, the claim representative determines the amounts payable under any policies that apply to the loss. Sally, as an innocent passenger, would have collected from Fred had he had either insurance in effect at the time of the loss or any assets that could be attached. However, liability may also be attributed to Margaret as driver of the vehicle in which Sally was a passenger. Sally will be paid for her damages under John's policy, which covers the car he owned and his daughter Margaret as an insured. Sally can collect her compensatory damages under John's liability and uninsured motorist coverage up to a total limit of $500,000. The final amounts will be determined by negotiation or by a court award.

Margaret has no easy recourse against Fred. She may choose to initiate an uninsured motorist claim against her father's policy, which could potentially compensate her up to the UM policy limit of $250,000. Her damages would include all medical expenses, forfeited tuition, and the loss of wages from the job she accepted. However, because she was a college student at the time of the accident and not employed, she would likely be able to successfully claim only those wages she would have earned for the time she was unable to work at the job she accepted. Once she has recovered physically, returned to school, completed her education, and obtained an equivalently paying job, she would not be entitled to any more loss wages.

Sally sued Margaret, as driver, and John, as owner, of the convertible. She hired an attorney to protect and defend their interests. In defending the claim, the insurer might consider retaining two attorneys for the defendant, if their interests differ—one representing Margaret and one representing her father John. The PAP provides for defense attorney fees in addition to the limits of liability. See the exhibit "Results of Analysis."

Results of Analysis

The DICE analysis helped the claim representative determine that the two PAPs applied to the losses from the accident and to determine applicable dollar limits that may be applied to this loss. (If the available limits are insufficient to satisfy the injured parties, the claim representative must inform the insured immediately. In this case it appears that the available limits are sufficient to satisfy all injured parties.)

Individual Involved	Liability Coverage Bodily Injury John's Policy	Medical Payments Coverage John's Policy	Medical Payments Coverage Jean's Policy	Uninsured Motorist Coverage John's Policy
Margaret	0	$500	0	$250,000
Sally	$250,000	$500	$1,000	$250,000
Fred	0	0	0	0

[DA05892]

SUMMARY

The Personal Auto Policy (PAP) is used to insure autos owned by individuals and families, such as cars, vans, and station wagons. The PAP includes a Declarations page, an Agreement and Definitions section, and six coverage sections. The PAP may also include one or more endorsements that modify or expand the coverage provided.

Most insurance policies include a separate Definitions section that explains both common terms and less frequently used insurance-specific wording to assist policyholders in understanding the coverage they have purchased. These definitions clarify to whom, to what, and when coverage, exclusions, insuring agreements, and other policy provisions apply. Consequently, these definitions are crucial to understanding the policy provisions and, in some cases, coverage can be extended or excluded based on the details in these definitions.

Part A—Liability Coverage of the PAP pays damages for bodily injury or property damage for which the insured is legally responsible because of an auto accident. The Insuring Agreement of Part A provides a broad grant of coverage, which can be either extended or narrowed by the following policy provisions: Supplementary Payments, Exclusions, Limit of Liability, Out of State Coverage, Financial Responsibility, and Other Insurance.

Part B—Medical Payments Coverage of the PAP provides auto accident medical coverage that pays reasonable and necessary medical and funeral expenses, regardless of who is at fault for an auto accident. The coverage granted by the Insuring Agreement in Part B is limited by Exclusions, Limit of Liability, and Other Insurance provisions in the same part.

Part C—Uninsured Motorists Coverage pays for bodily injury to an insured who is injured by an uninsured motorist, a hit-and-run driver, or a driver whose insurer becomes insolvent. The coverage is limited by a set of exclusions and is further modified by the Limit of Insurance, Other Insurance, and Arbitration provisions in Part C.

UIM coverage is an outgrowth of UM coverage. Unlike UM coverage, UIM coverage applies in situations in which a negligent driver is insured for at least the minimum required financial responsibility limits but has liability limits that are insufficient to pay the insured's damages.

The PAP is used to protect against financial loss resulting from an auto accident. The financial loss includes injury to the insured, passengers, and persons in another vehicle, as well as damage to the insured vehicle and other vehicles.

The DICE analysis assists the claims representative in determining what may be included under the various coverages afforded. If coverage applies to the loss, the claim representative determines the amounts payable.

ASSIGNMENT NOTES

1. *Sheldon v. Hartford Insurance Company*, 144 N.M. 562, 189 P.3d 695, (2008).

2. Includes copyrighted material of Insurance Services Office, Inc., with its permission. Copyright, ISO Properties, Inc., 2003.

3. Includes copyrighted material of Insurance Services Office, Inc., with its permission. Copyright, ISO Properties, Inc., 2005.

4. Includes copyrighted material of Insurance Services Office, Inc., with its permission. Copyright, ISO Properties, Inc., 2005.

5. Includes copyrighted material of Insurance Services Office, Inc., with its permission. Copyright, ISO Properties, Inc., 2005.

6. Includes copyrighted material of Insurance Services Office, Inc., with its permission. Copyright, ISO Properties, Inc., 2005.

4

Personal Auto Insurance: Physical Damage and Endorsements

Educational Objectives

After learning the content of this assignment, you should be able to:

▷ Summarize each of the provisions in Part D—Coverage for Damage to Your Auto of the Personal Auto Policy.

▷ Given a case describing an auto physical damage claim, determine whether Part D—Coverage for Damage to Your Auto of the Personal Auto Policy would cover the claim and, if so, the amount the insurer would pay for the claim.

▷ Describe the insured's duties following a covered auto accident or loss as shown in Part E of the Personal Auto Policy.

▷ Summarize each of the general provisions in Part F of the Personal Auto Policy.

▷ Describe the Personal Auto Policy endorsements that are used to handle common auto loss exposures.

▷ Given a case describing a claim involving an individual or a family with a Personal Auto Policy, determine what is covered, excluded, or limited, and for what amounts.

Personal Auto Insurance: Physical Damage and Endorsements

4

PART D—COVERAGE FOR DAMAGE TO YOUR AUTO

The most expensive investment for many people, aside from their residence, is their automobile. Insurance is a way to protect that investment.

Part D of the Personal Auto Policy (PAP) provides **physical damage coverage** for damage to or theft of a covered auto.

Part D includes these provisions:

- Insuring Agreement
- Transportation Expenses
- Exclusions
- Limit of Liability
- Payment of Loss
- No Benefit to Bailee
- Other Sources of Recovery
- Appraisal

Insuring Agreement

In the Part D insuring agreement, the insurer promises to pay for any direct and accidental loss to "your covered auto" or a "non-owned auto" as defined in the PAP, minus the **deductible** shown on the PAP Declarations page. Direct and accidental losses to an auto fall into two categories: collision losses and other than collision (OTC) losses.

Collision Coverage

The PAP declarations indicate whether a named insured has bought collision coverage for a specified auto as well as the amount of the premium for that coverage. Collision is defined in the PAP as the upset of or impact of "your covered auto" or a "non-owned auto" with another vehicle or object. Examples of collision losses covered under Part D of the PAP include those resulting from a car colliding with another car, hitting a tree, overturning after a driver loses control, or being damaged when a passenger in a parked car opens a car door, striking the insured vehicle parked next to it.

Physical damage coverages
There are four kinds: comprehensive—pays for loss to covered auto or its equipment from any cause not excluded, except collision or overturn; specified causes of loss—provides named peril coverage; collision—covers loss to a covered auto or its equipment by collision with another object or by overturn; and towing—provides coverage for towing and labor performed at the place of disablement.

Deductible
A portion of a covered loss that is not paid by the insurer.

Collision losses are paid regardless of fault, as in these examples:

- If Frank is responsible for an accident that damages his car, his collision coverage will pay for any physical damage to his own car, minus any deductible that applies.

- If the driver of another car causes the accident that damages Frank's car, Frank can collect either from the other driver (or the driver's insurer) or from his own insurer. If Frank collects from his own insurer, his insurer has the right to recover payment from the driver who caused the accident (or the driver's insurer). This recovery is referred to as subrogation.

If two or more autos that have collision coverage under the same policy are damaged in the same collision, only the highest deductible applies. For example, Bob owns three cars, all of which are covered under the same PAP. While turning into his driveway during a winter storm, Bob's car skids on the snow and collides with both of his other cars. Bob's PAP includes a $250 collision deductible on two of the cars and a $500 collision deductible on the third car. In settling this loss, Bob's PAP insurer will apply a single $500 deductible to the total damage to all three cars.

Other Than Collision Coverage

Other than collision (OTC) coverage

Coverage for physical damage to a covered auto resulting from any cause of loss except collision or a cause of loss specifically excluded.

Similar to collision coverage, **other than collision (OTC) coverage** is effective only if the declarations indicate that it is provided for that auto. The distinction between collision coverage and OTC coverage is relevant: many motorists purchase only OTC coverage because it is less expensive than collision coverage. Also, the OTC coverage often has a lower deductible than that of collision coverage.

OTC coverage insures auto physical damage losses that are not caused by collision and are not specifically excluded in the policy. This coverage was previously referred to as "comprehensive," and many insurance professionals still use that label. The term was changed because "comprehensive" implies coverage for everything; however, like virtually all other coverages, OTC coverage is subject to exclusions.

While collision is specifically defined in the PAP, OTC is not. However, the policy does list certain causes of loss that are considered OTC:

- Missiles or falling objects
- Fire
- Theft or larceny
- Explosion or earthquake
- Windstorm
- Hail, water, or flood
- Malicious mischief or vandalism
- Riot or civil commotion

- Contact with a bird or animal
- Breakage of glass

The causes of loss covered by OTC are not limited to those specifically listed. Any "direct and accidental loss" that is not due to collision and is not specifically excluded would be covered as an OTC loss. For example, if a covered auto is used to take an injured person to the hospital, resulting in blood stains to the covered auto's upholstery, OTC coverage would apply. The same coverage would apply to exterior damage to a covered auto when it is splattered with paint while parked next to a house being painted.

Two points about OTC are especially important. First, colliding with a bird or an animal is an OTC loss. Such a loss is therefore subject to the OTC deductible, which is usually lower than the collision deductible. Second, if glass breakage is caused by a collision, the insured can elect to have the glass breakage covered as part of the collision loss. As a result, the deductible for collision coverage would also apply to the glass breakage. If the insured instead elects to have the glass breakage covered under OTC, both deductibles could apply.

Nonowned Autos

The Part D coverages also apply to a "non-owned auto." Therefore, if Lois borrows a car that belongs to her friend Sean, any physical damage coverage that applies to Lois's covered auto also applies to the borrowed vehicle. (However, Lois's coverage would be excess over any physical damage coverage Sean has on his car.)

An insured can occasionally drive a rented or borrowed auto, and the insured's physical damage insurance will cover the vehicle. However, if the insured regularly drives a rented or borrowed vehicle, or if one is made available for an insured's regular use, the insured's coverage does not apply. For example, if Rosa is in an accident while driving a company car furnished by her employer or a car made available for her regular use in a carpool, the Part D coverages of her PAP do not apply. The determining factor is not how frequently Rosa drives a nonowned auto, but whether the nonowned auto is made available for her regular use.

The definition of nonowned auto also includes any auto or trailer that is being used as a temporary substitute for a covered auto or trailer that is out of normal use because of its breakdown, repair, servicing, loss, or destruction. For example, if a mechanic loans Jim a car to use while his is being repaired, Jim's physical damage insurance applies to the loaner car.

If a nonowned auto is damaged by a covered cause of loss, the PAP provides the broadest coverage applicable to any covered auto shown in the declarations. For example, Oscar owns two cars that are insured by his PAP. One car is covered for both collision and OTC, while the second car is covered only for OTC. If Oscar borrows his neighbor's car, it is covered by Oscar's PAP for both collision and OTC.

Deductibles

Deductibles require the insured to share covered losses with the insurer. Part D requires deductibles for three reasons: to reduce small claims, to hold down premiums, and to encourage insureds to be careful in protecting their cars against damage or theft.

A deductible of $100, $250, $500, or some higher amount specified in the policy declarations typically applies to each covered collision loss. A separate, often lower, deductible applies to OTC losses. For example, a PAP may have a $500 collision deductible and a $250 OTC deductible.

Transportation Expenses

Transportation expenses

Coverage extension for substitute transportation costs incurred when a private passenger type auto has been stolen.

Part D also provides an additional coverage known as **transportation expenses**. Following a covered physical damage loss to a covered auto, the insurer will reimburse the insured for temporary transportation expenses, such as auto rental fees or taxi fares, up to $20 per day, to a maximum of $600 for each covered loss. The same limits apply to a nonowned auto when the insured is legally responsible to the auto's owner for the owner's transportation expenses. A nonowned rental car is also subject to the transportation expense limits when the car's owner claims a loss of income because the car cannot be rented while it is being repaired and the named insured is legally responsible for the renter's loss of income.

The transportation expense coverage provided by the PAP applies only to expenses incurred when the cause of loss is covered by the policy. For example, if the insured did not purchase collision coverage, the policy would not apply to transportation expenses incurred due to a collision. Or if an insured has to rent a car because of mechanical difficulty, the rental car expenses are not covered.

Transportation expenses are not subject to a dollar-amount deductible. However, they are subject to a waiting period, which is essentially a deductible stated in time rather than in dollars. While a forty-eight-hour waiting period applies to total theft losses under OTC coverage, a twenty-four-hour waiting period applies to loss by other perils under both collision and OTC.

Because stolen cars often require repairs after they are recovered, transportation expenses coverage extends until the time the stolen auto is returned to use (or the insurer pays for the auto). For example, Luisa's covered auto is stolen and recovered seventeen days later. Her car has been damaged, and repair parts must be ordered. Luisa's car is in the repair shop a total of twenty days. Her PAP, which includes OTC coverage, will pay Luisa's transportation expenses for thirty-five days (17 + 20 − 2), where the two days is the waiting period, up to $20 per day, but subject to a maximum of $600.

Exclusions

A number of exclusions narrow the broad coverage in the PAP Part D insuring agreement.

Public or Livery Conveyance

Physical damage insurance does not apply while the vehicle is used as a public or livery conveyance, such as a taxi or a bus. As with comparable exclusions under other coverages of the PAP, this exclusion does not apply to a share-the-expense car pool.

Wear and Tear, Freezing, Breakdown, and Road Damage to Tires

Damage "due and confined to" wear and tear, freezing, mechanical or electrical breakdown or failure, and road damage to tires is excluded. This exclusion eliminates coverage for losses that either occur inevitably or can often be prevented by regular maintenance or the exercise of care. This exclusion does not apply if the damage results from the total theft of a covered auto or a nonowned auto. If the tires on Bill's covered auto are damaged beyond repair because he strikes a pothole, the cost of replacing the tires would not be covered. However, if a thief damages the tires by driving the wrong way across the spikes in a parking lot, the tire loss would be covered because it results from the car's theft.

As an illustration of how the policy language of "due and confined to" applies, consider an electrical failure resulting from a short-circuit. The electrical failure causes a fire, destroying the car. The ensuing loss to the car would be covered, and the exclusion would be confined to the electrical component that failed.

Radioactive Contamination or War

Loss due to radioactive contamination, discharge of a nuclear weapon, war (declared or undeclared), civil war, insurrection, rebellion, or revolution is excluded. For example, if a covered auto is damaged from radioactive contamination because of a nuclear accident at a public utility plant, the damage is excluded.

Electronic Equipment

Loss to any electronic equipment that reproduces, receives, or transmits audio, visual, or data signals is excluded. This includes radios and stereos, tape decks, compact disk systems, navigation systems, Internet access systems, personal computers, video entertainment systems, telephones, televisions, two-way mobile radios, scanners, and citizens band radios. However, the exclusion does not apply to electronic equipment that is permanently installed in "your covered auto" or a nonowned auto. When such electronic equipment is permanently installed, the high theft potential is reduced.

Media and Accessories

Tapes, records, disks, and other media used with sound, video, or data equipment are not part of the auto and are therefore not covered under the PAP. For example, the theft of videotapes or computer software from an insured's car is not covered even if the car is locked.

Government Destruction or Confiscation

The PAP excludes coverage for a total loss to a covered auto or nonowned auto due to destruction or confiscation by governmental or civil authorities. However, this exclusion does not apply to the interests of any loss payees (such as banks or other lending institutions) in the covered auto.

Trailer, Camper Body, or Motor Home

If the policy contains an appropriate endorsement, a trailer, camper, or motor home may be shown in the declarations as a covered auto. Physical damage loss to a trailer, camper, or motor home that is not shown in the declarations is excluded. However, the exclusion does not apply to a nonowned trailer. Also not excluded is a camper body or trailer acquired during the policy period if the insurer is asked to cover it within fourteen days after the insured becomes the owner.

Nonowned Auto Used Without Reasonable Belief of Being Entitled

As with other coverages, the PAP provides no physical damage coverage for loss to a nonowned auto when it is used by the insured or a family member who does not reasonably believe that he or she is entitled to use it.

Radar and Laser Detection Equipment

Loss to equipment designed to detect radar or laser beams is excluded. The exclusion is based on the theory that these devices promote unsafe driving.

Customizing Equipment

Many pickup trucks and vans are customized with special equipment, such as furniture, bars, or murals. Part D excludes loss to any custom furnishings or equipment in or on any pickup or van. However, if a covered auto is a pickup, the customized equipment exclusion does not apply to a cap (a hard cover over the bed of a pickup), a cover (usually made of canvas or other cloth to cover a pickup bed), or bedliner (a layer of resilient plastic over the floor and sides of a pickup bed).

Nonowned Auto Used in Garage Business

Also excluded under Part D is loss to a nonowned auto maintained or used in the business of selling, repairing, servicing, storing, or parking vehicles designed for use on public highways, including road testing and delivery. For example, if Ross is employed as an auto mechanic and damages a customer's car while road-testing it, the physical damage loss to the car is not covered under Ross's PAP. This commercial loss exposure should be insured by the repair shop.

Racing

Loss to a covered auto or a nonowned auto is excluded if the auto is damaged while located in a facility designed for racing if the auto is being used to prepare for, practice for, or compete in any prearranged racing or speed contest.

Rental Vehicles

If an insured's PAP provides physical damage coverage for an owned auto, the policy also provides physical damage coverage for nonowned vehicles—including rental vehicles. However, the exclusion states that the PAP will not pay for loss to, or loss of use of, a rental auto if the rental agreement includes a damage waiver or if applicable state law precludes the rental company from recovering from the insured for the loss.

Auto rental companies usually offer their customers a damage waiver at substantial extra cost. If purchased, this waiver eliminates or substantially reduces the individual's financial obligation to the rental company for damage to the car in an auto accident. Physical damage protection for rental autos is also provided as a benefit by some credit card companies, provided their card is used to charge the rental.

Limit of Liability

The insurer's limit of liability for a physical damage loss to a covered auto is the lower of either the **actual cash value (ACV)** of the damaged or stolen property or the amount necessary to repair or replace the property with other property of like kind and quality. In determining ACV, an adjustment is made for depreciation and physical condition of the damaged property.

Actual cash value (ACV)
Cost to replace property with new property of like kind and quality less depreciation.

When a vehicle sustains only a partial loss (such as a damaged fender), the insurer usually pays the cost of repairing it, less any applicable deductible. However, if the damage to the vehicle is extensive and the cost of repairs exceeds the vehicle's ACV, the car may be declared a total loss. In such a case, the amount the insurer will pay is limited to the ACV of the damaged vehicle, less any applicable deductible.

The insurer's maximum obligation for electronic equipment that reproduces, receives, or transmits audio, visual, or data signals and that is permanently installed but not in the locations used by the original manufacturer of the auto, is limited to $1,000. Also, the maximum amount paid for physical damage to a nonowned trailer is $1,500.

Payment of Loss

The insurer has the option of paying for the loss in money or repairing or replacing the damaged or stolen property. If a stolen auto is returned to the insured, the insurer pays the cost to return it and also pays for any damage resulting from the theft. However, the insurer has the right to keep all or part of the stolen property and pay the insured an agreed or appraised value. Payment for the loss includes the applicable sales tax for the damaged or stolen property.

No Benefit to Bailee

The No Benefit to Bailee provision states that the policy will not benefit, either directly or indirectly, any bailee (a person who assumes custody of the property of others for business purposes). If one of Midtown Parking Garage's employees negligently damages Donna's car by a covered cause of loss while it is in Midtown's custody, Donna's PAP insurer will pay for the damage to her car. The No Benefit to Bailee provision preserves the right of Donna's insurer to recover from Midtown if the garage was negligent. Although Donna receives prompt recovery, Midtown does not benefit from Donna's insurance.

Other Sources of Recovery

If a loss is covered by sources of recovery other than the PAP, the PAP insurer will pay only its share of the loss: the proportion that its limit of liability bears to the total applicable limits.

For example, an insured trailer with an ACV of $3,000 is destroyed by a fire in the insured's garage. The insured's OTC coverage applies to the loss. The PAP insurer's limit of liability for the loss is $3,000, the ACV of the trailer. The insured's homeowners insurance also covers the fire loss to the trailer, subject in this case to a $1,000 sublimit. The total of the applicable limits is $4,000 ($3,000 + $1,000). The PAP insurer's proportional share of the loss is $3,000/$4,000, or 75 percent. Thus, the PAP insurer's share is 75 percent of $3,000 ($2,250). The loss payment would be reduced by the amount of the insured's OTC deductible.

Any physical damage coverage provided by the PAP for a nonowned auto is excess over any other collectible source of recovery. Other sources of recovery could include coverage provided by the owner of the nonowned auto, any other applicable physical damage insurance, and any other source of recovery that applies to the loss.

For example, if Andy borrows Barry's car and damages it, Barry's physical damage insurance applies first, and Andy's insurance is excess, subject to his deductible. If Barry's collision deductible is $200 and Andy's collision deductible is $100, and the damage is $1,000, Barry's policy pays $800 ($1,000 – $200) and Andy's policy pays $100 ($200 – $100). The remaining $100 would have to be paid either by Andy or by Barry. If Andy acted negligently and Barry's car was damaged as a result, Barry's insurer may choose to subrogate against Andy for the $800 it paid to repair Barry's car. Andy's insurer will not pay the $800 under Part A—Liability Coverage because of the exclusion for property damage to property used by or in the care of the insured.

Appraisal

In the event of a disagreement on the amount of loss, either party may demand an **appraisal** of the loss. According to the Appraisal provision in the PAP, each party selects a competent and impartial appraiser. The two appraisers then select an "umpire." If the appraisers cannot agree on the ACV and the amount of loss, any differences are submitted to the umpire. A decision by any two of the three is binding on all. Each party pays its chosen appraiser and shares equally the expenses of the appraisal and the umpire. If the insurer agrees to an appraisal, it does not waive any of its rights under the policy (that is, the policy conditions and exclusions would still apply).

> **Appraisal**
> A method of resolving disputes between insurers and insureds over the amount owed on a covered loss.

PART D—COVERAGE FOR DAMAGE TO YOUR AUTO CASE STUDY

Applying Part D—Coverage for Damage to Your Auto of the Personal Auto Policy (PAP) to auto accidents involves unique coverage issues not associated with the other parts of the PAP. Several types of losses often occur in a single accident.

Part D—Coverage for Damage to Your Auto can extend to a wide range of loss exposures that includes claims for other than collision and loss of use. The circumstances of each accident will determine whether coverage for a particular claim applies.

Case Facts

Given the facts presented in this case, will the other than collision and loss of use claims be covered? If so, what amounts will the insurer pay for each claim?

Joe drove his car to the grocery store. When he returned to where he had parked his car, he discovered it had been stolen. Joe called his insurer and the police to inform them of the theft. Four days later, the police found his car. However, stolen from the vehicle were all four wheels, a factory-installed compact disk (CD) player, and several compact disks. Five days later, all the stolen parts had been replaced, the car was back in use, and Joe had incurred these costs to replace the stolen parts (including labor):

- Four wheels (rims and tires)—$1,200
- CD player—$500
- Estimated cost of replacing the stolen disks—$150

While his car was out of use, Joe rented a substitute auto for $30 a day, totaling $270 for the nine-day period.

To confirm the facts of this loss were accurate, the insurer relied on police reports, recorded statements from the insured and witnesses, rental car receipts, repair invoices, and appraisal of the covered auto.

Joe has his own PAP and, as part of that policy, paid a premium for other than collision (OTC) coverage for the car that was stolen. The OTC coverage is subject to a $500 deductible. His loss of use coverage is limited to $20 a day, not to exceed a maximum of $600. He has submitted a claim for the losses he incurred as a result of the theft. His PAP does not contain any endorsements that would affect coverage for damage to his car. See the exhibit "Overview of Joe's Policy."

Overview of Joe's Policy

Insured	Joe
Type of policy and coverage limits	Joe's PAP—$500 deductible for other than collision and for loss of use; $20 per day for a maximum of $600.
Endorsements that affect the case	None.
Other policy information	No other relevant information.
Background	The insured has complied with the policy conditions.

[DA00321]

Case Analysis Tools

To determine whether Joe's policy provides coverage for the damages to his auto, the insurance or risk management professional should have copies of the policy forms, any applicable endorsements that are indicated on the Declarations page of the policy, and the Declarations page itself. See the exhibit "Joe's Policy Declarations."

Joe's Policy Declarations

Personal Auto Policy Declarations

POLICYHOLDER:
(Named Insured)

Joe Insured
816 Brookside Drive
Anytown, USA 41234

POLICY NUMBER:

286 D 465211

POLICY PERIOD: **FROM:** June 18, 20XX
TO: Dec. 18, 20XX

But only If the required premium for this period has been paid, and for six-month renewal periods If renewal premiums are paid as required. Each period begins and ends at 12:01 A.M. standard time at the address of the policyholder.

**INSURED VEHICLES AND
SCHEDULE OF COVERAGES**

VEHICLE	COVERAGES	LIMITS OF INSURANCE		PREMIUM
1	20XX Honda Civic	VINXXX		
	Coverage A—Liability	$ 300,000	Each Occurrence	$ 203.00
	Coverage B—Medical Payments	$ 5,000	Each Person	$ 36.00
	Coverage C—Uninsured Motorists	$ 300,000	Each Occurrence	$ 61.80
	Coverage D—Other Than Collision	Actual Cash Value Less	$500	$ 41.60
	—Collision	Actual Cash Value Less	$500	$ 131.00
			TOTAL	$ 473.40

POLICY FORM AND ENDORSEMENTS: PP 00 01

COUNTERSIGNATURE DATE: June 18, 20XX

AGENT: A. M. Abel

Copyright, ISO Properties, Inc. [DA00313]

Determination of Coverage

To examine the policy forms to determine whether coverage applies to the losses, the insurance or risk management professional can apply the four steps of the DICE method to determine whether Joe's PAP provides coverage for his car. See the exhibit "DICE Analysis."

DICE Analysis

A DICE analysis is a logical method to approach a coverage determination for most types of loss. DICE is an acronym for these policy parts:

- Declarations
- Insuring agreements
- Conditions
- Exclusions

The claim representative reviews the policy language in a logical order to determine whether coverage applies and, if it does, what dollar limit amounts may apply.

DICE analysis involves four steps:

- Review the declarations page to determine whether it covers the person or the property at the time of loss.
- Review the insuring agreement to determine whether it covers the loss.
- Review the policy conditions to determine compliance.
- Review the policy exclusions to determine whether they preclude coverage of the loss.

By carefully performing the four steps described and reviewing policy terms and any other policy endorsements with the facts of the loss, the claim representative can determine what—if any—coverage may apply to a loss.

[DA05891]

The first DICE step is to determine whether the driver or vehicle is described on the insured's PAP Declarations page and whether the theft occurred during the policy period. Joe is listed as the named insured on his own PAP. The car that was stolen is listed as a covered auto. The theft occurred during the policy period.

The second DICE step is to determine whether the event triggers coverage under the PAP's physical damage insuring agreement. See the exhibit "Personal Auto Policy Liability Insuring Agreement."

Personal Auto Policy Liability Insuring Agreement

PART D – COVERAGE FOR DAMAGE TO YOUR AUTO

INSURING AGREEMENT

We will pay for direct and accidental loss to "your covered auto" or any "non-owned auto", including their equipment, minus any deductible shown in the Declarations.

...

We will pay for loss to "your covered auto" caused by:

1. Other than "collision" only if the Declarations indicate that Other Than Collision Coverage is provided for that auto.

In this policy provision, the insurer agrees to pay for any direct and accidental loss to "your covered auto" or a "non-owned auto," less the deductible shown on the declarations page.

The theft of the car is a direct and accidental loss from Joe's perspective. Because the loss is not the result of a collision or any other excluded cause of loss, it falls under OTC coverage. As established in the first DICE step, Joe's car is a covered auto for physical damage coverage, thus satisfying another requirement stated in the insuring agreement.

The third DICE step is to determine whether all policy conditions (for example, Joe's timely reporting of his loss to his insurer) have been complied with. For the purposes of this case study, the student should assume that they have been.

The fourth DICE step is to determine whether one or more exclusions preclude coverage the insuring agreements have granted. See the exhibit "Personal Auto Policy Exclusions, Electronic Equipment."

Personal Auto Policy Exclusions, Electronic Equipment

PART D – COVERAGE FOR DAMAGE TO YOUR AUTO

EXCLUSIONS

We will not pay for:

...

    4. Loss to any electronic equipment that reproduces, receives or transmits audio, visual or data signals. This includes but is not limited to:

...

      c. Compact disk systems;

...

    This exclusion (4.) does not apply to electronic equipment that is permanently installed in "your covered auto" or any "non-owned auto".

Copyright, ISO Properties, Inc., 2003. [DA05640]

Two exclusions may apply in this case. The first involves electronic equipment. Loss to any electronic equipment that reproduces, receives, or transmits audio, visual, or data signals is excluded. The CD player stolen from Joe's car would fall into that category. However, the exclusion does not apply to electronic equipment that is permanently installed in the car, as Joe's CD player was. Therefore, the stolen CD player is covered.

The second exclusion eliminates coverage for tapes, records, disks, or other media used with sound, video, or data equipment. The compact disks that were stolen from Joe's car would be considered media as defined by the policy;

therefore, Joe's insurer would not pay for the cost of replacing them. See the exhibit "Personal Auto Policy Exclusions, CDs."

Personal Auto Policy Exclusions, CDs

PART D – COVERAGE FOR DAMAGE TO YOUR AUTO

EXCLUSIONS

We will not pay for:

...

    5. Loss to tapes, records, disks or other media used with equipment described in Exclusion **4**.

Copyright, ISO Properties, Inc., 2003. [DA05641]

In summary, Joe's OTC coverage applies to the stolen wheels and CD player but not to the disks. Also, because Joe incurred temporary transportation expenses resulting from a covered loss to a covered auto, the Transportation Expenses coverage in Part D of the PAP covers his cost of renting a temporary substitute auto (subject to the per day and total limits).

Determination of Amounts Payable

Determining the amounts payable for Joe's loss under Part D of the PAP involves application of the Limit of Liability provision, the OTC deductible, and the Transportation Expenses coverage provision. See the exhibit "Personal Auto Policy Limit of Liability."

Personal Auto Policy Limit of Liability

PART D – COVERAGE FOR DAMAGE TO YOUR AUTO

LIMIT OF LIABILITY

  A. Our limit of liability for loss will be the lesser of the:

    1. Actual cash value of the stolen or damaged property; or

    2. Amount necessary to repair or replace the property with other property of like kind and quality.

       However, the most we will pay for loss to:

    ...

    2. Electronic equipment that reproduces, receives or transmits audio, visual or data signals, which is permanently installed in the auto not used by the auto manufacturer for installation of such equipment, is $1,000.

Copyright, ISO Properties, Inc., 2003. [DA05643]

The insurer's limit of liability for a physical damage loss is the lower of the actual cash value of the damaged or stolen property or the amount necessary to repair or replace the property with other property of like kind and quality.

Because the car was recovered with only a few of its parts stolen, it is considered a partial, rather than a total, loss. The insurer will pay Joe the cost of replacing the covered stolen parts (the wheels and the CD player) because it is less than the car's actual cash value.

The Limit of Liability provision also limits the coverage for stolen electronic equipment to $1,000 if the equipment was permanently installed in a location not used by the original manufacturer. However, Joe's CD player was factory-installed and had a value of only $500; therefore, the $1,000 limit does not affect the amount payable.

The total covered physical damage loss can now be calculated as $1,200 (for replacement of wheels) plus $500 (for replacement of CD player), or $1,700. The OTC deductible of $500 is subtracted from this amount to arrive at a payment of $1,200.

Although Joe's cost of renting a temporary substitute auto is insured under the Transportation Expenses coverage, that coverage is limited to $20 a day, not to exceed a maximum of $600. Moreover, because this was a total theft of the car, the policy imposes a two-day waiting period before reimbursement of Joe's transportation expenses begins. The car was out of service for a total of nine days—four days for the police to find the car and another five days to replace all the stolen parts. Therefore, following the two-day waiting period, Joe will receive reimbursement of up to $20 per day for his transportation expenses for seven days. The insurer will reimburse Joe for $140 of the $270 he spent to rent a temporary substitute auto. See the exhibit "Personal Auto Policy Transportation Expenses."

Joe will receive a total claim payment of $1,340, consisting of $1,200 for the stolen auto parts and $140 for his temporary transportation expenses. See the exhibit "Determination of Amounts Payable."

Personal Auto Policy Transportation Expenses

PART D – COVERAGE FOR DAMAGE TO YOUR AUTO

TRANSPORTATION EXPENSES

    A. In addition, we will pay, without application of a deductible, up to a maximum of $600 for:

        1. Temporary transportation expenses not exceeding $20 per day incurred by you in the event of a loss to "your covered auto". We will pay for such expenses if the loss is caused by:

           a. Other than "collision" only if the Declarations indicate that Other Than Collision Coverage is provided for that auto.

    ...

    B. Subject to the provisions of Paragraph A., if the loss is caused by:

        1. A total theft of "your covered auto" or a "non-owned auto", we will pay only expenses incurred during the period:

           a. Beginning 48 hours after the theft; and

           b. Ending when "your covered auto" or the "non-owned auto" is returned to use or we pay for its loss.

Copyright, ISO Properties, Inc., 2003. [DA05642]

Determination of Amounts Payable

- For the other than collision claim that included cost to replace the wheels and the compact disk player, the insurer will pay $1,200, which includes subtracting the $500 deductible.
- The cost to replace the compact disks is excluded.
- For the Transportation Expense loss of use claim, the insurer will pay $140.
- The total payment from the insurer is $1,340.

[DA05644]

PART E—DUTIES AFTER AN ACCIDENT OR LOSS

The Personal Auto Policy (PAP) contains a section outlining several important duties with which the insured must comply in order for the policy to provide coverage.

Before an insurer is obligated to pay for an accident or loss covered under the Personal Auto Policy (PAP), the insured must comply with certain requirements, such as notifying the insurer when a loss has occurred, cooperating in the investigation and settlement of the claim, and performing several other duties. Part E of the PAP specifies these general duties the insured must perform after an accident or a loss.

The insurer has no obligation to provide coverage if the insured's failure to comply with these requirements is prejudicial to the insurer (that is, if the insured's action is detrimental to the insurer). For example, if an insured does not promptly notify the insurer when a loss occurs, the insurer may not be required to provide coverage under the PAP. The insured must also perform additional duties if seeking protection under Part C—Uninsured Motorists Coverage or Part D—Coverage for Damage to Your Auto. See the exhibit "Part E—Duties After an Accident or Loss."

Part E—Duties After an Accident or Loss

General Duties	Additional Duties for Uninsured Motorists Coverage	Additional Duties for Physical Damage Coverage
Provide prompt notice to the insurer	Notify police if a hit-and-run driver was involved in the accident or loss	Take reasonable steps to prevent further loss
Cooperate with the insurer	Submit legal papers to the insurer	Notify police if the covered auto is stolen
Submit legal papers to the insurer		Permit inspection and appraisal of the damaged property
Submit to a physical exam if requested		
Agree to an examination under oath		
Authorize release of pertinent medical records to the insurer		
Submit a proof of loss		

[DA00169]

General Duties

A person seeking coverage under the PAP must perform specified general duties after an accident or a loss in order to receive payment under all of the policy's coverages:

- Provide prompt notice to the insurer—The insurer must be notified promptly of how, when, and where the accident or loss happened. The notice also should include the names and addresses of any witnesses and injured persons. Notice to the insurer can be initiated with a phone call or a fax to the insurer's claim department.

- Cooperate with the insurer—The person seeking coverage must cooperate with the insurer in the investigation, settlement, or defense of any claim or suit related to the accident or loss. Cooperation can include providing details of the loss, names of witnesses to the accident or loss, police reports, and other important information related to the settlement and appropriate defense of the claim.

- Submit legal papers to the insurer—The person seeking coverage must promptly submit to the insurer copies of any notices or legal documentation received in connection with the accident or loss. This submission assists the insurer in fairly settling the claim and in defending any legal case that may arise.

- Submit to physical examination—The person seeking coverage must agree to submit to a physical examination conducted by a doctor chosen by the insurer upon request. The insurer pays for such examinations.

- Agree to examination under oath—The person seeking coverage must agree to an examination under oath if required by the insurer.

- Authorize release of medical records—The person seeking coverage must authorize the insurer to obtain medical reports and other pertinent records related to the claim.

Proof of loss

A statement of facts about a loss for which the insured is making a claim.

- Submit proof of loss—The person seeking coverage must submit a **proof of loss** when required by the insurer. The insured swears to the contents of this statement and its contents.

Additional Duties for Uninsured Motorists Coverage

A person seeking coverage under Part C—Uninsured Motorists Coverage must perform additional duties:

- Notify police—The person seeking coverage must promptly notify police if a hit-and-run driver was involved in the accident. This requirement is designed to discourage the filing of fraudulent claims.

- Submit legal papers—If the person seeking coverage sues the uninsured motorist, the insured must submit to the insurer a copy of the legal documentation related to the suit. This requirement ensures that the insurer has as much information as possible to prepare its legal case if a covered party enters into a lawsuit with a third party.

Additional Duties for Physical Damage Coverage

Additional duties are also required under Part D—Coverage for Damage to Your Auto:

- Prevent further loss—The person seeking coverage must take reasonable steps after a loss to protect a covered auto or nonowned auto and its equipment from further loss. The insurer will pay the reasonable expenses the insured incurs to protect the vehicle from further damage. For example, the insurer will pay for a tow truck to transport the damaged auto to another location for safekeeping.

- Notify police—If a covered auto or nonowned auto is stolen, the person seeking coverage must promptly notify police of the theft. Prompt notification may increase the possibility that the stolen vehicle will be recovered.

- Permit inspection and appraisal—The person seeking coverage must permit the insurer to inspect and appraise the damaged property before its repair or disposal. For small losses, the insurer sometimes waives its right to inspect and appraise the damaged auto and instead allows the person seeking coverage to submit two or three repair estimates that serve as the basis for the loss settlement.

PART F—GENERAL PROVISIONS

The Personal Auto Policy includes terms and conditions that apply throughout the policy. These are contained in Part F of the policy.

Part F—General Provisions is the final part of the Personal Auto Policy (PAP). It contains general provisions and conditions that apply to the entire policy. These conditions include items that specify aspects of PAP coverage, such as how the insurer handles changes in the policy or policy cancellations.

Bankruptcy of Insured

This provision states that if the insured declares bankruptcy or becomes insolvent, the insurer is not relieved of any obligations under the policy. For example, if the insured is sued for an amount exceeding the policy limits and declares bankruptcy in an attempt to escape payment of the rest of the judgment, the insurer is still required to pay the part of the judgment covered by insurance.

Changes in the Policy

This provision indicates that the policy contains all the agreements between the named insured and the insurer. The terms of the policy cannot be changed or waived except by an endorsement issued by the insurer. If a change requires a premium adjustment, the adjustment is made in accordance with the manual rules of the insurer. Changes during the policy term that can result in a premium increase or decrease include changes in these elements:

- The number, type, or use of insured vehicles
- The operators using insured vehicles

- The place of principal garaging of insured vehicles
- The coverage provided, deductibles, or limits of liability

Liberalization Clause

A policy condition providing that if a policy form is broadened at no additional premium, the broadened coverage automatically applies to all existing policies of the same type.

Another portion of this provision, sometimes referred to as a **liberalization clause**, automatically provides broadened coverage under some conditions. According to this provision, if the insurer makes a change to the PAP that broadens its coverage without an additional premium, the change automatically applies to the insured's existing policy on the date the revision is effective in the insured's state. This provision does not, however, apply to changes that include both broadenings and restrictions of coverage or those that are implemented in a general program revision either by a new edition of the policy or by an amendatory endorsement.

Fraud

This provision says that no coverage exists for any insured who makes fraudulent statements or engages in fraudulent conduct in connection with any accident or loss for which a claim is made. For example, if an insured deliberately abandons a covered auto and then reports the car as stolen, the insurer does not cover the insured for that claim.

Legal Action Against the Insurer

According to this policy provision, no legal action can be brought against the insurer until the insured has fully complied with all of the policy terms. In addition, under Part A—Liability Coverage, no legal action can be brought against the insurer unless the insurer agrees in writing that the insured has an obligation to pay damages or the amount of the insurer's obligation has been finally determined by a judgment after a trial. No person or organization has any right under the policy to involve the insurer in any action to determine the liability of an insured unless all policy conditions have been met.

Insurer's Right to Recover Payment

The policy provision regarding an insurer's right to recover payment is often called the subrogation clause. If the insurer makes a loss payment to a person who has the right to recover damages from a third party that either caused or is legally liable for the loss, the insurer has a legal right of subrogation against that third party. For example, Joe, who is insured with Insurer A, is involved in an accident with Mary, who is insured with Insurer B. It is determined that Mary is legally liable for the accident and for Joe's injuries. If Insurer A makes payments to Joe, it can recover those payments from Mary or from Insurer B. The covered person must do whatever is necessary to enable the insurer to exercise its subrogation rights. In addition, the person to whom the loss payment was made is not allowed to do anything after the loss that would prejudice or impede the insurer's right of subrogation.

The subrogation provision does not apply to physical damage coverages in regard to any person who is using a covered auto with a reasonable belief that he or she is entitled to do so. For example, if Sue borrows Irene's car with her permission and damages the car in a collision, Irene's collision coverage will pay for the damage to the car. According to the terms of this provision, Irene's insurer cannot subrogate against Sue or her insurer.

Finally, if a person receives a loss payment from an insurer and also recovers damages from another party, that person is required to hold the proceeds of the second recovery in trust for the insurer and to reimburse the insurer to the extent of the insurer's loss payment.

Policy Period and Territory

The PAP applies only to accidents and losses that occur during the policy period shown on the Declarations page and within the policy territory.

The policy territory includes the United States, U.S. territories and possessions, Puerto Rico, and Canada. The policy also applies to a covered auto while being transported among ports of the U.S., Puerto Rico, or Canada. Coverage does not apply anywhere outside the policy territory. It is important to note that the policy territory does not include Mexico. Under Mexican law, a motorist from the U.S. who has not purchased valid insurance from a Mexican insurer and is involved in an accident can be detained in jail, have his or her car impounded, and be subject to other penalties. Motorists who are planning to drive into Mexico should purchase the Limited Mexico Coverage endorsement.

Termination

The PAP contains a provision that applies to **policy termination** by either the insured or insurer. The termination provision consists of four parts:

- Cancellation
- Nonrenewal
- Automatic termination
- Other termination provisions

Policy termination
The ending of the contractual relationship between the insured and insurer by cancellation, expiration, or nonrenewal.

All states have laws that restrict the insurer's right to cancel or nonrenew an auto policy, such as provisions for the number of days' notice that an insured must be given prior to cancellation. In many states, these laws differ from the termination provision in the PAP. Changes mandated by state laws are usually incorporated into the policy by means of a state endorsement that must be attached to all auto policies issued in that state. Whenever state laws and policy provisions conflict, state law supersedes the policy provisions.

Cancellation

Cancellation

Termination of a policy, by either the insurer or the insured, during the policy term.

Under the cancellation provision, the named insured normally can cancel anytime during the policy period by returning the policy to the insurer or by giving advance written notice of the date the **cancellation** is to become effective.

The insurer has more limited cancellation rights. If the policy has been in force for fewer than sixty days and is not a renewal or continuation policy, the insurer can cancel by mailing a cancellation notice to the named insured. Thus, the insurer has sixty days to investigate and determine whether a new applicant meets the insurer's underwriting standards. If the cancellation is for nonpayment of premium, the insurer must give the named insured at least ten days' notice; in all other cases, at least twenty days' notice must be given.

After the policy has been in force for sixty days, or if it is a renewal or continuation policy, the insurer can cancel the policy only for one of three reasons:

- The premium has not been paid.
- The insured's driver's license has been suspended or revoked during the policy period (or since the last annual anniversary of the original effective date if the policy is for other than one year).
- The policy has been obtained by a material misrepresentation. For example, if an insured knowingly provides false information to the insurer, the insurer has the right to cancel that person's coverage after the correct information is discovered.

Nonrenewal

This policy provision outlines the terms under which a policy is not renewed. Rather than cancel a policy, the insurer may decide to let the policy remain in force during the policy period but not to renew the policy for another term. If the insurer decides not to renew, the named insured must be given at least twenty days' notice before the end of the policy period. The conditions under which the insurer can nonrenew vary according to the length of the policy period:

- If the policy period is less than six months, the insurer has the right to nonrenew every six months, beginning six months after the policy's original effective date.
- If the policy period is six months or longer, but less than a year, the insurer has the right to nonrenew at the end of the policy period.
- If the policy period is one year or longer, the insurer has the right to nonrenew at each anniversary of the policy's original effective date. For example, after the policy has been in effect for at least one year, an insurer may decide to nonrenew a policy due to excessive loss amounts.

Automatic Termination

Under the automatic termination provision, if the insurer offers to renew the policy but the named insured does not accept the offer, the policy automatically terminates at the end of the current policy period. Failure to pay the renewal premium means that the named insured has not accepted the insurer's offer to renew the policy. That is, once the named insured is billed for another period, the premium must be paid, or the policy automatically terminates on its expiration date. Although in practice some insurers allow a short period of time for an insured to pay an overdue premium, the policy itself provides no grace period.

If the named insured obtains other insurance on a covered auto, the PAP coverage on that auto automatically terminates on the effective date of the other insurance. Suppose, for example, that Dennis has a PAP from Insurer X covering his sedan. He subsequently buys a sports car and purchases a new auto policy from Insurer Z covering both the sports car and the sedan. Dennis's PAP from Insurer X automatically terminates on the effective date of his new policy from Insurer Z, even if he does not notify his PAP insurer. If Dennis becomes involved in a serious accident while driving his sedan, he cannot claim coverage under both policies.

Other Termination Provisions

The policy contains three additional termination provisions:

- The insurer may choose to deliver the cancellation notice rather than mail it. However, proof of mailing (to the named insured at the address as shown in the declarations) of any cancellation notice is considered sufficient proof of notice.
- If the policy is canceled, the named insured may be entitled to a premium refund. Any premium refund is computed according to the insurer's manual rules. Making or offering to make the refund is not a condition of cancellation.
- The effective date of cancellation stated in the cancellation notice becomes the end of the policy period.

Transfer of Insured's Interest in the Policy

This provision stipulates that the named insured's rights and duties under the policy cannot be assigned to another party without the insurer's written consent. This means that if the insured sells his or her vehicle, he or she cannot transfer the insurance policy to the new owner of the vehicle. However, if the named insured dies, the coverage is automatically continued to the end of the policy period for both the surviving spouse (if he or she is a resident of the same household at the time of the named insured's death) and the legal representative of the deceased person (but only with respect to the representative's legal responsibility to maintain or use a covered auto).

Two or More Auto Policies

If two or more auto policies issued to the named insured by the same insurer apply to the same accident, the insurer's maximum limit of liability is the highest applicable limit of liability under any one policy. The intent of this provision is to prevent the "stacking" (adding together) of policy limits when two or more auto policies are issued by the same insurer.

COMMON ENDORSEMENTS TO THE PERSONAL AUTO POLICY

Insurance professionals should be aware that, while the Personal Auto Policy (PAP) provides extensive coverage, additions or modifications may be necessary in some scenarios.

Because the unmodified Insurance Services Office, Inc. (ISO) PAP contains eligibility restrictions, coverage exclusions, and coverage limitations, it does not completely meet every customer's auto insurance needs. However, several policy endorsements provide coverage additions or modifications for customers who have coverage needs beyond the unendorsed PAP. See the exhibit "Frequently Used Personal Auto Endorsements."

Miscellaneous Type Vehicle Endorsement

The unmodified PAP excludes coverage for vehicles that have fewer than four wheels and vehicles designed for off-public-road use. The Miscellaneous Type Vehicle Endorsement (PP 03 23 01 05) provides coverage for a motor home, a motorcycle or similar type of vehicle, an all-terrain vehicle, a dune buggy, or a golf cart, none of which are included in the PAP's definition of covered auto. The endorsement clarifies the PAP provisions to apply to miscellaneous type vehicles rather than to private passenger vehicles, vans, or pickup trucks. The endorsement schedule lists each covered vehicle and the corresponding applicable coverages, limits of liability, and premiums.

An optional passenger hazard exclusion, which excludes liability coverage for bodily injury to any person occupying the covered vehicle, can be activated as part of the endorsement. For example, a motorcycle owner who never carries passengers can elect this exclusion in exchange for a lower premium.

Part D (physical damage) of the endorsement excludes coverage for loss to clothing or luggage, business or office equipment, sales samples, or articles

Frequently Used Personal Auto Endorsements

Endorsement Name	Exposure Covered
Miscellaneous Type Vehicle Endorsement	Covers motor homes, motorcycles, and other vehicles with fewer than four wheels that are designed for off public road use
Snowmobile Endorsement	Provides coverage for snowmobiles other than vehicles propelled by airplane-type propellers or fans
Trailer/Camper Body Coverage (Maximum Limit of Liability)	Covers trailers or camper bodies, including related facilities or equipment
Extended Non-Owned Coverage	Provides liability and medical payments coverages for drivers of vehicles furnished or made available for the regular use of the named insured and/or family members
Named Non-Owner Coverage	Provides liability, medical payments, uninsured, and underinsured motorists coverages for drivers who do not own an auto but regularly or occasionally drive another person's vehicle or a rental vehicle
Auto Loan/Lease Coverage	Amends physical damage coverage for leased vehicles or vehicles with outstanding loan amounts to include an unpaid amount due on the lease or loan
Limited Mexico Coverage	Provides excess liability coverage over Mexican auto insurance for an insured who is involved in an accident or loss in Mexico within twenty-five miles of the United States border on a trip of ten days or less
Excess Electronic Equipment Coverage	Increases the $1,000 limit that applies to electronic equipment installed in the vehicle in locations not intended for that purpose by the auto manufacturer
Coverage for Damage to Your Auto (Maximum Limit of Liability)	Covers each described vehicle for a stated amount of insurance as indicated in the endorsement schedule that applies to collision and OTC losses
Optional Limits Transportation Expenses Coverage	Increases the limit for Coverage for Transportation Expenses under Coverage D (physical damage)
Towing and Labor Costs Coverage	Covers the towing of a disabled covered or nonowned auto, including costs for labor performed at the place of disablement.

[DA00170]

used in exhibits. It also limits the amount paid for physical damage losses to the lowest of these values:

- The stated amount shown in the schedule or declarations
- The actual cash value of the stolen or damaged property
- The amount necessary to repair or replace the property (less any deductible)

The determination of actual cash value includes an adjustment for the depreciation and physical condition of the damaged vehicle.

Snowmobile Endorsement

Coverage for snowmobiles can be added to the PAP by attaching a Snowmobile Endorsement (PP 03 20 01 05). A snowmobile is defined as a land motor vehicle propelled solely by wheels, crawler-type treads, belts, or similar mechanical devices and designed for use mainly off public roads on snow or ice. Under this definition, a vehicle propelled by airplane-type propellers or fans is not considered a snowmobile.

Available snowmobile coverages include liability, medical payments, uninsured motorists, collision, and other than collision. Each covered snowmobile is listed in a schedule that states the applicable coverages, limits of liability, and premiums.

The liability coverage for snowmobiles has several exclusions and modifications:

- Coverage does not apply if the snowmobile is used in any business.
- Coverage does not apply when the snowmobile is used in a race or speed contest or in practice or preparation for a race, regardless of whether the race is prearranged or organized.
- Coverage is excluded for any person or organization, other than the named insured, while renting or leasing a snowmobile.
- A passenger hazard exclusion can be activated that excludes liability for bodily injury to any person while occupying or being towed by the snowmobile.

The provisions of this endorsement regarding the amount paid for physical damage losses are the same as those of the Miscellaneous Type Vehicle Endorsement.

Trailer/Camper Body Coverage (Maximum Limit of Liability)

Under the Trailer/Camper Body Coverage (Maximum Limit of Liability) (PP 03 07 01 05) endorsement, coverage is extended to direct and accidental loss to a trailer or camper body described in the policy declarations or the schedule of the endorsement. The endorsement also provides coverage for related facilities or equipment, including, but not limited to, cooking, dining, plumbing, or refrigeration facilities, as well as awnings or cabanas. Loss to clothing or luggage, business or office equipment, and sales samples or articles used in exhibitions is excluded. The PAP exclusions for electronic equipment and media, radar detectors, and custom furnishings or equipment still apply. If necessary, such items can be covered under other PAP endorsements.

The provisions of this endorsement regarding the amount paid for physical damage losses are the same as those of the Miscellaneous Type Vehicle Endorsement.

Extended Non-Owned Coverage—Vehicles Furnished or Available for Regular Use

The unendorsed PAP excludes liability and medical payments coverage for vehicles furnished or made available for the regular use of the named insured and family members. This exclusion can be eliminated by adding the Extended Non-Owned Coverage—Vehicles Furnished or Available for Regular Use (PP 03 06 01 05) endorsement to the PAP. The endorsement's coverage applies only to the individual(s) named in the endorsement schedule. However, coverage can be extended to the named individual's family members. (Such an extension is indicated by a checkbox on the endorsement.)

The liability coverage provided by the endorsement is excess over any other applicable insurance on the nonowned vehicle. The endorsement schedule also indicates separate premiums for liability and for medical payments coverage.

The endorsement provides liability coverage for any vehicle furnished or available for the regular use of the named individual and for family members who are indicated in the schedule. For example, if Alice is furnished with a company car by her employer, this endorsement would provide liability and/or medical payments coverage on an excess basis.

Named Non-Owner Coverage

People who do not regularly own an auto or who occasionally drive another person's vehicle or a rental vehicle can secure coverage for the loss exposures arising out of their use of a nonowned auto by purchasing a PAP with the Named Non-Owner Coverage (PP 03 22 01 05) endorsement. This endorsement is used in conjunction with the PAP to provide liability coverage, medical payments coverage, uninsured motorists coverage, and underinsured motorists (but not physical damage) coverage for a driver who does not own an auto.

This coverage applies only to a person who is actually named in the endorsement. The named insured's spouse or other resident family members are not automatically covered. Coverage for family members can be included by indicating such coverage on the endorsement schedule.

The liability insurance under a PAP with the named nonowner endorsement is excess over any other applicable liability insurance on the nonowned auto. The endorsement provides important protection to the named insured who drives a nonowned auto with inadequate liability limits or perhaps no insurance at all.

The endorsement provides the named insured with liability, medical payments, uninsured motorists, and underinsured motorists coverage on a newly acquired vehicle for up to fourteen days. Coverage automatically terminates when the named insured purchases separate insurance on the vehicle. Unlike the Extended Non-Owned Coverage—Vehicles Furnished or Available for Regular Use Endorsement, named non-owner coverage is designed for individuals who only occasionally use another person's vehicle.

Auto Loan/Lease Coverage

If an insured under the PAP leases or has an outstanding loan for a vehicle that experiences a total loss, the balance of the loan or lease may exceed the vehicle's actual cash value. However, the lending institution or leasing company still will require the outstanding balance on the vehicle, even though it has been destroyed. The Auto Loan/Lease Coverage (PP03 35 01 05) endorsement amends the Part D (physical damage) coverage of the PAP so that, in the event of the loss, coverage is included for the unpaid amount due on the lease or loan. In such a situation, the endorsement provides coverage for the difference between the outstanding loan amount and the amount that would have been paid based on the limit of liability as stated in the unendorsed policy (actual cash value or the amount necessary to repair or replace the property with like kind and quality). This allows the insured to satisfy any outstanding loan or lease payments.

Under the Auto Loan/Lease endorsement, none of these would be included in any loss payment:

- Lease or loan payments that were overdue at the time of loss
- Penalties imposed under a lease for excessive use, abnormal wear and tear, or high mileage
- Security deposits not refunded by a lessor
- Costs for extended warranties; credit life insurance; or health, accident, or disability insurance purchased with the loan or the lease
- Balances transferred from previous loans or leases

The endorsement schedule includes a description of the covered auto(s) and premiums for other than collision and/or collision coverage. See the exhibit "Auto Loan/Lease Coverage Example."

> ## Auto Loan/Lease Coverage Example
>
> Karl has a forty-eight-month loan on a two-year-old vehicle whose actual cash value is $31,000. The vehicle is totally destroyed in an accident. At the time of the loss, Karl's loan amount is $33,450, of which $595 is the remaining cost of an extended warranty. An unendorsed PAP would pay Karl the $31,000 actual cash value. If the policy includes the Auto Loan/Lease Coverage endorsement, the payment would be $32,855 (the $33,450 loan amount less the $595 warranty cost).

[DA05772]

Limited Mexico Coverage

The unendorsed PAP does not provide any coverage in Mexico; however, the Limited Mexico Coverage (PP 03 21 01 05) endorsement can be added to the PAP. This endorsement extends the PAP coverages to an insured who is involved in an accident or loss in Mexico within twenty-five miles of the United States border on a trip of ten days or less.

The coverage provided by this endorsement does not meet Mexico's auto liability insurance requirements. The endorsement is effective only if primary liability coverage is also purchased from a licensed Mexican insurer. Mexican insurance usually can be purchased from a licensed agent at the border. The stipulations requiring a Mexican insurance policy are displayed in boldface print at the top of the endorsement under a "Warning" header.

The liability insurance provided by the endorsement is excess over the Mexican insurance and over any other valid and collectible insurance. The major advantage of the endorsement is that it provides additional liability insurance beyond that provided by the Mexican policy, as well as providing the other standard PAP coverages, such as physical damage coverage.

Excess Electronic Equipment Coverage

The unendorsed PAP excludes coverage for loss to any electronic equipment that is not permanently installed in the insured vehicle and also excludes coverage for loss to tapes, records, disks, or other media. The PAP also includes a $1,000 limit on electronic equipment that reproduces, receives, or transmits audio, visual, or data signals that are permanently installed in locations not intended for that purpose by the auto manufacturer. This includes navigation systems, Internet access systems, audio equipment, and other similar electronic equipment. The Excess Electronic Equipment Coverage (PP 03 13 01 05) endorsement can be used to increase the limit on such equipment from $1,000 to a limit shown in the endorsement schedule. The endorsement schedule also includes a description of the covered vehicle and the limit of liability and premiums for excess electronic equipment.

The Excess Electronic Equipment Coverage endorsement also provides coverage for direct and accidental loss to tapes, records, disks, or other media owned by the named insured or the named insured's family member. Coverage is provided for the lesser of the actual cash value or the amount necessary to repair or replace the stolen or damaged property, subject to a maximum limit of $200 for all such media. The media must be in or upon the covered auto or any nonowned auto at the time of loss.

Coverage for Damage to Your Auto (Maximum Limit of Liability)

The Coverage for Damage to Your Auto (Maximum Limit of Liability) (PP 03 08 06 94) endorsement to the PAP allows owners of high-value antique cars or restored show cars to establish the car's insurable value when the policy is written by inserting a stated amount of insurance in the policy. Under this endorsement (often called a "stated amount" endorsement), each vehicle is described, and a stated amount of insurance is shown that applies to collision loss and other than collision loss.

Even though the endorsement indicates a stated amount of insurance, it may not provide coverage for that amount in the event of a total loss to the vehicle. Rather, the insurer's maximum limit of liability for a covered loss is limited to the lowest of these values:

- The stated amount shown in the schedule or in the declarations
- The actual cash value of the stolen or damaged property
- The amount necessary to repair or replace the property with other property of like kind and quality

If, for example, the stated amount of insurance is less than the vehicle's actual cash value or the amount necessary to repair or replace the property, the stated amount is used as the basis of the loss settlement. However, if the stated amount of insurance is greater than the vehicle's actual cash value or the amount necessary to repair or replace the property, the lower amount is the basis for payment. In any case, the amount paid is reduced by any applicable deductible shown in the endorsement schedule or policy declarations.

When determining the vehicle's actual cash value in the event of a total loss, an adjustment is made for depreciation and the physical condition of the vehicle. This endorsement also states that if a repair or replacement of the vehicle results in better than like kind or quality, the insurer will not include the amount of betterment in any loss payment.

Optional Limits Transportation Expenses Coverage

The temporary transportation expenses associated with the loss of use of an auto can be significant when the owner has to rent a substitute auto until his or her owned auto is repaired or replaced. The PAP provides coverage up to a limit of $20 per day for such temporary transportation expenses. Depending on the prices charged by local rental car providers and the type of transportation needed, the cost could exceed this limit.

Increased limits for loss of use are available under the Optional Limits Transportation Expenses Coverage Endorsement (PP 03 02). The endorsement allows the insured to increase coverage to one of three limits, which can be applied to the costs of a substitute vehicle for the period reasonably required to repair or replace the auto:

- $30 per day, subject to a maximum of $900
- $40 per day, subject to a maximum of $1,200
- $50 per day, subject to a maximum of $1,500

Towing and Labor Costs Coverage

Available in limits of $25, $50, or $75, the Towing and Labor Costs Coverage Endorsement (PP 03 03) provides coverage for the costs of towing the covered auto when it is disabled. The cost of labor performed to repair the auto at the place of disablement is also covered up to the limit. A single limit per disablement applies whether it is used for towing or labor costs. However, a separate limit applies to each disablement. Thus, if a vehicle is disabled five times during the policy period, the limit is reinstated for each incident.

Variation on the ISO PAP

Many insurers choose to use only ISO PAP forms when providing personal auto insurance coverage to their insureds. However, some insurers may choose to offer a non-ISO policy that responds to an insured's unique needs. For example, such a policy can provide enhanced vehicle disablement coverage.

This coverage applies in the event the covered auto is disabled because of a covered loss that occurs beyond a certain distance (such as fifty miles) from the insured's residence. In such a circumstance, the coverage applies to commercial transportation fees for the occupants of the auto to return home or the costs to reach their destination and the cost of extra meals and lodging needed when the loss results in delays.

[DA05771]

PERSONAL AUTO POLICY COVERAGE CASE STUDY

Being able to apply the Personal Auto Policy (PAP) to a claim situation is a critical skill for the insurance practitioner.

This case helps the student apply the coverages found under the PAP to a given set of facts.

Case Facts

Given the following facts, will both of the auto claims be covered in their entirety? If so, what will be paid under the policy including any applicable endorsements?

Joshua was driving on the interstate when road conditions deteriorated from blowing snow. He was taking his wife, Javiera, to an appointment with her dentist. Their three-year-old daughter, Mandy, was in her car seat in the rear of the vehicle. Joshua owns the vehicle they were riding in and uses it regularly in his farming business. The traffic on the highway was moderately heavy, and most people were driving below the speed limit because of the weather conditions. Glancing in his rear view mirror, Joshua noticed a vehicle weaving in and out of traffic at a rapid speed. Suddenly, Benjamin, the driver of that vehicle, appeared to lose control and ran into Joshua's vehicle, forcing it off the highway, where it rolled over twice and landed upside down in a field.

The police arrived at the scene and, after taking statements from witnesses, charged Benjamin with dangerous driving. The victims were transported from the scene to a hospital. Joshua suffered minor injuries, but Javiera, who had not been wearing her seatbelt, was critically injured. Mandy had a broken arm and cuts and bruises. Joshua was treated and released from the hospital on the day of the accident. Mandy remained in the hospital overnight for observation, had a cast put on, and required some rehabilitation. Javiera stayed in the intensive care unit for one month and died as a result of her injuries.

Benjamin's injuries included cracked ribs and a punctured lung. He was in the hospital for ten days and off work for six weeks.

Joshua's vehicle was a total loss. Benjamin's vehicle had damage to the front end and the passenger door.

Joshua and Benjamin live in a state that does not have a no-fault auto insurance law.

The claim representative will confirm facts about the accident by reviewing police reports, witness statements, and medical records. He will also inspect the accident scene and the vehicles involved. Both Benjamin and Joshua notified their insurers within twenty-four hours of the accident and complied with all other policy conditions.

Joshua initiated a lawsuit against Benjamin for these amounts:

- $195,000—Medical and funeral expenses for Javiera
- $19,000—Medical and rehabilitation expenses for Mandy
- $5,000—Medical expenses for Joshua

Benjamin's medical expenses totaled $57,350. Joshua's vehicle was a total loss, with an ACV of $27,500. The damage to Benjamin's vehicle was $2,850. Both Joshua and Benjamin had to rent temporary vehicles. Joshua rented a vehicle for twenty-one days at a cost of $30 per day. Benjamin's rental was for ten days, also at $30 per day. Benjamin was required by his insurer to take four days off from work to appear in court. See the exhibit "Accident Expenses."

Accident Expenses

Accident Expense Amounts	Joshua	Benjamin
Medical Expenses	$195,000 (Javiera) $19,000 (Mandy) $5,000 (Joshua)	$57,350
Physical Damage to Autos	$27,500	$2,850
Temporary Replacement Vehicles	$630	$300
Lost Wages for Court Appearance	N/A	$480
Legal Fees	$8,600	$31,450

[DA05928]

The court ruled in Joshua's favor and awarded the full $219,000 ($195,000 for Javiera; $19,000 for Mandy; and $5,000 for Joshua) of the claim as damages, plus prejudgment interest in the amount of $4,000.

Both Joshua and Benjamin have PAPs that apply on the date of the accident. Joshua's PAP contains an endorsement for underinsured motorists coverage. In the state where Joshua and Benjamin reside, a limit trigger applies to underinsured motorists coverage. See the exhibit "Coverage Facts."

Coverage Facts

Joshua's PAP		Benjamin's PAP	
Part A—	$250,000 per person	Part A—	$300,000
Liability Coverage	$500,000 per accident	Liability Coverage	Combined single limits
Part B—	$5,000 per person	Part B—	$5,000 per person
Medical Payments		Medical Payments	
Part D—	$1,000 deductible— OTC	Part D—	$500 deductible
Damage to Your Auto	$1,000 deductible— Collision	Damage to Your Auto	OTC only; no collision coverage
Underinsured Motorists Coverage Endorsement	$100,000		N/A

[DA05929]

Case Analysis Tools

To determine whether Joshua's PAP, Benjamin's PAP, or both provide coverage for this accident, a claim representative should have copies of the policy forms and any applicable endorsements indicated on the declarations pages of the policies. The Declarations page identifies the covered parties, vehicles, and policy period. A description of the insured autos is included, as well as the coverages that apply, the limits of insurance for each coverage, and any endorsements that apply to the policy. See the exhibit "DICE Analysis."

DICE Analysis

A DICE analysis is a logical method to approach a coverage determination for most types of loss. DICE is an acronym for these policy parts:

- Declarations
- Insuring agreements
- Conditions
- Exclusions

The claim representative reviews the policy language in a logical order to determine whether coverage applies and, if it does, what dollar limit amounts may apply.

DICE analysis involves four steps:

- Review the declarations page to determine whether it covers the person or the property at the time of loss.
- Review the insuring agreement to determine whether it covers the loss.
- Review the policy conditions to determine compliance.
- Review the policy exclusions to determine whether they preclude coverage of the loss.

By carefully performing the four steps described, and reviewing policy terms and any other policy endorsements, with the facts of the loss, the claim representative can determine what—if any—coverage may apply to a loss.

[DA05891]

Determination of Coverage

To determine whether a policy covers a loss, many insurance professionals apply the DICE method. ("DICE" is an acronym for categories of policy provisions: declarations, insuring agreement, conditions, and exclusions.) The DICE method has four steps:

1. Review of the declarations page to determine whether it covers the person or the property at the time of the loss
2. Review of the insuring agreement to determine whether it covers the loss
3. Review of policy conditions to determine compliance
4. Review of policy exclusions to determine whether they preclude coverage of the loss

The first step in the DICE method is to review the declarations page of the policies to determine whether the accident occurred during the policy period and whether the drivers and vehicles are described on the declarations page. The declarations page on Joshua's PAP lists him as the named insured and describes the auto involved in the accident. Benjamin has a PAP that lists him as the named insured and describes the auto involved in the accident. The accident occurred during the policy period of both policies.

The second step in the DICE method is to review the policies to determine whether the event has triggered coverage under either of the PAP's insuring agreements.

The PAP insuring agreement under Part A—Liability Coverage provides coverage for bodily injury or property damage an insured is legally responsible for because of an auto accident. Benjamin's collision with Joshua's vehicle would be considered an auto accident. Also, Joshua's lawsuit naming Benjamin and demanding payment for injuries as a result of the auto accident triggers liability coverage under the PAP:

> PAP—Part A—Liability Coverage
>
> A. We will pay damages for "bodily injury" or "property damage" for which any "insured" becomes legally responsible because of an auto accident. Damages include prejudgment interest awarded against the "insured". We will settle or defend, as we consider appropriate, any claim or suit asking for these damages. In addition to our limit of liability, we will pay all defense costs we incur. Our duty to settle or defend ends when our limit of liability for this coverage has been exhausted by payment of judgments or settlements. We have no duty to defend any suit or settle any claim for "bodily injury" or "property damage" not covered under this policy.[1]

The third DICE step is to determine whether all policy conditions have been met. Both Benjamin and Joshua notified their insurers promptly, and all other policy conditions were satisfied.

The fourth DICE step is to review policy exclusions to determine whether one or more policy exclusions preclude coverage of the loss. The exclusion for "business use" should be reviewed because Joshua used his vehicle primarily for his farming business, and this exclusion may apply. After reviewing the exclusion, the claim representative determines that it does not apply to vehicles used for farming or ranching. Therefore, this exclusion does not apply to Joshua's use of this vehicle:

PAP—Part A—Liability Coverage

We do not provide Liability Coverage for any "insured"

7. Maintaining or using any vehicle while that "insured" is employed or otherwise engaged in any "business" (other than farming or ranching) not described in Exclusion A.6.

This Exclusion (A.7) does not apply to the maintenance or use of a:

a. Private passenger auto;

b. Pickup or van; or

c. "Trailer" used with a vehicle described in a. or b. above.[2]

Determination of Amounts Payable

Determining the amount payable under liability coverage involves analyzing the limit of liability available to pay losses and supplementary payments.

In this case, the court awarded Joshua and his family $219,000 as total damages due to bodily injury caused by Benjamin. In addition, the court ordered prejudgment interest of $4,000 against Benjamin.

The limits of liability on Benjamin's PAP are $300,000 combined single limits. This is sufficient to fully cover the damages Joshua suffered, so his underinsured motorists coverage doesn't come into play. In addition, attorneys' fees to defend Benjamin in the suit brought by Joshua totaled $31,450. Under the Coverage Part A—Insuring Agreement of Benjamin's PAP, this amount is paid in addition to the limit of liability and will be paid for the full amount. In the insuring agreement, the insurer agrees to defend the insured and pay all legal costs the insured may incur in a liability suit, even if the combined costs exceed the limit of liability. Joshua's legal fees of $8,600 will be paid by his insurer:

PAP—Part A—Liability Coverage

B. We will pay damages for "bodily injury" or "property damage" for which any "insured" becomes legally responsible because of an auto accident. Damages include prejudgment interest awarded against the "insured". We will settle or defend, as we consider appropriate, any claim or suit asking for these damages. In addition to our limit of liability, we will pay all defense costs we incur. Our duty to settle or defend ends when our limit of liability for this coverage has been exhausted by payment of judgments or settlements. We have no duty to defend any suit or settle any claim for "bodily injury" or "property damage" not covered under this policy.[3]

Only $5,000 of Benjamin's medical bills would be paid under Coverage Part B—Medical Payments of his PAP because this is the limit shown on the declarations page. Medical payments apply without regard to fault and are paid for the insured and occupants of the covered auto:

PAP—Part B—Medical Payments Coverage

A. We will pay reasonable expenses incurred for necessary medical and funeral services because of "bodily injury":

1. Caused by accident; and

2. Sustained by an "insured".

We will pay only those expenses incurred for services rendered within 3 years from the date of the accident.[4]

The damage to the vehicles would be covered under Coverage Part D—Coverage for Damage to Your Auto. This accident meets the policy's definition of collision, which includes "impact with another vehicle." Joshua's policy indicates on the declarations page that collision coverage is provided for the described auto. Benjamin's policy does not indicate collision coverage for the described auto.

For the damage to the vehicles, there would be no coverage for Benjamin's vehicle, as he didn't purchase collision coverage. The Part D insuring agreements in the PAP pay for collision damage only if the declarations indicate that collision coverage is provided for that auto. Benjamin's insurer covers the damage to Joshua's vehicle as "property damage" under Part A:

PAP—Part D—Coverage For Damage To Your Auto

A. We will pay for direct and accidental loss to "your covered auto" or any "non-owned auto", including their equipment, minus any applicable deductible shown in the Declarations. If loss to more than one "your covered auto" or "non-owned auto" results from the same "collision", only the highest applicable deductible will apply. We will pay for loss to "your covered auto" caused by:

1. Other than "collision" only if the Declarations indicate that Other Than Collision Coverage is provided for that auto.

2. "Collision" only if the Declarations indicate that Collision Coverage is provided for that auto.

If there is a loss to a "non-owned auto", we will provide the broadest coverage applicable to any "your covered auto" shown in the Declarations.[5]

Instead of waiting for the court to determine whether Benjamin is liable for the damage, Joshua could file a claim for the damage to his vehicle with his insurer. The insurer's limit of liability for physical damage to Joshua's covered auto is the lower of either the ACV of the damaged property or the amount necessary to repair or replace the property. In determining ACV, an adjustment is made for depreciation and physical condition of the damaged property. Thus, Joshua's insurer would pay him an ACV of $26,500 ($27,500 minus the deductible of $1,000).

If Joshua collects from his own insurer, his insurer has the right to recover payment from the driver who caused the accident. Once Benjamin is found to be at fault for the accident, Joshua's insurer may have rights of subrogation against Benjamin's insurer. Also, if Joshua were to recover damages from Benjamin or his insurer, he would be required to reimburse his insurer for the amount paid under his PAP.

Both Benjamin and Joshua rented vehicles as temporary transportation. Under Part D—Coverage for Damage to Your Auto, transportation expenses are paid at $20 per day to a maximum of $600. There is also a twenty-four-hour waiting period, and no deductible applies to this coverage provision. For an insured to benefit from this coverage, the vehicle must have collision coverage listed on the declarations page. Benjamin does not carry collision coverage for his vehicle, so this coverage does not apply under his policy. Joshua does carry collision coverage and rented the temporary vehicle for twenty days. He will receive $400 (20 days @ $20 = $400) because the once the car was determined to be out of use for more than one day, the form agrees to pay for transportation expenses from day one:

> PAP—Part D—Coverage for Damage to Your Auto—Transportation Expenses
>
> A. In addition, we will pay, without application of a deductible, to a maximum of $600 for:
>
> 1. Temporary transportation expenses not exceeding $20 per day incurred by you in the event of a loss to "your covered auto". We will pay for such expenses if the loss is caused by:
>
> a. Other than "collision" only if the Declarations indicate that Other Than Collision Coverage is provided for that auto.
>
> b. "Collision" only if the Declarations indicate that Collision Coverage is provided for that auto.
>
> B. Subject to the provisions of Paragraph A., if the loss is caused by:
>
> 1. A total theft of "your covered auto" or a "non-owned auto", we will pay only expenses incurred during the period:
>
> a. Beginning 48 hours after the theft; and
>
> b. Ending when "your covered auto" or the "non-owned auto" is returned to use or we pay for its loss.
>
> 2. Other than theft of a "your covered auto" or a "non-owned auto", we will pay only expenses beginning when the auto is withdrawn from use for more than 24 hours.
>
> Our payment will be limited to that period of time reasonably required to repair or replace the "your covered auto" or the "non-owned auto".[6]

Benjamin was required by his insurer to take four days off from work to testify at the trial, and his insurer paid him $480 ($120 per day) for loss of earnings. Under Coverage Part A, Supplementary Payments, if the insurer requests the insured to attend at trial, it will provide coverage up to $200 per day for loss of earnings. This payment does not reduce the limit of liability available under Coverage Part A.

Prejudgment interest of $4,000 is assessed against Benjamin. Prejudgment interest is interest that may accrue on damages before a judgment has been rendered. It is considered to be part of the award for damages, so it is subject to the applicable limit of liability for Part A.

Benjamin is convicted of dangerous driving. His insurer determines that Benjamin has prior convictions and now considers him a high-risk driver. Benjamin's insurer notifies him that it will not be renewing his policy. Benjamin lives in a state that has mandatory auto insurance requirements, so he will have to go to the residual market to obtain future auto insurance. The state offers an Automobile Insurance Plan for insuring high-risk drivers in which all auto insurers doing business in the state are assigned their proportionate share of such drivers based on the total volume of auto insurance written in the state. See the exhibit "Correct Answers."

Correct Answers

Joshua's PAP	Benjamin's PAP
COVERAGE A—Bodily Injury	COVERAGE A—Bodily Injury
Defense costs—$8,600	Javiera—$195,000
	Mandy—$19,000
	Joshua—$5,000
	TOTAL—$219,000
	Prejudgment interest—$4,000
	Defense costs—$31,450
	Loss of earnings—$480
	COVERAGE B—Medical Payments
	Benjamin—$5,000
Coverage D—Collision	Coverage D—Collision
Damage to Joshua's vehicle—$26,500 ($27,500 minus the deductible of $1,000)*	Not covered
Transportation expenses—$400	

*Subject to subrogation recovery from Benjamin's insurer

[DA05930]

SUMMARY

Under Part D—Coverage for Damage to Your Auto of the PAP, the insurer agrees to pay for direct and accidental loss to a covered auto or nonowned auto, less the applicable deductible. The coverage granted by the insuring agreement is extended or limited by other Part D provisions.

It is important to know how to apply physical damage coverages to the facts of a case. This is accomplished by first determining whether a loss is covered and, if so, determining how much an insurer should pay for the loss.

Part E of the PAP outlines duties that the insured must perform after a loss. If the failure of the insured to comply with the stated duties is deemed prejudicial to the insurer, the insurer can deny coverage. In such a case, the insurer would have no obligation to make any payment for loss.

The General Provisions part of the PAP contains provisions and conditions that apply to the entire policy, rather than to specific coverage parts. These provisions include bankruptcy of the insured, changes in the policy, fraud, legal action against the insurer, insurer's right to recover payment (subrogation), policy period and territory, termination, transfer of the insured's interest in the policy, and two or more auto policies.

The unendorsed PAP is designed to insure vehicles such as private passenger autos, vans, or pickup trucks owned and/or used by individuals and families. Some insureds, however, have coverage needs that go beyond the basic PAP and require endorsements to customize their insurance coverage.

Knowing how to apply the PAP and endorsements to the facts of a case is a critical skill. It involves, first, determining whether a loss is covered, using the DICE method, and, if so, determining how much the insurer should pay for the loss.

ASSIGNMENT NOTES

1. Includes copyrighted material of Insurance Services Office, Inc. with its permission. Copyright, ISO Properties, Inc., 2005.
2. Includes copyrighted material of Insurance Services Office, Inc. with its permission. Copyright, ISO Properties, Inc., 2005.
3. Includes copyrighted material of Insurance Services Office, Inc. with its permission. Copyright, ISO Properties, Inc., 2005.
4. Includes copyrighted material of Insurance Services Office, Inc. with its permission. Copyright, ISO Properties, Inc., 2005.
5. Includes copyrighted material of Insurance Services Office, Inc. with its permission. Copyright, ISO Properties, Inc., 2005.
6. Includes copyrighted material of Insurance Services Office, Inc. with its permission. Copyright, ISO Properties, Inc., 2005.

Homeowners Section I

Educational Objectives

After learning the content of this assignment, you should be able to:

▷ Describe how individuals and families can use the Insurance Services Office, Inc., (ISO) 2011 Homeowners insurance program to address their personal risk management needs.

▷ Describe the Homeowners 3—Special Form (HO-3) in terms of:

- Its structure and the coverages it provides

- The role of endorsements in modifying it

- The factors considered in rating it

▷ Describe what is insured by each of these coverages contained in the 2011 Homeowners 3—Special Form (HO-3) policy:

- Coverage A—Dwelling

- Coverage B—Other Structures

- Coverage C—Personal Property

- Coverage D—Loss of Use

- Additional Coverages

▷ Describe what is covered and what is excluded by these provisions in the 2011 Homeowners 3—Special Form (HO-3) policy:

- Perils Insured Against for Coverages A and B

- Perils Insured Against for Coverage C

- Section I—Exclusions

▷ Summarize each of the 2011 Homeowners 3—Special Form (HO-3) policy provisions in Section I—Conditions.

▷ Given a scenario describing a homeowners property claim, determine whether the 2011 HO-3 policy Section I—Property Coverages would cover the claim and, if so, the amount the insurer would pay for the claim.

ISO HOMEOWNERS COVERAGE

The Insurance Services Office, Inc. (ISO) Homeowners insurance program's policy forms are designed to meet the personal risk management needs of individuals and families.

The parties eligible for coverage under the ISO 2011 Homeowners (HO) insurance program fall into three general categories:

- Individuals and families who own a private home in which they reside—This is typically a single-family dwelling, but sometimes an eligible two to four-family dwelling. A mobile home is not eligible for unendorsed coverage. Dwelling and mobile home insurance policies are available for insuring residences that are not eligible for homeowners policies.

- People who rent or lease the premises in which they reside—The residence might be an apartment, a house (either a single-family house or other type), a mobile home, a trailer home, a house trailer, or a condominium unit.

- Individuals and families who own private condominium units used for residential purposes—Most insurers provide homeowners policies to people who own and live in condominium units. However, some insurers also provide such coverage when the insureds own but do not live in the condominium as long as the condominium unit is used as a residence by one family or by one or two tenants.

To address these parties' needs, the ISO Homeowners program offers six policy forms:

- Homeowners 2—Broad Form (HO-2)
- Homeowners 3—Special Form (HO-3)
- Homeowners 4—Contents Broad Form (HO-4)
- Homeowners 5—Comprehensive Form (HO-5)
- Homeowners 6—Unit-Owners Form (HO-6)
- Homeowners 8—Modified Coverage Form (HO-8)

Individuals and families should select a form based on their risk management needs and whether they meet the form's eligibility requirements. See the exhibit "How the ISO Homeowners Program Policy Forms Address Personal Risk Management Needs."

How the ISO Homeowners Program Policy Forms Address Personal Risk Management Needs

ISO Policy Form	Example of Personal Risk Management Need Addressed
HO-2—Broad Form	Meets most needs of owner-occupants for dwelling, other structures, and personal property coverage at a lower premium than the HO-3 or HO-5 coverages.
HO-3—Special Form	Meets the needs of owner-occupants of dwellings who want coverage on their dwellings and other structures that is broader than the HO-2 offers.
HO-4—Contents Broad Form	Meets the needs of tenants and other apartment or dwelling occupants who do not require coverage on the dwelling.
HO-5—Comprehensive Form	Meets the needs of owner-occupants of dwellings who want the broadest coverage available among ISO's forms for their dwellings, other structures, and personal property.
HO-6—Unit-Owners Form	Meets the needs of owners of condominium units and cooperative apartment shares.
HO-8—Modified Coverage Form	Meets the needs of owner-occupants of dwellings who may not meet insurer standards required for other policy forms.

[DA00300]

The HO-2—Broad Form (HO 00 02), simply known as the HO-2, provides named perils coverage for dwellings, other structures, and personal property. The HO-2 is designed to meet the risk management needs of owner-occupants of dwellings.

Forms HO-2, HO-3, HO-5, and HO-8 can be issued only to the owner-occupant of a one-, two-, three-, or four-family dwelling. Rules prohibit issuance to owners who do not occupy the dwelling. Further, the forms may not be issued to cover dwellings on farm premises. Persons purchasing a dwelling under a long-term installment contract, without legal title to the property, are eligible in the same manner as titled owners and occupants under a life estate arrangement. Also, a dwelling under construction is eligible if the named insured is the intended owner-occupant.

The HO-3—Special Form (HO 00 03), called the HO-3, provides special form coverage on dwellings and other structures (rather than the named perils coverage provided by the HO-2). Special form coverage, also known as open perils coverage, protects property against direct physical loss that is not otherwise excluded by the coverage form. Note that the HO-3 provides named perils coverage for personal property, as does the HO-2. The HO-3 is designed to meet the risk management needs of owner-occupants of dwellings who want broader coverage on their dwellings and other structures.

The HO-4—Contents Broad Form (HO 00 04), or HO-4, provides coverage for a tenant's personal property on a named perils basis. The HO-4 does not provide coverage for dwellings or other structures. This policy form is designed to meet the risk management needs of tenants and other occupants of apartments or dwellings. For example, a young woman who has recently graduated from college, started a new job, and moved into an apartment should obtain an HO-4 if she is no longer an official resident of her parents' insured household and would like her own personal property and liability insurance protection. Form HO-4 can be issued to a tenant who maintains a residence in any kind of structure. Persons who maintain a residence in a building that they own but that is not a one- or two-family dwelling are also eligible.

A homeowners policy (other than HO-4) may also be issued in the name of a trust and trustee(s) when legal title to a one-, two-, three-, or four-family dwelling or condominium unit is held solely by the trust and when the trustee, beneficiary, or grantor regularly resides there. If a portion of the premises is used for other-than-private-residential occupancy, eligibility rules permit (1) not more than two roomers or boarders per family unit and (2) an incidental business occupancy, such as an office, private school, or studio. Occasional rental of the premises to others is also allowed.

The HO-5—Comprehensive Form (HO 00 05), known as the HO-5, provides open perils coverage on dwellings, other structures, and personal property. The HO-5 is designed to meet the risk management needs of owner-occupants of dwellings who would like the broadest coverage available among ISO's forms for their property. A homeowner who desires the broadest available coverage for his home and contents, and is willing to pay the increased premium for it, should select the HO-5.

The HO-6—Unit-Owners Form (HO 00 06), or HO-6, provides coverage for personal property on a named perils basis, with limited dwelling coverage (unit improvements and betterments). The HO-6 is designed to meet the risk management needs of the owners of condominium units and cooperative apartment shares. The HO-6 is similar to the HO-4, but it includes special provisions for loss exposures inherent in condominium and cooperative unit ownership. For example, a couple that purchases a vacation unit in a seaside condominium community should obtain additional homeowners coverage under an HO-6.

Only owners of condominium units and cooperative apartment shareowners are eligible for the HO-6, although the insured is not required to be an occupant of the unit. If a two-, three-, or four-family dwelling is co-owned by the families who reside there, one of the owner-occupant forms may be issued in the name of one of the owner-occupants, with the others named on an Additional Insured Endorsement (HO 04 41) to cover each party's interest in the building. The other parties may be issued an HO-4 for their personal property. This combination of coverages gives all co-owners complete homeowners coverage.

Functional replacement cost

The cost of replacing damaged property with similar property that performs the same function but might not be identical to the damaged property.

The HO-8—Modified Coverage Form (HO 00 08), called the HO-8, provides coverage for a dwelling, other structures, and personal property on a limited, named perils basis. A special valuation clause specifies that damage will be covered on a **functional replacement cost** basis. The HO-8 is designed to meet the risk management needs of owners-occupants of dwellings that may not meet insurer underwriting standards required for other policy forms (such as when the replacement cost of a dwelling significantly exceeds the dwelling's market value). For example, a couple may own a historic home in a city where local property values, including the value of the historic home, are far below replacement cost. This couple may opt for homeowners coverage under an HO-8.

Apply Your Knowledge

A homeowner wishes the broadest possible coverage for his home and contents. Which of the six ISO Homeowners program forms would be most appropriate for his coverage needs?

Feedback: The HO-5—Comprehensive Form (HO 00 05), known as the HO-5, provides open perils coverage on dwellings, other structures, and personal property and is designed to meet the risk management needs of owner-occupants of dwellings who would like the broadest coverage available among ISO's forms for their property.

OVERVIEW OF HOMEOWNERS FORM HO-3

The Homeowners 3—Special Form (HO-3) provides insurance coverage for the majority of owner-occupied dwellings. The HO-3 form, coupled with available endorsements, is designed to meet the needs of individuals and families.

A widely used homeowners policy form is the Insurance Services Office, Inc. (ISO) Homeowners 3—Special Form (HO 00 03), commonly referred to as the HO-3. Learning the basic structure and coverages of an HO-3 policy is the basis for understanding a variety of HO forms. The HO-3 policy is designed for the owner-occupants of a one- to four-family dwelling, as opposed to owners who do not occupy the dwelling. It provides coverage for a house, its contents, and the occupants' liability and is designed to be broad enough to cover the property and liability insurance needs of most families. To meet an insured's specific needs, the HO-3 policy can be modified by endorsement. As with other homeowners policies, insurers charge a premium for coverage under the HO-3 that is based on homeowners rating factors and adjustments.

Structure of Homeowners Form HO-3

The HO-3 policy structure consists of these primary components:

- Declarations
- Agreement and Definitions
- Section I—Property Coverages
- Section II—Liability Coverages
- Endorsements

Sections I and II are both subject to exclusions and conditions. Section I includes perils insured against, while Section II offers additional coverages. See the exhibit "Policy Structure for the ISO Homeowners 3—Special Form."

Policy Structure for the ISO Homeowners 3—Special Form

Declarations

Agreement

Definitions

Section I—Property Coverages

    Coverage A—Dwelling

    Coverage B—Other Structures

    Coverage C—Personal Property

    Coverage D—Loss of Use

    Additional Coverages

Section I—Perils Insured Against

Section I—Exclusions

Section I—Conditions

Section II—Liability Coverages

    Coverage E—Personal Liability

    Coverage F—Medical Payments to Others

Section II—Exclusions

Section II—Additional Coverages

Section II—Conditions

Section I and II Conditions

Endorsements (if applicable)

Copyright, ISO Properties, Inc. [DA00350]

Declarations

The declarations provide essential information about the insured, the property covered, and the limits of coverage by answering these questions:

- Who is the policyholder?
- Where is the policyholder's residence?
- What are the coverage limits?
- What is the premium?
- What is the Section I deductible?
- What is the effective date of the policy?
- Which forms and endorsements apply to the policy?
- Who is the mortgage holder?

Agreement and Definitions

The agreement (also known as the insuring agreement) is usually the first sentence in the policy form. It establishes the basis for the contract and specifies what the insurer and the insured will do. The insurer agrees to provide coverage, and the insured agrees to pay the premium and comply with the policy conditions.

Definitions follow the agreement and continue for several pages. Definitions clarify what is and is not covered under the policy. Defined words have special meanings when they are used within the policy; a defined word or phrase might have a meaning that is different, narrower, or broader than the dictionary definition. Words or phrases defined in this section appear in the policy within quotation marks. For example, the terms "you" and "your" refer to the named insured shown in the policy declarations and his or her resident spouse, even if the spouse is not named.

If a word is used within a policy and no definition is provided, it is given the common definition provided by a dictionary.

Section I—Property Coverages

Section I—Property Coverages, the first of two major coverage sections in the HO-3 policy, specifies the property covered, the perils insured against, and the exclusions and conditions that affect property coverages and losses.

Section I is divided into four property coverages plus a group of Additional Coverages:

- Coverage A—Dwelling applies to the dwelling on the "residence premises" listed on the Declarations page. It also applies to structures attached to the dwelling, such as a garage or deck.
- Coverage B—Other Structures applies to structures on the residence premises, other than the dwelling building, that are not attached to the dwelling, such as storage sheds, detached garages, and swimming pools.

- Coverage C—Personal Property applies to the contents of the insured premises and to personal property owned or used by an insured anywhere in the world, such as personal luggage or borrowed skis that are stolen.

- Coverage D—Loss of Use applies to the insured's exposure to financial loss, apart from the property damage itself, if the premises where the insured resides are damaged so badly they are unfit for use.

- Additional Coverages apply to certain direct property losses or consequential expenses that are not covered by Coverages A, B, C, or D. An example of an Additional Coverage that insures direct property loss is Trees, Shrubs, and Other Plants. An example of an Additional Coverage that covers a consequential expense is Debris Removal.

Section II—Liability Coverages

Section II—Liability Coverages is divided into two parts:

- Coverage E—Personal Liability applies to third-party coverage for those who are injured or whose property is damaged by an insured, generally for a basic limit of $100,000.

- Coverage F—Medical Payments to Others covers the necessary medical expenses incurred by others (not an insured) within three years of an injury.

Role of Endorsements

As a self-contained insurance policy, the homeowners policy is a single document that forms a complete contract. The HO-3 meets the majority, but not all, of the homeowners insurance needs of most individuals and families. Many endorsements are available to modify the HO-3 policy. These have been developed for use nationwide and approved by the states. Endorsements can increase or decrease limits, add or remove coverages, change definitions, clarify policy intent, or recognize specific characteristics that require a premium increase or decrease.

For example, the Personal Property Replacement Cost Loss Settlement endorsement (HO 04 90 05 11) provides replacement cost coverage on personal property, awnings, carpeting, household appliances, and outdoor equipment. These items are covered on an actual cash value basis on an unendorsed HO-3 form.

Additional endorsements are available for condominiums, home businesses, mobile homes, additional perils, increased amounts of coverage, or a guard against inflation.

Factors Considered in Rating

Homeowners policy rating factors and adjustments can vary by insurer. However, they typically use a framework designed by ISO that includes the development of a base premium and adjustments. Insurers may make additional adjustments, outside the ISO framework, before arriving at the final premium.

A homeowners policy premium is determined by first developing the base premium. The base premium is based on factors such as the dwelling location, public protection class (classification used to rate the quality of community fire protection), construction factors, coverage amount, and the policy form selected.

Base premium adjustments are applied to reflect variations in the risk management requirements and loss exposures of individuals and families. Base premium adjustments can result from endorsements, deductible changes, and unusual construction types.

Final adjustments are applied to develop the final premium. These can include claim history, insurance score, and package policy credits. Final premium adjustments typically vary by insurer; for example, insurers may use one of the final adjustments (for example, claim history) on a consistent basis while not using others. See the exhibit "Rating Homeowners Policies."

Rating Homeowners Policies

   Base premium factors

+ Base premium adjustments

+ Final adjustments
                 _____

   Final homeowners premium

[DA00301]

HO-3 SECTION I—PROPERTY COVERAGES

The Insurance Services Office, Inc. (ISO) 2011 Homeowners 3—Special Form (HO-3) provides coverage for a house and its contents. It is designed to cover the property loss exposures that most individuals and families face.

Section I—Property Coverages of the HO-3 policy provides four basic property coverages and twelve Additional Coverages:

- Coverage A—Dwelling
- Coverage B—Other Structures
- Coverage C—Personal Property
- Coverage D—Loss of Use

Coverage A—Dwelling

Coverage A applies to the dwelling on the residence premises listed on the Declarations page. "Residence premises" includes not only a one-family dwelling, but also a two-, three-, or four-family dwelling where the named insured resides in at least one of the units. It also applies to structures (such as a garage or a deck) attached to the dwelling and to materials and supplies located on or next to the covered dwelling and used to construct or repair the dwelling. Coverage does not apply to the land at the residence premises.

Coverage B—Other Structures

Coverage B—Other Structures applies to structures on the residence premises that are not attached to the dwelling and are separated from it by "clear space." A fence, utility line, or similar connection linking another structure with the dwelling does not make it an attached structure.

An additional amount equal to 10 percent of the Coverage A limit is available for other structures. This 10 percent limit applies collectively to all "other structures" at the residence premises.

Coverage B has three important exclusions:

- A structure rented to anyone who is not a resident of the dwelling. However, a structure that is rented to others for use as a private garage is covered.

- A structure from which any business is conducted.

- A structure used to store business property. However, a structure containing business property is covered if the business property is solely owned by an insured or a tenant of the dwelling, provided that the business property does not include gaseous or liquid fuel, other than fuel in a permanently installed fuel tank of a vehicle or craft parked or stored in the structure.

Coverage C—Personal Property

Coverage C—Personal Property applies to items the insured owns or uses, anywhere in the world. It can also cover loss of or damage to personal property of others while that property is on the residence premises, if the named insured requests such coverage after a loss. Coverage C can also cover loss of or damage to personal property of a guest or residence employee while it is in any residence occupied by an insured.

The standard limit for Coverage C is 50 percent of the Coverage A limit, and it applies in addition to that limit. The Coverage C limit can be increased simply by changing the amount appearing on the Declarations page and charging an additional premium.

Only 10 percent of the Coverage C limit or $1,000 (whichever is greater) is available for property usually located at a residence other than the one listed on the Declarations page. This same limitation applies to property kept by an insured in a self-storage warehouse.

The 10 percent or $1,000 limitation does not apply to personal property removed from the residence premises because the house is being repaired, renovated, or rebuilt and is not fit to live in or to store property in. An insured who is moving from one principal residence to another will have the full limit of Coverage C available at both locations for thirty days.

Special Limits of Liability

Some categories of personal property are subject to sublimits, called special limits of liability, within the Coverage C limit. Items within these categories pose a higher-than-average risk of loss (for example, jewelry) or are types of property not contemplated in homeowners insurance premiums (for example, business property). The special limits for three personal property categories (jewelry and furs; firearms and related items; and silverware, goldware, platinumware, and pewterware) apply only when loss is caused by theft. The special limits for eight other categories of personal property apply when loss is caused by any covered peril. See the exhibit "Special Sublimits Within Coverage C."

Special Sublimits Within Coverage C

Personal Property	Special Limit of Liability
Liability Sublimits Applicable to All Covered Perils	
Money and precious metals, including stored value cards, such as gift cards	$200
Securities, documents, records, and stamps, including cost to research and replace information that has been lost	$1,500
Watercraft, including trailers, equipment, and motors	$1,500
Trailers (other than used with watercraft)	$1,500
Portable electronic equipment	$1,500
Antennas, tapes, wires, records, disks, or other media	$250
Property Used Primarily for Business Purposes	
On the residence premises	$2,500
Away from the residence premises	$1,500
Sublimits Applicable to Theft (No Sublimit for Other Perils)	
Jewelry, furs, precious stones, and semiprecious stones	$1,500
Firearms and related items	$2,500
Silverware, goldware, platinumware, and pewterware	$2,500

[DA07598]

Property Not Covered

The HO-3 policy specifically excludes all coverage for some categories of personal property. In most cases, these items are usually insured through policies other than a homeowners policy:

- Articles separately described and specifically insured in this or other insurance. (For example, jewelry separately described on an endorsement or in a separate policy is Property Not Covered.)
- Animals, birds, or fish.
- Motor vehicles, parts, and electronic equipment that operates solely from the vehicle's electrical system. (Coverage is provided for vehicles not required to be registered, such as riding mowers and wheelchairs.)
- Aircraft and hovercraft.
- Property of roomers and boarders unrelated to the insured.
- Property in an apartment rented to others. (Coverage for such property is provided as an Additional Coverage.)
- Property rented or held for rental to others off the residence premises.
- Business data, including drawings, stored either on paper or electronically.
- Credit cards or electronic fund transfer cards. (Coverage for such property is provided as an Additional Coverage.)
- Water or steam. (For example, there is no coverage for replacing water in a damaged swimming pool.)

Coverage D—Loss of Use

Coverage D applies to the insured's exposure to financial loss, apart from the property damage itself, if the residence premises are damaged so badly that they are not fit to live in. Coverage D applies only if the damage is the result of a loss that is covered under Section I—Property Coverages of the policy. The Coverage D limit is 30 percent of the Coverage A limit, and it applies in addition to the Coverage A limit. The limit can be increased by changing the amount on the Declarations page and paying an additional premium.

Three coverages are grouped under Coverage D:

- Additional living expense—If the insured must live elsewhere until the dwelling has been repaired, this pays for any necessary increase in living expenses required to maintain the household's normal standard of living.
- Fair rental value—If part of the residence is rented to others, the insurer will reimburse the insured the lost rental value (less expenses that do not continue) until repairs are made.
- Loss of use due to civil authority—Even if an insured's property is undamaged, civil authorities may prohibit access to the home because of damage to neighboring property. In this case, the expenses of living elsewhere and lost rental income are covered for a maximum of two weeks.

Additional Coverages

The Additional Coverages insure against various types of losses that would not otherwise be covered under Section I of the policy. In addition to the basic descriptions of coverage provided in the bulleted list, the exhibit states whether each Additional Coverage creates an additional amount of insurance (as opposed to being payable within the applicable policy limit), whether each is subject to the policy deductible, and whether each must be triggered by another covered loss:

- Debris Removal—Covers reasonable expenses for removing debris of covered property that has been damaged by an insured peril or by ash, dust, or particles from a volcanic eruption that has caused direct loss to a covered building or property in the building. It also covers, subject to special conditions, the cost to remove fallen trees, not to exceed $500 for any one tree or $1,000 in any one loss.

- Reasonable Repairs—Covers reasonable costs incurred to protect covered property or repair other property damaged by an insured peril.

- Trees, Shrubs, and Other Plants—Covers loss caused by fire or lightning, explosion, riot or civil commotion, aircraft, vehicles not owned or operated by a resident, vandalism or malicious acts, or theft up to an additional 5 percent of the dwelling limit with a maximum of $500 for any one item. Property grown for business purposes is excluded.

- Fire Department Service Charges—Pays up to $500 for fire department charges incurred to save or protect insured property from a covered loss if the responding unit is from beyond the property's regular fire protection district.

- Property Removed—Covers property removed from premises endangered by an insured peril. While removed, the property is covered for direct loss by any cause (not limited to perils insured against) for up to thirty days.

- Credit Card, Electronic Fund Transfer Card or Access Device, Forgery, and Counterfeit Money—Pays up to $500 for legal obligation due to unauthorized use or theft of a credit card or an electronic fund transfer card or access device. It also covers loss due to forgery of a negotiable instrument or acceptance in good faith of counterfeit paper currency. There is no coverage for a card used by a resident of the household or by someone to whom the card was entrusted, and the insured must have complied with all terms of the issuing company. Losses arising from business use or dishonesty of the insured are excluded.

- Loss Assessment—Pays up to $1,000 for assessments charged by a corporation or an association of property owners for loss to collectively owned property caused by an insured peril.

- Collapse—Covers abrupt collapse of a building or part of a building resulting from an insured peril, hidden decay, insect or vermin damage, weight of contents or inhabitants, weight of rain, or defective material or construction. There is no coverage if the building was showing visible signs of deterioration before the collapse.

- Glass or Safety Glazing Material—Covers breakage of building glass, including breakage caused by earth movement. Direct physical loss to covered property caused solely by the broken glass is covered, but not resulting damage caused because the glass is broken (for example, rain damage). There is no coverage if the dwelling has been vacant for more than sixty days.

- Landlord's Furnishings—Pays up to $2,500 of the policy limit to cover damage caused by an insured peril other than theft to appliances, carpeting, and other household furnishings in apartments rented to others.

- Ordinance or Law—Pays up to 10 percent of the Coverage A limit to cover increased costs incurred due to the enforcement of any ordinance or law regulating the construction, demolition, remodeling, renovation, or repair of the insured building. There is no coverage for any costs relating to pollutants.

- Grave Markers—Covers grave markers, including mausoleums, for damage by an insured peril, up to $5,000.

Additional Coverages

Additional Coverages	Does this coverage create an additional limit?	Does the deductible apply?	Is this coverage dependent on another covered loss?
1. Debris Removal	Yes, if primary limits are exhausted, an additional 5 percent of the limit of liability is available.	Yes*	Yes, damage to covered property by a covered peril or volcanic eruption must occur.
2. Reasonable Repairs	No.	Yes*	Yes, damage to covered property by a covered peril must occur.
3. Trees, Shrubs, and Other Plants	Yes, up to $500 is provided for each item up to a total of 5 percent of the Coverage A limit.	Yes*	No.
4. Fire Department Service Charge	Yes, payment up to $500 is an additional limit.	No	No, there must be a threat of a covered peril, but there is no requirement that the peril actually occur.
5. Property Removed	No.	Yes*	No, the removed property is covered against direct loss from any cause.
6. Credit Card, Electronic Fund Transfer Card or Access Device, Forgery, and Counterfeit Money	Yes, an additional total of $500 is available for any series of acts committed by any one person. Defense coverage is also provided.	No	No.
7. Loss Assessment	Yes, for an additional $1,000.	Yes**	No, not to property of the insured. But there must be a loss from a covered peril to association property.
8. Collapse	No.	Yes *	No, other property need not be damaged, but the collapse must result from a covered peril.
9. Glass or Safety Glazing Material	No.	Yes*	No, other property need not be damaged, but the glass breakage must result from a covered peril.
10. Landlord's Furnishings	No.	Yes*	No.
11. Ordinance or Law	Yes, an additional limit of 10 percent of Coverage A is available.	Yes*	Yes, to the dwelling or an "other structure."
12. Grave Markers	No.	Yes*	No.

*Not a separate deductible. Only one deductible is subtracted from the total loss of a covered event.

** Only one deductible applies per unit to the total amount of any one loss, regardless of the number of assessments.

[DA00379]

HO-3 SECTION I—PERILS INSURED AGAINST AND EXCLUSIONS

The Insurance Services Office, Inc. (ISO) Homeowners 3—Special Form (HO-3) protects policyholders against loss from a variety of perils to their homes, other structures, and personal property.

The HO-3 contains these divisions in Section I—Perils Insured Against:

- Coverage A—Dwelling and Coverage B—Other Structures are provided on a **special form coverage** basis, commonly referred to as open perils coverage.

- Coverage C—Personal Property is provided on a **named perils coverage** basis.

No covered perils are listed in Section I—Property Coverages for Coverage D—Loss of Use or for the policy's Additional Coverages, because Coverage D and three of the Additional Coverages apply only when other covered losses occur. The remaining Additional Coverages individually describe when coverage applies. Certain exclusions from coverage apply in Section I—Exclusions.

Special form coverage
Property insurance coverage covering all causes of loss not specifically excluded.

Named perils coverage
An insurance policy in which the covered causes of loss are listed or "named" in the policy.

Perils Insured Against for Coverages A and B

Insured perils for Coverage A—Dwelling and Coverage B—Other Structures are grouped together because both provide open perils coverage for real property with similar exposures to loss. Open perils coverage begins with this broad grant of coverage: "We insure against direct physical loss to property described in Coverages A and B."

This statement is followed by a list of excluded perils. Any peril not listed in these exclusions is covered. The excluded perils are these:

- Any peril excluded in Section I—Exclusions, discussed subsequently. Examples of excluded perils are flood, earthquake, and war.

- Collapse—However, collapse that results from some other cause is provided for under Section I—Property Coverages.

- Freezing of a plumbing, heating, air conditioning, or sprinkler system or a household appliance—If the insured fails to take reasonable precautions to prevent pipes and hoses from freezing and bursting, coverage is excluded for any resulting damage.

- Freezing, thawing, pressure, or weight of water or ice—Damage to external property (such as fences, pavement, patios, swimming pools, foundations, piers, and docks) caused by freezing, thawing, and water or ice pressure is excluded.

- Theft of construction materials—Theft in or to a dwelling under construction or of construction materials and supplies is excluded until the dwelling is finished and occupied.

- Vandalism and malicious mischief to vacant dwellings—Coverage for vandalism, including ensuing losses such as fire damage, is excluded for dwellings that have been vacant for more than sixty consecutive days.

- Mold, fungus, or wet rot—Coverage for loss resulting from these causes is excluded unless the mold, fungus, or wet rot is hidden and results from an accidental leak of water or steam from a plumbing, heating, sprinkler, or air conditioning system; from a household appliance; or from a storm drain or water, steam, or sewer pipes off the residence premises. Sump pumps and roof drains are not considered part of the plumbing, heating, sprinkler, or air conditioning system or household appliance.

- Natural deterioration—Losses caused by wear and tear, marring, deterioration, mechanical breakdown, latent defect, inherent vice, smog, rust, other corrosion, and dry rot are excluded.

- Smoke from agricultural smudging or industrial operations—Damage that results from smoke caused by agricultural smudging or industrial operations is excluded. Agricultural smudging intentionally creates a dense smoke to protect plants from frost.

- Pollutants—The policy excludes coverage for damage to property caused by pollutants. An exception is made if the pollutants are released or escape as the result of any of the perils insured under Coverage C.

- Settling of the dwelling—Losses caused by settling, shrinking, bulging, or expansion of foundations, footings, patios, pavements, bulkheads, and the building structure are excluded.

- Animals—The HO-3 excludes damage caused by animals that an insured owns or keeps or by birds, rodents, or insects.

Unless the loss is otherwise excluded, the HO-3 covers water damage resulting from an accidental discharge or overflow of water or steam from a plumbing, heating, air conditioning, or sprinkler system; from a household appliance; or from a storm drain or water, steam, or sewer pipe off the residence premises. Coverage is provided for damage caused by the water, including the cost of tearing out and replacing any part of the building to make repairs. However, the loss to a damaged system or appliance is not covered.

Ensuing losses not specifically excluded by the HO-3 are covered. For example, settling of foundations is excluded, but if a settling foundation causes a water pipe to break, the ensuing water damage would be covered.

Perils Insured Against for Coverage C

Coverage C covers the contents of a home and other personal property. In contrast with the open perils coverage for Coverages A and B, Coverage C applies on a named perils basis, meaning that coverage applies only if covered property is damaged as a result of a cause of loss named in the policy. While open perils and named perils cover many of the same causes of loss, open perils coverage sometimes includes causes of loss that are not among the named perils.

For example, melting snow can back up beneath roof shingles because of the accumulation of frozen water (called an "ice dam") in the roof gutters. The water then enters the building, causing water damage to the building and personal property within. Ice dam is not a named peril under Coverage C, but it is a covered peril for purposes of Coverages A and B because it is not excluded. Therefore, any resulting water damage to the building is covered by Coverage A or B, but water damage to personal property in the building is not covered by Coverage C.

These are named perils that apply to Coverage C:

- Fire or lightning.
- Windstorm or hail—However, damage caused by rain, snow, sleet, sand, or dust is covered only if wind (including hurricane and tornado) or hail first damages the building, causing an opening in a roof or wall through which the cause of damage enters. Watercraft and their equipment are covered only while inside a fully enclosed building.
- Explosion.
- Riot or civil commotion—State laws commonly define a "riot" as a violent disturbance involving three or more (in some states, two or more) people. Civil commotion is a more serious and prolonged disturbance or violent uprising.
- Aircraft.
- Vehicles—For example, damage to personal property in the back seat of a car involved in an auto accident would be covered.
- Smoke—Sudden and accidental smoke damage to personal property, including damage by soot, fumes, or vapors from a boiler or furnace, is covered. Loss caused by smoke from agricultural smudging or industrial operations is excluded.
- Vandalism or malicious mischief.
- Theft—Theft is generally understood to mean any unlawful taking of property. The theft peril states that it "includes attempted theft and loss of property from a known place when it is likely that the property has been stolen." Thus, for example, the peril includes damage to covered property that results from an attempted but unsuccessful theft, such as when thieves break through a door but flee before stealing anything because a burglar alarm sounds.
- Falling objects—Coverage is provided if a falling object breaks through the dwelling's roof or wall and damages the contents.
- Weight of ice, snow, or sleet—Coverage applies only for damage to property contained in a building.
- Accidental discharge or overflow of water or steam—The water or steam must be accidentally released by a plumbing, heating, air conditioning, or fire-protective sprinkler system or by a household appliance.
- Sudden and accidental tearing apart, cracking, burning, or bulging—Coverage applies if a hot water heating system, an air conditioning system, an automatic fire-protective sprinkler system, or an appliance for heating water suddenly and accidentally tears apart, cracks, burns, or bulges, resulting in a loss.

- Freezing—Damage resulting from the freezing of a plumbing, heating, air conditioning, or fire-protective sprinkler system or of a household appliance is covered provided that the insured has taken reasonable precautions to maintain the heat or has shut off and drained the system or appliance.
- Sudden and accidental damage from artificially generated electrical current—Loss to tubes, transistors, or electronic components or circuitry of appliances, computers, or home entertainment equipment is not covered.
- Volcanic eruption—This peril does not include loss caused by earthquake or tremors. Damage caused by airborne shock waves and ash, for example, is covered. An earthquake caused as a consequence of a volcanic eruption, however, is not covered.

Several noteworthy limitations apply to the theft peril. See the exhibit "Limitations Applicable to Theft Peril."

Limitations Applicable to Theft Peril

- Theft committed by an insured is excluded.
- Theft from a building under construction and theft of construction materials are excluded.
- Theft from a part of the insured premises rented to someone other than an insured is excluded.
- Theft of personal property from another residence the insured owns, rents, or occupies is excluded unless the insured is temporarily living there.
- Theft of property of an insured who is a student residing away from home (such as in a dormitory) is excluded unless the student has been there during the ninety days before the loss.
- Theft is excluded for watercraft, including furnishings and equipment, away from the residence premises.
- Theft of trailers, semi-trailers, and campers is excluded.

[DA07720]

Section I—Exclusions

The HO-3 Section I exclusions apply to Coverages A, B, and C:

- Ordinance or law—This exclusion eliminates coverage for losses resulting from any ordinance or law that reduces the value of the property; requires testing for or cleaning up of pollutants; or requires demolition, construction, or debris removal. However, the HO-3 Additional Coverages section provides limited ordinance or law coverage for buildings or structures damaged as a result of an insured peril. The Additional Coverage applies to losses resulting from any ordinance or law that requires construction, demolition, remodeling, renovation, or repair beyond the typical repairs needed to restore the structures after a loss.

- Earth movement—Earthquakes and other types of earth movement, such as landslides, mudslides, mudflows, subsidence, and sinkholes, are excluded perils. This exclusion applies regardless of the cause of the earth movement, whether natural or otherwise. Damage caused by an ensuing fire or explosion is covered.

- Water—Coverage for losses caused by flood, surface water, waves, water, or waterborne material such as sewage that backs up through sewers and drains is excluded regardless of the cause of the water-related loss. Losses resulting from the "escape, overflow, or discharge" of "water or waterborne material from a dam, levee, seawall, or any other boundary or containment system" are also excluded. Ensuing losses from fire, explosion, or theft resulting from water damage are covered.

- Power failure—Damage resulting from a loss of electrical power or utility service because of a problem away from the insured residence premises is not covered. However, if power is interrupted by an insured peril that occurs on the premises, resulting losses are covered.

- Neglect—An insured is expected to use all reasonable means to protect property during and after a loss. The HO-3 provides no coverage for losses that result from the insured's failure to do so. Under an Additional Coverage, the insurer agrees to pay the cost of reasonable repairs to protect damaged property.

- War—Losses that result from war, including the discharge of nuclear weapons (on purpose or by accident), are excluded. This exclusion includes undeclared war, civil war, insurrection, rebellion, revolution, or military war-like action. Destruction, seizure, or use of insured property for military purposes is also excluded.

- Nuclear hazard—Losses that occur because of a nuclear hazard are excluded. A nuclear hazard is defined in Section I—Conditions as any "nuclear reaction, radiation, or radioactive contamination."

- Intentional loss—The HO-3 excludes any loss arising out of an act any insured commits or conspires to commit with the intent to cause a loss.

- Governmental action—Property described in Coverages A, B, and C is not covered against destruction, confiscation, or seizure by order of any governmental or public authority. This exclusion does not preclude coverage for governmental action taken to prevent the spread of fire.

Section I—Exclusions contains three additional exclusions that apply only to Coverage A—Dwelling and Coverage B—Other Structures:

- Weather is an excluded peril only if it contributes to any of the previously excluded perils. For example, torrential rain that causes a mudslide would not be a covered peril, because earth movement (mudslide) is excluded. However, if the weight of rainwater that has collected on a roof causes the roof to collapse, coverage is provided under the Collapse form of Additional Coverage.

- Acts or decisions—including the failure to act or decide—of any person, group, organization, or government body are excluded.
- Damage that results from faulty planning, zoning, surveying, design specifications, workmanship, construction, renovation, materials, and maintenance is excluded. However, if faulty construction of a chimney in the insured's house results in a fire, the damage caused by the fire would be covered.

HO-3 SECTION I—CONDITIONS

Eighteen major conditions apply to the Section I coverages in the Insurance Services Office, Inc. (ISO) Homeowners 3—Special Form (HO-3). Both the insured and the insurer must meet these conditions.

Section I—Conditions of the ISO HO-3 policy describes the conditions that must be met by both the insured and the insurer and provides a majority of the information required for the insured and insurer to comply with the mutual "promise" made in the insuring agreement.

Insurable Interest and Limit of Liability

The Insurable Interest and Limit of Liability condition limits the maximum payment for any single loss to the applicable limits shown on the Declarations page, regardless of the number of insureds who have an insurable interest in the property. This condition further limits loss payment to any insured to the extent of that insured's insurable interest in the property at the time of the loss.

Deductible

The Deductible condition specifies that the policy deductible applies on a per-loss basis and that only the highest deductible applies when two or more apply to a loss. Before the 2011 revision, this condition had appeared after the Definitions section, but now follows the Insurable Interest and Limit of Liability condition in the Conditions section. This placement reinforces the policy's intent that the deductible only applies to Section I losses.

Additionally, the minimum deductible for the ISO Homeowners program is $500. This is an increase from the previous minimum deductible amount under Section I, which was $250.

Your Duties After Loss

The Your Duties After Loss condition lists the insured's duties after a property loss. Because the cooperation of an insured is essential to the investigation, settlement, or defense of any claim, this condition clarifies that the insurer can deny coverage when an insured fails to fulfill the contractual duties listed.

In any given claim settlement, the insurer's claims representative might not require the performance of all of the listed items. However, this clause entitles the representative to require performance of any of the duties that may be helpful in the claim settlement process. These are the listed duties:

- Give prompt notice
- Notify the police
- Notify the credit card, electronic fund transfer card company, or access device company
- Protect the property from further damage
- Cooperate with the insurer
- Prepare an inventory
- Verify the loss
- Sign a sworn proof of loss

Loss Settlement

The Loss Settlement condition establishes the process for determining the amount to be paid for a property loss. There are two settlement methods, with the first method established for Coverage C—Personal Property and other miscellaneous items, and the other established for Coverage A—Dwelling and Coverage B—Other Structures.

The deductible amount shown on the Declarations page is subtracted once from the total of all losses payable under Section I and caused by a single loss event. (Two additional coverages do not have the deductible applied to them—one dealing with fire department service charges and the other with credit cards and other types of money cards.)

Losses to personal property listed under Coverage C—Personal Property, as well as awnings, carpeting, appliances, antennas, outdoor equipment, structures that are not buildings, and grave markers or mausoleums, are settled at the lesser of two amounts:

- Actual cash value (ACV) at the time of the loss
- The amount required to repair or replace the items

The loss settlement for buildings depends on how the limit of insurance compares to the replacement cost value of the damaged buildings at the time of the loss. These are the methods for determining the loss settlement for a building:

- If the limit of insurance is 80 percent or more of the replacement cost, the insurer will pay for the replacement cost of the damage up to the limit of coverage.
- If the limit of insurance is less than 80 percent of the replacement cost, the insurer will pay the greater of two amounts. The first amount is the ACV of the damage. The second is the proportion of the cost to repair or replace the damage that the limit of insurance bears to 80 percent of the replacement cost. This second method is sometimes easier to understand as a formula.

$$\text{Loss payment} = \frac{\text{Limit of insurance}}{80\% \times \text{Replacement cost}} \times \text{Replacement cost of the loss}$$

Except for small losses, which are generally considered to be under $2,500, the insurer will not pay more than the ACV until repairs are completed. An insured who has not decided whether a structure should be rebuilt can seek loss settlement on an ACV basis. Should the insured then decide to complete the repairs, he or she has up to 180 days after the loss to notify the insurer of intent to complete the repairs and make settlement on a replacement cost basis rather than on the ACV basis. See the exhibit "Loss Settlement Examples."

Loss Settlement Examples

These are examples of how the loss settlement for a dwelling would be determined. (These simple examples ignore any deductible that might apply.)

Example 1—Dwelling limit equals or exceeds 80 percent of the replacement cost: An insured has a home with a $200,000 replacement cost and an HO-3 with a Coverage A limit of $180,000. Lightning strikes the central air conditioning unit and destroys it beyond repair. The unit has a replacement cost of $5,000 and is five years old. The dwelling is insured for more than 80 percent of replacement cost ($180,000 is 90 percent of $200,000).

The insured would receive $5,000 to replace the unit.

Example 2—Dwelling limit is less than 80 percent of the replacement cost: If this same insured has an HO-3 with a Coverage A limit of $100,000 (50 percent of the replacement cost), the insured's coverage would be below the 80 percent replacement cost requirement, and the second loss settlement method would be used. The insured would then receive the greater of the following:

- The ACV of the air conditioner. The ACV would be the $5,000 replacement cost minus depreciation. If a central air conditioner has a useful life of ten years and is now five years old, this air conditioner would depreciate by 50 percent. The ACV would equal $2,500.
- The limit is calculated:

$$\$100,000 \div (80\% \times \$200,000) \times \$5,000 = \$3,125$$

The insured would receive the greater amount of $3,125.

The insured is not required to rebuild a damaged or destroyed building on the same location. However, if the building is rebuilt on different premises, the insurer will pay no more than it would have if the building were repaired or replaced at the original premises. Regardless of the method used to determine the loss settlement amount, the limit of coverage shown on the Declarations page is the maximum amount that will be paid for any loss.

The Additional Limits of Liability for Coverages A, B, C, and D endorsement increases the Coverage A—Dwelling limit to equal the current replacement cost of the dwelling if that amount exceeds the limit appearing on the Declarations page. The limits of liability for Coverage B—Other Structures, Coverage C—Personal Property, and Coverage D—Loss of Use will be increased by the same percentage applied to Coverage A.

Loss to a Pair or Set

Often, items that are in pairs or sets are more valuable together than they are individually. Because of the increased value of pairs or sets, the Loss to a Pair or Set condition establishes the amount an insurer will pay if an item that is part of a pair or set is damaged or lost.

For example, Cindy has a custom-made brass lantern on each side of her driveway. The matching lanterns were recently fabricated at a cost of $2,000. As a pair, the lanterns have an ACV of $2,000. One lantern, by itself—not part of a pair—would have an ACV of $300 or could be exactly reproduced for $1,500. If one of Cindy's lanterns is stolen, the insurer has two options:

- Replace the missing lantern for $1,500 and restore the pair to its original value
- Pay Cindy the difference between the ACV of the lanterns as a pair and the ACV of the remaining single lantern ($1,700)

Replacing the missing lantern for $1,500 is the logical choice for the insurer in this case. However, if the missing lantern could not be replaced, the insurer might have no choice other than to pay $1,700 to compensate Cindy for the value lost. Whichever solution is chosen, the deductible will be subtracted from the final amount of the loss.

Appraisal

If the insured and the insurer cannot agree on the amount of a loss, the Appraisal condition outlines a method for resolving the disagreement. This method, commonly called the appraisal process, follows this procedure:

- The insurer and the insured each choose an appraiser to prepare an estimate of the value of the loss. Each party pays for its own appraiser.
- If the estimates differ, the two appraisers submit their differences to an umpire. The umpire is an impartial individual (often another appraiser or a judge) who resolves the differences. An agreement by any two of the

three will set the amount of loss. The insurer and the insured share the cost of the umpire.

Other Insurance and Service Agreement

If two or more insurance policies cover the same loss, the Other Insurance and Service Agreement condition states that the loss will be shared proportionally by all policies.

This example demonstrates how the share is apportioned between two policies:

John has an HO-3 with an $80,000 Coverage A—Dwelling limit. Maryanne, John's wife, did not realize that John had purchased a homeowners policy. She also purchased a homeowners policy with a $120,000 Coverage A—Dwelling limit.

A fire destroys the couple's home, which has a $100,000 replacement cost at the time of the loss. After the fire, John and Maryanne discover that two policies exist to cover their home, with a total of $200,000 in coverage available ($80,000 from John's policy plus $120,000 from Maryanne's policy).

The two policies will share the loss proportionally:

- The insurer that issued John's policy will pay 40 percent of the loss ($80,000 ÷ $200,000 = 0.40), or $40,000.
- The insurer that issued Maryanne's policy will pay 60 percent of the loss ($120,000 ÷ $200,000 = 0.60), or $60,000.

An insured home or item of personal property might also be covered by a service plan, property restoration plan, home warranty, or service warranty agreement. The homeowners policy makes it clear in the Other Insurance and Service Agreement condition that homeowners insurance coverage applies as excess over any amounts payable under any such agreement.

Our Option

Insurers usually settle claims by paying the value of the loss, and the insured is responsible for repairing or replacing the property. However, the Our Option condition reserves the right for the insurer to repair or replace damaged property with similar property, should it choose to do so. Sometimes insurers exercise this right because they can purchase repairs or obtain replacement items at a deep discount. Repairing or replacing property is the insurer's option. The insured cannot require the insurer to repair or replace damaged property.

Loss Payment

As provided for in the Loss Payment condition, the insurer will adjust all losses with the insured or the insured's spouse (unless another person is named in the policy or is legally entitled to receive payment). A loss is payable sixty days after the insurer receives a proof of loss and either an agreement has been reached by the insurer and the insured or a court judgment or an appraisal award has been entered. (Time periods may vary according to state requirements.)

Abandonment of Property

The Abandonment of Property condition provides that if the insured abandons the property after it is damaged or destroyed, the insurer need not take responsibility for it. For example, after collecting insurance proceeds for a loss, an insured might prefer to walk away from a burned-out home in a neighborhood where property values have declined and turn the property over to the insurer, rather than remain liable for the damaged building. However, the insurer is not obligated to accept the property.

Mortgage Clause

The Mortgage Clause condition establishes these rights of the mortgagee listed on the Declarations page:

- If a loss occurs to property covered by Coverage A—Dwelling or Coverage B—Other Structures, the loss is payable jointly to the mortgagee and the insured. Typically, the mortgagee relies on this right to ensure that the insured uses the money to repair the property. The mortgagee is satisfied as long as the property is repaired and the insured continues to make mortgage payments.

- A mortgagee has rights that are independent of the insured's rights. If the insurer denies the insured's loss (if, for example, arson by the insured is discovered), the mortgagee retains the right to collect from the insurer its insurable interest in the property.

- An insurer must mail notice of cancellation or nonrenewal of a policy to the mortgagee (in addition to notice sent to the insured) at least ten days before the cancellation or nonrenewal.

No Benefit to Bailee

The No Benefit to Bailee condition states that a bailee who holds the property of an insured is responsible for the care of that property. For example, a dry cleaner who negligently damages an insured's clothing cannot avoid responsibility for the damage because the insured has coverage under the homeowners policy.

Loss Payable Clause

In the Loss Payable Clause condition, the insurer agrees to include the named loss payee when a claim is paid involving that personal property. For example, the Loss Payable Clause condition applies to a homeowner who uses leased or rented furniture. The homeowner might be asked to name the furniture leasing company as an additional insured for this property. This information would appear in the policy declarations. Ordinarily, this means that a claim draft would be payable to both the named insured and the loss payee. The loss payee is also entitled to notification if the policy is canceled or nonrenewed. See the exhibit "Other Section I Conditions."

Other Section I Conditions

Suit Against Us—Bars an insured from bringing legal action against the insurer unless the insured has complied with all policy provisions. Any legal action must be started within two years of the loss.

Recovered Property—Provides that if the insurer pays a claim for the loss of property, and the property is later recovered, the insured has the option of taking the property and returning the claim payment or keeping the claim payment and allowing the insurer to take over the property.

Volcanic Eruption Period—All volcanic eruptions that occur within a seventy-two-hour period are considered to be one volcanic eruption. If multiple eruptions should occur within that period, only one coverage limit and one deductible would apply.

Policy Period—Specifies that coverage applies only to losses that occur during the policy period.

Concealment or Fraud—States any insured who conceals or misrepresents any material information, engages in fraudulent conduct, or makes false statements relating to the insurance is not covered under the policy. This condition applies whether the conduct occurred before or after a loss.

Nuclear Hazard Clause—Defines the nuclear hazard, for which coverage is excluded in the Section I—Exclusions. Excluded nuclear hazards encompass any radiation, contamination, explosion, or smoke resulting from a nuclear reaction. A direct loss by fire resulting from the nuclear hazard is covered.

[DA07730]

2011 HO-3 SECTION I—PROPERTY COVERAGE CASE STUDY

Knowing how to apply the Insurance Services Office, Inc. (ISO) Homeowners 3—Special Form (HO-3) policy to the facts of a case is an important skill. This case study will help you make the transition from knowing policy language to applying policy language to personal property losses to determine whether coverage applies. As you progress through this case study, you can check your understanding of the coverage provided by answering the Knowledge to Action questions.

Case Facts

Marvin and Lashonda own a single-family home, which is insured under an unendorsed HO-3 policy with a $300,000 dwelling limit. A carport is attached to the rear of the home, where Marvin stores a small fishing boat and trailer. On February 2, 20X1, as the couple is cooking dinner, visitors unexpectedly arrive. Marvin and Lashonda forget to remove a pot from the stove, the pot overheats, and a fire ensues. The fire department is called, and the couple and their guests safely escape. The fire, smoke, and water damage destroy the kitchen and several adjoining rooms and damage the carport area, which is adjacent to the kitchen. The boat and trailer are destroyed by the heat and fire. Kitchen furnishings and appliances are destroyed. The couple must temporarily live in a nearby hotel for one month until their home is safe to occupy. Marvin and Lashonda report the loss to their insurer promptly. They are in compliance with all policy conditions, including Coverage A replacement cost provisions. See the exhibit "Summary of Marvin and Lashonda's Damages."

Summary of Marvin and Lashonda's Damages

$50,000	Value of structural damage to home because of the fire
$3,000	Value of Marvin's fishing boat and trailer (total loss)
$8,000	Value of structural damage to the carport
$3,500	Cost to live in a hotel while damage to home is repaired
$25,000	Value of damage to furnishings and appliances, including those items valued at a total loss

[DA07743]

Given the facts presented in the case, will the claim for fire and related damage be covered under the HO-3? If so, what amount will the insurer pay for the claim? When answering the questions in this case-based activity, consider only the information provided as part of this case.

Necessary Reference Materials

To determine whether the HO-3 policy provides coverage for the losses Marvin and Lashonda incurred as a result of the fire and the ensuing damage, you need copies of the HO-3 policy form and the Declarations page.

Overview of Steps

When examining the policy forms to determine whether coverage applies to the loss(es), you can apply the four steps of the DICE method. ("DICE" is an acronym for categories of policy provisions: declarations, insuring agreement, conditions, and exclusions.) Doing this involves analyzing these provisions and determining whether any information found at each step precludes coverage at the time the losses occurred. You should also examine other categories of policy provisions, such as the insured's duties, general provisions, endorsements (if applicable), and terms defined in the policy in relation to the declarations, insuring agreement, conditions, and exclusions.

Next, you should determine the amounts payable for the losses under the applicable policy or policies. Doing this involves analyzing the limits of insurance and any deductibles that apply. It also involves determining whether more than one policy provides coverage for the same loss.

Determination of Coverage

To determine whether HO-3 coverage applies for Marvin and Lashonda's submitted fire claim, you can move sequentially through the four steps of the DICE method of policy analysis.

DICE Analysis Step 1: Declarations

The first DICE step is to review the Declarations page of Marvin and Lashonda's policy to determine whether it covers the loss. See the exhibit "Excerpt From Marvin and Lashonda's Declarations Page."

Excerpt From Marvin and Lashonda's Declarations Page

Homeowners Policy Declarations

| **POLICYHOLDER:** (Named Insured) | Marvin and Lashonda Smith 216 Brookside Drive Anytown, USA 40000 | **POLICY NUMBER:** | 296 H 578661 |

| **POLICY PERIOD:** | **Inception:** March 30, 20XX **Expiration:** March 30, 20X1 | **Policy period begins 12:01 A.M. standard time at the residence premises.** |

[DA07744]

Knowledge to Action

Action Task: Review the Declarations page in Marvin and Lashonda's policy.

According to your analysis of the excerpt of Marvin and Lashonda's Declarations page, is coverage applicable for the property and individuals in question during the coverage period?

Feedback: The Declarations page confirms Marvin and Lashonda as insureds for the premises damaged. The loss occurred during the policy period.

DICE Analysis Step 2: Insuring Agreement

The second DICE step is to review Marvin and Lashonda's insuring agreement to determine whether it is applicable to the described loss.

Knowledge to Action

Action Task: Review the relevant portions of the insuring agreement in the HO-3 policy.

According to your analysis of the excerpt of the insuring agreement, did this loss trigger coverage under the HO-3 Insuring Agreement?

Feedback: Yes, coverage is triggered under the HO-3, in which the insurer agrees to pay for direct physical loss to property described in Coverages A and B (subject to certain exclusions) and for direct physical loss under Coverage C for certain named perils, including fire and subsequent smoke and water damage.

DICE Analysis Step 3: Conditions

The third DICE step is to review the policy conditions to determine whether they preclude coverage at the time of the loss. See the exhibit "HO-3 Policy Form (Unendorsed) With $500 Deductible."

HO-3 Policy Form (Unendorsed) With $500 Deductible

Marvin and Lashonda's Coverages

Marvin and Lashonda Smith
216 Brookside Drive
Anytown, USA

Policy Period: From 03/30/X0 to 03/30/X1 (12:01 a.m. Standard time at the location of
            the residence premises)

Cov. A—Dwelling	$300,000	Cov. B—Other Structures	$30,000	Cov. C—Personal Property	$150,000	Cov. D—Loss of Use	$90,000

[DA07745]

Knowledge to Action

Action Task: Determine whether the HO-3 policy conditions preclude coverage for Marvin and Lashonda's loss.

According to your analysis of the excerpt of the HO-3 policy conditions, is coverage precluded for Marvin and Lashonda's loss?

Feedback: No, coverage is not precluded for Marvin and Lashonda's loss. They reported the claim promptly and are in compliance with all policy conditions. The $300,000 coverage under Coverage A meets the 80 percent Coverage A Replacement Cost provision.

DICE Analysis Step 4: Exclusions

The fourth DICE step is to review the policy exclusions to determine whether they exclude or limit coverage of the loss. See the exhibit "Special Limits of Liability."

Knowledge to Action

Action Task: Review the "Special Limits of Liability" exhibit to determine whether one or more exclusions exclude or limit coverage of Marvin and Lashonda's loss.

According to your review of the "Special Limits of Liability" exhibit, do one or more exclusions exclude or limit coverage of Marvin and Lashonda's loss?

Feedback: Yes, one coverage limitation in Marvin and Lashonda's HO-3 applies to Coverage C—Personal Property. Under Coverage C, a $1,500 limit applies per loss to watercraft, including trailers and related equipment. This limitation would apply to Marvin's fishing boat and trailer.

Special Limits of Liability

3. Special Limits Of Liability

The special limit for each category shown below is the total limit for each loss for all property in that category. These special limits do not increase the Coverage C limit of liability.

   a. $200 on money, bank notes, bullion, gold other than goldware, silver other than silverware, platinum other than platinumware, coins, medals, scrip, stored value cards and smart cards.

   b. $1,500 on securities, accounts, deeds, evidences of debt, letters of credit, notes other than bank notes, manuscripts, personal records, passports, tickets and stamps. This dollar limit applies to these categories regardless of the medium (such as paper or computer software) on which the material exists.

   This limit includes the cost to research, replace or restore the information from the lost or damaged material.

   c. $1,500 on watercraft of all types, including their trailers, furnishings, equipment and outboard engines or motors.

   d. $1,500 on trailers or semitrailers not used with watercraft of all types.

   e. $1,500 for loss by theft of jewelry, watches, furs, precious and semiprecious stones.

   f. $2,500 for loss by theft of firearms and related equipment.

   g. $2,500 for loss by theft of silverware, silver-plated ware, goldware, gold-plated ware, platinumware, platinum-plated ware and pewterware. This includes flatware, hollowware, tea sets, trays and trophies made of or including silver, gold or pewter.

   h. $2,500 on property, on the "residence premises", used primarily for "business" purposes.

   i. $500 on property, away from the "residence premises", used primarily for "business" purposes. However, this limit does not apply to loss to electronic apparatus and other property described in Categories j. and k. below.

   j. $1,500 on electronic apparatus and accessories, while in or upon a "motor vehicle", but only if the apparatus is equipped to be operated by power from the "motor vehicle's" electrical system while still capable of being operated by other power sources.

   Accessories include antennas, tapes, wires, records, discs or other media that can be used with any apparatus described in this Category j.

   k. $1,500 on electronic apparatus and accessories used primarily for "business" while away from the "residence premises" and not in or upon a "motor vehicle". The apparatus must be equipped to be operated by power from the "motor vehicle's" electrical system while still capable of being operated by other power sources.

   Accessories include antennas, tapes, wires, records, discs or other media that can be used with any apparatus described in this Category k.

[DA00338]

Determination of Amounts Payable

Now that you have completed the DICE analysis, you can determine the amounts payable. Doing this involves analyzing the limit(s) of insurance available to pay for the loss and any deductibles that apply. It also involves determining whether more than one policy provides coverage for the same loss.

Knowledge to Action

Under Coverage A, how much will Marvin and Lashonda receive for fire damage to their home?

Feedback: Under Coverage A, Marvin and Lashonda will receive $49,500 ($50,000 less the $500 deductible) for fire damage to the home (within the $300,000 Coverage A limit) at full replacement cost because the policy dwelling limit complies with policy replacement cost provisions (Note that for purposes of this case, the policy deductible is being applied here).

Under Coverage A, how much will Marvin and Lashonda receive for fire damage to their carport?

Feedback: Under Coverage A, Marvin and Lashonda will receive $8,000 for fire damage to their carport (considered part of the dwelling, not an "other structure"; within the $300,000 Coverage A limit).

Under Coverage C, before an adjustment is made for the depreciation and physical condition of the furnishings and appliances, how much would Marvin and Lashonda be entitled to receive for fire, smoke, and water damage to those items?

Feedback: Under Coverage C, Marvin and Lashonda would be entitled to receive $25,000 for fire, smoke, and water damage to furnishings and appliances (within the $150,000 coverage limit). However, the amount that they would actually receive would be reduced based on the actual cash value of the furnishings and appliances, which would reflect a diminished value based on the extent to which they've depreciated.

Under Coverage C, before an adjustment is made for the depreciation and physical condition of the boat and the trailer, how much would Marvin and Lashonda be entitled to receive for fire damage to each?

Feedback: Under Coverage C, Marvin and Lashonda will receive $1,500 for fire damage to the boat and trailer (leaving a $1,500 balance unpaid because of the special limit of liability; within $150,000 coverage limit). However, the amount that they would actually receive would be reduced based on the actual cash value of the boat and trailer, which would reflect a diminished value based on the extent to which they've depreciated.

Under Coverage D, how much will Marvin and Lashonda receive for the additional living expenses required for a one-month hotel stay while their home is made habitable?

Feedback: Under Coverage D, Marvin and Lashonda will receive $3,500 for their additional living expenses (within the $90,000 coverage limit).

SUMMARY

Individuals and families have a variety of personal risk management needs related to their homes and personal liability. The ISO Homeowners program offers a selection of homeowners forms to meet these various needs. The forms vary according to the types of property eligible for coverage and type of coverage provided.

The Homeowners 3—Special Form (HO 03) meets the needs of most homeowners and families. It includes several sections: Declarations, Agreement and Definitions, Section I—Property Coverages, and Section II—Liability Coverages. Endorsements can be added to modify the coverage provided. The premium for the coverage consists of a base premium and adjustments.

HO-3 Section I—Property Coverages contains four property coverages: Coverage A—Dwelling, Coverage B—Other Structures, Coverage C—Personal Property, and Coverage D—Loss of Use. Section I also includes twelve Additional Coverages, which provide limited coverage for various types of losses that would not otherwise be covered under Section I.

HO-3 provides open perils coverage for property described in Coverage A—Dwelling and Coverage B—Other Structures and named perils coverage for property described in Coverage C—Personal Property. Coverages A, B, and C are all subject to the Section I—Exclusions. Coverages A and B are also subject to several other exclusions that help to define the scope of open perils coverage.

HO-3 Section I—Conditions describes the eighteen major conditions applying to the property coverages that both the insured and the insurer must meet.

You should now be able to apply policy language to personal property losses to determine whether the losses are covered and, if so, the amount for which they are covered.

6

Homeowners Section II

Educational Objectives

After learning the content of this assignment, you should be able to:

▷ Determine whether the 2011 Homeowners 3—Special Form (HO-3) policy provisions in the following Section II—Liability Coverages provide coverage for a given loss or loss exposure:

- Coverage E—Personal Liability

- Coverage F—Medical Payments to Others

- Additional Coverages

▷ Determine whether one or more exclusions preclude the coverage provided by Section II of the 2011 Homeowners 3—Special Form (HO-3) policy provisions in Section II—Exclusions.

▷ Summarize each of these 2011 Homeowners 3—Special Form (HO-3) policy provisions:

- Conditions applicable to Section II

- Conditions applicable to Sections I and II

▷ Compare the coverage provided by each of the following 2011 homeowners forms to the coverage provided by the 2011 Homeowners 3—Special Form (HO-3):

- HO-2 Broad Form

- HO-4 Contents Broad Form

- HO-5 Comprehensive Form

- HO-6 Unit-Owners Form

- HO-8 Modified Coverage Form

▷ Given a case describing a homeowners liability claim, determine whether the Homeowners Section II—Liability Coverages would cover the claim and, if so, the amount the insurer would pay for the claim.

Homeowners Section II

HO-3 SECTION II—LIABILITY COVERAGES

Individuals and families are exposed to liability through the property they own and use and through their personal activities. Section II—Liability Coverages in the Insurance Services Office, Inc. (ISO) Homeowners 3—Special Form (HO-3) form addresses this and other personal liability loss exposures.

Homeowners forms are not all alike. Some insurers draft their own homeowners forms and endorsements. Also, state-by-state variations on all forms are common. ISO homeowners policy forms combine property and liability coverages (Section I and Section II) to meet the common loss exposures faced by individuals and families. Of the ISO homeowners forms, the HO-3 is used most frequently. The forms can be endorsed to meet certain uncommon loss exposures. Section I of the ISO homeowners policy forms provides coverage for an insured's first-party loss exposures. Section II provides coverage for an insured's **third-party** loss exposures.

The HO-3's Section II contains the same coverage provisions found in the other ISO Homeowners program policy forms (HO-2, HO-4, HO-5, HO-6, and HO-8). The basic coverage provided by the HO-3 Section II—Liability Coverages applies to losses related to an insured's premises (dwelling location); personal activities (for example, pet ownership); and other incidental sources of personal liability, such as residence employees.

Section II of the ISO HO-3 contains two primary coverages and an additional coverages section:

- Coverage E—Personal Liability
- Coverage F—Medical Payments to Others
- Section II—Additional Coverages

Coverage E—Personal Liability

The Coverage E—Personal Liability Coverage provisions provide coverage if a claim is made or a suit is brought against an insured because of **bodily injury** or **property damage** arising from a covered **occurrence**. If the claim or suit brought by the third party does not allege bodily injury or property damage as defined in the policy, or if the bodily injury or property damage occurs before or after the policy period, the insurer is not obligated to pay any damages under Coverage E or to defend the insured.

Third party
A person or business who is not a party to the insurance contract but who asserts a claim against the insured.

Bodily injury
Physical injury to a person, including sickness, disease, and death.

Property damage
Physical injury to, destruction of, or loss of use of tangible property.

Occurrence
An accident, including continuous or repeated exposure to substantially the same general harmful conditions.

The term "occurrence" is particularly important in the homeowners insuring agreement. Liability coverage applies only to bodily injury and property damage that result from an occurrence during the policy period. One accident is an occurrence, even if it involves injury to more than one person or damage to more than one piece of property. Also, an occurrence can be a sudden event, a gradual series of incidents, or a continuous condition, as long as it is fortuitous. An example of a nonsudden occurrence is the gradual yet accidental seepage of pollutants from an insured's defective septic system into a neighbor's supply of drinking water.

The insurer pays up to the limit of liability for the damages for which an insured is legally liable. Liability coverage, which applies worldwide, applies to bodily injury and property damage arising from the insured's activities or premises. In most instances, such liability arises from the insured's negligence. Basic personal liability limits are $100,000 per occurrence, with higher limits available for an additional premium.

The circumstances under which personal liability can arise may be illustrated by examining the circumstances surrounding a loss. For example, if a policyholder's poodle bites and seriously injures a neighbor's one-year-old child in the child's own yard, the insured will likely be held liable for the resulting injuries and damages. In this example, a claim notice to the insurer is sufficient for the insurer to investigate and settle the loss. However, if the insured's dog bites a trespasser who enters the insured's fenced yard and mistreats the animal, the insured's liability might be questionable. In such a case, the insurer might deny the claim on the grounds that the insured does not appear to be liable for the injury. However, if the injured trespasser brings a suit against the insured, the insurer would be obligated to provide for the insured's defense and pay damages if the insured is found liable.

Defense costs coverage, which is supplemental to the liability limit, is provided even if a suit is groundless, false, or fraudulent. For example, if an individual falsely claims he tripped on an insured's sidewalk and sustained a back injury, the insurer would have to respond to the suit. The insurer provides for defense costs in addition to any coverage. If the insured is found liable, the insurer also covers the damages, up to the personal liability limit, that might apply to the trip-and-fall claim.

The insurer's obligation to defend ends only when the liability limit for the occurrence is exhausted by payment of a settlement or judgment (even if policy limits are exhausted by the costs of the claim). For example, in the trip-and-fall occurrence, assume the claimant's injuries are legitimately caused by the insured. If the individual claims $200,000 in damages and the insured's homeowners coverage has a $100,000 personal liability limit, the insurer cannot simply pay $100,000 and avoid further litigation. Rather, the insurer must defend the insured until a settlement is reached. If a settlement can be reached for $150,000, the insurer's obligations end when it pays defense costs and pays the claimant's $100,000 in damages (the policy limit). See the exhibit "Policy Definitions and How They Apply to Section II."

Policy Definitions and How They Apply to Section II

Who is an insured for liability coverage?

- The policyholder (the named insured) shown on the Declarations page and the named insured's spouse if a resident of the same household. The policyholder and resident spouse are identified as "you" in the policy.

- Residents of the household who are relatives of the named insured or spouse.

- Residents of the household who are under the age of twenty-one and in the care of the named insured or resident relatives.

- A full-time student who resided in the household before moving out to attend school. This person must be either under the age of twenty-one and in the care of the named insured or resident relatives, or a relative of the named insured under the age of twenty-four. The policyholder's twenty-two-year-old daughter who is a full-time college student would therefore qualify as an insured.

- Any person or organization legally responsible for animals or watercraft that are covered by the policy and owned by a person defined in the first three bulleted items. For example, a neighbor who walks the named insured's dog while the insured is on vacation is protected as an insured for liability coverage under the named insured's homeowners policy if the dog causes an injury while in the neighbor's care.

- Anyone employed by a person defined in the first three bulleted items, with respect to any motor vehicle covered by the policy. For example, a gardener who accidentally hits a neighbor's car while using the named insured's riding lawn mower to mow the named insured's lawn is an insured for liability coverage under the named insured's homeowners policy.

- Other persons using any vehicle covered by the policy on an insured location, with the consent of the named insured or spouse, are insureds for liability coverage. For example, if a neighbor takes the named insured's all-terrain vehicle for a test drive in the named insured's yard and accidentally strikes and injures a child, the neighbor becomes an insured for liability coverage under the named insured's homeowners policy.

Who is a residence employee versus other employees?

Coverage F—Medical Payments to Others applies to insured "residence employees," but not to other "employees." The policy defines both terms. Residence employees include domestic workers whose duties relate to maintaining or using the household premises or performing domestic or household services. Four Section II exclusions—an insured's premises that are not an insured location, motor vehicles, watercraft, and aircraft—do not apply to bodily injury sustained by a "residence employee" in the course of employment by an insured. Therefore, Coverages E and F will cover a residence employee's injuries in some situations.

An employee, as defined by the policy, is an employee of an insured who is not a residence employee.

[DA07776]

Coverage F—Medical Payments to Others

Coverage F—Medical Payments to Others covers medical payments incurred by others (not insureds or regular household residents) within three years of an injury. These medical expenses include reasonable charges for medical, surgical, x-ray, dental, ambulance, hospital, professional nursing, and funeral services, and prosthetic devices. Medical Payments to Others coverage is automatically included in all homeowners policies for a limit generally set at $1,000 per person for a single accident. This limit can be increased for an additional premium. The limit for Coverage F is shown on the declarations page.

Medical Payments to Others coverage (sometimes simply called "medical payments") may be considered to overlap with bodily injury liability coverage. However, liability coverage applies only when an insured is legally responsible for damages. Claims for medical payments are often paid when the insured feels a moral obligation to another person, even though the insured is not negligent or legally responsible. When a bodily injury claim involves a relatively small amount of money, paying it as a Medical Payments to Others claim simplifies matters by eliminating any need to determine whether an insured was legally responsible for the injuries. For example, an invited guest falls and breaks his wrist in a well-lit and properly maintained hallway in the insured's home, requiring a trip to the emergency room that costs $850. Even though the insured is not liable for the injury, the Medical Payments to Others coverage will provide reimbursement of the $850.

Coverage F—Medical Payments to Others coverage applies under these conditions:

- The injury occurs to a person who has the insured's permission to be at the insured location. For example, medical payments coverage applies if an insured's dog bites a party guest at the insured's home. Coverage does not apply if the insured's dog bites a burglar.

- The injured person is away from the insured location, and bodily injury arises out of a condition at the insured location or on property immediately adjoining the insured location. For example, if an insured is draining water from a pool into a gutter that empties at the bottom of his street and a neighbor slips in the water and breaks his wrist, the insured's medical payments coverage applies.

- A person is injured while away from the insured location by an activity performed by an insured. For example if an insured plays soccer on weekends and accidentally breaks a teammate's nose, the insured's medical payments coverage applies.

Section II—Additional Coverages

The Section II—Additional Coverages provisions supplement the protection provided by Coverages E and F. Amounts payable under this portion of the policy are in addition to the Coverage E—Personal Liability and Coverage F—Medical Payments to Others limits of liability. Section II—Additional Coverages claims are usually incidental in nature or related to claims already made by an insured under Coverages E and F.

Section II—Additional Coverages includes four additional coverages:

- Claim Expenses
- First Aid Expenses
- Damage to Property of Others
- Loss Assessment

Claims Expenses

The Claim Expenses additional coverage specifies expenses the insurer will pay when handling a claim. In addition to any judgment or settlement an insurer pays (subject to the Coverage E liability limit) on behalf of an insured, an insurer covers these claims expenses:

- "Expenses we incur"—For example, the insurer pays for the insured's legal representation when a claim or suit occurs.
- Premiums on bonds—For example, if any bonds are required in the defense of a suit, the insurer pays the bond premiums. However, the insurer will not pay the premium on bonds that exceed the policy's Coverage E limit.
- Reasonable expenses—For example, if an insurer requests an insured's assistance in the investigation or defense of a claim or suit, the insurer pays for any reasonable expenses incurred by the insured, including loss of earnings, up to $250 per day. Reasonable expenses can include parking costs, meals, and mileage.
- Postjudgment interest—For example, after a judgment has been made against an insured, interest can accrue on the amount owed to a plaintiff until the insurer actually makes that payment. Postjudgment interest amounts can be substantial if the insurer appeals the judgment to a higher court. Postjudgment interest pays for any interest expense that accrues.

First Aid Expenses

The First Aid Expenses additional coverage states that an insurer will reimburse an insured for expenses the insured has incurred when rendering first aid to others as a result of any bodily injury covered under the policy. For example, if a guest is injured in an insured's home and the insured uses supplies from her first aid kit to bandage the wound, the insured can collect reimbursement from her insurer for the first aid supplies used. The insurer will not reimburse expenses for first aid to an injured insured.

Damage to Property of Others

The Damage to Property of Others additional coverage, sometimes called "voluntary property damage" coverage, pays up to $1,000 for damage to property of others caused by an insured, regardless of fault or legal liability.

For example, an insured borrows a friend's digital camcorder to record his daughter's piano recital. During the event, he drops the camcorder and breaks it. The insured will have coverage for up to $1,000 to replace the device without having to prove that he was responsible for the loss. This coverage allows an insured to maintain goodwill by paying for relatively minor losses to another person's property, and it allows the insurer to avoid litigation expenses on small property damage claims to determine whether the insured was at fault.

An insurer will not pay under this additional coverage for property damage to the extent of any amount recoverable under Section I of the policy. For example, if the camcorder had been damaged by fire, a peril covered under Section I, the insurer would pay only the deductible amount under the Damage to the Property of Others coverage; the remaining amount would be payable under Section I.

The insurer will not pay for any property damage in these circumstances:

- The damage is caused intentionally by an insured thirteen years of age or older. (Intentional damage caused by children under thirteen is covered.)
- Property owned by an insured is damaged.
- Property owned by or rented to a tenant of an insured or a resident of the named insured's household is damaged.
- The damage arises out of a business engaged in by an insured.
- The damage is a result of an act or omission in connection with premises (other than an insured location) that the insured owns, rents, or controls.
- The damage arises out of the ownership, maintenance, or use of any motor vehicle, watercraft, aircraft, or hovercraft (other than a recreational vehicle designed for use off public roads that is not subject to motor vehicle registration and not owned by an insured).

Loss Assessment

Homeowners are sometimes billed with an assessment by their homeowners associations or other similar organizations when the organization sustains a loss for which their officers failed to secure a sufficient amount of insurance. The Loss Assessment additional coverage provides up to $1,000 for an insured's share of a loss assessment charged to the insured by a corporation or an association of property owners for these types of losses:

- Bodily injury or property damage that is not excluded under Section II of the homeowners policy

- Liability that results from an act of an elected and unpaid director, officer, or trustee

As an example, the recreation center of a condominium association (jointly owned by the individual homeowners) might sustain severe damage to its roof in an ice storm or snowstorm. If the officers are found liable for not adequately insuring the building, the association's bylaws may permit it to assess each owner for a share of the uninsured loss. The Loss Assessment additional coverage will cover that assessment for up to $1,000.

Apply Your Knowledge

Ralph is mowing the grass in his front yard when the blade on his mower strikes a rock, causing it to fly toward Sam, his next door neighbor. Sam was in Ralph's front yard walking toward him to return a hedge trimmer he had borrowed from Ralph. Sam immediately fell down, grabbed his chest, and called out for an ambulance. Upon investigation, it was determined the rock bounced off the hedge trimmer, never striking Sam. Sam sued Ralph for bodily injury. Ralph is insured by an HO-3 policy, which was in effect at the time of the accident.

Will Coverage E—Personal Liability Coverage of Ralph's HO-3 policy respond to Sam's claim?

Feedback: Yes, Coverage E—Personal Liability Coverage provisions provide coverage if a claim is made or a suit is brought against an insured because of bodily injury arising from a covered occurrence. Mowing the yard is a covered activity, and the accident occurred during the policy period. There is no indication that the occurrence was not accidental.

How will the fact that the rock never struck Sam affect the defense Ralph's insurer provides him?

Feedback: Defense costs coverage, which is supplemental to the liability limit, is provided even if a suit is groundless, false, or fraudulent. The fact that Sam is, at best, exaggerating any injury does not relieve Ralph's insurer of the cost of defending him.

HO-3 SECTION II—EXCLUSIONS

Individuals and families commonly use homeowners insurance policies to address real and personal property loss exposures and liability loss exposures that may arise as a consequence of property ownership or activities. Exclusions help limit the scope of the personal liability coverage these policies provide.

HO-3 Section II—Exclusions contains exclusions common to all of the home-owners forms used in the Insurance Services Office, Inc. (ISO) Homeowners program. Exclusions are designed to limit or preclude coverage, but because of how some exclusion provisions are worded, limited personal liability coverage may, in fact, be provided by a particular provision. Therefore, the provisions contained in Section II—Exclusions should be carefully considered with the general terms of coverage provided by Coverage E—Personal Liability and Coverage F—Medical Payments to Others, as well as Section II—Additional Coverages and Section II—Conditions, to determine the full scope of Section II coverage.

HO-3 Section II contains twenty-two exclusions that are divided into sets. Some sets apply to all of Section II, and some apply only to Coverage E or Coverage F.

Motor Vehicle and Other Motorized Craft—Exclusions

The first four exclusions of Section II apply to losses arising out of motor vehicles, watercraft, aircraft, and hovercraft. These exclusions are defined in the Definitions section of the homeowners policy and apply to both Coverages E and F. With respect to these vehicles or craft, coverage does not apply for claims arising out of these conditions:

- The ownership, maintenance, occupancy, operation, use, loading, or unloading of a motor vehicle or craft by any person unless it appears in a specific exception to the exclusion
- Negligent entrustment, by an insured, of an excluded motor vehicle or craft
- An insured's failure to supervise, or negligently supervising, a person
- An insured's "vicarious liability" for the actions of a child or minor

Motor Vehicle Liability

The homeowners policy defines a motor vehicle as any self-propelled vehicle, including an attached trailer. The Section II Motor Vehicle Liability exclusion, which applies to both Coverages E and F, is designed to limit the majority of personal motor vehicle loss exposures that would typically be insured under a Personal Auto Policy (PAP). Coverage does not apply to a motor vehicle that meets any of these criteria:

- It is required by law to be registered for use on public roads or property.
- It is involved in an organized race.
- It is rented to others.
- It is used to carry persons or cargo for a charge.
- It is used for any business purpose, except for motorized golf carts used on a golf course.

Although the motor vehicle exclusion is intended to allow the auto policy to provide virtually all motor vehicle liability coverage, the homeowners policy provides some Section II—Liability coverages for certain motor vehicles. These are examples of motor vehicles covered under Section II—Liability coverages:

- Motor vehicle designed as a toy vehicle for use by children under seven years of age that is powered by one or more batteries and has not been modified after being manufactured to exceed five miles per hour on level ground.
- Motor vehicle in dead storage on an insured location.
- Motor vehicle used solely to service a residence. (Note that with the 2011 revision, this is expanded to include not only the insured's residence but also any residence.)
- Motor vehicle designed for assisting people who are handicapped.
- Motor vehicle designed for recreational use off public roads and not owned by an insured or owned only while on an insured location.
- Motorized golf carts not capable of exceeding twenty-five miles per hour, owned by an insured, and used to play golf or used legally within a private residential association.
- Trailers currently not towed by, hitched to, or carried on another motor vehicle.

Watercraft Liability

The watercraft exclusions, which apply to both Coverages E and F, are similar to the motor vehicle exclusions. However, watercraft might be covered under one of the exceptions to the watercraft exclusions. In general, small, low-powered watercraft, or watercraft the insured uses but does not own, are included for Section II coverage. See the exhibit "Watercraft Exposures Covered by Section II of the Homeowners Policy Forms."

Watercraft Exposures Covered by Section II of the Homeowners Policy Forms

Covered Watercraft Liability Loss Exposures	Examples
Watercraft that are stored	A 30-foot sailboat stored out of the water at a marina for the winter
Sailboats (with or without auxiliary power) shorter than 26 feet	A 17-foot catamaran owned by the insured
Sailboats (with or without auxiliary power) longer than 26 feet *not owned by or rented* to an insured	A 32-foot sailboat the insured borrowed from her brother for a vacation
Inboard or inboard-outdrive watercraft with engines of 50 horsepower or less that are *not owned* by an insured	A 50-horsepower jet ski rented by an insured
Inboard or inboard-outdrive watercraft of more than 50 horsepower *not owned* by or rented to an insured	A 150-horsepower inboard motor boat borrowed from a neighbor
Watercraft with one or more outboard engines or motors with 25 total horsepower or less	A fishing boat with a 15-horsepower motor, owned by the insured
Watercraft with one or more outboard engines or motors with more than 25 total horsepower that are *not owned* by an insured	A boat with a 75-horsepower outboard motor, borrowed from a friend

Includes copyrighted material of Insurance Services Office, Inc., with its permission. Copyright, ISO Properties, Inc., 2010. [DA00180]

Watercraft not covered by the insured's homeowners policy can be properly covered by a separate watercraft policy.

Aircraft and Hovercraft Liability

The homeowners policy excludes all aircraft liability under Coverages E and F. However, because model airplanes or hobby aircraft that do not carry people or cargo are excluded from the policy's aircraft definition, they are covered.

As with aircraft, hovercraft liability is excluded under Coverages E and F. Hovercraft are self-propelled motorized ground-effect air-cushion vehicles. No exceptions to this exclusion are available in the homeowners policy.

Coverage E—Personal Liability and Coverage F—Medical Payments to Others

Some bodily injury and property damage loss exposures are beyond the scope of a homeowners policy or are effectively covered under other policies. Eight exclusions apply to both Coverages E and F.

Expected or Intended Injury

The Expected or Intended Injury exclusion applies to any bodily injury or property damage caused by an insured when the bodily injury or property damage is intentional or expected, even if the actual injury or damage resulting from the action was unintended when the intentional action took place. For example, assume an insured detects someone in her home late at night whom she believes to be a burglar, and, because of the darkness, she grabs a gun and shoots the burglar. The "burglar" is, in fact, a neighbor who is suffering from dementia and has accidentally wandered through the insured's open back door. Although the insured had no intention of shooting her neighbor, she undoubtedly intended to cause bodily injury when she shot him. Therefore, coverage is excluded. However, the insured may rely on an exception to the exclusion that stipulates that the exclusion does not apply to bodily injury or property damage resulting from the use of reasonable force to protect persons or property.

Business

The Business exclusion is designed to exclude coverage for bodily injury or property damage arising out of the business activities of an insured while providing coverage for occasional or part-time activities, such as insureds under the age of twenty-one selling lemonade, delivering newspapers, maintaining lawns, or babysitting. The exclusion states that the policy provides no coverage for bodily injury or property damage relating to a business operated from the residence premises or another insured location.

Business is broadly defined in the Definitions section of the policy to include a full-time, a part-time, or an occasional trade, profession, or occupation, or any other activity engaged in for money or other compensation, with these exceptions:

- Activities for which the insured received $2,000 or less during the year preceding the policy period
- Volunteer activities
- Home daycare services not involving compensation but possibly involving an exchange of services
- Home daycare services rendered to a relative

Renting property to others qualifies as a business, as defined by the policy. However, these three exceptions to this exclusion allow for some common rental situations:

- Rental of an insured location on an occasional basis is a covered loss exposure if the location is used only as a residence. For example, a homeowner lives in a town that hosts a popular annual arts festival. During the festival, the homeowner leaves on vacation and rents her home to festival attendees. Section II coverage would be provided to the insured during the time the home is rented.

- Rental of part of an insured location as a residence is a covered loss exposure as long as the occupying family takes no more than two roomers or boarders in a single-family unit. For example, a homeowner renting out an apartment in the residence (perhaps an apartment over an attached garage) would have Section II coverage arising out of the normal rental of that apartment.

- Rental of part of an insured location is a covered loss exposure if it is used only as an office or a school, studio, or private garage. For example, an insured could rent out a room or an apartment in the residence for use as an office, and Section II coverage would apply.

Several endorsements related to home business insurance, business pursuits, and incidental occupancies are available to provide limited liability coverage for certain business activities of the insured.

Other Coverage E and Coverage F Exclusions

These are the remaining exclusions applicable to Section II—Coverages E and F:

- Professional Services—Coverages E and F exclude coverage for the insured's rendering of or failure to render professional services. For example, an architect might be liable for a loss resulting from providing improper drawings to a client. This business loss exposure should be addressed by a professional liability policy.

- Insured's Premises Not an Insured Location—Coverages E and F are excluded for bodily injury or property damage arising out of any premises that is owned by or rented to an insured, or is owned and rented to others by an insured but is not an insured location.

- War—Section II of the HO-3 excludes any bodily injury or property damage that results from war.

- Communicable Disease—Coverages E and F exclude coverage for any bodily injury or property damage that arises from the transmission of a communicable disease by an insured.

- Sexual Molestation, Corporal Punishment or Physical or Mental Abuse—Coverages E and F exclude coverage for any loss that arises out of sexual molestation, corporal punishment, or physical or mental abuse by an insured.

- Controlled Substance—Coverages E and F exclude any loss that results from the use, sale, manufacture, delivery, transfer, or possession of controlled substances as defined by the Federal Food and Drug Law (such as cocaine, marijuana, and other narcotic drugs, or steroids).

Exclusions That Apply Only to Coverage E

Six exclusions apply only to Coverage E—Personal Liability and not to Medical Payments to Others:

- Loss Assessment and Contractual Liability—Coverage E does not provide coverage for liability arising from any **loss assessment** charged against an insured as a member of a homeowners or condominium association or corporation. Additionally, the policy excludes liability assumed under contract or agreement. However, exceptions apply, and liability coverage is provided for two types of written contracts. The first are contracts relating to the ownership, maintenance, or use of an insured location. The second is liability of others assumed by the named insured before an accident occurs.

- Damage to the Insured's Property—Personal liability coverage is intended to address third-party liability loss exposures. An insured cannot collect payment under Section II—Liability Coverages for damage to his or her own property, even if the property repairs might serve to prevent a liability claim. For example, an insured cannot expect his homeowners policy to pay the cost of repairing a cracked and damaged sidewalk, even if the sidewalk repairs might help avoid a personal liability claim.

- Damage to Property in the Insured's Care—Coverage E does not apply to property rented to, occupied by, or in the care of an insured. However, an exception to this exclusion applies to property damage caused by fire, smoke, or explosion. If the insured rents a beach cottage for a summer vacation, Coverage E would apply if the insured accidentally starts a fire in the kitchen that results in smoke and fire damage to the cottage. However, Coverage E would not apply if the insured strikes the cottage with a vehicle, because vehicle damage to the cottage is not a result of fire, smoke, or explosion, and the cottage is in the insured's care.

- Bodily Injury to Persons Eligible for Workers Compensation Benefits— Coverage is excluded under Coverage E for bodily injury to any person who is eligible to receive or who is provided benefits by an insured under a state's workers compensation law.

- Nuclear Liability—Coverage E excludes bodily injury or property damage liability that would normally be covered under a nuclear energy liability policy.

- Bodily Injury to an Insured—Coverage E does not apply to the named insured, resident relatives, and other residents under the age of twenty-

Loss assessment
A charge by the condominium association against the unit owners for the cost of uninsured losses.

one in the insured's care for their own bodily injury, even if the injury is caused by another insured.

Exclusions That Apply Only to Coverage F

Four exclusions apply only to Coverage F—Medical Payments to Others. These exclusions are in addition to the exclusions common to both personal liability and the medical payments coverage exclusions:

- Residence Employee Off Premises—Coverage F excludes bodily injury to a residence employee if an injury occurs off the insured's location and the injury does not arise out of the employee's work. Not excluded under Coverage F, and therefore included, is coverage for residence employees while they are working away from the insured location or on the insured location whether working or not.

- Bodily Injury Eligible for Workers Compensation Benefits—Any person eligible to receive payment under any workers compensation law, non-occupational disability law, or occupational disease law will not receive compensation for bodily injury under Coverage F. This exclusion applies regardless of whether the benefits are to be provided by an insured.

- Nuclear Reaction—Coverage F excludes bodily injury from any nuclear reaction, nuclear radiation, or radioactive contamination, regardless of the cause.

- Injury to Residents—Coverage F excludes bodily injury to any person who regularly resides at the insured location (other than a residence employee).

HO-3 SECTION II—CONDITIONS

A homeowners insurance policy contains various sections describing what the policy covers and what it doesn't cover and in what amounts. Conditions applicable to Section II and conditions applicable to both Sections I and II provide a framework for the rest of the policy sections by describing the rights and duties of the insured and the insurer in order to maintain the policy in good standing and to facilitate prompt claim settlement.

The Homeowners 3—Special Form (HO-3) policy contains conditions also found in the other forms in the Insurance Services Office, Inc. (ISO) Homeowners program. Conditions applicable to Section II apply to liability coverage, specifically to the policy provisions described in Coverage E— Personal Liability and Coverage F—Medical Payments to Others. Conditions applicable to Sections I and II apply to both property and liability coverage and are related to policy period, cancellation, nonrenewal, and other matters.

Conditions Applicable to Section II

Section II—Conditions establishes the duties and responsibilities of the insurer and the insured. Additional requirements are described for third parties making a claim under Section II. The duties and responsibilities described for the insurer, insured, and third parties include how Section II claims will be handled. HO-3 Section II—Conditions contains ten conditions. See the exhibit "General Functions of Section II Conditions in Homeowners Policy Forms."

Limit of Liability

The Section II Limit of Liability provision stipulates that the limit of Coverage E—Personal Liability appearing on the Declarations page is the total limit of coverage for any one occurrence. This limit does not increase, regardless of the number of insureds, claims made, or people injured.

The Limit of Liability condition also states that all bodily injury and property damage that result from continuous or repeated exposure to the same harmful conditions are considered to be one occurrence. For example, assume the insured's gardener becomes ill over a period of weeks after using an insecticide the insured purchased. Even though the occurrence that caused the injury was not a single event and took place over several months, the injury is considered the result of a single occurrence. Therefore, the insurer is exposed to one limit of liability.

This condition further states that the limit of liability applicable to Coverage F—Medical Payments to Others for all medical expenses for bodily injury to one person as the result of an accident cannot exceed the Coverage F limit shown on the Declarations page. For example, an insured with a $1,000 limit for Coverage F would have $1,000 in coverage available for each guest injured in an accident in the insured's home. The limit can apply to more than one person per accident.

Severability of Insurance

For some occurrences, a claim can involve several insureds. Under the **Severability of Insurance condition**, each insured seeking protection is treated as if he or she has separate coverage under the policy. So the policy will cover a claim brought by one insured against another insured. However, the insurer's limit of liability stated in the policy is not increased for any one occurrence if more than one insured is involved.

Severability of Insurance condition
Policy condition that applies insurance separately to each insured; does not increase the insurer's limit of liability for any one occurrence.

Duties After "Occurrence"

The Duties After "Occurrence" condition describes several requirements the insured must fulfill if an occurrence occurs under Section II. If the insured does not fully perform the required duties following an occurrence and the

General Functions of Section II Conditions in Homeowners Policy Forms

Section II Condition	General Function
Limit of Liability	Describes maximum limitations of and conditions for payment under Coverage E—Personal Liability and Coverage F—Medical Payments to Others.
Severability of Insurance	Stipulates that for any covered occurrence, each insured covered under the policy is treated as if he or she had separate coverage; however, the insurer's limit of liability is not increased, regardless of the number of insureds involved.
Duties After "Occurrence"	Describes requirements an insured must fulfill after an occurrence or else an insurer may deny coverage.
Duties of an Injured Person—Coverage F—Medical Payments to Others	Describes requirements an injured person must fulfill after an occurrence or else an insurer may deny coverage.
Payment of Claim—Coverage F—Medical Payments to Others	Stipulates that if an insurer pays a claim under Coverage F, the payment is not an admission of either the insurer's or insured's liability.
Suit Against Us	Describes the conditions that must be met and terms under which a suit can be filed against the insurer.
Bankruptcy of an Insured	Stipulates that the bankruptcy of an insured does not release the insurer from responsibility under the homeowners policy.
Other Insurance	Stipulates that any limits applicable to a Coverage E occurrence are paid in excess over any collectible insurance unless the other insurance is written specifically as an excess policy.
Policy Period	States that the bodily injury and property damage coverage limits apply only within the policy period covered by the policy.
Concealment or Fraud	Stipulates that Section II coverage is excluded only for an insured who is proven to have made false or fraudulent statements. Innocent insureds not involved in the fraud are not barred from protection.

insurer is therefore hindered in performing its duties, the insurer is not obligated to pay the claim.

Duties after an occurrence include these requirements:

- Give written notice to the insurer as soon as practical.
- Cooperate with the insurer's investigation, settlement, and defense activities.
- Forward legal documents promptly to the insurer.
- Provide claims assistance to the insurer in making a settlement, enforcing any right of contribution against another party, attending hearings and trials, securing and giving evidence, and obtaining the attendance of witnesses.
- Submit evidence for damage to property of others when a claim is made under the additional coverage for damage to property of others; the insured must submit to the insurer a sworn statement of loss and show the damaged property to the insurer.
- Do not make voluntary payment; if the insured does so, it will be at the insured's own expense.

Duties of an Injured Person—Coverage F—Medical Payments to Others

This Section II—Coverage F condition stipulates that if an individual makes a claim for an occurrence under Medical Payments to Others coverage, the injured person must fulfill these requirements:

- Give the insurer written proof of the claim as soon as possible.
- Authorize the insurer to obtain copies of medical reports and records.
- Submit (the injured person) to a physical exam by a doctor chosen by the insurer as often as the insurer requires such examinations.

Note that it is the injured third party, not the insured, who must perform these duties to receive payment under Coverage F.

Payment of Claim—Coverage F—Medical Payments to Others

This Coverage F condition stipulates that the insurer's payment of a Medical Payments to Others claim is not an admission of liability by the insured or the insurer. The purpose of Section II medical payments coverage is to prevent suits or to reduce the possible damages resulting from claims by providing prompt payment for injured parties' medical expenses without the need to determine fault.

Suit Against Us

The Suit Against Us condition states that an insurer cannot be sued under the homeowners policy until certain provisions and terms have been met:

- The insured has met all of its obligations under Section II of the policy.

- The insurer cannot be joined as a party to any action against an insured.

- The obligation of the insured has been determined by a final judgment or agreement signed by the insurer.

Additional Section II Conditions

The Bankruptcy of an Insured condition stipulates that if the insured becomes bankrupt or insolvent, the insurer is still obligated to handle the occurrence as it normally would. The insurer is not relieved of any obligations under the policy by the insured's financial status. The Other Insurance condition causes Section II—Coverage E limits to be paid as excess over any other collectible insurance unless the other insurance is written specifically to provide excess coverage (such as a personal umbrella liability policy).

The Policy Period condition stipulates that coverage applies only to bodily injury and property damage that occurs during the policy period, which is indicated in the Declarations page. The claim may be filed at any time, even after the policy has expired.

The Concealment or Fraud condition excludes coverage only for the insured(s) involved in the concealment or fraud, or those making false statements. Other innocent insureds would not be excluded from liability coverage. Under Section I, concealment or fraud by any insured bars property coverage for all insureds.

Conditions Applicable to Sections I and II

The final section of the HO-3 policy includes seven conditions that apply to both Sections I and II. See the exhibit "General Functions of Sections I and II Conditions in Homeowners Policy Forms ."

Liberalization Clause

The Liberalization Clause specifies how broadened coverage applies to the policy. Only homeowners with the same edition of a policy that is subsequently changed by the insurer are affected by this condition.

As an example of the application of the Liberalization Clause, suppose that in order to attract new customers, an insurer provides replacement cost coverage on contents to all insureds at no additional charge by attaching a personal property replacement cost endorsement to all new and renewal homeowners policies. On the date the additional coverage becomes effective, all existing

General Functions of Sections I and II Conditions in Homeowners Policy Forms

Sections I and II Condition	General Function
Liberalization Clause	Stipulates that when an insurer broadens coverage on new and renewal policies, the current policies of the insurer also receive the broader coverage
Waiver or Change of Policy Provisions	States that an insurer's representative cannot modify the policy and relinquish a right unless the insurer does so in writing
Cancellation	Describes the procedures required for the insured or the insurer to terminate a policy
Nonrenewal	Describes the procedures required for the insurer to not renew a policy
Assignment	States that the insured cannot assign the policy to another party without the written consent of the insurer
Subrogation	Stipulates that an insured can waive all rights of recovery against another party but must do so in writing and before the loss occurs
Death	Stipulates that if the named insured dies, the insurer will cover the decedent's representative as an insured

Includes copyrighted material of Insurance Services Office, Inc., with its permission. Copyright, ISO Properties, Inc., 2010. [DA07788]

homeowners policies issued by the insurer automatically include the additional coverage, even if the insureds are unaware of the change.

Waiver or Change of Policy Provisions

A waiver or change of provision condition states that a **waiver** of a right or change of a policy provision is valid only if the insurer makes it in writing. Despite this condition, courts have permitted use of oral waivers by claims representatives made during the adjustment of a loss and after the written policy was issued, because claims representatives are the insurer's representatives and have **apparent authority** to modify policy conditions. As the insurer's agents, insurance agents with **binding authority** also are authorized to make policy changes through an oral binder that is effective until a written policy change endorsement is produced.

Waiver

The intentional relinquishment of a known right.

Apparent authority

A third party's reasonable belief that an agent has authority to act on the principal's behalf.

Binding authority

An insurance agent's authority to effect coverage on behalf of the insurer.

Cancellation

The Cancellation condition specifies the requirements for a valid termination of the policy by either the insured or the insurer. It states that the policyholder may cancel the policy at any time by returning it to the insurer or by contacting the insurer in writing and advising the insurer of the date when cancellation is to take effect. The insurer, conversely, can cancel the policy only for certain stated reasons (determined by state regulation) by delivering a written notice of cancellation to the insured within the stipulated number of days (also determined by state regulation).

Nonrenewal

The insurer has the right to decide not to renew a policy when it expires. The Nonrenewal condition requires the insurer to provide at least thirty days' written notice to the insured if it does not plan to renew the policy. Some states require a longer period of notification. The nonrenewal notice is mailed to the address on the declarations. This constitutes sufficient proof that the insurer mailed the notice, even if the insured does not receive it.

Assignment

An insurance policy is a personal contract between the insurer and the policyholder. Therefore, the insurer must be able to choose whom it will insure. The Assignment condition states that any assignment of the policy without the insurer's written consent is invalid.

Subrogation

Subrogation refers to the insurer's right to recover its claim payment to an insured from the party responsible for the loss. Under the Subrogation condition, the insured can waive all rights to recovery against any person, provided the waiver is in writing and is made before a loss. Tenants, for example, often sign lease agreements that waive their rights against landlords for loss caused by the landlord. In the absence of any pre-loss waiver, an insurer can require the insured to assign all rights of recovery against another person to the insurer to the extent of the insurer's payment of a loss.

Death

The Death condition stipulates that if the named insured or his or her spouse should die, the insurer agrees to cover the decedent's legal representative (usually the executor or administrator of the estate) as an insured, but only to the extent that the decedent had an interest in the property covered in the policy. The term "insured" also includes resident relatives and custodians of the deceased's property as identified in the Death condition.

COVERAGE VARIATIONS IN ISO HOMEOWNERS FORMS

The homeowners insurance program developed by Insurance Services Office, Inc. (ISO) includes five coverage forms in addition to the widely used HO-3 form. To meet customers' needs and preferences, an insurance professional must understand the differences between these forms.

The ISO homeowners insurance program includes six coverage forms:

- Homeowners 2—Broad Form, or HO-2
- Homeowners 3—Special Form, or HO-3
- Homeowners 4—Contents Broad Form, or HO-4
- Homeowners 5—Comprehensive Form, or HO-5
- Homeowners 6—Unit-Owners Form, or HO-6
- Homeowners 8—Modified Coverage Form, or HO-8

While HO-3 is the most widely used, the other forms address different coverage needs or preferences:

- Apartment dwellers and condominium unit owners do not need full insurance on the buildings in which they live.
- Some customers will accept more restricted coverage than the HO-3 provides in exchange for lower premiums.
- Some customers are willing to pay for broader coverage than the HO-3 provides.
- Some older homes that have depreciated substantially are not well-suited for the replacement cost coverage provided by the HO-3.

An ISO homeowners form exists to address each of these situations. The primary differences between the HO-3 form and the other homeowners forms are in each form's Section I—Property Coverages. The Agreement, Section II—Liability Coverages, and Section II—Conditions are identical in all ISO homeowners forms. See the exhibit "Homeowners Forms Comparison."

HO-2 Broad Form Compared With HO-3

Like the HO-3, the HO-2 is designed for the owner-occupant of a house. An HO-2 has a slightly lower premium than an HO-3, while covering the same property for the same limits. The lower premium results from the fact that the HO-2 covers the dwelling and other structures against fewer causes of loss.

The HO-3 provides open perils coverage (also known as special form coverage) for Coverage A—Dwelling and Coverage B—Other Structures and provides named perils coverage for Coverage C—Personal Property. In contrast, the HO-2 provides named perils coverage for Coverages A, B, and C. In

Homeowners Forms Comparison

Form	Used for Insuring	Coverage A— Dwelling	Coverage B— Other Structures	Coverage C— Personal Property	Section II— Liability Coverages
HO-2 Broad Form	Owner-occupied dwellings	Named perils	Named perils	Named perils	Same in all forms
HO-3 Special Form	Owner-occupied dwellings	Open perils	Open perils	Named perils	Same in all forms
HO-4 Contents Broad Form	Tenants in residential buildings	N/A	N/A	Named perils	Same in all forms
HO-5 Comprehensive Form	Owner-occupied dwellings	Open perils	Open perils	Open perils	Same in all forms
HO-6 Unit-Owners Form	Owners of condominium or cooperative units	Named perils	N/A Included in Coverage A	Named perils	Same in all forms
HO-8 Modified Coverage Form	Owner-occupied dwellings	Modified named perils	Modified named perils	Modified named perils	Same in all forms

[DA09181]

both forms, Coverage D—Loss of Use is triggered by any loss covered under Coverage A, B, or C that makes the building unusable.

In addition to insuring against more causes of loss than named perils coverage, open perils coverage has another advantage, which involves the burden of proof:

- With named perils coverage, such as the HO-2, the insured must prove the loss was caused by a covered cause of loss for coverage to apply. The burden of proof is on the insured.

- With open perils coverage, if a loss to covered property occurs, the initial assumption is that it is covered. To deny coverage, the insurer must prove the loss was caused by an excluded cause of loss. In this case, the burden of proof is on the insurer.

By shifting the burden of proof, open perils coverage can provide an important advantage to an insured who suffers a property loss as a result of an unknown cause.

The list of named perils in the HO-2 encompasses most common insurable perils faced by homeowners. It closely resembles the list of named perils applicable to Coverage C in the HO-3 with a few minor differences. These are two examples:

- The vehicles peril is found in both policies, but the HO-2 policy has an exclusion for loss to a fence, driveway, or walk caused by a vehicle owned or operated by a resident of the premises.

- For accidental discharge or overflow of water or steam, the HO-2 excludes coverage if the building is vacant for more than sixty consecutive days. The HO-3 does not mention vacancy under this peril.

HO-4 Contents Broad Form Compared With HO-3

The HO-4 is designed specifically for people who live in rented houses or apartments. The HO-4 is essentially the same as an HO-3 without Coverages A and B. The HO-4 differs from the HO-3 in other ways, including these:

- HO-4 Coverage C is written at a limit the insured selects as adequate to cover personal property. In the HO-3, HO-2, and HO-5, the Coverage C limit is typically 50 percent of the Coverage A limit.

- Coverage D in the HO-4 is provided automatically at 30 percent of the Coverage C limit, rather than as 30 percent of the Coverage A limit, as in the HO-2 and HO-3.

- The HO-4 provides an additional coverage for building additions and alterations, with a limit equal to 10 percent of the Coverage C limit.

- The HO-4 does not include an additional coverage for furnishings provided by a landlord, because the occupant-insured of the apartment does not have an insurable interest in such property.

- Both the HO-3 and the HO-4 provide an additional coverage for increased costs imposed by a building ordinance or law. The HO-3 limit is 10 percent of the Coverage A limit, while the HO-4 limit is 10 percent of the building additions and alterations limit.
- Trees, shrubs, and other plants are covered for 10 percent of the Coverage C limit in the HO-4 policy, while the HO-3 provides coverage for up to 5 percent of the Coverage A limit.

HO-5 Comprehensive Form Compared With HO-3

The HO-5 provides the broadest property coverage of any ISO homeowners form. The HO-5 is essentially an HO-3 modified to provide open perils coverage, not only for the dwelling and other structures, but also for Coverage C—Personal Property.

The HO-5 broadens personal property coverage in some areas simply by not excluding an exposure that has been excluded by the HO-3 policy:

- The HO-5 covers water damage, including flood damage, for personal property away from a location owned, rented, occupied, or controlled by an insured.
- The HO-5 covers personal property damaged by rain through an open window, door, or roof opening, even if the building itself is not damaged.

The HO-5 special limits of $1,500 for jewelry and furs, $2,500 for firearms, and $2,500 for silverware apply not only to items that are stolen, but also to items that are misplaced or lost. The HO-3 does not cover, for any amount, items that are misplaced or lost.

HO-6 Unit-Owners Form Compared With HO-3

Condominium

A real estate development consisting of a group of units, in which the air space within the boundaries of each unit is owned by the unit owner, and all remaining real and personal property is owned jointly by all the unit owners.

Cooperative corporation

A form of real property ownership in which the real property is owned by a corporation whose shareholders are the tenants of the property.

The HO-6 is closely related to the HO-4. This form is tailored to cover the exposures faced by unit owners in a **condominium** or a **cooperative corporation**. The HO-6 provides coverage for unit owners' property and liability exposures. It differs from the HO-3 in these ways:

- The HO-6 defines residence premises as the unit where the insured resides. The HO-3 definition includes a one- to four-family dwelling where the insured resides.
- The HO-6 description of Coverage A—Dwelling under Section I—Property Coverages includes: (1) alterations, appliances, fixtures, and improvements that are part of the building contained within the insured unit; (2) items of real property that pertain exclusively to the insured unit; (3) property that is the unit owner's responsibility under a condominium or cooperative association's property owners' agreement; and (4) structures owned solely by the insured at the residence location (such as a storage shed or garage).

- Coverage A—Dwelling in the HO-6 provides a basic limit of $5,000, which can be increased if needed.

- Coverage B—Other Structures coverage is eliminated from the HO-6 because Coverage A of the HO-6 includes other structures owned solely by the insured.

- Coverage C—Personal Property is subject to a limit the insured selects.

- Coverage D—Loss of Use is provided automatically at a limit that is 50 percent of the Coverage C limit, rather than 30 percent of the Coverage A limit.

- Section I—Perils Insured Against in the HO-6 provides named perils coverage for Coverages A and C, similar to the coverage provided in the HO-2.

- Loss Assessments coverage is identical in the HO-3 and the HO-6, although it is more applicable to a condominium or cooperative corporation than a private dwelling. Condominiums and cooperatives have many elements, such as driveways, outdoor lighting, and swimming pools, that belong to all unit owners collectively. Damage to any of these commonly owned elements could result in an assessment against each individual unit owner.

- Trees, shrubs, and other plants are covered for up to 10 percent of the Coverage C limit, in contrast to the HO-3 limit of 5 percent of the Coverage A limit. In the HO-6, this coverage applies to plants solely owned by the named insured on grounds at the insured unit (such as those in the yard of a townhouse-style condominium).

- The additional coverage for landlord's furnishings is not included in the HO-6 policy.

- In the HO-6 policy, coverage for debris removal does not cover the cost to remove trees that damage a covered structure or block a driveway or ramp. This cost would be the condominium corporation's responsibility.

HO-8 Modified Coverage Form Compared With HO-3

The HO-8 is designed for use when the replacement cost of an owner-occupied dwelling significantly exceeds its market value.

An example of a dwelling that might be covered under the HO-8 is an older house with obsolete construction or features that would be expensive to replace, such as hand-carved wooden moldings. Such a house could have a market value of $100,000, but the cost to rebuild might be $200,000. A homeowner may be unwilling to pay the high premium necessary to buy $200,000 of insurance on a house purchased for $100,000. In addition, the homeowner could receive more money by collecting the insurance proceeds than by selling the house, which creates an obvious moral hazard. As a result, many insurers are unwilling to write an HO-3 on such a house.

The HO-8 provision addresses this problem under Section I—Conditions. A provision in this section specifies that if the insured makes repairs after a loss, the insurer will not pay more than the cost of "common construction materials and methods" that are "functionally equivalent to and less costly than obsolete, antique, or custom construction."

The HO-8 policy covers only ten named perils, and it limits or eliminates other coverages found in the HO-3 policy. The additional coverages for collapse, landlord's furnishings, ordinance or law, and grave markers are not included in the HO-8 policy. The HO-8 policy provides limited coverage for property not on the insured premises. There are no special limits for jewelry, firearms, silverware, and similar items because the theft peril provides coverage only up to $1,000.

These are other limitations in an HO-8 policy:

- Smoke from a fireplace is an exclusion in the HO-8 that is not found in the HO-3.
- Glass or safety glazing material is limited to $100.
- Under debris removal coverage, the amount available is included in the policy limit with no additional insurance available if the policy limit is exhausted. The HO-3 provides for an additional 5 percent if policy limits are exhausted.
- Windstorm is the only peril covered for trees, shrubs, and plants and only up to a limit of $250 per item ($500 in the HO-3). The occurrence limit is the same as the limit in the HO-3 policy, which is 5 percent of the dwelling limit.
- There is no coverage for personal property owned by a guest or residence employee while the property is in any residence occupied by an insured.
- The theft peril provides off-premises coverage limited to property in banks, trust companies, self-storage facilities, and similar locations.

DETERMINING WHETHER HOMEOWNERS SECTION II—LIABILITY COVERAGES COVERS A CLAIM

Section II—Liability Coverages of any homeowners policy provides coverage for liability exposures arising from the ownership and use of the covered property and from personal activities. The application of coverage depends on the circumstances of the loss.

Knowing how to apply the liability coverages of a homeowners policy to the facts of a case is an important skill. This case study will help you make the transition from knowing policy language to determining whether policy language provides coverage for specific claims. As you progress through this case study, you can check your understanding of the coverage provided by answering the Knowledge to Action questions.

Case Facts

Sally and Jeff live in a single-family home with their five-year-old son, Matthew. Sally and Jeff maintain a homeowners policy covering their home. They do not maintain an umbrella policy or any concurrent policies.

Sally and Jeff's neighborhood regularly gathers to celebrate the Fourth of July. This year, Sally and Jeff agreed to host dinner. Their neighbor, Jean, agreed to provide dessert and host the fireworks display. On July 3, Jeff had dental surgery. Despite being under the influence of prescribed narcotics on July 4, Jeff prepared, grilled, and served hamburger patties to ten of his neighbors.

After dinner, the party moved to Jean's house. Matthew rode his battery-powered toy truck, specifically designed for children under the age of seven. The vehicle's top speed is four mph. While Matthew was driving his truck around the adults on Jean's patio, Linda, a guest, stepped backward into his path. Matthew hit Linda with his truck, causing her to lose her balance and fall against Jean's kitchen window. The window glass broke and cut Linda's hand. The party quickly ended, as Linda had to go to the emergency room for medical attention.

In the weeks following, Sally and Jeff received notice of several claims:

Claim 1: Six dinner guests became seriously ill several hours after the party. The guests allege that Jeff served them contaminated meat and that the contamination resulted from Jeff's negligent preparation. Based on a review of hamburger-meat recalls and illnesses reported by the United States Food and Drug Administration, there is no indication that the meat was contaminated before Jeff handled it. The six individuals collectively hire an attorney and file suit against Jeff, seeking compensation for medical expenses, lost wages, pain, and suffering. They demand $180,000, or $30,000 per individual.

Claim 2: Linda seeks reimbursement for $5,250 in medical expenses, including stitches and pain medication. Linda recovered without complication and foresees no additional treatment. Linda realizes it is not feasible to sue a five-year-old for negligence. To preserve her relationship with her neighbors, she does not want to file suit against Sally and Jeff for negligent parental supervision of Matthew.

Claim 3: Jean, citing Matthew's actions, demands reimbursement from Sally and Jeff for replacement of her kitchen window. The replacement cost was $200.

To meet their duty following a loss, Sally and Jeff provide prompt written notice to their insurer of the three claims and cooperate in the investigation. To confirm that the facts of these incidents are accurate, Sally and Jeff's insurer relies on recorded statements from claimants and witnesses, medical records, and inspections of the premises where the loss occurred. For the first claim, the insurer assumes Jeff's defense in the bodily injury liability lawsuit. For Linda's injury, the insurer helps her file a claim under Sally and Jeff's Medical Payments coverage. For Jean's window damage, the insurer opens a liability claim for Damage to Property of Others.

Given the facts presented in the case, will Section II—Liability Coverages of the homeowners policy cover the three claims? If so, what amount will the insurer pay for each claim? When answering the questions in this case-based activity, consider only the information provided as part of this case. See the exhibit "Case Facts."

Case Facts

Insureds	Sally and Jeff Jones
Types of policies and coverage limits	E—Personal Liability—$500,000 Each Occurrence
	F—Medical Payments to Others—$5,000 Each Person
Endorsements that affect the case	None
Other policy information	No other relevant information
Background	The insureds have complied with the policy conditions.

[DA00330]

Necessary Reference Materials

To determine whether Sally and Jeff's homeowners policy provides coverage for the three claims, you should have copies of the policy form, which is available in the *The Institutes' Handbook of Insurance Policies*; any applicable endorsements indicated on the Declarations page of the policy; and the Declarations page itself. See the exhibit "Excerpt of Homeowners Policy Declarations."

Overview of Steps

To determine whether the losses are covered and the amount the insurer would pay, you can apply the four steps of the DICE method, which stands for Declarations, Insuring Agreement, Conditions, and Exclusions. This involves analyzing the policy declarations, insuring agreement, conditions, and exclusions to determine whether any information found at each step precludes coverage at the time of the losses. Next, you determine the amounts payable for the losses by analyzing the limits of insurance.

Excerpt of Homeowners Policy Declarations

Homeowners Policy Declarations

POLICYHOLDER (Named Insured) Jeff and Sally Jones
2 Oak Lane
Anytown, USA 12345

POLICY NUMBER: 456-7890

POLICY PERIOD Inception: **January 7, 20X1**

Expiration: **January 7, 20X2**

Policy period begins 12:01 A.M. standard time at the residence premises.

We will provide the insurance described in this policy in return for the premium and compliance with all applicable policy provisions.

SECTION II COVERAGES	LIMIT
E—Personal Liability	$500,000 **Each Occurrence**
F—Medical Payments to Others	$ 5,000 **Each Person**

Copyright, ISO Properties, Inc. [DA07789]

Determination of Coverage

Apply the DICE method to the case facts for each of the three losses.

DICE Analysis Step 1: Declarations

The first step in the DICE method is to review the Declarations page to determine whether the individuals are covered and whether the incidents occurred during the policy period. In this case, the policy lists Jeff and Sally as named insureds, and the party occurred during the policy period.

DICE Analysis Step 2: Insuring Agreement

The second DICE step is to determine whether each event triggers coverage under an insuring agreement.

Knowledge to Action

Action Task: Refer to the policy to review the Coverage E and Coverage F insuring agreements and the definition of "insured," which is used in both agreements.

In Claim 3, Jean demands reimbursement from Sally and Jeff for the replacement of her kitchen window, citing the actions of their minor child, Matthew.

Under Sally and Jeff's homeowners policy, who fits the policy definition of insured?

a. Only Jeff

b. Only Jeff and Sally

c. Jeff, Sally, and Matthew

d. Only Sally

Feedback: c. The insureds that are defined in the policy as "you" are the named insureds as shown in the declarations, in this case Jeff and Sally. The policy definition of "insured" also includes residents of the named insureds' household who are their relatives. Therefore, their son, Matthew, also qualifies as an insured.

Claim 1: Coverage E—Personal Liability provides coverage if a claim is made or a suit is brought against an insured for bodily injury or property damage. Illness caused by contaminated food meets the definition of bodily injury. The resulting lawsuit against Jeff is sufficient to trigger coverage under Section II.

Claim 2: With respect to Linda's injuries, Coverage F—Medical Payments to Others covers medical expenses incurred within three years of the date of an accident. The coverage also applies to a person who is off the insured location and whose bodily injury is caused by the activities of an insured. Because Matthew's driving of the toy truck on Jean's patio caused the injury, Linda can seek coverage under Coverage F.

Claim 3: The damage to Jean's window is covered under Section II—Additional Coverages, which includes Damage to Property of Others caused by an insured. This coverage does not include damage caused intentionally by an insured age thirteen or older. However, the damage was not intentional, and Matthew is only five years old. The property also is not owned by the insured or a tenant of the insured. Therefore, the coverage applies.

DICE Analysis Step 3: Conditions

The third DICE step is to determine whether all policy conditions have been met. Sally and Jeff followed policy conditions outlining their duties after an occurrence, including providing written notice to the insurer as soon as practical and cooperating in the investigation and defense of any claim or suit.

Knowledge to Action

Action Task: Refer to the policy and review Section II—Conditions.

Linda may have to comply with which of the following conditions to be paid for her injuries? Select all answers that are correct:

a. Provide the insurer with written proof of loss
b. Authorize the insurer to obtain copies of any medical reports
c. Submit to a physical exam if requested by the insurer
d. Provide the insurer with the opportunity to direct care

Feedback: a, b, and c. In Section II—Conditions, Duties of an Injured Person—Coverage F—Medical Payments to Others, the injured person may be required to perform each of these tasks to be paid.

DICE Analysis Step 4: Exclusions

The fourth DICE step is to determine whether one or more exclusions preclude coverage the insuring agreements have granted.

Knowledge to Action

Action Task: Refer to the policy and review Section II—Exclusions.

Does the Controlled Substances exclusion apply to the neighbors' claim against Jeff, given that he was under the influence of prescribed narcotics on July 4?

Feedback: No. The Controlled Substances exclusion eliminates coverage for bodily injury or property damage arising out of a person's use of a controlled substance. However, the exclusion contains an exception for the use of prescription drugs at the direction of a licensed medical provider. Therefore, the exclusion does not apply to this case.

Determination of Amounts Payable

Now that you have completed the DICE analysis, you can determine the amounts payable. This involves analyzing the limits of insurance available to pay for the loss.

Claim 1: At the direction of the insurer, defense counsel successfully negotiates a settlement with the plaintiffs through their attorney. The agreed settlement is $120,000 in total, apportioned as $20,000 to each of the six guests who became ill. Because Sally and Jeff's policy has a limit of $500,000 for each occurrence under Coverage E, the full $120,000 is covered.

Claim 2: Linda's final medical bills totaled $5,250. Because the limit for Coverage F under Sally and Jeff's policy is $5,000 per person, Linda's recovery would be limited to $5,000. That means $250 of the submitted medical bills would not be covered.

Claim 3: The Additional Coverage for Damage to Property of Others in Section II of the policy provides limits of up to $1,000 per occurrence. Therefore, the $200 cost to replace the glass in Jean's kitchen window would be fully covered. See the exhibit "Determination of Amounts Payable."

Determination of Amounts Payable

Claim	Coverage Available	Amount Payable
Guests who became ill	Coverage E—$500,000	$120,000
Linda's claim for medical expenses	Coverage F—$5,000	$5,000
Replace the broken glass in neighbor's kitchen window	Additional Coverage for Property of Others—$1,000	$200

[DA07790]

SUMMARY

The HO-3's Section II—Liability Coverages is designed to meet the common liability loss exposure needs of individuals and families. Section II includes two of the primary coverages listed in the homeowners policy declarations: Personal Liability and Medical Payments to Others. Section II also contains some additional coverages that apply to first aid expenses and damage to property of others, as well as other incidental personal loss exposures.

Section II—Exclusions of the HO-3 contains twenty-two exclusions, some of which apply to Section II and some of which apply to Coverage E or Coverage F. Because of how some of the exclusion provisions are worded, limited coverage may, in fact, be provided by a specific provision. Therefore, exclusion provisions should be carefully considered with the rest of the Section II terms and conditions to determine the full scope of personal liability coverage.

These are the ten conditions that apply to Section II of the HO-3 and establish the duties and responsibilities of the insured, the insurer, and third-party claimants in a liability claim: Limit of Liability, Severability of Insurance, Duties After "Occurrence," Duties of an Injured Person—Coverage F—Medical Payments to Others, Payment of Claim—Coverage F—Medical Payments to Others, Suit Against Us, Bankruptcy of an Insured, Other Insurance, Policy Period, and Concealment or Fraud. These seven conditions apply to both Sections I and II of the HO-3: Liberalization Clause, Waiver or Change of Policy Provisions, Cancellation, Nonrenewal, Assignment, Subrogation, and Death.

In addition to form HO-3, the ISO homeowners program includes five forms—HO-2 (Broad Form), HO-4 (Contents Broad Form), HO-5 (Comprehensive Form), HO-6 (Unit-Owners Form), and HO-8 (Modified Coverage Form)—that meet coverage needs or preferences that the HO-3 does not address.

The DICE method can be used to determine whether, and for what amount, a claim is covered under Section II—Liability Coverages of a homeowners policy.

7

Using Homeowners Endorsements to Meet Individual Needs

Educational Objectives

After learning the content of this assignment, you should be able to:

▷ For each of the homeowners policy endorsements for modifying limits and adding special deductibles, explain when each endorsement is needed or used and how the endorsement modifies the homeowners form to which it is attached.

▷ For each of the homeowners policy endorsements for modifying the perils insured against, explain when each endorsement is needed or used and how the endorsement modifies the homeowners form to which it is attached.

▷ For each of the homeowners policy endorsements for modifying property valuation provisions, explain when each endorsement is needed or used and how the endorsement modifies the homeowners form to which it is attached.

▷ For each of the homeowners policy endorsements for insuring business exposures, explain when each endorsement is needed or used and how the endorsement modifies the homeowners form to which it is attached.

▷ For each of the homeowners policy endorsements for insuring rental exposures, explain when each endorsement is needed or used and how the endorsement modifies the homeowners form to which it is attached.

▷ For each of the homeowners policy endorsements for addressing miscellaneous exposures, explain when each endorsement is needed or used and how the endorsement modifies the homeowners form to which it is attached.

▷ Given a description of an individual's or a family's loss exposures, recommend an appropriate homeowners form and endorsements for covering those exposures.

Using Homeowners Endorsements to Meet Individual Needs

7

HOMEOWNERS ENDORSEMENTS FOR MODIFYING LIMITS AND ADDING SPECIAL DEDUCTIBLES

Understanding which endorsements are available to modify limits and add special deductibles will allow an insurance professional to address many of the unique needs presented by individual insureds and insurers.

Several endorsements can be used to modify limits or add special deductibles within a homeowners policy. For example, if Fred wants to keep $1,000 cash in his home for unforeseen emergencies, the $200 special limit on money may be raised to $1,000 with the Coverage C Increased Special Limits of Liability endorsement (HO 04 65). If Fred has personal property valued at $20,000 at a self-storage facility, but his homeowners policy provides only $10,000 coverage for such property (calculated as 10 percent of Fred's $100,000 Coverage C limit), he could use the Increased Amount of Insurance for Personal Property Located in a Self-Storage Facility endorsement (HO 06 14) to increase the limit on his stored property to $20,000. If an insurer is struggling to remain financially solvent after a hurricane struck the northeast coast of the United States, it may require all future homeowners policies sold in the area to be written with a separate special deductible for losses caused by windstorm or hail during a hurricane by using the Hurricane Deductible endorsement (HO 03 18).

The homeowners endorsements that modify limits and add special deductibles include these:

- Additional Limits of Liability for Coverages A, B, C and D (HO 04 11)
- Increased Limits on Business Property (HO 04 12)
- Specified Additional Amount of Insurance for Coverage A—Dwelling (HO 04 20)
- Inflation Guard (HO 04 46)
- Other Structures on the Residence Premises—Increased Limit (HO 04 48)
- Personal Property at Other Residences (HO 04 50)
- Credit Card, Electronic Fund Transfer Card or Access Device, Forgery and Counterfeit Money Coverage (HO 04 53)
- Scheduled Personal Property Endorsement (HO 04 61)
- Coverage C Increased Special Limits of Liability (HO 04 65)
- Ordinance or Law Increased Amount of Coverage (HO 04 77)
- Increased Amount of Insurance for Personal Property Located in a Self-Storage Facility (HO 06 14)
- Windstorm or Hail Percentage Deductible (HO 03 12)
- Hurricane Deductible (HO 03 18)

Description of Homeowners Endorsements for Modifying Limits and Adding Special Deductibles

ENDORSEMENTS FOR MODIFYING LIMITS

Title and Number	When Needed or Used	How It Modifies the HO Form to Which It Is Attached
Additional Limits of Liability for Coverages A, B, C and D HO 04 11	The insured wants the percentage increase provided by HO 04 20 to apply not only to the Coverage A limit but also to the limits for Coverages B, C, and D.	Increases the Coverage A limit in the same way that HO 04 20 does; in addition, increases the Coverage B, C, and D limits by the same percentage, but only if the Coverage A limit is increased as a result of a Coverage A loss. For example, a loss to personal property alone would not activate an increase in the Coverage C limit.
Increased Limits on Business Property HO 04 12	The insured keeps business property on the residence premises that exceeds the special limit in category h., and the insured wants such property to be covered for a higher limit.	Increases the special limit applicable to category h. to the total limit shown in the schedule. In addition, the category i. limit that applies to business property away from the residence premises is increased to an amount that is 60 percent of the total limit shown in the schedule.
Specified Additional Amount of Insurance for Coverage A—Dwelling HO 04 20	The insured wants to be able to collect an amount of insurance in addition to the Coverage A limit for a loss to the dwelling. This might be especially desirable for dwellings located in areas that are susceptible to loss by hurricane or other catastrophes, because increased demand for labor and materials following a catastrophe can result in escalation of repair or replacement costs.	Enables the insured to collect an additional amount of insurance equal to the Coverage A limit multiplied by the percentage shown in the schedule, subject to these conditions: • The insured must have allowed the insurer to adjust the Coverage A limit in accordance with the insurer's property evaluations and increases in inflation • The insured must have notified the insurer, within 30 days of completion, of any improvements that increase the building's replacement cost by 5 percent or more.
Inflation Guard HO 04 46	To automatically increase the limits for Coverages A, B, C, and D for inflation.	The limits for Coverages A, B, C, and D are automatically increased annually by the percentage amount shown in the schedule and applied pro rata during the policy period.
Other Structures on the Residence Premises—Increased Limits HO 04 48	The insured has, on the residence premises, one or more "other structures" whose value exceeds the Coverage B limit (which is ordinarily 10 percent of the Coverage A limit). For example, the insured has a home valued at $350,000 and a detached four-car garage with an upstairs apartment, valued at $100,000. The Coverage B limit is only $35,000, so an additional $65,000 is needed.	Each structure on the residence premises that is described in the schedule is covered for the limit shown in the schedule for that structure. The limit shown in the schedule is payable in addition to the Coverage B limit. Thus, the limit shown in the schedule should reflect the amount that is needed in addition to the Coverage B limit to provide adequate coverage on the structure(s) shown in the schedule.
Personal Property at Other Residences HO 04 50	The insured has personal property usually located in a residence other than the residence premises and the value of this property exceeds 10 percent of the Coverage C limit or $1,000, whichever is greater.	For each location shown in the schedule, increases the Coverage C limit, as shown, for personal property usually located at that location.
Credit Card, Electronic Fund Transfer Card or Access Device, Forgery and Counterfeit Money Coverage HO 04 53	The insured wants to increase the $500 limit applicable to this additional coverage.	Increases the limit for this additional coverage as shown in the schedule.

Title and Number	When Needed or Used	How It Modifies the HO Form to Which It Is Attached
Scheduled Personal Property Endorsement HO 04 61	The insured wants to insure jewelry, furs, cameras, musical instruments, silverware, golf equipment, fine arts, stamp collections, or coin collections for adequate limits that are separate from the Coverage C limit and not subject to the Coverage C special limits.	The schedule shows an amount of insurance for each category or item of property listed. In addition, additional limitations apply to some classes of property. For example, when coins or stamps are covered on a blanket basis, the insurer will pay no more than $1,000 on any unscheduled coin collection nor more than $250 for any one stamp or coin. Also, coverage for jewelry, furs, cameras, or musical instruments acquired after policy inception is limited to 25 percent of the amount of insurance for that class or $10,000, whichever is less.
Coverage C Increased Special Limits of Liability HO 04 65	The insured has property of a type that is listed in category a, b, e, f, g, or j of the special limits applicable to Coverage C, and the value of the property exceeds the special limit.	Allows any of the special limits applicable to categories a, b, e, f, g, or j to be increased to an amount that meets the insured's needs, subject to the limits the insurer is willing to extend.
Ordinance or Law Increased Amount of Coverage HO 04 77	The insured wants to increase the amount that will be collectible under this Additional Coverage.	Increases the limit for the Ordinance or Law additional coverage from 10% of the Coverage A limit to the percentage shown in the schedule.
Increased Amount of Insurance for Personal Property Located in a Self-Storage Facility HO 06 14	The insured has property in a self-storage facility and the value of the property exceeds 10 percent of the Coverage C limit or $1,000, whichever is greater.	Increases the limit for property in a self-storage facility to the amount shown in the schedule.

ENDORSEMENTS FOR ADDING SPECIAL DEDUCTIBLES

Title and Number	When Needed or Used	How It Modifies the HO Form to Which It Is Attached
Windstorm or Hail Percentage Deductible HO 03 12	To apply a percentage deductible to the peril of windstorm or hail. In contrast with a flat deductible, a percentage deductible increases in proportion to the dollar amount of the loss. This approach makes it more feasible for insurers to accept properties in areas that have catastrophic wind or hail potential.	The deductible applicable to any one loss caused by windstorm or hail is the Coverage A limit times the deductible percentage amount shown in the schedule. Under ISO filed rules, the available percentages are 1, 2, 5, 7.5, and 10 percent.
Hurricane Deductible HO 03 18	To apply either a flat deductible or a percentage deductible to loss caused by windstorm or hail during a hurricane.	The deductible shown in the schedule can be either a stated dollar amount or a stated percentage of the Coverage A limit. This deductible applies only to loss caused by windstorm or hail during the period that begins when a hurricane watch or warning is issued or declared for any part of the insured's state (or the District of Columbia, Puerto Rico, Guam, or U.S. Virgin Islands) by the National Hurricane Center of the National Weather Service and ends 24 hours following the termination of the last hurricane watch or warning for any part of the state.

HOMEOWNERS ENDORSEMENTS FOR MODIFYING PERILS INSURED AGAINST

Some insureds need more coverage for certain perils than is provided by an unendorsed homeowners policy. To meet such needs, an insurance professional must know which coverages can be modified by endorsement.

Insureds can choose among multiple endorsements to increase their homeowners coverage for select perils. For example, if Charlie is concerned that his aging shower pan may develop a crack that results in wet rot and mold damage, the insurer can add the Limited Fungi, Wet or Dry Rot, or Bacteria Coverage endorsement (HO 04 27) to Charlie's HO-3 policy. If Charlie is concerned about identity theft after a co-worker described the expenses she incurred when someone stole her identity, the Identity Fraud Expense Coverage endorsement (HO 04 55) could be added. If floods occur in Charlie's neighborhood but not in his house, which is on a hill, he may still be concerned that water could back up through his sewer or drains. The Limited Water Back-Up and Sump Discharge or Overflow Coverage endorsement (HO 04 95) could be added to cover the water damage.

The homeowners endorsements that modify perils insured against include these:

- Special Computer Coverage (HO 04 14)
- Limited Fungi, Wet or Dry Rot, or Bacteria Coverage (HO 04 26, HO 04 27, or HO 04 28)
- Loss Assessment Coverage for Earthquake (HO 04 36)
- Earthquake (HO 04 54)
- Identity Fraud Expense Coverage (HO 04 55)
- Scheduled Personal Property Endorsement (HO 04 61)
- Limited Water Back-Up and Sump Discharge or Overflow Coverage (HO 04 95)
- Refrigerated Property Coverage (HO 04 98)
- Sinkhole Collapse (HO 04 99)
- Special Personal Property Coverage (HO 05 24)
- Unit-Owners Coverage C Special Coverage (HO 17 31)
- Unit-Owners Coverage A Special Coverage (HO 17 32)

Description of Homeowners Endorsements for Modifying Perils Insured Against

Title and Number	When Needed or Used	How It Modifies the HO Form to Which It Is Attached
Special Computer Coverage HO 04 14	The insured wants to insure computer equipment on an open perils basis. This endorsement is used only when the insured does not already have open perils coverage on personal property.	Covers computer hardware, software, operating systems, networks, and peripherals on an open perils basis. The endorsement does not increase the Coverage C limit, modify the Coverage C special limits, or modify the Coverage C Property Not Covered provisions.
Limited Fungi, Wet or Dry Rot, or Bacteria Coverage HO 04 26 HO 04 27 HO 04 28	To provide limited amounts of coverage for property and liability claims resulting from fungi, wet or dry rot, or bacteria. • HO 04 26 is used with HO-2, HO-4, and HO-6. • HO 04 27 is used with HO-3 and HO-5. • HO 04 28 is used with HO-4 and HO-6 if they have been endorsed to provide open perils coverage.	• Modifies Section I—Property Coverages to cover loss to covered real or personal property damaged by fungi, wet or dry rot, or bacteria on the residence premises. Under ISO rules, the basic limit of $10,000, which applies on an aggregate basis, can be increased to $25,000 or $50,000. • Modifies Section II—Liability Coverages to pay damages because of bodily injury or property damage involving the inhalation of, ingestion of, contact with, exposure to, existence of, or presence of any fungi, wet or dry rot, or bacteria. Under ISO rules, the basic limit of $50,000, which applies on an aggregate basis, can be increased to $100,000.
Loss Assessment Coverage for Earthquake HO 04 36	The insured unit-owner or the condominium association wants the unit-owner's insurance to include coverage for loss assessments for earthquake damage.	Adds earthquake, including land shock waves or tremors before, during, or after a volcanic eruption, as an insured peril for purposes of loss assessment coverage only. Flooding resulting from an earthquake is excluded. The earthquake deductible for any one assessment is determined by multiplying the amount of insurance shown in the schedule by the deductible percentage amount. In no event will the deductible be less than $500.
Earthquake HO 04 54	The insured or the insured's mortgageholder wants the policy to cover earthquake losses.	Adds earthquake, including land shock waves or tremors before, during, or after a volcanic eruption, as an insured peril. An exclusion of exterior masonry veneer applies unless the exclusion is deleted as indicated in the schedule. Flooding resulting from an earthquake is also excluded, as is the cost of filling land. The earthquake deductible is determined by multiplying either the Coverage A or Coverage C limit (whichever is greater) by the deductible percentage amount shown in the schedule. In no event will the deductible be less than $500.
Identity Fraud Expense Coverage HO 04 55	The insured wants to be protected against expenses resulting from identity fraud committed against an insured.	Pays up to $15,000 for any of several specified types of expenses incurred by an insured as the result of identity fraud first discovered during the policy period. Defines identity fraud as "the act of knowingly transferring or using, without lawful authority, a means of identification of an 'insured' with the intent: a. To commit or b. To aid or abet another to commit any unlawful activity that constitutes a violation of federal law or a felony under any applicable state or local law."
Scheduled Personal Property Endorsement HO 04 61	The insured wants open perils coverage on scheduled categories or items of jewelry, furs, cameras, musical instruments, silverware, golf equipment, fine arts, stamp collections, or coin collections.	The scheduled categories or items of eligible property are covered on an open perils basis without several exclusions that normally apply to open perils coverage. For example, breakage of covered property (such as an expensive violin or a camera) is covered without the usual requirement that the breakage must be caused by a specified peril such as fire. However, some additional exclusions apply to fine arts, postage stamps, and coins. For example, fading, creasing, denting, scratching, tearing, or thinning of stamps or coins is excluded.
Limited Water Back-Up and Sump Discharge or Overflow Coverage HO 04 95	The insured wants the policy to cover loss resulting from water that backs up through sewers or drains or is discharged from a sump, sump pump, or related equipment.	Covers direct physical loss, not caused by the negligence of an insured, caused by water or waterborne material that originates from within the dwelling where the named insured resides and backs up through sewers or drains; or is discharged from a sump, sump pump, or related equipment. The mechanical breakdown and water exclusions do not apply to the coverage provided by the endorsement.

Title and Number	When Needed or Used	How It Modifies the HO Form to Which It Is Attached
Refrigerated Property Coverage HO 04 98	The insured wants the policy to cover spoilage of refrigerated property resulting from power outage or mechanical failure of the unit that stores the property.	The insurer will pay that part of a covered loss that exceeds $100, up to a total loss payment of $500. Coverage applies only if the named insured has maintained the refrigeration unit in proper working condition immediately before the loss occurs.
Sinkhole Collapse HO 04 99	The insured or the insured's mortgageholder wants the policy to cover loss caused by sinkhole collapse.	Modifies the Earth Movement exclusion so that it does not apply to sinkhole collapse, which the endorsement defines as physical damage caused by sudden settlement or collapse of the earth supporting the property. "The settlement or collapse must result from subterranean voids created by the action of water on limestone or similar rock formations."
Special Personal Property Coverage HO 05 24	The insured under an HO-4 wants open perils, instead of named perils, coverage on personal property.	Replaces the named perils applicable to Coverage C of the HO-4 with open perils provisions similar to those applicable to Coverages A and B in HO-3.
Unit-Owners Coverage C Special Coverage HO 17 31	The unit-owner is insured under an HO-6 and wants open perils, instead of named perils, coverage on personal property.	Replaces the named perils applicable to Coverage C of the HO-6 with open perils provisions similar to those applicable to Coverages A and B in HO-3.
Unit-Owners Coverage A Special Coverage HO 17 32	The unit-owner is insured under an HO-6 and wants open perils, instead of named perils, coverage on the types of real property (such as alterations, appliances, and fixtures) that are covered by Coverage A of this form.	Replaces the named perils applicable to Coverage A of the HO-6 with open perils provisions similar to those applicable to Coverages A and B in HO-3.

Includes copyrighted material of Insurance Services Office, Inc., with its permission. Copyright, Insurance Services Office, 1999, 2010. [DA09098]

HOMEOWNERS ENDORSEMENTS FOR MODIFYING VALUATION PROVISIONS

To effectively meet the needs of the insured and insurer, an insurance professional must know the options that are available by endorsement when deciding which valuation basis to use for property loss covered by Section I of the homeowners policy.

Several endorsements are available for modifying the regular valuation provisions contained in a homeowners policy. For example, the unendorsed homeowners policy covers fences on an actual cash value basis. If Mike, the insured, wants to be paid enough to buy a new plastic fence in the event his old one is damaged by a covered peril, the Replacement Cost Loss Settlement for Certain Non-Building Structures on the Residence Premises endorsement (HO 04 43) can be added to his homeowners policy. If Mike wants to be paid an agreed amount in the event his golf clubs are stolen, the Scheduled Personal Property Endorsement (With Agreed Value Loss Settlement) endorsement (HO 04 60) can be added. If an insurer has recently paid a large number of claims for hail-damaged roofs and must improve its underwriting results but doesn't want to nonrenew an otherwise-good book of business, it can use the Actual Cash Value Loss Settlement Windstorm or Hail Losses to

Roof Surfacing endorsement (HO 04 93). This endorsement changes the loss settlement on hail-damaged-roof claims from a replacement cost to an actual cash value basis.

All but one of the endorsements discussed in this section modify the valuation basis for one type of property. For example, one endorsement applies to non-building structures, another to personal property, and another to roof surfacing. Knowing which endorsement modifies the valuation basis for which type of property may help in understanding when they should be used.

The homeowners endorsements that modify the basis used in determining how much to pay for a covered property loss include these:

- Replacement Cost Loss Settlement for Certain Non-Building Structures on the Residence Premises (HO 04 43)
- Scheduled Personal Property Endorsement (With Agreed Value Loss Settlement) (HO 04 60)
- Actual Cash Value Loss Settlement (HO 04 81)
- Personal Property Replacement Cost Loss Settlement (HO 04 90)
- Actual Cash Value Loss Settlement Windstorm or Hail Losses to Roof Surfacing (HO 04 93)
- Functional Replacement Cost Loss Settlement (HO 05 30)

Description of Homeowners Endorsements for Modifying Valuation Provisions

Title and Number	When Needed or Used	How It Modifies the HO Form to Which It Is Attached
Replacement Cost Loss Settlement for Certain Non-Building Structures on the Residence Premises HO 04 43	The insured wants to extend replacement cost loss settlement to structures that would otherwise be covered on an actual cash value basis.	Applies replacement cost loss settlement to reinforced masonry walls; metal or fiberglass fences; fences made of plastic or resin materials; non-wooden patios and walks; driveways; and inground or semi-inground swimming pools, therapeutic baths, or hot tubs with walls and floors made of reinforced masonry, cement, metal, or fiberglass.
Scheduled Personal Property Endorsement (With Agreed Value Loss Settlement) HO 04 60	The insured wants scheduled personal property coverage to apply on an agreed value basis instead of on an actual cash value or a replacement cost basis. When property is covered on an agreed value basis, the insurer agrees, in the event of loss, to pay the scheduled value shown for the property.	• Makes the same amendments of the HO policy as the regular Scheduled Personal Property Endorsement, HO 04 61, except for the Loss Settlement condition. • States that the insurer will pay, for each article or property described in the schedule, the full amount shown in the schedule for the article or property. • At the insurer's request, the insured must surrender damaged property to the insurer if the property is not lost or stolen.
Actual Cash Value Loss Settlement HO 04 81	The insured or the insurer (usually the latter) wants to limit loss settlement on all covered property to actual cash value.	Replaces the entire Loss Settlement condition with a statement that covered property losses will be settled at actual cash value at the time of loss, not to exceed the cost to repair or replace.
Personal Property Replacement Cost Loss Settlement HO 04 90	The insured wants to insure personal property on a replacement cost basis instead of on an actual cash value basis.	• Applies replacement cost loss settlement to Coverage C and (if covered by the policy) awnings, outdoor antennas, outdoor equipment, carpeting, and household appliances. • Applies replacement cost loss settlement to the types of property covered by endorsement HO 04 61 if they are separately described and specifically insured in the policy and not subject to agreed value settlement. • Describes these types of property as ineligible for replacement cost coverage and therefore covered at actual cash value: antiques, fine arts, collector's items, articles not in good or workable condition, and outdated items not being used. • Insurer will pay no more than the least of the following amounts: replacement cost at the time of loss without deduction for depreciation; full cost of repair; Coverage C limit; any applicable special limit; or the limit that applies to an item that is separately described and specifically insured.
Actual Cash Value Loss Settlement Windstorm or Hail Losses to Roof Surfacing HO 04 93	To limit loss settlement to actual cash value for windstorm or hail damage to roof surfacing.	Modifies the Section I Loss Settlement conditions so that actual cash value loss settlement will apply to covered damage to roof surfacing caused by windstorm or hail.
Functional Replacement Cost Loss Settlement HO 05 30	The insured wants building loss settlement to be based on the cost to repair or replace using common materials and methods. Owners of old homes often prefer this approach over regular replacement cost loss settlement because the building limit can be set for a lower amount, thus reducing the policy premium to a more affordable level.	• Defines "functional replacement cost" as "the amount it would cost to repair or replace the damaged building with less costly common construction materials and methods which are functionally equivalent to obsolete, antique or custom construction materials and methods used in the original construction of the building." • Changes the usual replacement cost loss settlement provisions to apply on the basis of functional replacement cost.

HOMEOWNERS ENDORSEMENTS FOR INSURING BUSINESS EXPOSURES

A variety of loss exposures arise when an insured conducts business from his or her home. Given how common home businesses are, an insurance professional should know how to meet the needs of insureds and the challenges of insuring such a business with an endorsed homeowners policy.

Multiple endorsements are available to address many of the exposures that arise when an insured conducts a business from his or her residence premises. For example, Nancy, a CPA who operates an accounting firm from her home, leases the office furniture she uses. The lease agreement requires her to insure the furniture, which can be done using the Home Business Insurance Coverage endorsement (HO 07 01). The same endorsement will also provide liability coverage for Nancy if a client were to slip and fall on the premises and seek damages from Nancy. Also, because Nancy is operating an accounting firm, she may want to increase her valuable papers and records coverage from $2,500 to a more adequate amount. This increase can be implemented using the Valuable Papers and Records Coverage Increased Limits endorsement (HO 07 56).

The list of homeowners endorsements that are used for insuring business exposures includes these:

- Home Business Insurance Coverage (HO 07 01)
- Additional Insured—Managers or Lessors of Premises Leased to an Insured (HO 07 50)
- Additional Insured—Vendors (HO 07 51)
- Loss Payable Provisions (HO 07 52)
- Exclusion—Personal and Advertising Injury (HO 07 53)
- Liquor Liability Exclusion and Exception for Scheduled Activities (HO 07 54)
- Special Coverage—Spoilage of Perishable Stock (HO 07 55)
- Valuable Papers and Records Coverage Increased Limits (HO 07 56)
- Permitted Incidental Occupancies—Residence Premises (HO 04 42)
- Permitted Incidental Occupancies—Other Residence (HO 24 43)
- Home Day Care Coverage Endorsement (HO 04 97)
- Business Pursuits (HO 24 71)

Description of Homeowners Endorsements for Insuring Business Exposures

Title and Number	When Needed or Used	How It Modifies the HO Form to Which It Is Attached
Home Business Insurance Coverage HO 07 01	The insured has a business conducted at or from the residence premises and wishes to insure business property and general liability exposures by endorsement to the HO policy instead of by purchasing a separate businessowners policy. The business must be owned by the named insured or by a partnership, joint venture, or other organization whose partners, members, or stockholders are the named insured and residents of the named insured's household. The coverage provided by the endorsement should be carefully compared with the insured's business loss exposures. Even if the endorsement is added, the insured must acquire additional policies to cover any auto, workers compensation, management liability, professional liability, cyber risk, crime, or other exposures not covered by the endorsed HO policy. Several endorsements are available for use exclusively with HO 07 01.	*Section I—Property Coverages:* • Provides a separate limit of insurance for an "other structure" described in the schedule and used for business. • Adds additional coverages for loss of business income and extra expense (up to 12 consecutive months following the physical loss), accounts receivable ($2,500), and valuable papers and records ($2,500). • Applies Coverage C to business personal property of others in the named insured's care, and to leased personal property that the named insured has a contractual duty to insure. • States that the special limit of $2,500 on property, on the residence premises, used primarily for business purposes does not apply to property pertaining to your business, thus allowing the full Coverage C limit to apply. • Provides a $5,000 special limit on business property (other than money, securities, and similar items) away from the residence premises. • Increases the special limit on money, precious metals, and similar items to $1,000. *Section II—Liability Coverages:* • Adds coverage for liability for bodily injury, property damage, and personal and advertising injury arising out of "your product," "your work," or the use of the residence premises to conduct the insured's business. • Adds an annual aggregate limit for products-completed operations liability (same amount as the Coverage E limit). • Adds an annual aggregate limit for all other business liability (twice the combined limits of Coverages E and F). • Expands the definition of insured to include the named insured's employees (subject to the usual exceptions found in commercial liability form) and the named insured's real estate manager. • Expands the definition of coverage territory to include the limited international extensions commonly included in businessowners policies. • Adds several liability and medical payments exclusions commonly found in businessowners policies.
Additional Insured—Managers or Lessors of Premises Leased to an Insured HO 07 50	The insured is leasing the residence premises from the current owner(s) under a long-term installment sales contract, and the owner(s) or their managers ask to be named as additional insureds for purposes of Coverage E—Personal Liability. For use with HO 07 01 only.	• Extends the definition of insured to include the person or organization named in the schedule, but only with respect to liability for the part of the premises rented to the named insured and described in the declarations. • Adds three additional exclusions.
Additional Insured—Vendors HO 07 51	The insured uses an agent or independent contractor to sell the insured's products, and this person or organization (called a vendor) asks to be named as an additional insured for purposes of Coverage E—Personal Liability. For use with HO 07 01 only.	• Extends the definition of insured to include the vendor named in the schedule, but only with respect to bodily injury or property damage arising out of the products described in the schedule that are distributed or sold in the regular course of the vendor's business. • Adds nine additional exclusions.

Title and Number	When Needed or Used	How It Modifies the HO Form to Which It Is Attached
Loss Payable Provisions HO 07 52	The insured is required to name another person or organization as a loss payee. For use with HO 07 01 only.	• Sets forth the three sets of loss payable conditions: A. Loss Payable, B. Lender's Loss Payable, C. Contract of Sale. • Provides a schedule for identifying loss payees, describing the property for which the loss payees are covered, and indicating which set of loss payable conditions apply.
Exclusion—Personal and Advertising Injury HO 07 53	The insurer wants to exclude personal and advertising injury liability coverage from the Home Business endorsement. For example, the insured's home business is advertising, and the insurer does not wish to cover the insured's potential liability for advertising liability. For use with HO 07 01 only.	Deletes the provisions for personal and advertising injury liability and adds an exclusion of any claim involving personal and advertising injury.
Liquor Liability Exclusion and Exception for Scheduled Activities HO 07 54	The insurer wants to exclude liquor liability under certain circumstances but is willing to cover liquor liability arising out of specified activities or events. For use with HO 07 01 only.	Adds a liquor liability exclusion that applies only if the insured manufactures, sells, or distributes alcoholic beverages; serves or furnishes alcoholic beverages for a charge; or serves or furnishes alcoholic beverages without a charge, if a license is required for such activity. However, the exclusion does not apply to liquor liability arising out of any activity or event described in the schedule.
Special Coverage—Spoilage of Perishable Stock HO 07 55	The insured wants to obtain coverage for spoilage of perishable stock such as cut flowers used in a floral business. For use with HO 07 01 only.	• Covers perishable stock described in the schedule against direct physical loss resulting from "breakdown," "contamination," or "power outage" as those terms are defined in the endorsement. • With respect to spoilage of perishable stock only, omits all of the exclusions in the HO form except for Earth Movement, War, Nuclear Hazard, Governmental Action, and Water; and adds five new exclusions.
Valuable Papers and Records Coverage Increased Limits HO 07 56	The insured wants to increase the $2,500 limit. For use with HO 07 01 only.	Increases the limit for the Valuable Papers and Records additional coverage from $2,500 to the amount shown in the schedule.
Permitted Incidental Occupancies—Residence Premises HO 04 42	If the insured has certain incidental business or professional occupancies, coverage for the occupancy is limited under Section I and excluded under Section II. The endorsement extends the HO form to cover a permitted incidental occupancy in the dwelling or in an "other structure" on the residence premises. Examples of permitted incidental occupancies are offices used for business or professional purposes; private schools; and studios for music, dance, or photography.	*Section I—Property Coverages:* • Provides a separate limit of insurance for an "other structure" described in the schedule. • Provides that the Coverage C limit applies to property of the business described in the schedule. • Modifies the $2,500 special limit applicable to property, on the residence premises, used primarily for business purposes so that it applies only to such property other than furnishings, supplies, and equipment of the described business. *Section II—Liability Coverages:* • Modifies the Business exclusion so that it does not apply to the use of the residence premises to conduct the described business. • Excludes bodily injury to any "employee" arising out of the business described in the schedule.

Title and Number	When Needed or Used	How It Modifies the HO Form to Which It Is Attached
Permitted Incidental Occupancies—Other Residence HO 24 43	The insured has an incidental occupancy of the type that could be covered by HO 04 42, but the incidental occupancy is in a residence other than the residence premises. For example, during the regular school year, Mike works as a music teacher in a public school system. During the summer, he gives private music lessons in his secondary (seasonal) residence.	• Does not modify Section I—Property Coverages in any way. • Extends the definition of insured location to include the premises described in the schedule, from which an insured conducts the business described in the schedule. • States that the insurer covers, under Section II—Liability Coverages, the business described in the schedule. • Modifies the Business exclusion so that it does not apply to the use of the premises described in the schedule to conduct the described business. • Excludes bodily injury to any "employee" arising out of the business described in the schedule.
Home Day Care Coverage Endorsement HO 04 97	The insured wants to extend the HO policy to cover property and liability exposures arising out of a home day care business being conducted at the residence premises.	*Section I—Property Coverages:* • Provides a separate limit of insurance for an "other structure" described in the schedule and used for business. • Provides that the Coverage C limit applies to property of the business described in the schedule. • Modifies the $2,500 special limit applicable to property, on the residence premises, used primarily for business purposes so that it applies only to such property other than furnishings, supplies, and equipment of the described business. *Section II—Liability Coverages:* • Provides that the Section II coverages apply to BI and property damaging arising out of home day care services regularly provided by an insured and for which an insured receives compensation. • Modifies the Business exclusion so that it does not apply to the covered provided by this endorsement. • Excludes liability arising out of draft or saddle animals or vehicles used with them, motor vehicles, aircraft, hovercraft, and watercraft. • Adds an annual aggregate limit applicable to Coverages E and F, equal to the limit shown in the declarations for Coverage E.
Business Pursuits HO 24 71	An insured wants to be covered for liability arising out of his or her business activities. To qualify for this endorsement, the insured must not own the business, be a partner in it, or financially control it. Home businesses owned by an insured can be insured under the Home Business Insurance Coverage endorsement, HO 07 01. For example, an insured who is employed by a manufacturer as a traveling sales representative could be insured under HO 24 71. A self-employed manufacturers' representative could not.	• Excludes liability for business pursuits in connection with a business owned or financially controlled by the insured or by a partnership of which the insured is a partner or member. • Excludes liability arising out of professional services other than teaching. • Excludes bodily injury to a fellow employee of the insured in the course of employment. • When the insured is a member of the faculty or teaching staff of any school or college, excludes liability arising out of draft or saddle animals, aircraft, hovercraft, motor vehicles, or watercraft; and bodily injury to any pupil arising out of corporal punishment by or at the direction of the insured unless the schedule shows that corporal punishment coverage applies.

HOMEOWNERS ENDORSEMENTS FOR INSURING RENTAL EXPOSURES

To meet the needs of an insured who rents a residence to a tenant, an insurance professional must know which endorsements can modify a homeowners policy and how each would protect the insured.

An insured who rents residential property to others has multiple loss exposures as a result of this activity. Many of these exposures can be covered by endorsements to the insured's homeowners policy. For example, if Jane owns a house that has a detached garage apartment that she rents to Jeff, she needs coverage for damage to the garage structure. She can acquire this coverage with the Structures Rented to Others endorsement (HO 04 40). This same endorsement will also provide liability coverage for Jane if Jeff were to become injured due to her negligence as a landlord, such as if she were to hire an incompetent electrician who causes an electrical fire that burns Jeff.

Without such an endorsement, coverage for both the garage structure and liability arising out of renting this structure would be excluded in an unendorsed homeowners policy. Also, if the garage apartment is rented to Jeff fully furnished, Jane may need to increase the $2,500 limit on Landlord's Furnishings. This can be done using the Landlord's Furnishings—Forms HO 00 02, HO 00 03 and HO 00 05 Only endorsement (HO 05 46).

The list of homeowners endorsements that are used to modify homeowners forms to insure rental exposures includes these:

- Structures Rented to Others (HO 04 40)
- Extended Theft Coverage for Residence Premises Occasionally Rented to Others (HO 05 41)
- Landlord's Furnishings—Forms HO 00 02, HO 00 03 and HO 00 05 Only (HO 05 46)
- Unit-Owners Rental to Others (HO 17 33)
- Additional Residence Rented to Others 1, 2, 3 or 4 Families (HO 24 70)

Description of Homeowners Endorsements for Insuring Rental Exposures

Title and Number	When Needed or Used	How It Modifies the HO Form to Which It Is Attached
Structures Rented to Others HO 04 40	The insured rents an "other structure" on the residence premises for dwelling purposes. The endorsement is needed because HO-2, HO-3, HO-5, and HO-8 all exclude an "other structure" rented or held for rental to any person not a tenant of the building, unless used solely as a private garage.	• For purposes of Section I—Property Coverages, states that the insurer covers the structure(s) described in the schedule that is on the residence premises, rented to any person not a tenant of the dwelling, and used as a private residence. • For purposes of Section II—Liability Coverages, modifies the definition of insured location to include the structure(s) described in the schedule and states that the Business exclusion does not apply to such structure(s).
Extended Theft Coverage for Residence Premises Occasionally Rented to Others HO 05 41	The insured occasionally rents the residence premises in whole or in part to a tenant, roomer, or boarder and wants to have coverage for theft committed by such persons. This endorsement is not needed when the insured is covered under an HO-5, or under an HO-4 or HO-6 that has been endorsed to provide open perils coverage.	Amends the wording of the theft peril so that it covers theft committed by an occasional tenant, roomer, or boarder, excluding various types of precious items that are attractive to thieves, such as money, precious metals, coins, securities, jewelry, watches, furs, and precious and semi-precious stones.
Landlord's Furnishings—Forms HO 00 02, HO 00 03 and HO 00 05 Only HO 05 46	The insured holds one or more apartments on the residence premises for rental and wants to increase the $2,500 limit on the Landlord's Furnishings additional coverage.	For each rental unit, shows an increase in the $2,500 limit of the additional coverage.
Unit-Owners Rental to Others HO 17 33	When the insured regularly rents the insured unit to others, the unendorsed HO-6 does not provide any coverage under Coverage C—Personal Property or Section II—Liability Coverages.	• Modifies the Coverage C exclusion of property in an apartment regularly rented to others by an insured so that it does not apply to the residence premises • Deletes the exclusion of theft from that part of a residence premises rented by an insured to someone other than another insured • Excludes theft from the residence premises of a variety of precious property items, such as money, precious metals, securities, and jewelry • Modifies the Business exclusion in Section II so that it does not apply to the rental of an insured location under any circumstances
Additional Residence Rented to Others 1, 2, 3 or 4 Families HO 24 70	If the insured owns an additional residence and rents it to others continuously, the residence is ineligible for an HO policy because it is not owner-occupied. In this situation, property insurance for the additional residence can be provided in a dwelling policy, and HO 24 70 can be added to the insured's HO policy to extend Section II—Liability Coverages to the rental property.	• Modifies the definition of insured location to include the location of the additional residence listed in the schedule • Modifies the Business exclusion in Section II—Liability Coverages so that the exception to the exclusion includes the location of the additional residence

HOMEOWNERS ENDORSEMENTS FOR ADDRESSING MISCELLANEOUS EXPOSURES

An insurance professional must be able to recognize the miscellaneous loss exposures that arise in a variety of circumstances to know when an endorsement to a homeowners policy can be used to meet the insured's or insurer's particular needs.

A homeowners policy can often be modified more efficiently than issuing a new policy or modifying another policy in order to provide coverage for an insured with a miscellaneous exposure.

For example, instead of writing a separate renter's policy for Paul, who is a twenty-four-year-old doctoral student away at school, it is more efficient to extend his parents' homeowners policy to cover Paul's personal property and liability exposures. This extension of coverage was included, without endorsement, in his parents' homeowners policy while he was younger than twenty-four, but his parents must now use the Additional Insured—Student Living Away From the Residence Premises endorsement (HO 05 27).

Paul's dad, Phillip, plays golf and uses a golf cart that he would like to insure for collision. This can be accomplished using the Owned Motorized Golf Cart Physical Loss Coverage endorsement (HO 05 28).

A few miscellaneous exposures are covered by the standard homeowners policy but need to be excluded for an insurer to be willing to write the coverage. For example, if a homeowner has a vicious dog that has bitten several people in the past, the homeowner's insurer may refuse to provide liability coverage for future bites by the dog. This exclusion of liability coverage can be implemented using the Canine Liability Exclusion Endorsement (HO 24 77).

The list of homeowners endorsements that are used for addressing miscellaneous exposures includes these:

- Assisted Living Care Coverage (HO 04 59)
- Coverage B—Other Structures Away From the Residence Premises (HO 04 91)
- Specific Structures Away From the Residence Premises (HO 04 92)
- Additional Insured—Student Living Away From the Residence Premises (HO 05 27)
- Owned Motorized Golf Cart Physical Loss Coverage (HO 05 28)
- Property Remediation for Escaped Liquid Fuel and Limited Lead and Escaped Liquid Fuel Liability Coverages (HO 05 80, HO 05 81, and HO 05 82)
- Incidental Low Power Recreational Motor Vehicle Liability Coverage Endorsement (HO 24 13)
- Owned Snowmobile (HO 24 64)

Description of Homeowners Endorsements for Miscellaneous Exposures

Title and Number	When Needed or Used	How It Modifies the HO Form to Which It Is Attached
Assisted Living Care Coverage HO 04 59	To extend the insured's HO coverages to a relative who regularly resides in an assisted living facility.	• Extends Coverage C to include personal property owned and used by the person named in the schedule, subject to additional special limits for items such as hearing aids, eyeglasses, false teeth, and wheelchairs. • Excludes property regularly located away from the facility; property owned by an insured; and property of the facility that is rented to or used by the person named in the schedule. • Provides additional living expense, not to exceed $500 per month for up to 12 months, if a covered loss makes the facility unfit to live in. • States that Coverage F—Medical Payments to Others does not apply to the endorsement. • Adds these exclusions to Coverage E—Personal Liability: "liability assumed by the facility prior to an occurrence," and "bodily injury to a care facility professional or support staff that occurs while such person is on or off duty and attending to the person named in the Schedule."
Coverage B—Other Structures Away From the Residence Premises HO 04 91	To cover an "other structure" that is located away from the residence premises and therefore not covered under Coverage B—Other Structures in the insured's HO form. For example, the insured has a tool and equipment shed located on a separate parcel of land near the residence premises. This endorsement should be used only when the total value of all other structures on and off the residence premises does not exceed 10 percent of the Coverage A—Dwelling limit. HO 04 92 can be used to cover other structures off the residence premises for a separate, adequate limit.	• Extends Coverage B to cover other structures owned by the named insured and located away from the residence premises, if the named insured uses the other structure(s) in connection with the residence premises. • Excludes other structures off the residence premises if used (or capable of being used) as a dwelling, if used to conduct any business, if used to store business property, or if rented or held for rental to any person not a tenant of the dwelling. • Limits recovery for other structures on or away from the residence premises to 10 percent of the Coverage A limit. • Modifies the Loss Settlement condition so that losses to other structures off the residence premises are settled at actual cash value rather than replacement cost.
Specific Structures Away From the Residence Premises HO 04 92	To cover an "other structure" that is located away from the residence premises, for which the insured wants a limit of insurance that is separate from the limit applicable to other structures on the residence premises. For example, the insured has a boat house located on a separate parcel of land across the street from the residence premises. The value of the boat house is $50,000 and the limit applicable to other structures on the residence premises is $35,000.	Applies the same terms of coverage as HO 04 91 except that each structure described in the schedule is covered for up to the limit shown for that structure.

- Watercraft (HO 24 75)
- Canine Liability Exclusion Endorsement (HO 24 77)
- Personal Injury Coverage (HO 24 82)

Title and Number	When Needed or Used	How It Modifies the HO Form to Which It Is Attached

Additional Insured – Student Living Away From the Residence Premises
 	
HO 05 27
	To provide insured status to someone who formerly resided in the insured's household before moving out to attend school and who is also one of the following:
	
	• A relative age 24 or older
	
	• A relative of any age and attending school part-time
	
	• A nonrelative who is in the care of the insured or of another resident relative and under the age of 21 and a part-time student
	
	Without endorsement, the policy covers relatives under age 24 if full-time students, and covers nonrelatives under age 21 if full-time students.
		Extends the definition of insured to include the person named in the schedule, but only if that person meets both of these requirements:
		
		1. Was a resident of your household before moving out to attend the school named in the Schedule above; and
		
		2. Resides at the address shown in the Schedule and
		
		   a. Is your relative; or
		
		   b. Is an other person under the age of 21 and in your care or in the care of a relative who is a resident of your household.
		
		To be covered, the named person must also be enrolled at the school and residing at the address shown in the schedule. There is no requirement that the student be a full-time student.

Owned Motorized Golf Cart Physical Loss Coverage HO 05 28	To cover physical loss to a golf cart of the type covered under Section II—Liability Coverages. Because they meet the policy definition of "motor vehicle," golf carts are not covered property under Coverage C—Personal Property. However, ISO manual rules permit eligible golf carts to be covered against physical loss.	• Covers the golf cart for which a limit is shown in the schedule. • Covers (for up to 10 percent of the highest golf cart limit in the schedule) accessories, equipment, or parts that, at the time of loss, are at the insured's residence or in the golf cart while away from the insured's residence. • The covered property is insured on an open perils basis, subject to the Section I—Exclusions in the HO policy form and a set of additional exclusions in the endorsement. • Collision is covered only if the insured pays an additional premium. • A $500 deductible applies, regardless of any other deductible that applies to the policy. • Loss settlement is limited to the least of the actual cash value, the cost to repair or replace, or the applicable limit in the schedule.
Property Remediation for Escaped Liquid Fuel and Limited Lead and Escaped Liquid Fuel Liability Coverages HO 05 80 HO 05 81 HO 05 82	To provide environmental coverages needed by insureds with liquid fuel and lead liability exposures. • HO 05 80 is used with HO-2, -3, -5, and -8 • HO 05 81 is used with HO-4 • HO 05 82 is used with HO-6	• Adds Property Remediation for Escaped Liquid Fuel, which covers loss to "covered real property" (including land) and "covered personal property" resulting from the escape of liquid fuel from a covered fuel system. • Adds Limited Lead and Escaped Liquid Fuel Liability Coverage for bodily injury (BI) or property damage (PD) resulting from the escape of liquid fuel from a covered fuel system, BI resulting from the absorption, ingestion, or inhalation of lead on an insured location, and PD resulting from contamination by lead that came from an insured location • The basic limits under ISO rules are $10,000 for property remediation and $50,000 for the liability coverage. Higher limits are available at the insurer's option.
Incidental Low Power Recreational Motor Vehicle Liability Coverage Endorsement HO 24 13	To extend Section II—Liability Coverages to certain types of recreational motor vehicles.	Modifies the Motor Vehicle Liability exclusion so that it does not apply to a motor vehicle designed for recreational use off public roads that is either not owned by an insured or, if owned by an insured, meets several additional requirements regarding location of the occurrence, maximum maximum speed capacity (15 mph), and type of vehicle.

Title and Number	When Needed or Used	How It Modifies the HO Form to Which It Is Attached
Owned Snowmobile HO 24 64	To extend Section II—Liability Coverages to a snowmobile owned by an insured and used off an insured location. Without being endorsed, the HO forms cover liability for use of a snowmobile on an insured location (with some exceptions).	Covers motor vehicle liability involving a snowmobile owned by an insured and described in the schedule.
Watercraft HO 24 75	To extend Section II—Liability Coverages to scheduled watercraft that exceed the power, type, or length requirements for watercraft coverage under the HO forms. In most cases, a separate boatowners policy will provide better liability and physical damage coverage for boats than a homeowners policy can.	Two categories of watercraft can be scheduled in the endorsement: • Watercraft with one or more outboard engines or motors of more than 25 total horsepower or other watercraft with inboard or inboard-outboard engines or motors • Sailing vessels 26 feet or more overall length, with or without auxiliary power The endorsement adds exclusions of racing (which does not apply to a sailing vessel), rental to others, carrying persons or cargo for a charge, use for any business purpose, and bodily injury to an employee.
Canine Liability Exclusion Endorsement HO 24 77	The insurer wants to exclude liability for a dog owned by or in the care of an insured. Under ISO rules, the named insured must acknowledge the exclusion in writing.	Adds an exclusion, applicable to Coverage E—Personal Liability and Coverage F—Medical Payments, of bodily injury or property damage arising out of direct physical contact with a canine described in the schedule.
Personal Injury Coverage HO 24 82	To extend Coverage E—Personal Liability to cover personal injury as defined in the endorsement.	• Adds an insuring agreement stating that the insurer will defend any insured against a claim or suit alleging damages because of "personal injury" to which the insurance applies and to pay any such damages for which the insured is held liable, up to the Coverage E limit. • Defines personal injury to include one or more of the following offenses if committed during the policy period: false arrest, detention, or imprisonment; malicious prosecution, wrongful eviction, slander or libel; and violation of a person's right of privacy. • Adds eleven exclusions (a through k) applicable to personal injury coverage.

Includes copyrighted material of Insurance Services Office, Inc., with its permission. Copyright, Insurance Services Office, 1999, 2010. [DA09097]

RECOMMENDING HOMEOWNERS FORMS AND ENDORSEMENTS

Being able to recommend an appropriate homeowners form and endorsements to meet an insured's particular circumstances and coverage needs is an essential skill for insurance professionals.

When arranging homeowners coverage for an individual or a family, you must first select the homeowners form for which the insured is eligible and that will meet the insured's coverage needs and preferences. The 2011 Homeowners Program of Insurance Services Office, Inc. (ISO) includes these six policy forms:

- Homeowners 2—Broad Form, or HO-2
- Homeowners 3—Special Form, or HO-3
- Homeowners 4—Contents Broad Form, or HO-4

- Homeowners 5—Comprehensive Form, or HO-5
- Homeowners 6—Unit-Owners Form, or HO-6
- Homeowners 8—Modified Coverage Form, or HO-8

You must then determine whether the insured has any loss exposures that are not adequately covered by the selected form but could be covered by adding one or more endorsements to the policy. Once the needed endorsements have been identified, they can be recommended for the insured's consideration. In some cases, an insured might decline to purchase an appropriate endorsement because of its cost.

The scenarios that follow show how various ISO endorsements might be used to modify ISO's 2011 homeowners policy forms to meet different insureds' needs. The scenarios omit endorsements that are routinely added to most policies, such as the Inflation Guard endorsement (HO 04 46). The scenarios also omit endorsements that insurers use to restrict coverage so that they can accept risks that would otherwise be unacceptable. For example, an insurer might require the Hurricane Deductible endorsement (HO 03 18) for a dwelling situated in a coastal area susceptible to hurricanes.

Young Family on a Tight Budget

Fred and Colleen are a young married couple with two children ages one and three. They live in a single-family dwelling that they recently bought. Fred is employed in automobile sales, and Colleen supplements her husband's income by providing daycare services in their house for children in the neighborhood.

Fred and Colleen's house was constructed in the early 1900s and has a slate roof and brick walls that would be very expensive to replace using the original materials and construction methods. Fred and Colleen want to keep their homeowners policy effective but affordable ("no frills"), as they are on a tight budget. However, they are not interested in the reduced coverage they would receive under an HO-8 policy.

Recommend an ISO homeowners form and endorsements for insuring Fred and Colleen's property and liability loss exposures.

Recommendations for Fred and Colleen

Fred and Colleen could consider either an HO-2 or an HO-3. They might be able to save a small amount of premium by going with the HO-2, but they should be informed that the usually small additional cost for an HO-3 expands coverage on the dwelling and other structures to an open perils, instead of a named perils, basis.

The Home Day Care Coverage Endorsement (HO 04 97) should be added to cover exposures arising out of Colleen's daycare business. Fred and Colleen should also consider the savings (by way of a lower dwelling limit) that they could realize by selecting the Functional Replacement Cost Loss Settlement (HO 05 30) endorsement.

Artist's Apartment and Studio

Mark is an artist who has just rented a loft apartment in a renovated warehouse. The apartment has an area of 1,500 square feet, which Mark will use as his regular residence and as a studio where he will give art lessons to private students for a fee.

The personal property that will be contained in Mark's apartment and studio include his clothing, furniture, art supplies and equipment (used for Mark's own artwork and in his art classes), and an art collection that is valued at $35,000. Mark, who also pursues photography as a hobby, owns cameras valued at $15,000.

Mark makes only a modest income giving art lessons, but he receives additional income from a trust fund and is open to buying broader terms of coverage, particularly for his art collection and cameras. Recommend an ISO homeowners form and endorsements for insuring Mark's property and liability loss exposures.

Recommendations for Mark

As a tenant, Mark is eligible only for an HO-4 policy. He may wish to upgrade the HO-4's covered causes of loss from broad named perils to open perils by use of the Special Personal Property Coverage endorsement (HO 05 24). Similarly, he may wish to upgrade the actual cash value loss settlement provisions of the HO-4 to replacement cost by use of the Personal Property Replacement Cost Loss Settlement endorsement (HO O4 90).

If Mark is content to obtain open perils coverage on only his art collection and cameras, and not the rest of his personal property, he can omit the Special Personal Property Coverage endorsement and purchase the Scheduled Personal Property Endorsement (HO 04 61), which in some respects provides broader coverage than HO 05 24.

The Permitted Incidental Occupancies—Residence Premises (HO 04 42) endorsement should be adequate for covering Mark's business personal property and his liability for bodily injury or property damage arising out of conducting art classes on the residence premises.

Wealthy Married Couple

Stan and Peggy are a married couple who live in a high-hazard earthquake area in California. Stan is a sales representative employed by a sporting goods company, and Peggy is an attorney who works for a firm in Los Angeles.

Their dwelling has a replacement cost value of $1.5 million, and a guesthouse on the residence premises has a replacement cost value of $200,000. Stan and Peggy want to insure their dwelling, guesthouse, in-ground pool, and personal property on an open perils basis with replacement cost loss settlement on all these categories of property.

Peggy's jewelry is valued, in total, at $100,000, on a replacement cost basis, which greatly exceeds the maximum limit for theft, misplacing, or losing of jewelry that the insurer will provide under the Coverage C Increased Special Limits of Liability endorsement (HO 04 65).

As a sales representative, Stan stores merchandise and sales samples in the dwelling. This business property is owned by his employer, but Stan, by agreement with his employer, is responsible for loss to this property while it is in Stan's custody and therefore wants it to be covered by his homeowners property coverage. The value of this property substantially exceeds the Coverage C special limits of $2,500 and $1,500 applicable to business property on and off the residence premises.

Stan is responsible for the welfare of his elderly mother, who lives nearby in an assisted living facility. Even though she does not meet the policy definition of an insured, he wants her to have personal property and liability coverage under his homeowners policy.

Recommend an ISO homeowners form and endorsements for insuring Stan's and Peggy's property and liability loss exposures during the coming year.

Recommendations for Stan and Peggy

An HO-5 policy will provide the open perils coverage that Stan and Peggy want on their property. The HO-5 will cover their dwelling and guesthouse for replacement cost loss settlement, but it will cover their personal property and in-ground pool on an actual cash value basis because the Loss Settlement provisions in the HO-5 state that losses to personal property and non-building structures, such as a swimming pool, are settled at actual cash value.

Their personal property can be covered on a replacement cost basis by attaching the Personal Property Replacement Cost Loss Settlement endorsement (HO 04 90), and the in-ground pool can be covered on a replacement cost basis by attaching the Replacement Cost Loss Settlement for Certain Non-Building Structures on the Residence Premises endorsement (HO 04 43).

Because the Coverage B—Other Structures limit is set at 10 percent of the Coverage A—Dwelling limit, Stan and Peggy will need to increase the Coverage B limit to the appropriate amount for covering the guesthouse and swimming pool. If, for example, the dwelling is insured for $1.5 million, the Coverage B limit will be $150,000 unless modified by endorsement. The Residence Premises—Increased Limits endorsement (HO 04 48) can be used to increase the $150,000 limit to an amount sufficient for covering the guesthouse and pool on a full replacement cost basis.

Peggy can insure her jewelry on an open perils basis including theft, misplacing, or losing using the Scheduled Personal Property Endorsement (HO 04 61). This endorsement will provide replacement cost loss settlement on the covered items of jewelry as long as the Personal Property Replacement Cost Loss Settlement endorsement (HO 04 90) is also attached to the policy. The Scheduled Personal Property Endorsement (With Agreed Value Loss Settlement) (HO 04 60) could be used instead of endorsement HO 04 61 if Stan and Peggy prefer that the jewelry be insured on an agreed value basis.

Stan can insure, to an appropriate value, the business property in his custody by purchasing the Increased Limits on Business Property endorsement (HO 04 12).

Stan can cover his mother's personal property and liability exposures at the assisted living facility by purchasing the Assisted Living Care Coverage endorsement (HO 04 59).

Stan and Peggy's policy can be amended to cover earthquake losses by adding the Earthquake endorsement (HO 04 54).

Married Couple With Home Business and Rental Property

Rick and Marie are a married couple who live in a single-family dwelling that has a replacement cost value of $275,000.

Marie owns an accounting business that she operates in a detached garage building on the residence premises. The garage has been converted into an office, and the replacement cost value is $50,000. Rick and Marie would like to obtain, under their homeowners policy, property and liability coverage for Marie's accounting business.

Rick is retired but manages a four-family dwelling building at another location owned by the couple. The building is not eligible for homeowners property coverage because it is not owner occupied. Therefore, Rick and Marie insure the building against property loss under a separate dwelling policy. However, the dwelling policy does not include liability coverage, so Rick and Marie want to obtain liability coverage for this building under their homeowners policy so that they do not need to buy a separate liability policy on the rental property.

Rick spends his spare time fishing and hunting. He owns an old aluminum fishing boat with a twenty-horsepower outboard motor. The boat, motor, and boat trailer are valued at $1,300. Rick does not want to go to the trouble and expense of buying a separate boatowners policy for this boat, so he is looking only for basic property and liability coverage for the boat under the homeowners policy.

Rick and Marie have one son, Dave, who is twenty-five and attends graduate school in a nearby city, living in a college dormitory. To spare their son the cost of buying an HO-4 policy, Rick and Marie want his personal property and liability exposures to be covered under their homeowners policy.

Rick and Marie want to be insured under an HO-3 policy. To avoid a higher premium, they prefer to insure their personal property for actual cash value loss settlement.

Recommend any ISO homeowners endorsements that will be needed to insure Rick and Marie's property and liability loss exposures during the coming year.

Recommendations for Rick and Marie

Rick and Marie can extend their homeowners policy to cover property and liability exposures arising out of Marie's accounting business by adding the Home Business Insurance Coverage endorsement (HO 07 01). This endorsement will provide a separate limit of insurance for Marie's office building, which should be set at an amount sufficient to cover the building for its full replacement cost. Marie may wish to increase the $2,500 limit applicable to valuable papers and records in endorsement HO 07 01. This change can be made by adding the Valuable Papers and Records Coverage Increased Limits endorsement (HO 07 56).

Rick and Marie can obtain liability coverage on their rental property by purchasing the Additional Residence Rented to Others endorsement (HO 24 70).

Physical loss by a covered peril to Rick's boat, motor, and boat trailer will be insured under Coverage C for up to the property's actual cash value, not to exceed the $1,500 special limit on watercraft and their trailers. Rick's liability arising out of the ownership, maintenance, or use of the boat will also be covered under the homeowners policy because the outboard motor is not more than twenty-five horsepower. There is no need to add the Watercraft endorsement (HO 24 75) to the policy.

Dave's personal property and liability exposures while he is living in the dormitory can be covered by adding the Additional Insured—Student Living Away From the Residence Premises endorsement (HO 05 27) to his parents' homeowners policy.

Professor's Condominium Unit

Sheila is a college professor who owns a condominium unit. She lives in her unit while she is teaching foreign language classes during the fall and winter semesters, but during the summer she normally goes to Europe to teach, travel, and improve her fluency in foreign languages.

While Sheila is away for the summer, she rents her furnished unit to a trustworthy graduate student or a visiting professor. Sheila wants to make sure that her unit and its contents, as well as her personal liability exposures, will be covered as usual while she is away.

Sheila also wants her homeowners policy to cover liability she might incur as a result of her teaching activities.

Sheila is a risk-averse person who prefers to have the most favorable terms of coverage for perils insured against and valuation of losses. Recommend the appropriate ISO homeowners form and endorsements for insuring Sheila's property and liability loss exposures during the coming year.

Recommendations for Sheila

As a residential condominium unit-owner, Sheila is eligible only for an HO-6 policy. To maintain her HO-6 property and liability coverages while her unit is rented to others, Sheila can obtain the Unit-Owners Rental to Others (HO 17 33) endorsement.

Because of her desire to obtain favorable terms of coverage, Sheila may also wish to obtain the Unit-Owners Coverage C Special Coverage endorsement (HO 17 31) and Unit-Owners Coverage A Special Coverage endorsement (HO 17 32) to upgrade her HO-6 from broad named perils to open perils coverage.

Similarly, Sheila may also wish to upgrade the HO-6 actual cash value loss settlement provisions on personal property to replacement cost loss settlement through the Personal Property Replacement Cost Loss Settlement endorsement (HO 04 90).

Finally, Sheila can purchase the Business Pursuits endorsement (HO 24 71) to cover liability arising out of her teaching activities.

SUMMARY

Several endorsements can be used to modify limits or add special deductibles within a homeowners policy. Understanding when to use each endorsement appropriately and how the endorsement modifies the homeowners form to which it is attached will allow an insurance professional to address many of the unique needs presented by individual insureds and insurers.

Multiple endorsements are available to modify the perils insured against in homeowners forms. Understanding how the perils insured against can be modified will allow an insurance professional to address the needs of insureds seeking additional protection.

Several endorsements can be used to modify the valuation provisions in homeowners forms. Understanding how these endorsements modify the homeowners form to which they are attached enables an insurance professional to meet both the insured's and the insurer's needs.

A variety of loss exposures can arise when an insured conducts a business from his or her residence premises. Multiple endorsements to homeowners forms are available to address many of these exposures.

An insured who rents residential property to others has multiple loss exposures from this activity. An insurance professional who knows how to endorse a homeowners policy to cover many of these exposures can meet the needs of the landlord insured.

An insurance professional who can recognize the miscellaneous exposures that arise in a variety of circumstances and knows when an endorsement to a homeowners policy is available to cover or exclude coverage for such exposures can better meet the needs of an insured or an insurer.

Every individual or family can have unique residential loss exposures. An insurance professional who is familiar with the various ISO homeowners forms and endorsements and makes the effort to ascertain and understand the insured's loss exposures can recommend an appropriate form and endorsements to meet the insured's particular needs.

Other Residential Insurance Coverages

Educational Objectives

After learning the content of this assignment, you should be able to:

▷ Contrast the Dwelling Property 3—Special Form (DP-3) policy with the Homeowners 3—Special Form policy in regard to each of the following:

- Types of property covered

- Other coverages

- Perils insured against

- Exclusions and conditions

- Coverage for liability and theft losses

▷ Given a case describing a dwelling claim, determine whether the Dwelling Property—Special Form (DP-3) policy would cover the claim and, if so, the amount the insurer would pay for the claim.

▷ Summarize the coverages provided by personal inland marine policies.

▷ Summarize the coverage provided by each of the following types of farm insurance coverages:

- Insurance Services Office, Inc. (ISO) Farm Program

- ISO Homeowners endorsements

- Specialty farm and ranch programs

▷ Describe the operation of FAIR plans and beachfront and windstorm plans and the coverage they provide.

▷ Describe the operation of the National Flood Insurance Program and the coverage it provides.

▷ Given a case describing a claim involving an individual or a family with a National Flood Insurance Policy, determine what is covered, excluded, or limited, and for what amounts.

Other Residential Insurance Coverages

8

DWELLING POLICIES

Because dwelling policies are used widely, particularly to insure rental dwellings, an understanding of the coverages provided by the Insurance Services Office, Inc. (ISO) Dwelling Property 3—Special Form (DP 00 03) (DP-3) and how they differ from the Homeowners 3—Special Form (HO-3) policy is important.

Some residences are not eligible for homeowners coverage for various reasons. Here are some of those reasons:

- The residence is not owner-occupied.
- The value of the dwelling is below the minimum limit for a homeowners policy.
- The residence does not otherwise meet an insurer's underwriting guidelines.

An insured might not want a homeowners policy for either or both of two reasons: The insured might not want or need the full range of homeowners coverages, and a homeowners policy might cost more than the insured is willing to pay.

A dwelling policy can be used to cover owner and nonowner-occupied residences or to meet the needs of customers who do not want or need a homeowners policy. Although many differences exist between the dwelling and homeowners policies, among the most important differences is the fact that the unendorsed DP-3 policy does not provide any theft coverage for personal property or any liability coverages. However, both of these coverages can be added to the dwelling policy by an endorsement or a supplement.

Structures Eligible for Dwelling Policies

The HO-3 policy covers owner-occupied one- to four-family dwellings. Dwelling policies are designed principally for insuring one- to four-family dwellings, whether owner-occupied or tenant-occupied. However, dwelling policies may also be used for four other kinds of property and activities:

- A dwelling in the course of construction
- Mobile homes at a permanent location

- Houseboats, in some states
- Certain incidental business occupancies, if the businesses are operated by the owner-insured or by a tenant of the insured location

Coverages

The DP-3 offers property coverages on a dwelling and its contents that are similar to the coverages under Section I (property) of the HO-3 and other homeowners forms.

The dwelling form includes five coverages:

- Coverage A—Dwelling
- Coverage B—Other Structures
- Coverage C—Personal Property
- Coverage D—Fair Rental Value
- Coverage E—Additional Living Expense

Unlike the HO-3 policy, the dwelling policy does not automatically include all the property coverages. A limit for each desired coverage (dwelling, other structures, and personal property) must be shown on the Declarations page (with appropriate premium charges). Loss of use coverages (fair rental value and additional living expense), however, are automatically included in the DP-3.

Although a dwelling policy can be used for insuring only personal property with no dwelling or structures coverage, this is rarely done. The DP-3 form is more commonly used to cover only the dwelling and other structures (for example, to insure a house rented unfurnished to tenants) or to cover the dwelling, other structures, and personal property.

The DP-3 form provides coverage for the dwelling on the described location shown in the declarations and specifies that the structure must be used principally for dwelling purposes. The HO-3 form refers to the dwelling on the residence premises, including attached structures. The dwelling form also specifically states that, if not covered elsewhere in the policy, building equipment and outdoor equipment used for the service of the premises and located on the described location are covered. For example, if the insured owns a lawn mower kept in the garage of the insured dwelling and uses it to cut the grass at the insured location, the lawn mower would be included under Coverage A (if the insured did not purchase Coverage C—Personal Property). The remainder of the Coverage A language is similar in the dwelling and homeowners forms.

Although the dwelling and homeowners forms have some minor differences in their wording, their coverage for other structures is essentially the same. Structures set apart from the dwelling by clear space or connected to the dwelling by only a fence, utility line, or similar connection are defined as included under Coverage B. As in the HO-3 policy, Coverage B includes detached structures, such as garages and storage sheds, on the insured premises. Grave markers and mausoleums are specifically excluded under Other Structures in the DP-3 form, whereas the HO-3 policy provides up to $5,000 for grave markers as an additional coverage.

If Coverage C is selected, coverage under the dwelling form applies to personal property usual to the occupancy of a dwelling that is owned or used by the insured or resident family members. Coverage applies while the property is at the described location.

Unlike the homeowners form, the dwelling form has no special limits that apply to any specific type of personal property. For example, the homeowners form has special limits on theft losses to jewelry, furs, firearms, silverware, and similar types of property; the dwelling form has no such limits. Because the unendorsed dwelling form has no theft coverage, such theft limitations are not necessary. The homeowners policy has a special sublimit on money and related items, but the dwelling form excludes coverage for money altogether. The homeowners policy provides a special sublimit on watercraft (including their furnishings, equipment, and outboard motors), but the dwelling form excludes boats other than rowboats and canoes.

To cover personal property, the insured chooses a Coverage C limit in the dwelling form. If an insured is a landlord and has no personal property in the insured dwelling (or chooses not to insure personal property), he or she can choose to purchase only Coverage A under the DP-3. The HO-3 policy has no such option.

Coverages D and E in the DP-3 form correspond roughly to Coverage D—Loss of Use in the HO-3 form, which includes both fair rental value and additional living expense coverages. Coverage D covers the fair rental value of a property rented to others when it becomes unfit for its normal use because of a loss by a covered peril. Coverage E covers the increase in living expenses for the insured if the described property becomes unfit for its normal use because of a loss by a covered peril.

Other Coverages

Many of the other coverages provided in the dwelling policy correspond to the additional coverages in the homeowners policy, but there are some differences. Loss assessment coverage, which is included automatically (up to $1,000) in the homeowners policy, can be added to the dwelling policy by endorsement for an additional premium. The additional coverages in the homeowners policy for landlord's furnishings and for credit cards, transfer cards, forgery, and counterfeit money are not available in the dwelling policy.

The DP-3 form provides up to 10 percent of the Coverage A limit for Coverage B—Other Structures as outlined in the Other Coverages provision. This coverage is additional insurance and does not reduce the Coverage A limit for the same loss.

The debris removal coverage of the DP-3 form is included in the limit that applies to the damaged property. In contrast, the HO-3 provides an additional 5 percent of the applicable coverage limit for debris removal if the amount to be paid for the damage to the property plus the debris removal expense exceeds the coverage limit for the damaged property. The debris removal coverage under the HO-3 also provides coverage for trees, shrubs, and plants, subject to sublimits. There is no debris removal coverage for trees, shrubs, and plants in the DP-3 form.

The DP-3 form provides 10 percent of the Coverage C limit as additional insurance to cover a tenant's improvements, alterations, and additions for loss by a covered peril. No comparable coverage exists in the HO-3 form.

The DP-3 form provides up to 10 percent of the Coverage C limit for loss to the property covered under Coverage C, except rowboats and canoes, while that property is anywhere in the world. The HO-3 form provides worldwide coverage for personal property owned or used by an insured, with no limitation except that a 10 percent limitation applies to property usually located at a secondary residence of the insured.

The DP-3 form provides up to 20 percent of the Coverage A limit for losses under both Coverage D—Fair Rental Value and Coverage E—Additional Living Expense as outlined in the Other Coverages provision. This coverage is additional insurance and does not reduce the Coverage A limit for the same loss. Under the HO-3 form, the corresponding additional limit for loss of use is 30 percent of the Coverage A limit.

The DP-3 form, like the HO-3 form, provides coverage for the cost of reasonable repairs made after the occurrence of a covered loss solely to protect covered property from further damage. This coverage does not increase the limit of liability that applies to the covered property.

Under both the DP-3 and HO-3, covered property is protected if it is removed from the premises because it is endangered by an insured peril. Under both policies, this coverage applies to direct loss from any cause (as long as an insured peril necessitated the removal) for thirty days. In the dwelling form, as in the homeowners form, the limit for this coverage is the same as the limit for the property being moved.

In both the HO-3 and the DP-3 forms, the maximum limit that can be applied (as an additional amount of insurance) to trees, shrubs, other plants, or lawns is 5 percent of the Coverage A limit. The limit for any one tree, plant, or shrub is $500, and only specified perils are covered. This coverage can be expanded by endorsement to include the perils of wind and hail.

The DP-3 form, like the HO-3 form, will pay up to $500 for fire department service charges. Coverage is not provided if the property is located within the limits of the city, municipality, or protection district furnishing the fire department response. This coverage is additional insurance, and no deductible applies.

The DP-3 form offers coverage for building collapse due to specified perils. As in the HO-3 form, coverage is for direct physical loss to covered property resulting from collapse caused by any of six perils:

- Coverage C—Personal Property perils
- Decay that is hidden from view
- Hidden insect or vermin damage, unless the insured is aware of the damage prior to the collapse
- Weight of contents, equipment, animals, or people
- Weight of rain collecting on a roof
- Use of defective materials or methods of construction

Collapse coverage does not increase the limit of liability that applies to the damaged covered property.

The DP-3 form provides coverage for breakage of glass or safety glazing material that is part of a building, storm door, or storm window, and for damage to covered property caused by breakage of such glass or safety glazing material. The coverage does not apply if the dwelling has been vacant for more than sixty consecutive days before the loss. This coverage does not increase the limit of liability that applies to the damaged property. Similar coverage is included in the HO-3 form.

The DP-3 form provides coverage for increased costs the insured incurs because of the enforcement of any ordinance or law. If the insured has purchased Coverage A, ordinance or law coverage is provided up to 10 percent of the Coverage A limit. If there is no Coverage A limit, up to 10 percent of the Coverage B limit is provided for ordinance or law coverage. This coverage is additional insurance. Coverage under the HO-3 form is similar and provides up to 10 percent of Coverage A for ordinance or law coverage as additional insurance.

If the insured is a tenant at the described location, the limit applying to ordinance or law coverage is up to 10 percent of the limit that applies to improvements, alterations, and additions.

Perils Insured Against

The perils insured against for both the DP-3 and HO-3 differ depending on whether Coverage A, B, or C are involved.

The DP-3, like the HO-3, uses the special form approach and insures against "risk of direct loss to property" (as opposed to named perils coverage) under Coverage A—Dwelling and Coverage B—Other Structures. In both the DP-3 and the HO-3 forms, the coverage for direct physical loss to real property is determined by the causes of loss that are excluded. Those causes of loss that are not excluded are covered. For example, the DP-3 form excludes coverage for theft of any property that is not part of a covered building or structure. It also excludes loss caused by wind, hail, ice, snow, or sleet to outdoor radio and television antennas and aerials, and to trees, shrubs, other plants, or lawns. Other exclusions in the DP-3 are essentially the same as those in the HO-3.

Although the Coverage C named perils under the DP-3 form are similar to the named perils coverage in the HO-3 form, there are some differences. Theft of personal property is not covered under the DP-3, but coverage is provided for damage to covered property caused by burglars, unless the dwelling has been vacant for more than sixty days. For example, if burglars break down a door, damage a table, and steal a television, the damage to the door and the table would be covered, but the loss of the stolen television would not be covered. The DP-3 specifically excludes pilferage, theft, burglary, and larceny under the peril of vandalism or malicious mischief.

The windstorm or hail coverage in the DP-3 also differs slightly from the HO-3. The DP-3 specifically excludes wind or hail damage to canoes and rowboats; the HO-3 covers such damage to watercraft and their trailers, furnishings, equipment, and outboard motors, but only while the items are inside a fully enclosed building.

Dwelling Policy General Exclusions

The general exclusions in the DP-3 track closely with the Section I exclusions in the HO-3. These exclusions include loss caused directly or indirectly by several perils or events:

- Ordinance or law, except as provided in the Other Coverages section
- Earth movement, such as an earthquake
- Water damage, such as flood and backup of sewers and drains
- Power failure that occurs off the described location
- Neglect on the part of the insured
- War
- Nuclear hazard
- Intentional loss
- Weather conditions that contribute to any of the preceding excluded causes of loss
- Acts or decisions of other persons, groups, organizations, or governmental bodies
- Faulty construction, planning, materials, or maintenance

Dwelling Policy Conditions

The DP-3 form contains a single section of conditions. Similar conditions are found in the HO-3 policy, but some HO-3 conditions apply only to Section I, while others apply to both Section I and Section II (liability). Because the

DP-3 form has no Section II (liability) coverage, there is no need to specify the section to which the conditions apply. These conditions include the insured's duties after a loss, loss to a pair or set, other insurance, mortgage clause, and other similar conditions regarding the coverage. See the exhibit "Comparison of the HO-3 and the DP-3 Forms."

Coverage for Liability and Theft Losses

Although the ISO dwelling forms do not provide coverage for liability or theft losses, such coverages are available by adding a personal liability supplement and a theft endorsement.

Liability coverage may be written as an addendum to the dwelling policy or as a separate policy using the personal liability supplement (DL 24 01). An insured who has both a homeowners policy on his or her residence and a dwelling policy on a rental dwelling also has the option of obtaining liability coverage for the rental dwelling by purchasing the homeowners additional residence rented to others endorsement (HO 24 70) for an additional premium.

The personal liability supplement provides Coverage L—Personal Liability and Coverage M—Medical Payments to Others. These coverages are similar in format and language to Coverage E—Personal Liability and Coverage F—Medical Payments to Others in Section II of the homeowners policy.

The exclusions and additional coverages in the personal liability supplement attached to the DP-3 are virtually the same as those applicable to Section II of the homeowners policy. The main difference is that the additional liability coverage for loss assessment provided (up to a limit of $1,000) in the HO-3 form is not provided in the personal liability supplement.

An insured may choose between two endorsements to the dwelling form to provide theft coverage similar to that provided in the homeowners policy.

The first endorsement, the Broad Theft Coverage (DP 04 72) endorsement, provides coverage against the perils of theft, including attempted theft, and vandalism or malicious mischief as a result of theft or attempted theft on-premises and off-premises. Off-premises coverage is available only if the insured purchases on-premises coverage. The endorsement includes special limits similar to the sublimits included in the HO-3 form, such as those for money, jewelry, and firearms. See the exhibit "Broad Theft Coverage—Special Limits of Liability."

The second endorsement, the Limited Theft Coverage (DP 04 73) endorsement, covers only on-premises theft, attempted theft, and vandalism or malicious mischief as a result of theft or attempted theft. The endorsement includes special limits only for watercraft and their trailers, trailers not used for watercraft, and firearms and related equipment. It does not cover off-premises theft. See the exhibit "ISO Dwelling Fire Policy Comparison Chart."

Comparison of the HO-3 and the DP-3 Forms

Coverage	HO-3	DP-3
A—Dwelling	Limit selected by insured	Same
	Replacement cost coverage if limit is at least 80% of replacement cost	Same
	Automatically included	Included only if limit selected and shown on Declarations page
B—Other Structures	10% of Coverage A	10% of Coverage A
	Automatically included	Provided in the Other Coverages section
	Replacement cost coverage if limit is at least 80% of replacement cost	Same
C—Personal Property	50% of Coverage A automatically included	Included only if limit selected and shown on Declarations page
	Worldwide coverage up to Coverage C limit	Worldwide coverage only up to 10% of Coverage C
	ACV (actual cash value) coverage	Same
D—Loss of Use	30% of Coverage A	Coverage D—Fair Rental Value and Coverage E—Additional Living Expense
	Automatically included	20% of Coverage A Provided in the Other Coverages section for both Coverage D and Coverage E
Additional/Other Coverages		
• Loss assessment	$1,000	None (can be added by endorsement)
• Credit card, electronic fund transfer card or access device, forgery and counterfeit money	$500	None
• Landlord's furnishings	$2,500 at residence	None included in the Other Coverages section, but if the dwelling is rented, the owner/landlord's furnishings are covered up to the Coverage C limit
• Debris removal	Additional 5% of limit of liability available	Included in limit of coverage
	Includes coverage for trees, shrubs, and plants, subject to a sublimit	No coverage for trees, shrubs, and plants
• Improvements, alterations, and additions	None	Tenant may use up to 10% of Coverage C (additional insurance)

• Reasonable repairs	Included in limit	Same
• Property removed	Covered up to 30 days from date of loss	Same
• Trees, shrubs, plants	5% of Coverage A, up to $500 per item for limited perils (not including wind or hail)	Same
	Additional insurance	Additional insurance
• Fire dept. service charge	$500	Same
• Collapse	Covered for limited perils	Same
• Glass or safety glazing material	Covered	Covered
• Ordinance or law	10% of Coverage A	10% of Coverage A. If no Coverage A, 10% of Coverage B. If insured is tenant, 10% of improvements, alterations, and additions limit
Personal Property— Special Limits/ Exclusions	$200 for money	Money excluded
	$1,500 for securities and other documents	Securities and documents excluded
	$1,500 for watercraft	Watercraft excluded (except rowboats and canoes)
Perils Insured Against		
• Coverages A & B	Special-form coverage (risk of direct loss, subject to exclusions)	Same
• Coverage C	Named perils (broad form)	Same
	Theft coverage included by endorsement	No theft coverage (theft can be added)
Section II—Liability		
• E—Personal Liability	Automatically included	None
• F—Medical Payments to Others	Automatically included	None
		Liability and medical payments can be added by purchase of personal liability supplement

This comparison is based on Insurance Services Office (ISO) forms. It can be used as a quick reference and as an easy method to compare the HO-3 and DP-3 policies. However, only the actual policy forms contain complete coverage information, and those forms should be used to determine coverage wording.

[DA05619]

Regardless of whether a certain peril is covered within a policy there are risk control measures an insured can use to avoid or mitigate a loss. The risk control measures suggested will depend on the type of loss exposure being avoided or mitigated. The exhibit provides examples of such risk control measures. See the exhibit "Examples of Risk Control Measures for DP-3 Loss Exposures."

Broad Theft Coverage—Special Limits of Liability

Category	Limit
Money, bank notes, bullion, gold	$200
Securities, accounts, deeds	$1,500
Watercraft of all types, including their trailers	$1,500
Trailers or semitrailers, other than those used with watercraft	$1,500
Jewelry, watches, furs	$1,500
Firearms and related equipment	$2,500
Silverware, goldware, platinumware, and pewterware	$2,500

[DA05620]

DWELLING COVERAGE CASE STUDY

Knowing how to apply the Dwelling Property—Special Form (DP-3) dwelling policy to the facts of a case is an important skill. This case study can help the student begin to make the transition from knowing policy language to knowing how to apply policy language to losses.

This case helps the student to apply the Insurance Services Office, Inc. (ISO) DP-3 dwelling policy to a given set of facts. The unendorsed DP-3 policy covers the dwelling but does not include liability coverage.

Case Facts

Based on the facts presented in this case, will the property claim be covered? If so, what amount would the insurer pay for the claim?

Wally and Dawn are a young married couple who have just purchased their first home. They had been saving money for over a year so that they could make this purchase, and now their funds are limited. The three-bedroom home was a bargain but will require a lot of work over the next few years. Before obtaining insurance coverage for the home, Wally and Dawn received several quotes from different insurers. They discovered that the cost of an HO-3 homeowners policy was much higher than that of a DP-3 dwelling policy. Although the homeowners policy provided broader coverage, the couple decided to purchase the dwelling policy to save money. The policy does not include any endorsements.

About six months after Wally and Dawn obtained the policy, the home was damaged as a result of an electrical fire in the basement. Most of the fire damage was restricted to the basement, but there was smoke damage throughout the home. The total cost of home repairs was $35,000. The washer and

ISO Dwelling Fire Policy Comparison Chart

Perils Insured Against	DP-1—Basic Form	DP-2—Broad Form	DP-3—Special Form	DP-8—Modified Loss Settlement
Fire or Lightning, Internal Explosion	Coverages A, B, and C	Coverages A, B, and C	Coverage C	Coverages A, B, and C
Windstorm or Hail	Coverages A, B, and C	Coverages A, B, and C	Coverage C	Coverages A, B, and C
Explosion	Optional	Coverages A, B, and C	Coverage C	Optional
Riot or Civil Commotion	Optional	Coverages A, B, and C	Coverage C	Optional
Aircraft	Optional	Coverages A, B, and C	Coverage C	Optional
Vehicles	Optional	Coverages A, B, and C	Coverage C	Optional
Smoke	Optional	Coverages A, B, and C	Coverage C	Optional
Volcanic Eruption	Optional	Coverages A, B, and C	Coverage C	Optional
Vandalism or Malicious Mischief	Optional	Coverages A, B, and C	Coverage C	Optional
Damage by Burglars	Not covered	Coverages A, B, and C	Coverage C	Not covered
Falling Objects	Not covered	Coverages A, B, and C	Coverage C	Not covered
Weight of Ice, Snow, or Sleet	Not covered	Coverages A, B, and C	Coverage C	Not covered
Accidental Discharge or Overflow of Water or Steam	Not covered	Coverages A, B, and C	Coverage C	Not covered
Sudden and Accidental Tearing Apart, Cracking, Burning, or Bulging	Not covered	Coverages A, B, and C	Coverage C	Not covered
Freezing	Not covered	Coverages A, B, and C	Coverage C	Not covered
Sudden and Accidental Damage From Artificially Generated Electrical Current	Not covered	Coverages A, B, and C	Coverage C	Not covered
All risk of direct physical damage not otherwise excluded	Not covered	Not covered	Coverages A, and B	Not covered
Loss Settlement:	Coverages A, B, and C Actual cash value (ACV)	Coverages A and B replacement cost Coverage C actual cash value (ACV)	Coverages A and B replacement cost Coverage C actual cash value (ACV)	Coverages A and B replacement cost Coverage C actual cash value (ACV)

[DA05899]

Examples of Risk Control Measures for DP-3 Loss Exposures

Type of Loss Exposure	Examples of Risk Control Measures (in Addition to Insurance and Risk Retention)
Freezing of a plumbing, heating, air conditioning, or automatic fire protective sprinkler system or of a household appliance	• Maintain heat in the building • Shut off the water supply and drain all systems and appliances of water
Theft of property not part of a covered structure	• Lock all doors and windows • Install a security system • Store valuables in a safety deposit box at a bank
Vandalism and malicious mischief, theft or attempted theft at a vacant dwelling	• Do not leave the dwelling vacant • Have the dwelling checked daily
Seepage or leakage from within a plumbing, heating, air conditioning, or automatic fire protective sprinkler system or from within a household appliance.	• Check systems regularly • Perform regular maintenance
Maintenance perils (that is, wear and tear; mechanical breakdown; rust, mold, or rot; settling, shrinking, bulging or expansion, including resultant cracking; or birds, vermin, rodents, insects or domestic animals)	• Perform regular and ongoing maintenance • Fumigate for insects • Close up openings that could allow animals to enter
Fire or Lightning	• Install smoke detectors, fire extinguishers, or central station fire and security alarm • Locate close to hydrants and fire hall • Install lightning rods • Install surge suppressors
Windstorm or Hail	• Avoid locating in windstorm or hail-prone areas • Keep property indoors that is susceptible to damage • Install storm shutters

dryer also needed to be replaced, and there was damage to some personal property stored in the basement, which amounted to a total actual cash value (ACV) of $2,350. Wally and Dawn could not live in the house for one month after the fire and rented an apartment for $725 for the month. Also, while the house was being repaired, a burglary occurred. During the night, someone broke in through the back door, and a television and some stereo equipment valued at $2,800 were stolen. The cost to repair the damage to the door and its framing was $3,150.

To confirm that the facts about an accident are accurate, insurers frequently rely on police reports, recorded statements from claimants and witnesses, and inspections of the premises where the loss occurred. See the exhibit "Case Facts."

Type of Loss Exposure	Examples of Risk Control Measures (in Addition to Insurance and Risk Retention)
Explosion	• Have furnaces and other heat sources inspected regularly • Work carefully with explosive materials such as solvents, propane, or gasoline
Riot or Civil Commotion	Avoid locating in areas prone to civil disturbance
Aircraft	Avoid locating close to airports
Vehicles	Avoid dwellings located close to busy roads
Smoke	Have boilers, furnace or related equipment checked and maintained regularly
Vandalism or Malicious Mischief	• Avoid locating in areas prone to vandalism • Do not leave premises unoccupied or vacant
Damage By Burglars	• Have premises well-lit at night • Install a security system with a local alarm
Falling Objects	• Trim any trees that overhang the premises • Check and maintain items, such as antennas, that might fall
Weight of Ice, Snow, or Sleet	Remove accumulated snow, ice, or sleet from roof
Accidental Discharge or Overflow of Water or Steam; Sudden and Accidental Tearing Apart, Cracking, Burning or Bulging	• Check systems regularly • Perform regular maintenance
Sudden and Accidental Damage From Artificially Generated Electrical Current	• Have the dwelling's wiring inspected • Ensure that appliances, fixtures, computers, home entertainment units or other types of electronic apparatus are in good repair
Volcanic Eruption	Avoid locating in areas prone to volcanic eruption

[DA05900]

Case Analysis Tools

To determine whether Wally and Dawn's DP-3 provides coverage for the damage to the home, the insurance or risk management professional should have copies of the applicable policy forms. See the exhibit "Dwelling Fire Policy."

Case Facts

Insureds	Wally and Dawn Jones
Types of policies and coverage limits	DP-3 Policy • Coverage A—Dwelling ($145,000 limit) • Coverage B—Other Structures (10 percent of Coverage A limit) • Coverage C—Personal Property ($25,000 limit) • Coverage E—Additional Living Expenses (20 percent of Coverage A limit) $500 deductible applies
Endorsements that affect the case	None
Other policy information	No other relevant information
Background	The insureds have complied with the policy conditions.

[DA05621]

To determine whether a policy covers a loss, many insurance professionals apply the DICE method. ("DICE" is an acronym for categories of policy provisions: declarations, insuring agreement, conditions, and exclusions.) The DICE method has four steps:

1. Review of the declarations page to determine whether it covers the person or the property at the time of the loss
2. Review of the insuring agreement to determine whether it covers the loss
3. Review of policy conditions to determine compliance
4. Review of policy exclusions to determine whether they preclude coverage of the loss

Each of these four steps is used in every case. Other categories of policy provisions should be examined. For example, endorsements and terms defined in the policy should be reviewed in relation to the declarations, insuring agreement, exclusions, and conditions.

Determination of Coverage

To examine the policy forms and determine whether coverage applies to the losses, the insurance professional can apply the DICE method, which involves four steps.

Dwelling Fire Policy

DWELLING FIRE POLICY

POLICYHOLDER
(Named Insured)

Wallace & Dawn Jones
32 Happy Lane
Anytown, USA 123456

POLICY NUMBER: ABC-DEF

POLICY PERIOD

Inception: March 5, 20XX

Expiration: March 5, 20XX

Policy period begins 12:01 A.M. standard time at the described location.

FIRST MORTGAGEE AND MAILING ADDRESS:

Anytown Bank & Trust
Main Street
Anytown, USA 12345

We will provide the insurance described in this policy in return for the premium and compliance with all applicable policy provisions.

COVERAGES	LIMIT
A—Dwelling	$145,000
B—Other Structures	Included
C—Personal Property	$ 25,000
D—Rental Value	Included
E—Additional Expense	Included

Deductible: $500.

CONSTRUCTION: Frame	**NO. FAMILIES:** One	**TYPE ROOF:** Approved
YEAR BUILT: 1948	**PROTECTION CLASS:** 6	

POLICY PREMIUM: $ 987.00   **COUNTERSIGNATURE DATE:** March 1, 20XX

AGENT: J. Smith

The first DICE step is to review the Declarations page to determine whether the individuals are covered and whether the incidents occurred during the policy period. In this case, Wally and Dawn are listed as named insureds on the Declarations page, and the losses occurred during the policy period.

The second DICE step is to determine whether the loss triggers coverage under the DP-3 dwelling policy. Coverage for the fire damage is triggered under the DP-3 policy for both Coverage A and Coverage C. For Coverage A, the perils insured against cover risk of direct physical loss to property, subject to exclusions. Because neither fire nor smoke is specifically excluded, the damage to the home is covered. See the exhibit "Perils Insured Against."

Perils Insured Against

PERILS INSURED AGAINST

A. Coverage A – Dwelling And Coverage B – Other Structures

1. We insure against risk of direct physical loss to property described in Coverages A and B.

2. We do not insure, however, for loss:

    a. Excluded under General Exclusions

Copyright, ISO Properties, Inc., 2002. [DA05623]

For Coverage C—Personal Property, the perils of fire or lightning and the peril of smoke are both listed as covered perils, so the damaged washer, dryer, and other personal property are covered. See the exhibit "Coverage C—Personal Property."

Coverage C—Personal Property

B. Coverage C – Personal Property

We insure for direct physical loss to the property described in Coverage C caused by a peril listed below unless the loss is excluded in the General Exclusions.

1. Fire Or Lightning …

7. Smoke

This peril means sudden and accidental damage from smoke, including the emission or puffback of smoke, soot, fumes or vapors from a boiler, furnace or related equipment.

This peril does not include loss caused by smoke from agricultural smudging or industrial operations.

Copyright, ISO Properties, Inc., 2002. [DA05624]

The cost to rent an apartment would also be covered under Coverage E—Additional Living Expense. This coverage provides for "any necessary increase in living expenses" incurred to maintain a normal standard of living, as long as the loss is covered under the Coverage A or C perils. The peril must also cause the premises to be unfit for its normal use; in this case, the insurer has agreed that this is so. See the exhibit "Coverage E—Additional Living Expense."

Coverage E—Additional Living Expense

E. Coverage E – Additional Living Expense

1. If a loss to property described in Coverage A, B or C by a Peril Insured Against under this policy makes the Described Location unfit for its normal use, we cover any necessary increase in living expenses incurred by you so that your household can maintain its normal standard of living.

    Payment will be for the shortest time required to repair or replace the Described Location or, if you permanently relocate, the shortest time required for your household to settle elsewhere.

Copyright, ISO Properties, Inc., 2002. [DA05625]

The burglary loss of the television and stereo equipment is not covered because theft is not listed as one of the covered perils under Coverage C. The damage to the door, however, is covered under the "Damage by Burglars" peril, which covers damage to covered property that is caused by burglars. The wording of this peril specifically emphasizes that theft of property is not covered. Also, there is no coverage if the dwelling has been vacant for more than sixty days (however, a dwelling under construction is not considered vacant). In this case, the home was vacant, but only for thirty days. Furthermore, the home was under construction at the time of the loss, so coverage for the damage to the door will be covered. See the exhibit "Damage By Burglars."

Damage By Burglars

9. Damage By Burglars

    a. This peril means damage to covered property caused by burglars.

    b. This peril does not include:

        (1) Theft of property; or

        (2) Damage caused by burglars to property on the Described Location if the dwelling has been vacant for more than 60 consecutive days immediately before the damage occurs. A dwelling being constructed is not considered vacant.

Copyright, ISO Properties, Inc., 2002. [DA05626]

The third DICE step is to determine whether all policy conditions have been met. Wally and Dawn have complied with all policy conditions, including promptly notifying the insurer of the loss. Also, the policy limits meet all insurance-to-value requirements as outlined in the DP-3 policy.

The fourth DICE step is to determine whether one or more exclusions preclude coverage that the insuring agreements have granted. In this case, none of the exclusions applies.

Determination of Amounts Payable

Determining the amount payable for a loss under the DP-3 policy involves analyzing the limit of liability available to pay losses.

Because fire and smoke are covered under the DP-3 policy and the insurance-to-value requirements have been met, the $35,000 damage to the home is covered in full. The cost of replacing the washer, dryer, and other personal property are also covered in full for the ACV of $2,350. Wally and Dawn will pay the $500 deductible for these losses one time unless the insurer determines that the fire loss and the burglary loss are two separate events. In that case, Wally and Dawn may have to pay a single $500 deductible for all losses related to the fire and then another $500 deductible for the burglary damage. The cost of renting an apartment for one month while the home was unfit for normal use will also be covered for $725 under Coverage E—Additional Living Expenses because this is less than the limit of 20 percent of the Coverage A limit. The cost to repair the damage caused by burglars will be paid in the amount of $3,150. The theft loss is not covered, so the $2,800 for the television and stereo equipment will not be paid. See the exhibit "Determination of Amounts Payable."

Determination of Amounts Payable

$35,000 damage to the home—Covered in full because the Coverage A limit is $145,000 and the insurance-to-value requirements have been met.

$2,350 actual cash value of replacing the washer, dryer, and other personal property— Covered in full because the Coverage C limit is $25,000.

$725 cost of renting an apartment for one month while the home was unfit for normal use—Covered in full under Coverage E—Additional Living Expenses because the amount is less than the limit of 20 percent of the Coverage A limit.

$3,150 cost to repair the damage caused by burglars—Covered in full under "Damage by Burglars" peril.

$2,800 cost of stolen television and stereo equipment—Not covered because theft is not listed as a covered peril for Coverage C.

Deductible—Wally and Dawn will pay the $500 deductible for these losses one time unless the insurer determines that the fire loss and the burglary loss are two separate events. In that case, Wally and Dawn may have to pay a single $500 deductible for all losses related to the fire and another $500 deductible for the burglary damage.

[DA05627]

INLAND MARINE FLOATERS

A homeowners policy may not provide adequate insurance for some types of personal property. Often, such coverage needs can be met with a personal inland marine policy.

Inland marine insurance is designed to cover property that has special value or that frequently moves ("floats") from one location to another. Although these types of personal property are covered under a homeowners policy, they are usually subject to certain limitations. Examples of such property include jewelry, furs, fine arts, silverware, cameras, stamp and coin collections, clothes and luggage, sports equipment, and musical instruments.

Inland marine insurance
Insurance that covers many different classes of property that typically involve an element of transportation.

Characteristics and Components

The restrictive nature of some personal property coverages under a homeowners policy creates the need for personal inland marine policies, which can provide higher limits of insurance for losses of a particular type or that occur at a particular location. For example, homeowners coverage for theft of jewelry is frequently limited to $1,500 or less, homeowners coverage for coins and medals is limited to $200, and homeowners coverage is limited to $1,000 or less for personal property that is usually located at an insured's premises other than the **residence premises**.

Residence premises
The place where the insured resides as identified in the policy declarations.

Often, individuals who own these types of property insure them by adding an endorsement to the homeowners policy. Examples can illustrate some of the reasons people may prefer to obtain coverage under a separate personal inland marine policy:

- A couple owns highly valued paintings and sculptures, and their insurer is reluctant to provide the requested amount of coverage by endorsement to their homeowners policy.
- To insure his collection of costly cameras and lenses, an amateur photographer needs customized coverage that his homeowners policy cannot offer.
- A retired person owns valuable jewelry or golf equipment but lives in a retirement home and has no homeowners policy.
- A couple want to keep their homeowners premium separate from the premium on jewelry or collectibles because the homeowners premium is paid together with their mortgage payment.

Although personal inland marine insurance can be customized to meet a variety of coverage needs, personal inland marine policies share these general characteristics:

- The coverage is tailored to the specific type of property to be insured, such as jewelry, cameras, or musical instruments.
- The insured may select the appropriate policy limits.
- Policies are often written without a deductible.
- Most policies insure property worldwide with special form coverage (open perils), subject to exclusions.

Open Perils Coverage

Special form (open perils) coverage was formerly known as "all risks of physical loss or damage," but as a result of expansive court decisions, the word "all" was dropped.

[DA00845]

In addition to the shared characteristics, personal inland marine policies have a shared structure consisting of three components:

- Declarations page
- Common Policy Provisions
- Coverage form

The Declarations page lists the named insured, the policy period, the premium, any deductible, any forms attached, and other options. Together with the Declarations page, the Common Policy Provisions and a coverage form complete the policy.

Common Policy Provisions

The Common Policy Provisions of the Insurance Services Office, Inc. (ISO) personal inland marine policy include an insuring agreement, definitions, exclusions, and conditions. (Each personal inland marine policy also contains other conditions and exclusions that are listed in the particular coverage form selected.)

The insuring agreement states that the insurer is providing the insurance described in the policy in return for the premium paid by the insured and the insured's compliance with policy provisions.

The Definitions section describes which terms in the policy refer to the insured and which refer to the insurer.

The Common Policy Provisions exclude coverage for losses caused directly or indirectly by several perils:

- War
- Nuclear hazard
- Governmental action (such as property seized by a public authority)
- Intentional loss
- Neglect

The Conditions section of the Common Policy Provisions specifies that insured property may have **scheduled coverage** by which articles or items are specifically listed. With certain exceptions, the amount paid for a covered loss is the least of four amounts:

Scheduled coverage
Insurance for property specifically listed (scheduled) on a policy, with a limit of liability for each item.

- The actual cash value of the insured property at the time of loss or damage
- The amount for which the insured could reasonably be expected to have the property repaired to its condition immediately before loss
- The amount for which the insured could reasonably be expected to replace the property with property substantially identical to the lost or damaged article
- The amount of insurance stated in the policy

The Conditions section of the Common Policy Provisions also specifies that insured property may have unscheduled coverage by which articles are covered on a **blanket basis**, such as stamps or coins in a collection. Separate loss settlement conditions apply to unscheduled property, with limitations on an absolute dollar amount (such as $250 per any one stamp or coin) and limitations determined by the proportion of the loss amount to the amount of blanket insurance provided.

Blanket basis
A basis for insuring all items within a single amount of insurance without specifically identifying each item.

A personal inland marine policy generally extends coverage to the named insured and members of the insured's family living in the same household.

Coverages

In the ISO personal inland marine program, two types of coverage forms are available: specialized and general.

Specialized forms are used to cover a single category of personal property, such as outboard motors and boats, fine arts, cameras, or motorized golf carts. In addition to the wide variety of specialized ISO forms, insurers often offer their own versions of these forms, making personal inland marine a highly customized line of business.

General forms are broader and generic in nature. These three general forms are commonly used to provide coverage on a single form for many kinds of personal property:

* Personal Articles Standard Loss Settlement Form
* Personal Property Form
* Personal Effects Form

Personal Articles Standard Loss Settlement Form

The Personal Articles Standard Loss Settlement Form provides special form coverage for any of several classes of personal property, including jewelry, furs, cameras, musical instruments, silverware, golfer's equipment, fine arts, and stamp and coin collections. A specific amount of insurance is shown in the policy for each class of property or for each specific article. (An agreed value version of the endorsement is also available.)

Inherent vice

A quality of or condition within a particular type of property that tends to make the property destroy itself.

In addition to the exclusions listed in the Common Policy Provisions, the Personal Articles Standard Loss Settlement Form excludes losses caused by wear and tear, deterioration, **inherent vice**, or insects or vermin.

Additional exclusions apply to fine arts. The Personal Articles Standard Loss Settlement Form excludes coverage for breakage of fragile articles unless the breakage is caused by fire or lightning; explosion, aircraft, or collision; windstorm, earthquake, or flood; malicious damage or theft; or derailment or overturn of a conveyance.

Personal Property Form

The Personal Property Form provides special form coverage on unscheduled personal property owned or used by the insured and normally kept at the insured's residence. The form also provides worldwide coverage on the same property when it is temporarily away from the residence premises. The Personal Property Form can be used to insure thirteen classes of unscheduled personal property. Coverage applies when a separate amount of insurance is shown for any of these classes:

* Silverware
* Clothing

- Draperies and rugs
- Electronic equipment and musical instruments
- Objects of art
- China and glassware
- Cameras
- Sports equipment and supplies
- Major appliances
- Bedding and linen
- Furniture
- Professional personal property and all other personal property
- Building additions and alterations

The total amount of insurance in each category is the maximum limit of recovery for any single loss to property in that category. The total amount for the thirteen categories is the total policy limit. Many of the exclusions that apply in the Personal Articles Standard Loss Settlement Form also apply to the Personal Property Form.

Personal Effects Form

The Personal Effects Form is designed for frequent travelers. It provides special form coverage on personal property such as luggage, clothes, cameras, and sports equipment normally worn or carried by tourists and travelers. The form covers property worldwide, but only while the property is away from the insured's permanent residence. **Personal effects** are not covered when in storage. Many of the exclusions that apply in the Personal Articles Standard Loss Settlement Form and the Personal Property Form also apply to the Personal Effects Form.

Personal effects
Personal property items owned by individuals that are personal in nature, such as jewelry, clothes, wallets, or purses.

The Personal Effects Form specifically excludes these types of property:

- Accounts, bills, currency, deeds, securities, passports
- Animals
- Artificial teeth or limbs
- Contact lenses
- Bicycles, hovercraft, motors, motor vehicles, watercraft
- Household furniture
- Merchandise for sale or exhibition
- Physicians and surgeons instruments
- Salesperson's samples
- Theatrical property
- Contraband property in the course of illegal transport or trade

Because the homeowners policy covers personal property worldwide, most homeowners do not see any need to purchase coverage under an inland marine Personal Effects Form. Coverage is occasionally sold to those who are ineligible for homeowners policies or to travelers who want the broadest possible protection on their luggage and other personal effects.

FARM INSURANCE COVERAGES

Farm loss exposures are unique in that they often involve a combination of personal lines and commercial lines loss exposures. Understanding the various ways in which farm loss exposures can be treated allows insurance professionals to best meet the needs of their farm clients.

Farms can range in size from a few acres to several thousand acres. They can produce a wide variety of products, such as vegetables, grains, livestock, trees, or fish. They can require various kinds of facilities, machinery, and equipment. And their owners face many different loss exposures, which can be insured using these common farm insurance forms:

- Insurance Services Office, Inc. (ISO) Farm Program
- ISO Homeowners endorsements
- Specialty farm and ranch programs that cover unique loss exposures

ISO Farm Program

Farms generally fall into one of two categories: those owned by families who live and work on their own land, and those owned by agribusiness corporations that are worked by employees who may or may not live on the property. As a result, farm policies are typically modular and can be tailored to cover farm business loss exposures, residential loss exposures, or both. ISO and the American Association of Insurance Services (AAIS) both file farm insurance policy forms, and some of the leading writers of farm insurance have developed their own forms.

The ISO forms and endorsements can be used separately or in combination to cover residential structures and personal property; farm personal property, such as farm machinery and livestock; and nonresidential structures such as barns and silos.

Farm personal property can be insured on either a scheduled or an unscheduled basis. The types of property that can be scheduled include farm machinery; rented or borrowed farm machinery, vehicles, and equipment; livestock; poultry; bees, worms, and fish; grain and feed; hay, straw, and fodder; farm products, materials, and supplies; and computers.

Although farm machinery and equipment and livestock are covered under the Farm Personal Property Coverage Form, individuals who want to insure either or both of these classes of property, and no others, can obtain coverage under these inland marine forms:

- Mobile Agricultural Machinery and Equipment Coverage Form (FP 00 30)
- Livestock Coverage Form (FP 00 40)

Coverage can be provided for basic, broad, or special causes of loss. While many of the perils covered are found in most property policies, additional causes of loss reflect those loss exposures particular to farming. These include, for example, electrocution of covered livestock, attacks on covered livestock by dogs or wild animals, accidental shooting of covered livestock, drowning of covered livestock, and loading/unloading accidents (livestock only).

The ISO farm liability form combines elements of homeowners liability coverage and commercial general liability coverage, and it includes special provisions to address liability loss exposures unique to farms. Umbrella and excess forms are also available to provide limits in excess of underlying policies for farm liability, auto liability, farm employers liability, recreational motor vehicle liability, and watercraft liability. See the exhibit "ISO Farm Insurance Program Components."

ISO Homeowners Endorsements

Farm-related loss exposures are not strictly limited to full-scale farming operations. Some homeowners may have incidental farming loss exposures arising out of activities such as selling fruit, produce, poultry, or other agricultural products raised on their residence premises. ISO provides two endorsements to cover incidental farming loss exposures:

- Incidental Farming Personal Liability Endorsement
- Farmers Personal Liability Endorsement

Incidental Farming Personal Liability Endorsement

The Incidental Farming Personal Liability Endorsement (HO 24 72) protects insureds against liability arising from the farming operations described in the endorsement's schedule. The endorsement is intended to cover farming or gardening operations that are not the insured's principal occupation. For example, a homeowner who works at a full-time job away from his residence as his primary source of income owns twenty acres of grassland. Each fall, he cuts and bales the hay to sell to local farmers. An Incidental Farming Personal Liability endorsement would insure his liability if a buyer were injured while transferring hay from the homeowner's shed to a trailer.

Farmers Personal Liability Endorsement

A homeowner may have an expanded incidental farm operation that includes a part-time or full-time farm employee, raising a few cows or sheep, or the

ISO Farm Insurance Program Components

Form #	Form Title	Contents
FP 00 12	Farm Dwellings, Appurtenant Structures and Household Personal Property Coverage Form	Four insuring agreements for covering residential structures and personal property on a farm
FP 00 13	Farm Personal Property Coverage Form	Two insuring agreements for covering farm personal property on either a scheduled or an unscheduled basis
FP 00 14	Barns, Outbuildings and Other Farm Structures Coverage Form	Single insuring agreement for covering nonresidential buildings and structures used in farming
FP 15 01	The Causes of Loss Form—Farm Property	Provisions for basic, broad, and special causes of loss
FP 00 90	The Other Farm Provisions Form	Provisions for various additional coverages, conditions, and definitions that are common to more than one of the other farm forms
FL 00 20	The Farm Liability Coverage Form	Three insuring agreements for covering bodily injury and property damage liability, personal and advertising injury liability, and medical payments
FB 00 01	The Farm Umbrella Liability Policy	Two insuring agreements for covering bodily injury and property damage liability and personal and advertising injury liability in excess of the retained limit
FE 00 01	Farm Excess Liability Policy	Single insuring agreement for covering farm liability in excess of the retained limit

Copyright, ISO Properties, Inc. [DA05765]

sale of "home-grown" vegetables to a local restaurant. The Farmers Personal Liability Endorsement (HO 24 73) provides coverage for these farm liability exposures.

The Farmers Personal Liability Endorsement deletes the standard business-related exclusion found under the homeowners policy and replaces it with its own conditions and exclusions, providing coverage for these farms and employees:

- Farms owned and operated or rented and operated by the insured or the insured's employees
- Farms owned by the insured and rented to others
- Insured farm employees

All farm premises and employees must be scheduled in order for coverage to be provided. Additionally, the endorsement adds exclusions particular to the farm exposure, including a pollution liability exclusion, a crop-dusting exclusion, and an exclusion of bodily injury to an uninsured farm employee (an unscheduled employee) arising out of his or her employment by the insured.

Specialty Farm and Ranch Programs

Family farms, larger farming operations, and agribusiness enterprises often have loss exposures that are not covered by basic farm policies and endorsements. For example, the coverage that standard farm policies provide for crops and livestock is inadequate for these insureds. Various types of specialty crop insurance and livestock insurance are available from private insurers and from the United States government to meet the needs of these operations:

- Crop-hail insurance— **Crop-hail insurance** is a traditional type of crop coverage offered by private insurers. In addition to covering hail damage to growing crops, crop hail policies are often extended to cover additional perils such as fire, windstorm accompanying hail, and damage caused by livestock and vehicles. Such policies may also cover harvested crops against named perils while being transported to the first place of storage.

- Multiple Peril Crop Insurance—The Federal Crop Insurance Corporation (FCIC) offers several crop insurance programs. One such plan provides Multiple Peril Crop Insurance (MPCI), which insures farmers against unexpected production losses (as measured against the insured farmer's production history) resulting from natural causes, including drought, excessive moisture, hail, wind, frost, insects, and disease.

- Animal mortality insurance— **Animal mortality insurance** is essentially term life insurance on animals. It generally covers against loss of the insured animal by (1) death resulting from accident, injury, sickness, or disease or (2) theft, subject to exclusions. It provides much broader protection than conventional livestock coverage under a farm policy. Moreover, an animal mortality policy can be written for whatever limit of insurance is agreeable to the insurer and the owner of the insured animal. A prize bull, for example, might be insured for $250,000, in contrast with the $2,000 per head livestock limit in a standard farm policy.

- Feedlot insurance—A second type of livestock coverage is **feedlot insurance**, which covers animals while in the custody of a commercial **feedlot** operator. The feedlot operator usually does not take ownership of the

Crop hail insurance
Insurance offered by private insurers that covers crops against loss caused by hail and often other perils.

Animal mortality insurance
Insurance that covers loss of valuable animals by (1) death resulting from accident, injury, sickness, or disease or (2) theft, subject to exclusions.

Feedlot insurance
A specialized type of livestock coverage that covers animals while in the custody of a commercial feedlot operator.

Feedlot
A commercial facility that fattens a farmer's animals and then markets them for slaughter at the best possible time.

animals but is paid on a commission basis. Feedlot operators have a bailee liability exposure for animals in their custody. They may also assume liability by contract for loss resulting from causes that would not otherwise be a bailee's responsibility. Feedlot insurance meets these coverage needs.

- Federal Crop Insurance—Livestock policies are also available from the Federal Crop Insurance Corporation for insuring cattle, swine, and lambs in eligible states. These policies provide protection against the loss of gross margin (market value of livestock minus feed costs) on covered livestock or price decreases for covered livestock during the policy period.

☑ Reality Check

Agritainment and Agritourism: Fun at the Farm or Blooming Liability?

"A decade or so ago, when Keith Harris mostly just grew corn and other vegetables on his family farm in Dayton, he called it River View Farm. But since then, in order to attract more fall customers and keep the place thriving, he's added a few attractions. Specifically, a six-acre corn maze, a corn launcher, a play area, farm animals, a tire pyramid, and oh by the way, pumpkins you can pick yourself. He says he made the changes to capitalize on the growing demand for 'agritainment' and 'agritourism' opportunities."[1]

Today's family farmers feel increasing pressure to find new ways to generate farm revenue and to avoid selling off the family farm to developers. Agritainment (offering entertainment to attract visitors) and agritourism (offering a family entertainment destination) offer farmers two increasingly popular options for raising additional funds. These options require offering public access to their properties and activities such as hayrack rides, corn mazes, "haunted" barns, petting zoos, produce picking, farm tours, concessions, horseback riding, and even overnight farm stays. Inviting commercial guests and offering such activities present increased loss exposures that might require specialty farm insurance coverages.

[DA05766]

FAIR AND BEACHFRONT AND WINDSTORM PLANS

Urban riots in the 1960s and windstorms affecting increasingly popular coastal communities have resulted in excessive property damage and, consequently, restricted insurance availability. State governments have therefore been prompted to develop programs that enable homeowners to purchase insurance for urban and coastal properties that are not insurable in the voluntary insurance market.

Most residences are insured under either a homeowners or a dwelling policy provided by a private insurer in the voluntary market, through which organizations willingly insure properties with average and below-average exposure to losses. However, insurers are reluctant to insure some residential dwellings that have greater-than-average exposure to losses. Examples of such homes include those in urban and coastal areas that are exposed to windstorm losses. Several government plans are available to insure such homes, which previously were uninsurable or were insurable only through the nonstandard market at very high premiums. (The nonstandard market is composed of organizations that insure properties with above-average exposure to losses.)

Examining two types of insurance plans, Fair Access to Insurance Requirements (FAIR) plans and beachfront and windstorm plans, illustrates how state governments have responded to the needs of homeowners who have difficulty insuring properties that face greater-than-average exposure to losses. A review of each of these plans focuses on the purposes and operations of the plan as well as the property that is eligible and the coverages available under the plan.

FAIR Plans

FAIR plans make standard lines of property insurance available for exposures located in areas underserved by the voluntary market. Participating private insurers and state insurance authorities coordinate efforts to provide such coverage. Each state with a FAIR plan has enacted its own legislation in response to local market needs, so the coverage provided and the methods of operation vary considerably.

Purpose and Operation

Lenders usually will not extend credit for the purchase of property unless the owner can obtain adequate property insurance coverages. FAIR plans make insurance coverage available when insurers in the voluntary market cannot profitably provide coverage at a rate that is reasonable for policyholders and provide the needed support for credit. Urban areas that are susceptible to damage caused by riots and civil commotion pose greater-than-average risk of loss for insurers in the voluntary market and are candidates for state-run FAIR plans. Some FAIR plans provide certain coverages for owners of coastal properties that pose greater-than-average exposure to windstorm damage. The potential hazard of brush fires in some wooded, suburban areas may also pose greater-than-average risk for insurers; consequently, some FAIR plans provide coverage for homes located in hazardous brush areas.

A property owner who is unable to obtain basic property insurance in the voluntary market can apply for insurance to the state's FAIR plan through an authorized insurance agent or broker. The FAIR plan might operate as a policy-issuing **syndicate**, in which the plan issues the policies and the plan's staff handles underwriting, processing, and possibly claim handling. In several

Syndicate

A group of insurers or reinsurers involved in joint underwriting to insure major risks that are beyond the capacity of a single insurer or reinsurer; each syndicate member accepts predetermined shares of premiums, losses, expenses, and profits.

states, the FAIR plan contracts with one or more voluntary insurers to act as servicing organizations. For a percentage of premium, these insurers perform underwriting, policyholder service, and claim handling functions. In the majority of plans, all licensed property insurers are required to share payment for plan losses in proportion to their share of property insurance premiums collected within the state.

Eligible Property

To be eligible for FAIR plan coverage, a property must be ineligible for coverage in the voluntary market, and the policyholder must have the property inspected by the FAIR plan administrator. Only property that meets the FAIR plan inspection criteria can be insured through the program. If the property fails to meet the basic safety levels (such as older houses in poor repair), owners can be required to make improvements as a condition for obtaining insurance. If the problems are not corrected, the state can deny insurance, provided the exposures are not related to the neighborhood location or to hazardous environmental conditions that are beyond the owner's control (such as a location next to a fireworks factory).

Under most FAIR plans, five types of exposures are considered uninsurable:

- Property that is vacant or open to trespass
- Property that is poorly maintained or that has unrepaired fire damage
- Property that is subject to unacceptable physical hazards, such as poor housekeeping or storage of flammable materials
- Property that violates a law or public policy, such as a condemned building (one that is considered unfit for human habitation)
- In some states, property that was not built in accordance with building and safety codes

Coverages

Some state FAIR plans provide limited homeowners coverage; however, most plans provide coverage only for fire and a limited number of perils, which often include vandalism, riot, and windstorm. Available limits of insurance and mandatory deductibles vary widely among plans.

Difference in conditions (DIC) policy, or DIC insurance

Policy that covers on an "all-risks" basis to fill gaps in the insured's commercial property coverage, especially gaps in flood and earthquake coverage.

When a policyholder wants greater coverage than that offered by the FAIR plan (such as when an expensive suburban home is written in the FAIR plan because it is located in a wooded area), a specialty insurer can write a **difference in conditions (DIC) policy**. This additional policy can cover risks of direct loss while excluding fire and the other perils covered under the FAIR plan policy. Because fire is the primary loss exposure for these suburban properties and FAIR plans provide coverage for that exposure, private insurers are willing to provide coverage for other perils.

Beachfront and Windstorm Plans

Properties located along the Atlantic and Gulf Coasts are especially vulnerable to windstorm loss. Serious winter storms can strike from the mid-Atlantic states northward, and the southern Atlantic and Gulf Coast states are subject to damage from hurricanes. Hurricanes in Florida and Hawaii have resulted in costly wind damage. Beginning in the late 1960s and beyond, insurers in the voluntary market withdrew from writing property coverage in coastal areas. Because these properties were uninsurable, numerous coastal states responded by developing beachfront and windstorm plans. Use of these plans and FAIR plans providing windstorm coverages has increased with the popularity and value of coastal properties.

Purpose and Operation

Beachfront and windstorm plans are similar to FAIR plans in that they make insurance coverage available for properties with greater-than-average exposure to loss and provide the needed support for credit. Most beachfront and windstorm plans provide insurance coverage for windstorm and hail losses that cannot be obtained in the voluntary market. Under these plans, losses from tidal water are generally excluded and should be covered under a flood insurance policy.

The operation of beachfront and windstorm plans is similar to that of FAIR plans. Some states that offer beachfront and windstorm plans operate using a single servicing organization that provides the underwriting, policyholder services, and claim handling services. Others operate as policy-issuing syndicates in which the plan issues the policies and the plan's staff provides services. In all plans, insurers that write property coverages in that state are required to share in plan losses in proportion to their share of state property insurance premiums.

Eligible Property

Properties eligible for coverage under beachfront and windstorm plans must be ineligible for coverage in the voluntary market and must be located in designated coastal areas. Furthermore, in some states, they must be located within a certain distance of the shoreline. Owners of property in coastal areas can obtain coverage for most real and personal property through these plans. Eligibility for coverage under each plan requires that buildings constructed or rebuilt after a specified date conform to an applicable building code. In addition to dwellings and other residential buildings, mobilehomes may be eligible if they meet certain construction and tie-down requirements.

As with FAIR plans, beachfront and windstorm plans will not insure certain types of property:

- Property that is poorly maintained or that has unrepaired damage
- Property that is subject to poor housekeeping
- Property that violates a law or public policy

Coverages

The perils insured against in beachfront and windstorm plans vary by state, but many such plans provide only windstorm and hail coverage. In those states, policyholders must obtain other property coverages through the voluntary insurance market or other nonstandard markets. A few states offer broader property coverages through the plans. The maximum limits of insurance available, as well as deductibles, vary among states. State plans generally contain a provision that no application for new coverage or increase in limits will be accepted when a hurricane has formed within a certain distance of the beach area where the property is located.

In recent years, some states have merged their FAIR and beachfront and windstorm plans as the popularity of coastal properties and these plans has grown. Florida and Louisiana have merged their FAIR and windstorm plans to create state-run property insurance companies: Florida Citizens Property Insurance Company (CPIC) and Louisiana Citizens Property Insurance Corporation (Louisiana Citizens), respectively. These state plans provide coverage for a range of exposures throughout the state; however, the primary loss exposure is beachfront windstorms.

THE NATIONAL FLOOD INSURANCE PROGRAM

Both homeowners and dwelling policies exclude flood losses. To make flood insurance available to property owners, the federal government provides it through the National Flood Insurance Program (NFIP) at subsidized rates for both dwellings and commercial buildings, as well as for the contents of both.

Because of the catastrophic loss potential of a flood, the cost to insure against flooding would raise property insurance rates significantly. The National Flood Insurance Act of 1968 (42 U.S.C. §§4001 et seq.) established the NFIP. Administered by the Federal Emergency Management Agency (FEMA), this program makes federal flood insurance available in all states, the District of Columbia, Puerto Rico, Guam, and the United States Virgin Islands.

NFIP flood insurance cannot be written everywhere in the U.S., nor can coverage be placed on every type of building or contents. Such insurance can be written only on an eligible building, or on eligible contents within an eligible building, located within an eligible community.

Community Eligibility

Flood insurance may be written only in communities that FEMA has designated as participating communities in the NFIP. A community's residents become eligible for flood insurance in one of two ways:

- The community applies to the Federal Insurance Administration (FIA) to be included in the NFIP.

- FEMA determines that an area is flood-prone and notifies the community that it has one year to decide whether to join the NFIP. The FIA notifies those communities and offers to help deal with their flood problems should they elect to join the NFIP. A community that chooses not to join the NFIP is not eligible for federal flood assistance. A community must participate in the flood program within one year of notification or risk denial of federal or federal-related construction, acquisition, and other assistance.

If a community identified as flood-prone does not wish to participate in the NFIP, it has two options: contest the designation or simply choose not to participate. A community that successfully contests the flood-prone designation is still eligible for federal aid if a flood occurs. If a community chooses not to participate in the NFIP, its access to federal funds is limited.

Community participation in the NFIP is voluntary, although some states require NFIP participation as part of their floodplain management program. Each identified flood-prone community must assess its flood hazard and determine whether flood insurance and floodplain management would benefit its residents and economy.

Incentives and Programs

A community has many incentives for participating in the NFIP. A community that includes a **special flood hazard area (SFHA)** must participate in the NFIP program for NFIP flood insurance to be available within that community. Furthermore, the law restricts development by prohibiting any form of federal financial assistance for acquisition or construction purposes in an SFHA. For example, only NFIP participating communities are eligible for loans guaranteed by the Department of Veterans Affairs, insured by the Federal Housing Administration, or secured by the Rural Housing Service.

If a disaster occurs as a result of flooding in a nonparticipating community, no federal financial assistance can be provided for the permanent repair or reconstruction of insurable buildings in SFHAs. Eligible applicants for disaster assistance may, however, receive forms of disaster assistance that are not related to permanent repair and reconstruction of buildings. If a community is accepted into the NFIP within six months of a disaster, these limitations on federal disaster assistance are lifted.

Special flood hazard area (SFHA)

Area that the NFIP has classified as being expected to experience flooding at least once in 100 years.

Emergency Program

Flood hazard boundary map

A temporary map designed to identify flood-prone areas in the community.

Once a community has submitted an application for flood insurance and all other necessary information to the FIA, the FIA prepares a **flood hazard boundary map** if one does not exist. A flood hazard boundary map is based on approximate data and identifies, in general, the SFHAs within a community. These maps not only identify flood hazard areas, but also define areas where people in SFHAs can buy coverages. They also are used in the NFIP's emergency program for floodplain management and insurance purposes. The FIA sends the community's map to the state coordinating agency, the state insurance commissioner, the regional FEMA flood specialist, and other federal agencies.

Emergency program

Initial phase of a community's participation in the National Flood Insurance Program in which property owners in flood areas can purchase limited amounts of insurance at subsidized rates.

Flood Insurance Rate Map (FIRM)

A map that shows exact boundaries for special flood hazard areas, the various flood zones, and base flood elevations.

When a community first joins the NFIP, property owners in special flood hazard areas can purchase limited amounts of insurance at subsidized rates under the **emergency program**. Although the community is eligible under the emergency program, the FIA arranges for a detailed study of the community and its susceptibility to flood. The study results in the publication of a **Flood Insurance Rate Map (FIRM)** that divides the community into specific zones to identify the probability of flooding in each zone.

The amount of coverage is based on the type of building or contents, and only four emergency premium rates apply:

- For residential buildings
- For residential contents
- For nonresidential buildings
- For nonresidential contents

These rates, which apply per $100 of insurance, are uniform in all eligible communities. The maximum limits are $35,000 for a single- or two- to four-family dwelling and $10,000 for its contents. Limits vary for states and territories that are not in the lower forty-eight states and for other types of residential and nonresidential buildings.

As an example of how emergency program coverage applies, consider Helen, who owns a home in a flood-prone area. Helen's home is valued at $60,000, and the contents of her home are worth $19,000. The community in which Helen lives has qualified under the emergency flood insurance program. Therefore, Helen can insure her house for $35,000 and the contents for $10,000, the maximum limits available.

Once the first layer of insurance coverage has been made available to individuals in a flood-prone area through the emergency program, they cannot obtain federal or federally insured loans for new construction unless they purchase flood insurance. New construction includes not only new buildings but also building repair, reconstruction, or improvement costs that amount to 50 percent or more of the building's market value before the project's start or, if the project is necessary to restore a damaged building, the building's market value at the time of the damage.

Regular Program

Under the emergency program, federally subsidized rates in limited amounts are available before completion of a community's Flood Insurance Study (FIS). After FEMA completes its assessment of a community's flood-prone area, establishes an accurate FIRM, and calculates actuarial rates, the community is promoted from the emergency program to the second and final NFIP phase, the **regular program**.

Full limits of coverage are available to communities in the regular program. The maximum limits are $250,000 for a single- or two- to four-family dwelling and $100,000 for its contents, with variations for nonresidential buildings. The conversion from the emergency program to the regular program depends on the community's enacting and enforcing floodplain management regulations. A community that fails to convert to the regular program is suspended from the program and is ineligible for any flood insurance.

The example involving Helen demonstrates how the coverage limits of the regular program function. Helen's home is valued at $60,000, and her contents are worth $19,000. Under the emergency program, she has $35,000 of insurance on her home and $10,000 worth of coverage for its contents. Once her community is under the regular program, Helen can apply for and pay premiums for full coverage (maximum available limits of $250,000 for a single-family home and $100,000 for contents). The coverage is subject to deductibles, which apply separately to building and to contents. See the exhibit "NFIP Flood Insurance Coverage Limits."

Regular program

Second phase of the National Flood Insurance Program in which the community agrees to adopt flood-control and land-use restrictions and in which property owners purchase higher amounts of flood insurance than under the emergency program.

NFIP Flood Insurance Coverage Limits

Coverage Type	Emergency Program Limit	Regular Program Limit
One- to four-family structure	$ 35,000*	$250,000
One- to four-family home contents	$ 10,000	$100,000
Other residential structures	$100,000**	$250,000
Other residential contents	$ 10,000	$100,000
Business structure	$100,000**	$500,000
Business contents	$100,000	$500,000
Renter contents	$ 10,000	$100,000

* In Alaska, Guam, Hawaii, and U.S. Virgin Islands, the amount available is $50,000.

** In Alaska, Guam, Hawaii, and U.S. Virgin Islands, the amount available is $150,000.

"Regular Program Limits," www.floodsmart.gov/floodsmart/pages/faqs/how-much-flood-insurance-coverage-is-available.jsp (accessed March 14, 2010), and "Emergency Program Limits," http://rifloods.wordpress.com/2009/10/01/changes-to-nfip-today/ (accessed March 14, 2010). [DA05801]

Flood Insurance Coverage

Three flood insurance policies are available:

- The dwelling form is used for any dwelling having an occupancy of no more than four families, such as single-family homes, townhouses, row houses, and individual condominium units.
- The general property form is used for all other occupancies—that is, multi-residential and nonresidential, except for residential condominium building associations.
- Residential condominium building associations are eligible for coverage under the residential condominium building association form.

All three policies protect insureds against direct losses to real and personal property from the flood peril. These policies do not cover indirect losses, such as additional living expenses; rent; rental value; and enforcement of any ordinance or law regulating the construction, repair, or demolition of buildings. See the exhibit "Standard Flood Insurance Policy Forms."

Waiting Period

To avoid adverse selection, the NFIP generally requires a thirty-day waiting period for new flood insurance policies and for endorsements that increase coverage on existing policies. Coverage does not become effective until thirty days after the date of the application or, in certain cases, thirty days after receipt of the application by the NFIP or its representative.

Absent the waiting period, property owners might delay purchase of flood insurance until an impending flood endangered their property. An exception to the waiting period is made for flood insurance that is purchased initially in connection with a new or an increased mortgage on a property. In such cases, the policy becomes effective at the time the mortgage becomes effective, provided that the policy is applied for at or before the transfer of ownership or date of mortgage.

For example, Alan purchases a home on riverfront property. The property settlement is scheduled for July 25 at noon, and the mortgage becomes effective at the same time. Alan submits an application and pays the appropriate premium to NFIP on July 24 for flood insurance on his new home. Alan's flood policy will become effective at noon on July 25 when the property is transferred to him. Because a new mortgage is involved, Alan's flood policy is not subject to the thirty-day waiting period.

Write-Your-Own (WYO) Program

The NFIP provides government-underwritten flood insurance through two mechanisms:

- A producer may write the business directly through the servicing representative designated by the FIA. FIA has elected to have state-licensed

Standard Flood Insurance Policy Forms

Policy Form	Description
Dwelling Policy Form	The Dwelling Policy Form may be issued to homeowners, residential renters, condominium unit owners, and owners of residential buildings containing two to four units. The policy provides building and/or contents coverage for: • A detached, single-family, non-condominium residence with incidental occupancy limited to less than 50 percent of the total floor area • A two- to four-family, non-condominium building with incidental occupancy limited to less than 25 percent of the total floor area • A dwelling unit in a residential condominium building • A residential townhouse/rowhouse • Manufactured mobile homes
General Property Policy Form	The General Property Policy Form may be issued to owners or lessees of non-residential buildings or units, or residential condominium buildings that are uninsurable under the Residential Condominium Building Association Policy (RCBAP). The policy provides building and/or contents coverage for these and similar "other residential" risks: • Hotel or motel with normal guest occupancy of six months or more • Apartment building • Residential cooperative building • Dormitory • Assisted-living facility It also can be used to cover these types of non-residential risks, among others: • Shop, restaurant, or other business • Mercantile building • Factory or warehouse • Nursing home
Residential Condominium Building Association Policy (RCBAP) Form	The Residential Condominium Building Association Policy Form may be issued to condominium associations to insure eligible residential condominium buildings.

Adapted from www.fema.gov/business/nfip/sfip.shtm (accessed March 14, 2010). [DA05802]

insurers' agents and brokers sell flood insurance to consumers. State regulators hold the insurers' agents and brokers accountable for providing NFIP customers with the same standards and level of service required of them in selling other lines of insurance. FIA underwrites the applications submitted by the servicing representatives and directly processes claims for losses under the policies. The servicing representatives receive a commission for the policies they write.

- A producer may place the business with an insurer participating in FIA's **Write-Your-Own (WYO) program**.

Write-Your-Own (WYO) program

A program allowing private insurers to write flood insurance under the National Flood Insurance Program (NFIP).

The WYO program is a cooperative undertaking of the insurance industry and the FIA. Insurers participating in the WYO program issue the majority of NFIP policies in force. WYO allows private insurers participating in the program to sell and service flood insurance under their own names.

Regardless of whether the NFIP or a WYO insurer issues a policy, the coverage provided is identical, and WYO insurers use exactly the same language used in policies that the NFIP issues directly. In the WYO program, the FIA determines rates, coverage limitations, and eligibility. The NFIP totally reinsures the coverage. Insurers receive an expense allowance for policies written and claims processed, while the federal government retains responsibility for losses. Insurers collect premiums, retain commissions, and use the remainder of the premiums to pay claims.

If flood losses exceed the amounts an insurer holds to pay flood claims, the federal government makes up the difference. However, if flood insurance premiums exceed losses, the insurer pays the excess to the federal government. Participating insurers issue and service flood insurance policies through their own operations and can retain approximately 30 percent of the premium to cover expenses.

The goals of the WYO program are to increase the number of flood policies written, to improve services, and to involve private insurers in the sale of flood insurance. More than 90 percent of all NFIP policies are written through private insurers under the WYO program.

Flood Insurance Reform

The Flood Insurance Reform Act of 2004 (Pub.L. 108-264) reformed the NFIP and the terms of the National Flood Insurance Act. It created a five-year pilot program to reduce losses to properties experiencing repetitive flood insurance claims. "Repetitively flooded" homes are those that have received four or more flood insurance claim payments of more than $5,000 each, with the cumulative amount exceeding $20,000, or two or more claim payments that cumulatively exceed the value of the property.

The reform act's preamble included congressional findings that quantify the motivation behind the act:

- The NFIP insured more than 4 million policyholders.
- About 48,000 properties in the program had experienced, within a ten-year period, two or more flood losses in which each loss was more than $1,000.
- About 10,000 repetitive-loss properties experienced two or three losses that cumulatively exceeded building value.
- These repetitive-loss properties cost taxpayers about $200 million annually.
- About 1 percent of insured properties accounted for 25 to 30 percent of claims.
- The majority of repetitive-loss properties were built before the 1974 implementation of floodplain management standards created under the original program and were eligible for subsidized flood insurance.

In an average year, fewer than 1 percent of all NFIP-insured properties represent 25 percent of all loss payments. This act provided a disincentive to property owners to live in repetitively flooded areas. Rather than encouraging rebuilding, the program provides repeatedly flooded homeowners with assistance in either elevating or moving their homes away from flood waters. Most mitigation offers involve elevation assistance. Those who refuse mitigation assistance pay for choosing to live in risky areas because refusal of a mitigation offer triggers the rate increases. Previously, many individuals and communities had no incentive to elevate their properties or to move.

To illustrate, the property owner of a repeatedly flooded property who refuses a reasonable mitigation offer will experience a flood insurance premium increase to 150 percent of the chargeable rate for the property at the time of the mitigation offer. Property owners can appeal rate increases following refusal of mitigation offers.

The act helps people move away from flood-prone areas by providing a $450 million increase over five years in an existing FEMA grant assistance program. The increase is to be used by local communities to relocate or elevate properties sustaining the most flood damage, saving an estimated $65 to $70 million annually by preventing or mitigating losses and paying for itself five to six years after program completion. In cases in which a buyout is the best option, the act includes a purchase offer and an appeals process, as well as safeguards to ensure continued home ownership.

Finally, the act reduces intensive development in repeatedly flooded areas to help restore the natural functions of floodplains, such as wildlife biodiversity and wetlands that absorb flood waters.

☑ Reality Check

Spring Rains Bring Disaster

The flooding problems that AccuWeather.com feared would ensue across the Northeast have evolved. Unfortunately, flooding will remain an issue for many communities through the next several days.

Melting snow was a significant contributor to the flooding across the central Appalachians. The arrival of colder air will slow the melting rate the rest of this weekend. A few mountain peaks will even have snowflakes.[2]

Individuals living in low-lying areas often look forward to spring with dread. Rather than thinking about warmer temperatures and budding flowers, these families and their communities start preparing for floods. This is particularly true when spring rains follow a winter season with heavy snow amounts. Thawing snow causes the ground to become saturated, and even minor downpours can cause significant flooding. A major storm system with many days of rain can only lead to disaster.

In 2008, floods in large areas of the Midwest caused billions of dollars in property damage and loss of life. Cedar Rapids, Iowa, suffered significant effects from this storm. In 2009 and 2010, heavy rains combined with melting snow caused flooding in the Red River Valley and particularly in Fargo, North Dakota, resulting in substantial property damage losses. Similar weather patterns also caused spring flooding and property damage in states along the East Coast and into New England in 2007.

Such events underscore the importance of flood insurance to individuals and businesses as well as the fact that the flood loss exposure is not limited to coastal locations.

[DA05803]

NATIONAL FLOOD INSURANCE PROGRAM COVERAGE CASE STUDY

Floods are typically catastrophic losses that affect large numbers of insureds at the same time. Claim representatives handling flood losses are generally under pressure to settle claims quickly and fairly when resources may be scarce and conditions difficult. A thorough understanding of how to determine coverage and the amount payable in a flood claim can help claim representatives manage challenging circumstances efficiently.

When adjusting a flood insurance claim, the claim representative must establish the facts of the case and then analyze the policy wording itself to determine whether coverage exists for the loss and, if so, the appropriate amount to offer in settlement of the insured's claim.

Case Facts

When a community has applied to the Federal Insurance Administration (FIA) to participate in the National Flood Insurance Program (NFIP), and has been approved for inclusion in the regular program, what happens when a flood occurs in that community? How are flood losses actually adjusted?

Anytown is located along the banks of the Winding River. The town participates in the NFIP regular flood program. It is spring, and melting snow and heavy rains have caused the Winding River to overflow, flooding many of the homes and businesses in town. The flooding lasts two weeks before the muddy water begins to recede.

William is an NFIP-certified flood adjuster who works for an independent adjusting firm. He and several coworkers have been sent to Anytown to assist in handling the numerous losses that have occurred. The first claim that William is assigned involves damage to the home of Max and Felicia, who have a separate HO-3 policy in addition to an NFIP Dwelling Form. The couple has owned the home for several years and has a mortgage on the property with the local savings and loan association. The NFIP policy limits are $175,000 on the dwelling and $60,000 on the contents. The policy deductible applies separately to the dwelling coverage and to the contents coverage. See the exhibit "Flood Insurance Coverage Facts."

Flood Insurance Coverage Facts

Insureds	Max and Felicia
Policy	NFIP Standard Flood Insurance Policy Dwelling Form
Building Limit	$175,000
Contents Limit	$60,000
Deductible	$1,000 Building coverage $1,000 Contents coverage
Endorsements that affect the case	None
Background	Insureds have complied with policy conditions

[DA05931]

As required under the terms of the policy, the insureds have submitted a proof of loss detailing the estimated value of their claim. These values exclude items of property contained in the basement, which are not covered under the NFIP Dwelling Form (see "Section III Property Covered" in the NFIP Dwelling Form). The flood damage to the couple's home is extensive in the basement and on the ground floor. All of the drywall and wall-to-wall carpeting needs to be replaced, and the furniture is damaged beyond repair. The refrigerator, stove, and built-in dishwasher cannot be salvaged, nor can the television, DVD player, or personal computer. In addition to the damage at their home, Max and Felicia incurred the cost of staying in a hotel during the flood and will continue to stay there while their claim is settled and their house and contents are repaired or replaced. See the exhibit "Max and Felicia's Estimate of the Value of Their Claim."

Max and Felicia's Estimate of the Value of Their Claim

Item	Estimate
Structural repairs to the home	$45,000
Carpeting	$7,000
Refrigerator, stove, and dishwasher	$3,000
Furniture	$30,000
Television, DVD player, and personal computer	$2,000
Hotel stay	$9,000

[DA05932]

Case Analysis Tools

To determine coverage, William will need a copy of Max and Felicia's NFIP Dwelling Form, including the policy declarations. The declarations page identifies who is covered, the location, and the policy period, as well as any endorsements that may apply. A description of the dwelling as well as the coverage limits are also listed on the declarations page. To determine whether the policy covers this loss, William will apply the DICE method. See the exhibit "DICE Decision Tree."

Determination of Coverage

As a first step in the DICE method of coverage determination, William examines the declarations page of Max and Felicia's policies. Because it has been determined that this loss resulted as a consequence of a flood (see the "Definitions" section of the NFIP Dwelling Form), the homeowners policy will not provide coverage. In reviewing the NFIP Dwelling Form, William notes that the property for which they are submitting their claim is the insured location on that policy. The loss occurred during the policy period. The policy limits are $175,000 on the home and $60,000 on the contents. The $1,000 deductible on the policy will apply to both the building portion of the loss and the contents portion. The local savings and loan association is listed as mortgagee on the policy.

DICE Decision Tree

To determine whether a policy covers a loss, many insurance professionals apply the DICE method. ("DICE" is an acronym for categories of policy provisions: declarations, insuring agreement, conditions, and exclusions.) The DICE method has four steps:

1. Review of the declarations page to determine whether it covers the person or the property at the time of the loss
2. Review of the insuring agreement to determine whether it covers the loss
3. Review of policy conditions to determine compliance
4. Review of policy exclusions to determine whether they preclude coverage of the loss

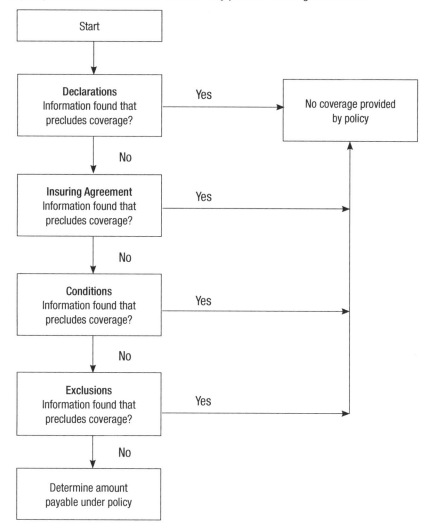

Each of these four steps is used in every case. Other categories of policy provisions should be examined. For example, endorsements and terms defined in the policy should be reviewed in relation to the declarations, insuring agreement, exclusions, and conditions.

[DA00232]

The second step in the process is to examine the policy's insuring agreement. William verifies that Max and Felicia have paid the correct premium, have complied with the terms and conditions of the policy, and have furnished accurate information. The insurer must, therefore, fulfill its obligations under the insuring agreement. However, the insurer is obligated to cover only direct physical loss. This means that Max and Felicia's claim for their hotel expenses is not covered because additional living expenses are an indirect loss rather than a direct loss. William explains this to the couple and shows them the applicable section of the policy wording:

I. AGREEMENT

The Federal Emergency Management Agency (FEMA) provides flood insurance under the terms of the National Flood Insurance Act of 1968 and its amendments, and Title 44 of the Code of Federal Regulations (CFR).

We will pay you for direct physical loss by or from flood to your insured property if you:

1. Have paid the correct premium;

2. Comply with all terms and conditions of this policy; and

3. Have furnished accurate information and statements.[3]

The third step in the DICE method is to examine the policy conditions. The NFIP Dwelling Form includes twenty-two conditions that outline the obligations of both the insurer and the insured and that clarify aspects of the coverage provided under the policy. William examines all of the conditions and determines that the two that are significant in this particular claim are the Mortgage Clause and the Loss Settlement condition.

The Mortgage Clause requires that William pay any Coverage A—Building loss to the mortgagee. In practice, the claim settlement check would be made payable to both the insureds and the mortgagee. In addition, even if for some reason Max and Felicia's claim were denied, their mortgagee's interest in their home could still be protected under the policy.

The Loss Settlement condition outlines how a flood loss is to be valued. Before valuing the loss, William will need to determine whether any policy exclusion applies. This will require him to examine two separate sections of the policy—V. Exclusions and IV. Property Not Covered.

V. EXCLUSIONS

A. We only provide coverage for direct physical loss by or from flood, which means that we do not pay you for:

1. Loss of revenue or profits;

2. Loss of access to the insured property or described location;

3. Loss of use of the insured property or described location;

4. Loss from interruption of business or production;

5. Any additional living expenses incurred while the insured building is being repaired or is unable to be occupied for any reason;

6. The cost of complying with any ordinance or law requiring or regulating the construction, demolition, remodeling, renovation, or repair of property, including removal of any resulting debris. This exclusion does not apply to any eligible activities that we describe in Coverage D - Increased Cost of Compliance; or

7. Any other economic loss.[4]

The only exclusion that applies to Max and Felicia's claim is that for additional living expenses. William has already discussed this with the insureds. A review of Section IV. Property Not Covered confirms that none of the items the insureds are claiming is included there. William advises the insureds that, with the exception of their additional living expenses, their claim will be covered. The next step is to determine the amount payable under the policy and make an appropriate settlement offer.

Determination of Amounts Payable

William begins the process of valuing the claim by verifying which items are covered under the building limit and which are considered to be contents. Section III. Property Covered specifies a list of items that are to be included under the building coverage. William determines that the dishwasher, carpeting, stove, and refrigerator fall under the building portion of the claim. He also verifies that no excluded items from the basement have been included in either the building or the contents claim.

7. The following items of property which are covered under Coverage A only:

a. Awnings and canopies;

b. Blinds;

c. Built-in dishwashers;

d. Built-in microwave ovens;

e. Carpet permanently installed over unfinished flooring;

f. Central air conditioners;

g. Elevator equipment;

h. Fire sprinkler systems;

i. Walk-in freezers;

j. Furnaces and radiators;

k. Garbage disposal units;

l. Hot water heaters, including solar water heaters;

m. Light fixtures;

n. Outdoor antennas and aerials fastened to buildings;

o. Permanently installed cupboards, bookcases, cabinets, paneling, and wallpaper;

p. Plumbing fixtures;

q. Pumps and machinery for operating pumps;

r. Ranges, cooking stoves, and ovens;

s. Refrigerators; and

t. Wall mirrors, permanently installed.[5]

William turns next to the Conditions section of the policy and examines the Loss Settlement condition. It specifies that the policy pays replacement cost on the building portion of the insured's loss, provided that the home is insured to at least 80 percent of its full replacement cost (or is the maximum amount of insurance available under the NFIP, which does not apply in this case). William determines that Max and Felicia's home is insured to value. The Loss Settlement condition further specifies that contents losses are paid on an actual cash value (ACV) basis.

2. Replacement Cost Loss Settlement

The following loss settlement conditions apply to a single-family dwelling described in V.1.a. above:

a. We will pay to repair or replace the damaged dwelling after application of the deductible and without deduction for depreciation, but not more than the least of the following amounts:

(1) The building limit of liability shown on your Declarations Page;

(2) The replacement cost of that part of the dwelling damaged, with materials of like kind and quality, and for like use; or

(3) The necessary amount actually spent to repair or replace the damaged part of the dwelling for like use.

4. Actual Cash Value Loss Settlement

The types of property noted below are subject to actual cash value [or in the case of V.4.a.(2) below, proportional] loss settlement.

a. A dwelling, at the time of loss, when the amount of insurance on the dwelling is both less than 80 percent of its full replacement cost immediately before the loss and less than the maximum amount of insurance available under the NFIP. In that case, we will pay the greater of the following amounts, but not more than the amount of insurance that applies to that dwelling:

(1) The actual cash value, as defined in II.B.2., of the damaged part of the dwelling; or

(2) A proportion of the cost to repair or replace the damaged part of the dwelling, without deduction for physical depreciation and after application of the deductible.

This proportion is determined as follows: If 80 percent of the full replacement cost of the dwelling is less than the maximum amount of insurance available under the NFIP, then the proportion is determined by dividing the actual amount of insurance on the dwelling by the amount of insurance that represents 80 percent of its full replacement cost. But if 80 percent of the full replacement cost of the dwelling is greater than the maximum amount of insurance available under the NFIP, then the proportion is determined by dividing the actual amount of insurance on the dwelling by the maximum amount of insurance available under the NFIP.

b. A two-, three-, or four-family dwelling.

c. A unit that is not used exclusively for single family dwelling purposes.

d. Detached garages

e. Personal property

f. Appliances, carpets, and carpet pads.

g. Outdoor awnings, outdoor antennas or aerials of any type, and other outdoor equipment.

h. Any property covered under this policy that is abandoned after a loss and remains as debris anywhere on the described location.

i. A dwelling that is not your principal residence.[6]

William calculates the value of the building portion of the insureds' loss at $55,000. This includes the structural repairs to the home and replacement of the carpeting, the refrigerator, the stove, and the dishwasher. Based on the age and condition of the contents immediately before the loss, William determines that their depreciated value, or actual cash value, is 50 percent of their replacement cost. Therefore, the value of the contents portion of the loss is $16,000, or 50 percent of the couple's initial replacement estimate of $32,000. Because the building limit on the policy is $175,000 and the contents limit is $60,000, both the building and contents portions of the loss are fully covered. After subtracting the deductible from both the building loss ($55,000 minus $1,000) and the contents loss ($16,000 minus $1,000), William makes a settlement offer of $69,000, which Max and Felicia accept. See the exhibit "Correct Answers."

Correct Answers

Item	Coverage	Estimate	Value
Structural repairs to the home	Building	$45,000	$45,000
Carpeting	Building	$7,000	$7,000
Refrigerator, stove, and dishwasher	Building	$3,000	$3,000
Total building loss			$55,000
Minus deductible			($1,000)
Final building settlement			$54,000
Furniture	Contents	$30,000	$15,000
Television, DVD player, and personal computer	Contents	$2,000	$1,000
Total contents loss			$16,000
Minus deductible			($1,000)
Final contents settlement			$15,000
Hotel stay	Excluded	$0	$0
Total loss settlement ($54,000 + $15,000)			$69,000

[DA05933]

SUMMARY

Homeowners policies are a common type of residential insurance. Not all residences, however, are eligible for homeowners coverage, and not all insureds want or need a homeowners policy. For these residences and customers, a dwelling policy may be more appropriate. Dwelling policies may be written for one- to four-family owner- or tenant-occupied dwellings, dwellings under construction, or mobile homes at a permanent location.

Knowing how to apply the dwelling policy to the facts of a case is a critical skill. The first stage in this process is determining whether a loss is covered, and, if so, the second stage involves determining how much an insurer should pay for the loss.

Inland marine insurance is designed to cover property that has special value or that frequently moves ("floats") from one location to another. Commonly used personal inland marine forms include the Personal Articles Standard Loss Settlement Form, the Personal Property Form, and the Personal Effects Form. Personal inland marine insurance can be used to provide coverage for personal property in circumstances when homeowners policy coverage is not available or is too restrictive.

Farm owners face a wide variety of loss exposures, which can be insured in several ways. Commonly used farm insurance forms include the ISO Farm Program, endorsements to homeowners policies, and special policies for unique loss exposures. Special insurance products include crop hail insurance, multiple peril crop insurance, animal mortality insurance, feedlot insurance, and Federal Crop Insurance livestock policies.

Fair Access to Insurance Requirements (FAIR) plans and beachfront and windstorm plans are provided by private insurers coordinating with state insurance authorities to provide insurance for properties with greater-than-average exposures to loss in areas underserved by the voluntary market. Property under both types of plans must meet state-specified eligibility requirements, and coverages under the plans usually correlate with the plan's purpose. FAIR plans for urban properties cover fire and a limited number of other perils, whereas beachfront and windstorm plans typically cover windstorm and hail. However, in recent years, the distinction has blurred, and some states have merged their plans.

The National Flood Insurance Act of 1968 established the National Flood Insurance Program (NFIP), administered by the Federal Emergency Management Agency (FEMA). Flood insurance may be written only in communities that FEMA has designated as participating communities in the NFIP. A community joins the NFIP by participation in two sequential programs: the emergency program and the regular program.

Amounts of insurance are limited for each program, and a waiting period applies. The Write-Your-Own (WYO) program is a cooperative undertaking between the NFIP and private insurers. In 2004, Congress passed the Flood

Insurance Reform Act to create a five-year pilot program to reduce losses to properties experiencing repetitive flood insurance claims.

When adjusting a flood insurance claim, the claim representative must first establish the facts of the case and then analyze the policy declarations, insuring agreement, conditions, and exclusions (the DICE method), as well as other policy sections, to determine whether coverage exists for the loss. Once coverage has been determined, the claim representative can value the loss to determine an appropriate amount to offer in settlement of the insured's claim.

ASSIGNMENT NOTES

1. Ray Routhier, "Let Us 'Agritain' You," AllBusiness.com, September 10, 2009, www.allbusiness.com/agriculture-forestry/agriculture-crop-production-fruit/12900473-1.html (accessed February 25, 2010).

2. "Latest on the Northeast Flooding," www.accuweather.com/blogs/news/story/26118/flood-situation-update-for-nor.asp (accessed March 14, 2010).

3. NFIP Standard Flood Insurance Policy—Dwelling Form.

4. NFIP Standard Flood Insurance Policy—Dwelling Form.

5. NFIP Standard Flood Insurance Policy—Dwelling Form.

6. NFIP Standard Flood Insurance Policy—Dwelling Form.

Direct Your Learning ▶▶

9

Watercraft, RVs, Mobile Homes, and Excess Liability

Educational Objectives

After learning the content of this assignment, you should be able to:

▶ Explain how individuals and families can use insurance to treat loss exposures related to the following miscellaneous vehicles:

- Motor homes and recreational trailers
- Motorcycles and other two-wheeled vehicles
- Snowmobiles
- Golf carts
- Antique and classic automobiles
- Other recreational vehicles

▶ Explain what loss exposures are covered and what is limited or excluded by the following types of mobile home coverages:

- The Insurance Services Office, Inc. (ISO) Mobilehome Endorsement
- Other ISO mobilehome endorsements
- Specialty insurers' mobile home policies

▶ Explain how individuals and families can treat their watercraft loss exposures using each of the following:

- Small boat policies
- Boatowners and yacht policies
- Insurance Services Office, Inc. (ISO) Personal Lines Watercraft Policy Program
- ISO Homeowners Coverage Forms
- Personal Auto Policy

9

▷ Summarize the coverage provided by the typical personal umbrella policy.

▷ Given a case describing a liability claim, determine the following:

- Whether the loss would be covered by a personal umbrella policy

- The dollar amount, if any, payable under the umbrella policy

- The dollar amount, if any, payable under the underlying insurance policies

- The dollar amount, if any, payable by the insured

Watercraft, RVs, Mobile Homes, and Excess Liability

9

COVERAGE FOR MISCELLANEOUS VEHICLES

The design and operation of certain vehicles, used primarily for recreation, create varied loss exposures. Different risk management techniques than those used for automobiles are necessary to address the needs of individuals and families who own these vehicles.

A wide variety of vehicles presents an equally wide variety of loss exposures that require effective risk management techniques. Insurance professionals and vehicle owners should have an understanding of the insurance options available in order to manage the financial risks associated with different types of recreational vehicles.

Motor Homes and Recreational Trailers

Motor homes are driveable units in which living quarters form an integral part of the vehicle. Truck-mounted campers featuring a detachable camper unit are in this class.

Recreational trailers also provide temporary mobile living quarters and must be towed by private passenger autos, trucks, or vans. The recreational trailer class also includes camping trailers and travel trailers.

The loss exposures of motor homes and recreational trailers, although similar, differ from automobile exposures in nature, frequency, and severity.

The use of these recreational vehicles as temporary dwellings creates exposures common to residences, such as fire and explosion. Camping vehicles can have a greater exposure to flood or windstorm damage than autos because campsites are often located in flood plains or in wooded areas.

Collision is a common cause of loss for both autos and recreational vehicles, but collision damage for recreational vehicles tends to be more frequent per miles driven than for personal autos. Trailers, for example, can jackknife and collide with the vehicles that tow them. Faulty hitches can become unsecured and cause runaway trailers that can collide with other vehicles and objects. Drivers often are not skilled at adjusting their driving habits for the different operating characteristics of motor homes or recreational trailers, and accidents result.

Loss exposures can be controlled through training of all operators in the vehicle's intended uses, limitations, and unique handling characteristics.

Proper maintenance of all propane equipment, such as stoves and heaters, can also help control losses.

Motor-home and recreational-vehicle owners should arrange for risk financing through insurance. Because motor homes and travel trailers may be expensive, property coverage as well as liability coverage is usually necessary. Insurance can be purchased for these vehicles using endorsements to the Insurance Services Office, Inc. (ISO) Personal Auto Policy (PAP).

Miscellaneous type vehicles

Vehicles such as motor homes, motorcycles, ATVs, dune buggies, and golf carts, which can be added by endorsement to the PAP.

The **Miscellaneous Type Vehicle** Endorsement (PP 03 23) is used with the Miscellaneous Type Vehicle Amendment (Motor Homes) (PP 03 28) to provide liability, medical payments, uninsured motorist, and property damage coverage for motor homes. The insured vehicle and the coverages for which it is insured must be named in the endorsement schedule. A passenger hazard exclusion can be activated that will reduce premium and provide medical payments coverage but not liability coverage for passengers in the vehicle.

Because many motor home owners rent or lend their motor homes to others, thus increasing risk, the amendment adds two exclusions for an insured motor home rented to a person or an organization other than the named insured:

- The policy provides no coverage when the motor home is rented to or used by a person other than the named insured except for liability coverage up to the financial responsibility or compulsory limits that apply in the state where the motor home is principally garaged. The excluded coverage can be added for an additional premium.
- Coverage is eliminated for any person who fraudulently acquires the motor home.

For travel trailers or campers, the Trailer/Camper Body Coverage Endorsement (PP 03 07) can be added. This endorsement provides coverage for the "trailer" or camper body described in the schedule or in the declarations and for attached facilities or equipment, such as cooking facilities and awnings or cabanas. The schedule or declarations must indicate whether coverage is provided for a loss caused by collision and/or by other than collision. The endorsement contains exclusions that eliminate coverage for clothing, luggage, and business supplies or equipment.

Many insurers that specialize in recreational vehicle insurance use independently filed forms (filed by the individual insurer with state governments) in which coverage differs considerably from the coverage provided by the ISO policies and endorsements. In many cases, the coverage is broader than that provided by the ISO endorsements. Most non-ISO policies designed for owners of motor homes and recreational trailers share some common features:

- A limited amount of coverage for personal property and household furnishings
- Vacation expense coverage to defray part of the additional costs incurred by an insured whose vehicle or trailer becomes uninhabitable because of

damage or destruction while on vacation away from home, such as the cost of a motel room

- A **lay-up provision** that allows payment of premium for only the portion of the year that the motor home or recreational trailer is in use

Motorcycles and Other Two-Wheeled Vehicles

Motorcycles, designed for use on public roads and subject to motor vehicle registration, are two-wheeled vehicles, although a sidecar with an additional wheel can be added. Motorcycles are capable of fast acceleration and high speeds.

Trail bikes and minibikes are usually ridden off the public roads and are usually slower and less expensive than motorcycles.

Mopeds, motorized bicycles that can be pedaled or operated by small, low-powered engines, are much slower and less expensive than motorcycles. Some states, however, consider mopeds to be motorcycles subject to motor vehicle registration.

Although motorcycles and other two-wheeled vehicles have similar loss exposures to those of automobiles, the bodily injury exposures are often more severe for several reasons:

- Vehicles designed for off-road use are exposed to operating conditions and ground surfaces that can increase the likelihood of bodily injury.
- Use of off-road vehicles by unlicensed, often youthful, and inexperienced operators increases the likelihood of accidents.
- Two-wheeled vehicles provide less protection than automobiles.

Loss exposures can be controlled by training of operators, adult supervision of youthful operators, the use of helmets, and special care by operators when riding in unfamiliar off-road areas.

The use of two-wheeled vehicles creates significant liability loss exposure, such as liability for bodily injury to a child, for owners of these vehicles. Liability insurance is necessary to transfer the financial risk of such exposures. Property damage exposures may be less significant than liability loss exposures for some of these vehicles, and either deductibles or retention may be used to manage the property loss exposure for smaller two-wheeled vehicles.

Insurance coverage for motorcycles and other two-wheeled vehicles is provided by the Miscellaneous Type Vehicle Endorsement to the PAP. This endorsement revises the liability exclusion in the PAP relating to vehicles with fewer than four wheels. A passenger hazard exclusion can also be activated. The endorsement can amend the medical payments coverage by allowing coverage for bodily injury resulting from the use of a vehicle with fewer than four wheels.

Lay-up provision

A provision that suspends certain coverages on recreational vehicles and watercraft for a specified period during seasons when they are in storage.

Independently filed non-ISO forms also provide insurance coverage specifically designed for motorcycles or other two-wheeled vehicles. Options such as coverage for custom parts and equipment are available through specialty policies.

Snowmobiles

Liability coverage for the use of any snowmobile on an insured location is automatically covered under ISO homeowners insurance policies. However, to obtain personal liability and medical payments to others coverage for snowmobiles owned by an insured and used away from an insured location, the insured must attach an ISO Owned Snowmobile Endorsement (HO 24 64). This endorsement expands coverage to include these individuals and situations:

- Any person or organization legally responsible for or using a snowmobile owned by the insured with the insured's permission
- **Vicarious liability** of parents for their children who may operate the snowmobile
- Negligent supervision by an insured
- Negligent entrustment when the snowmobile owner entrusts the snowmobile to someone who is unskilled or otherwise incompetent to operate it and an accident results

Vicarious liability

A legal responsibility that occurs when one party is held liable for the actions of a subordinate or an associate because of the relationship between the two parties.

The endorsement contains exclusions for snowmobiles subject to motor vehicle registration and for the use of snowmobiles for prearranged racing contests or business purposes.

Coverage for snowmobiles can also be provided by the ISO Snowmobile Endorsement (PP 03 20) to the PAP. This endorsement can provide coverage for physical damage to the snowmobile that is not provided by the homeowners policy, in addition to liability, medical payments, and uninsured motorists coverage. Some insurers may require a passenger hazards exclusion, while other insurers may offer this exclusion as an option to reduce premium. Exclusions apply for business or prearranged racing use of the snowmobile.

Non-ISO policies are also available for snowmobiles. A lay-up provision in a specialty snowmobile policy may be an attractive feature to snowmobile owners who use these recreational vehicles during only one season of the year. Specialty policies may offer features such as coverage for snowmobile accessories like safety gloves and boots and options for additional equipment like sleds designed to be pulled by the snowmobile.

Golf Carts

The ISO Homeowners 2000 policies provide liability coverage for motorized golf carts designed to carry up to four persons at a speed not to exceed twenty-five miles per hour on level ground. Coverage applies to losses occurring in specified uses and locations:

- Playing golf or other recreational activity within the legal boundaries of a golfing facility, including business use of the golf cart in a golfing facility
- Travel from a parking or storage area or across designated areas of public roads to access another part of the golfing facility
- Travel within a private residential community in which an insured's residence is located and in which motorized golf carts can legally travel

Coverage for property damage to the golf cart can be added with the Owned Motorized Golf Cart Physical Loss Coverage Endorsement (HO 05 28) to the homeowners policy. Coverage can also be obtained through the Miscellaneous Type Vehicle Endorsement to the PAP or a non-ISO policy designed for golf carts. Specialty policies often provide coverage for accessories and roadside assistance with additional options available.

Neighborhood Electric Vehicles can be used in a similar manner to golf carts. These vehicles are increasing in popularity because they are electrically powered and have low fuel cost and emissions.

 **Reality Check**

Neighborhood Electric Vehicles (NEVs)

Neighborhood Electric Vehicles (NEVs), also referred to as LowSpeed Vehicles (LSVs), are powered by rechargeable batteries and electric motors with zero emissions and designed for speeds of twenty to twenty-five miles per hour. In 1998 the National Highway Traffic Safety Administration designated a classification for NEVs. Some communities, for example certain retirement communities, feature trails designed exclusively for use by NEVs. Some NEVs have a turf mode for use on golf courses. Specialty policies designed for NEVs are available with options for off-road and licensed on-road vehicles as well as other coverage options.

Although some NEVs may resemble golf carts, especially those intended for use on golf courses, many of these vehicles look quite different. Some NEVs resemble small cars, while others have more unique designs, such as an animal print on the body or the stylistic features of a small spaceship.

[DA05843]

Antique and Classic Automobiles

Antique automobiles are usually defined as those that are over twenty-five years old. Classic cars may be less than twenty-five years old but have special value because of unusual styling or mechanical features. Liability coverage for antique and classic cars does not present any special problems and is regularly available under standard policies. Rate credits may be given for liability coverage for antique cars driven only in parades and other special events. In fact, many of the applications for coverage on these types of automobiles require the insured to warrant that the car will be used only in such show events.

Although securing liability coverage presents little or no problem for the producer, problems can arise in securing physical damage insurance. This difficulty stems from the fact that these cars generally appreciate rather than depreciate in value. The traditional definition of "actual cash value" (replacement cost less depreciation) does not apply because the vehicle's current value may exceed its original cost.

One possible solution to this problem is to insure the auto under a PAP and attach the Coverage for Damage to Your Auto (Maximum Limit of Liability) endorsement (PP 0308) to establish the vehicle's value. Many specialty insurers also offer policies for antique and classic vehicles.

Other Recreational Vehicles

Other recreational vehicles with more than two wheels include these:

- All-terrain vehicles (ATVs), equipped with three, four, or six oversized or balloon tires, are versatile vehicles designed for use on rugged terrain and in shallow water.
- Dune buggies, four-wheeled vehicles composed of an auto chassis and typically a fiberglass body, are similar in versatility to ATVs, often used on sand, and regulated as private passenger vehicles in most states because they are also driven on public roads.
- Go-carts, usually equipped with small gasoline-powered engines similar to those in power lawn mowers and large enough to carry only the operator, are designed for low-speed racing although sometimes modified to run at high speeds.
- Children's play cars are similar to go-carts but designed to operate at low speeds for use by children.

An Incidental Low Power Recreational Motor Vehicle Endorsement (HO 24 13) can be used to extend the homeowners insurance policy's liability and medical payments coverage to these vehicles except for those capable of traveling more than 15 miles per hour or subject to motor vehicle registration. For vehicles ineligible for this endorsement, insurance coverage can be provided through the Miscellaneous Type Vehicle Endorsement to the PAP or through a custom recreational vehicle policy. See the exhibit "Risk Management Techniques for Miscellaneous Vehicle Related Loss Exposures."

Risk Management Techniques for Miscellaneous Vehicle Related Loss Exposures

Vehicle Type Exposed to Loss	Liability Loss Exposure	Risk Control Techniques	Risk Financing Techniques	Property Loss Exposure	Risk Control Techniques	Risk Financing Techniques
Motor home	Increased collision frequency	Operator training	ISO Miscellaneous Type Vehicle Endorsement with Amendment (Motor Home) Specialty policy	Explosion and fire; Windstorm and flood	Maintenance of propane equipment; Placement in secure location	ISO Miscellaneous Type Vehicle Endorsement with Amendment (Motor Home); Specialty policy
Travel trailer	Increased collision frequency	Operator Training	ISO Miscellaneous Type Vehicle Endorsement; Specialty policy	Explosion and fire; Windstorm and flood	Maintenance of propane equipment; Placement in secure location	ISO Miscellaneous Type Vehicle Endorsement with Trailer/Camper Body Coverage Endorsement; Specialty policy; Deductible Retention for camping trailers
Motorcycle	Increased risk of injury to passenger	Helmet use	ISO Miscellaneous Type Vehicle Endorsement; Specialty Policy	Increased risk of collision with larger vehicle	Experience; Caution	ISO Miscellaneous Type Vehicle Endorsement; Specialty policy
Other two-wheeled vehicles (moped, dirt bike)	Increased risk of injury to youthful operators and passengers	Helmet use; Adult supervision; Caution on off-road terrain	ISO Miscellaneous Type Vehicle Endorsement; Specialty policy	Increased risk of crash on off-road terrain	Adult supervision; Caution on off-road terrain	ISO Miscellaneous Type Vehicle Endorsement; Specialty policy; Deductible Retention
Snowmobile	Risk of injury to youthful operators and passengers	Protective personal safety equipment; Adult supervision	ISO Homeowners Owned Snowmobile Endorsement; ISO Snowmobile Endorsement to PAP; Specialty policy	Collision with tree or another snowmobile; Overturning of the snowmobile	Adult supervision; Caution	ISO Snowmobile Endorsement to PAP; Specialty policy; Retention
Golf Cart	Risk of bodily injury to passengers or those in other golf carts	Operator knowledge of facility or community rules	ISO Homeowners; ISO Miscellaneous Type Vehicle Endorsement; Specialty policy	Collision with larger vehicle or another golf cart	Operator knowledge of facility or community rules	ISO Homeowners Golf Cart Endorsement; ISO Miscellaneous Type Vehicle Endorsement; Specialty policy
Antique and classic automobiles	No unique liability risk	Operator Training	ISO PAP; Specialty policy	Value appreciates rather than depreciates; ACV not applicable	Caution	ISO PAP Coverage for Damage to Your Auto (Maximum Limit of Liability) endorsement; Specialty policy
Other recreational vehicles (ATV, dune buggy, go-cart, play car)	Risk of bodily injury, especially to children operators and passengers	Adult supervision; Caution on off-road terrain	ISO Homeowners Low Power Recreational Vehicle Endorsement; ISO Miscellaneous Type Vehicle Endorsement; Specialty policy	Overturning of vehicle on rough terrain; Collision	Adult supervision of children; Caution on off-road terrain	ISO Miscellaneous Type Vehicle Endorsement; Specialty policy; Retention; Deductible

[DA05752]

MOBILE HOME INSURANCE

Mobile homes, although similar to houses after they are placed on permanent foundations, present different property loss exposures because of their portability, construction, and site locations. Mobile home policies—modified homeowners policies or stand-alone specialty policies—are designed to meet mobile home owners' unique needs.

Certain loss exposures are either unique or of special importance to mobile homes. Most mobile homes, unless they are permanently placed on a foundation, can be moved. Although a commercial mover must usually be hired, the mobile home owner is exposed to possible loss by collision or upset of a unit being transported. Many mobile homes are concentrated in mobile home parks, and this concentration increases the likelihood that a fire in one mobile home will spread to the next and the likelihood of windstorm damage when mobile homes are blown into one another. A mobile home is more likely than a house to be blown off its foundation or to be carried away by a severe storm. Tie downs, which anchor the frame of the unit to its foundation or the ground, are often required as a condition of insurance.

Mobilehome Endorsement

A homeowners endorsement form that broadens HO-2 or HO-3 coverage to include common mobilehome exposures.

These exposures create special needs for coverage. The Insurance Services Office, Inc. (ISO) **Mobilehome Endorsement** modifies homeowners policies to provide such coverage, and additional endorsements can further customize coverage. Specialty insurers also provide their own independent policy forms for mobile homes. See the exhibit " What is a Mobile Home?."

The ISO Mobilehome Endorsement

An ISO mobile home policy is created by attaching the Mobilehome Endorsement (MH 04 01) to an Homeowners 2, 3, or 4 (HO-2, HO-3, or HO-4) policy and a declarations page. The mobile home must usually be designed for portability and year-round living and must be at least ten feet wide and forty feet long to be eligible for coverage. The insurance is subject to all provisions of the homeowners policy except for the amended provisions shown in the Mobilehome Endorsement.

The Mobilehome Endorsement revises the Definitions section of the policy to define "residence premises" as the mobile home and other structures located on land that must meet certain requirements:

- The land is owned or leased by the insured.
- The land is where the insured resides.
- The land is shown as the "residence premises" in the declarations.

The Mobilehome Endorsement modifies the Property Coverages in Section I of the homeowners policy in several ways.

In addition to the mobile home and attached structures and utility tanks on the residence premises, Coverage A—Dwelling applies to other items that

What is a Mobile Home?

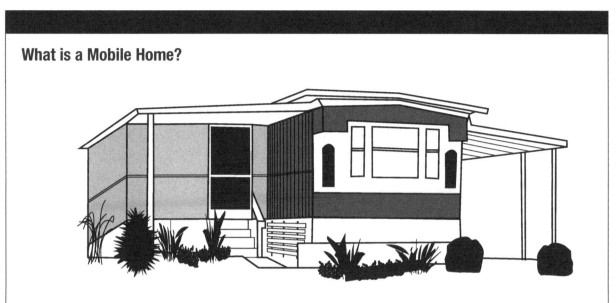

Designed for year-round living, mobile homes are more characteristic of dwellings than of recreational vehicles or travel trailers used as temporary living quarters. Although the U.S. Department of Housing and Urban Development (HUD) replaced the term "mobile home" with the term "manufactured home" for homes built in a factory on a permanent chassis in federal safety standards effective in 1976, most insurers still use the term "mobile home." Modular homes (also called panelized and pre-cut homes) are assembled on site from factory-built sections in accordance with building codes for the site location and are not typically considered to be manufactured homes.

U.S. Department of Housing and Urban Development, HUD.GOV (Accessed 2/6/10). [DA05793]

may be unique to the design of mobile homes, which have more built-in furnishings than typical dwellings:

- Floor coverings
- Appliances
- Dressers and cabinets
- Materials and supplies located on or next to the residence premises and used to construct, alter, or repair the mobile home or other structures on the residence premises.

The Conditions state that if a loss occurs to a series of pieces or panels of the mobile home, coverage is provided to repair or replace the damaged part to match the remainder as closely as possible, but there is no guarantee of the availability of replacements. The insurer is not liable to replace the entire series of pieces or panels if a part is lost or damaged.

Coverage B—Other Structures applies to structures on the residence premises that are not attached to the mobile home, such as a pool or storage shed. The limit of liability for Coverage B is not more than 10 percent of the limit that applies to Coverage A with a $2,000 minimum limit. Use of Coverage B does not reduce the Coverage A limit of liability. For example, if a windstorm caused damage to a pool on the premises of a mobile home valued at $10,000 and repair costs were $2,000, coverage for the repair would be insufficient without the minimum limit.

The limit for Coverage C—Personal Property is usually lower on ISO mobilehome policies than it is on homeowners policies because of the many built-in accessories and furniture that are covered as part of the dwelling. For example, ISO mobilehome policies would typically set the Coverage C limit for personal property at 40 percent of the Coverage A limit; ISO homeowners policies initially set the Coverage C limit of liability at 50 percent of the Coverage A limit.

The Mobilehome Endorsement for Property Removed provides additional coverage. If the mobile home is endangered by a covered peril and removal is necessary to avoid damage, the insurer will pay up to $500 for the removal and return of the mobile home. No deductible applies to this coverage. For example, if a mobile home park is threatened by a spreading forest fire, this coverage would pay up to $500 for an insured mobile home to be moved to a temporary location.

The Mobilehome Endorsement modifies the Mortgage Clause by changing the word "mortgagee" to include lienholder.

The Mobilehome Endorsement removes the additional coverage in the HO-3 policy for Ordinance or Law. A separate **Ordinance or Law Coverage endorsement** is required to restore this coverage.

Because the liability loss exposures for mobile homes are similar to those for other types of dwellings, the Mobilehome Endorsement does not amend Section II—Liability Coverage.

Ordinance or Law Coverage endorsement

Endorsement that covers three types of losses resulting from the enforcement of building ordinances or laws: (1) the value of the undamaged portion of a building that must be demolished, (2) the cost to demolish the building's undamaged portion and remove its debris, and (3) the increased cost to rebuild the property.

Other ISO Mobilehome Endorsements

In addition to typical homeowners policy endorsements, five endorsements are available only for the mobile home policy. See the exhibit "ISO Mobilehome Endorsements."

The Actual Cash Value Mobilehome Endorsement (MH 04 02) changes the loss settlement terms on the mobile home and other structures to apply an actual cash value (ACV) basis rather than a replacement cost basis. Because many mobile homes depreciate quickly, the insurer may require an ACV endorsement, which limits the insurer's obligation to the least of the following amounts:

- The cost of repairing the damage
- The cost of replacing the damaged property with similar property (not necessarily from the same manufacturer)
- The actual cash value of the damage
- The applicable limit of coverage

ISO Mobilehome Endorsements

Actual Cash Value Mobilehome Endorsement (MH 04 02)	Limits insurer's obligation to the least of the actual cash value, the cost of repair, a similar replacement, or the applicable coverage limit
Transportation/Permission to Move Endorsement (MH 04 03)	Covers perils of transporting and storing the mobile home for up to 30 days
Mobilehome Lienholder's Single Interest Endorsement (MH 04 04)	Provides coverage only to the lienholder for transportation exposures and any loss from the owner's embezzlement of the mobilehome
Property Removed Increased Limit Endorsement (MH 04 06)	Increases the limit for temporarily relocating a mobile home that is in danger from an insured peril
Ordinance or Law Coverage Endorsement (MH 04 08)	Provides coverage if a governmental authority or law orders repair, alteration, or removal of the mobile home or structures on the premises

[DA05754]

The Transportation/Permission to Move Endorsement (MH 04 03) provides coverage for perils of transportation (collision, upset, stranding, or sinking) and for the mobile home and other structures at the new location anywhere in the United States or Canada for thirty days from the effective date of the endorsement.

The Mobilehome Lienholder's Single Interest Endorsement (MH 04 04) provides coverage only to the lienholder for collision and upset transportation exposures, subject to numerous recovery conditions, and for any loss resulting from the owner's conversion, embezzlement, or secretion (concealment) of the mobilehome. Some lienholders require this endorsement. For example, John and Sue purchase a mobile home with a small down payment, and the seller finances the balance. John and Sue then move the mobile home to a state where the seller cannot enforce the lien and stop making payments. Without an endorsement to the policy, the mobilehome coverage does not protect the seller when the mobile home is not damaged or destroyed.

The Property Removed Increased Limit Endorsement (MH 04 06) allows the insured to increase the Mobilehome Endorsement's $500 limit for removing a mobile home endangered by an insured peril.

The Ordinance or Law Coverage Endorsement (MH 04 08) is identical to the Ordinance or Law additional coverage provision in the homeowners policy and provides coverage for an amount equal to a specified percentage of the Coverage A limit.

Specialty Insurers' Mobilehome Policies

In addition to ISO, another advisory organization, the American Association of Insurance Services (AAIS), has developed its own "Mobile-Homeowners" program with its own policy forms.

Several insurers specialize in insurance coverage for manufactured homes. Most of these insurers are independent filers (filing insurance rates with state governments independent of rating and advisory organizations). Although some of these insurers may use ISO or AAIS products, most provide their own independent "mobilehome," "mobile-homeowners," or mobile home forms. As with the ISO mobile home policy, policy endorsements are available for optional coverage. Liability coverage is also typically the same as that provided in the insurer's standard homeowners policies.

Specialty insurers, by focusing on a niche market such as mobile homes, can often provide expertise in risk management techniques from loss control to underwriting through the claim process. Owners of properties such as mobile homes may benefit from an insurer who understands their unique loss exposures.

Most insurers use a mobile home policy for mobile or manufactured homes and a standard homeowners policy for modular or panelized homes. Some insurers, however, use the term "manufactured home" to include modular homes and provide coverage with a mobile home or manufactured home policy.

PERSONAL WATERCRAFT INSURANCE

Many individuals and families own watercraft of diverse designs and sizes that present a variety of loss exposures. The financial risk associated with these loss exposures may be treated with insurance.

The ownership and use of watercraft create loss exposures that fall into several categories:

- Physical damage loss to the watercraft
- Medical expenses for injuries to the owners or their families and guests
- Bodily injury and property damage liability

Watercraft loss exposures for owners can be minimized through boating safety and navigation courses, adult supervision of youthful operators, the availability and use of life jackets, proper maintenance of the watercraft, the sobriety of the operators, and the installation of automatic safety devices, such as fire sprinkler systems in yachts.

Because of the potential for significant liability losses from injuries in a boating accident and property loss exposures to watercraft, insurance is an important risk management technique for transferring the financial risk of owning watercraft. Loss exposures associated with watercraft include perils common on land, such as fire, as well as **perils of the seas**. It is important for insurance professionals and watercraft owners to understand the coverage, options, and limitations of the various types of watercraft insurance policies. See the exhibit "Watercraft."

Perils of the sea
Accidental causes of loss that are peculiar to the sea and other bodies of water.

Small Boat Policies

Small boat policies are designed to cover boats up to a certain size (typically those that are twenty-six feet in length). Although these policies are not standard, they have certain common features regarding covered property, covered perils, and policy exclusions. These types of policies are designed to provide insurance coverage for the various loss exposures of individuals and families who own small boats.

The property small boat policies usually cover includes the boat, motor, equipment, and trailer. Most small boat policies are written on an actual cash value (ACV) basis and contain a deductible. Certain personal watercraft may not be classified as boats and may not qualify for coverage under the typical small boat policy. Coverage for such personal watercraft may require specialty policies or endorsements. Examples of watercraft that do not qualify as small boats include Jet Skis, WaveRunners, and Sea-Doos.

A small boat policy can be written to provide named-perils or special form ("all risks") coverage. Most small boat policies are of the special form type and cover all direct physical losses to covered watercraft except specifically excluded losses. Covered property losses include damage to the boat from collision with another object (such as a pier), theft of the boat's motor or equipment, lightning damage to the boat's electrical or navigational equipment, and wind damage to a sail.

Most small boat policies include liability insurance for bodily injury, loss of life, and property damage to third parties resulting from the ownership, maintenance, or use of the boat. Medical payments coverage is typically included for any insured person who sustains bodily injury while in, upon, boarding, or leaving the boat. For example, liability loss exposures covered under a small boat policy when the boat collides with a dock would include injuries sustained by a passenger, liability for damage to the dock, and liability for medical payments to a person on the dock who sustained a leg injury during the collision.

Watercraft

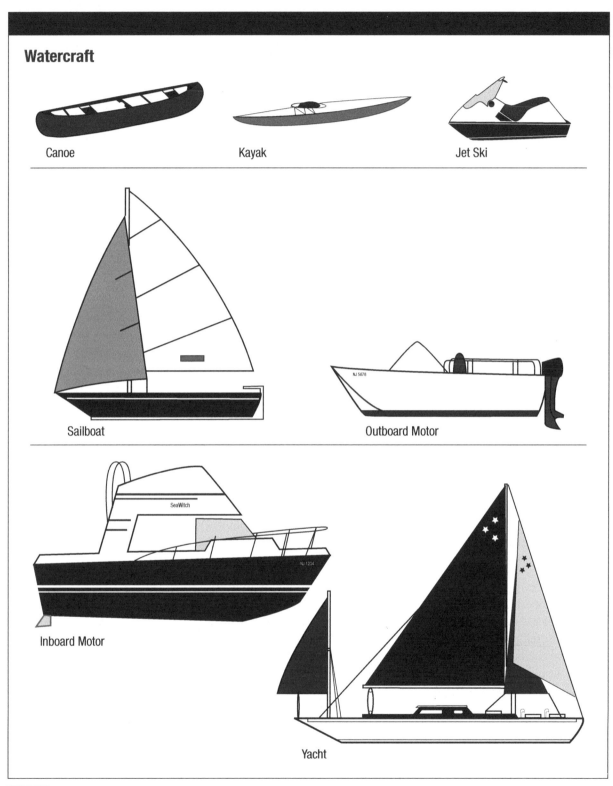

Canoe

Kayak

Jet Ski

Sailboat

Outboard Motor

Inboard Motor

Yacht

[DA05753]

Typical exclusions in small boat policies include these:

- Wear and tear, gradual deterioration, damage from vermin and marine life, mold, rust and corrosion, inherent vice, latent defect, mechanical breakdown, weathering, or damage from extremes of temperature
- Loss or damage from repair, renovation, refinishing, or service to the boat
- Loss or damage occurring during business use (rental of the boat or compensation for carrying passengers) or an official race

Boatowners and Yacht Policies

Many insurers offer boatowners and yacht policies. Individuals and families who own larger boats will usually receive more adequate insurance coverage with a yacht policy, but the insurer may require a professional survey of the yacht before writing the policy. Both types of policies combine physical damage, liability, and medical payments coverage in one policy and typically include perils of the sea coverage. Although these policies have no standard rules or forms, they contain certain common features.

Boatowners and yacht policies usually contain several **warranties**:

- The boat will be used only for private, pleasure purposes and not hired or chartered.
- The boat is in seaworthy condition.
- The boat will not be in operation during any lay-up provision period.
- The insured will not operate the boat outside the navigational limits specified in the policy.

Warranty

A written or an oral statement in a contract that certain facts are true.

The policies usually cover these persons:

- Those named on the declarations page
- Resident household relatives
- Persons under the age of twenty-one in the insured's care
- Paid captain and crew
- Other persons or organizations using the boat without charge

The physical damage coverage (also called **hull insurance**) contained in a boatowners or yacht policy can be on a special form basis or named-perils basis. Like the small boat policy, this coverage includes the boat (hull), equipment, accessories, motor, and trailer. These policies can be written on either a replacement cost basis or an ACV basis. Yachts are typically insured on an agreed value basis after a professional survey.

Hull insurance

Insurance that covers physical damage to vessels, including their machinery and fuel but not their cargo.

Boatowners and yacht policies typically include **protection and indemnity (P&I) insurance**, a broader form of coverage that protects an insured against liability for bodily injury and property damage arising from the ownership, maintenance, or use of the boat. Crew injuries are also covered.

Protection and indemnity (P&I) insurance

Insurance that covers shipowners against various liability claims due to operating the insured vessel.

Medical payments coverage in these policies usually includes coverage for bodily-injury-related expenses for the insured, family members, or any other person subject to the exclusions while in, upon, boarding, or leaving the covered watercraft.

Boatowners and yacht policies have typical property loss exclusions:

- Wear and tear, weathering, gradual deterioration, rust, corrosion, mold, wet or dry rot, marring, denting, scratching, inherent vice, latent or physical defect, insects, and damage from animal or marine life or atmospheric dampness

- Mechanical breakdown unless the loss was caused by fire or explosion

- Freezing and thawing of ice unless reasonable care was used to protect the property such as installation of a circulating water system to keep water from freezing around the boat in icy conditions

- Loss during any official race, except for sailboat racing in some policies

- Intentional loss

- War, nuclear hazard, and radioactive contamination

There are also typical liability loss exclusions in boatowners and yacht policies:

- Liability from losses occurring from illegal activities, rental or charter of the watercraft, or use of the watercraft for racing

- Damage resulting from transportation of the boat on land unless there is an endorsement or option for this coverage

- Liability for discharge of pollutants unless sudden or accidental

- Losses covered by workers compensation or similar law

Additional coverages may be added, such as coverage for the insured's legal obligation to remove a wrecked or sunken vessel following a loss, the costs of removing the watercraft from the water if a hurricane is approaching, and coverage for employers liability for captain and crew under the **Jones Act.**

Jones Act (United States Merchant Marine Act of 1920)

A federal statute that permits injured members of a vessel's crew (or survivors of a deceased crew member) to sue their employer for damages due to the employer's negligence.

ISO Personal Lines Watercraft Policy Program

In January 2010, to respond to the need for insurance coverage for the owners of recreational watercraft, Insurance Services Office, Inc. (ISO) introduced a Watercraft Policy (WT 00 01) that provides coverage for watercraft (except for personal watercraft not qualified as small boats) without length or horsepower limitations. Navigation territory may be customized, or may include losses occurring within the United States, its territories or possessions, Puerto Rico, or Canada:

- On land (during towing, for example)

- In inland waters (rivers and lakes)

- In coastal waters within twelve miles of the shoreline
- In the Great Lakes

The policy provides property damage coverage, with value determined separately for these items:

- Watercraft hull and boating equipment, including dinghies
- Outboard motors
- Watercraft trailers

Although these are insured as separate items, a single policy deductible applies. The policy is written on an ACV basis.

The policy provides medical payments coverage to the insured, any family member, or any other person injured while occupying, towed by, or struck in the water by the insured watercraft. It also provides liability coverage for bodily injury or property damage for which any insured becomes legally responsible because of a watercraft accident.

These optional coverage and endorsements are available:

- A Personal Watercraft endorsement adds coverage for small personal watercraft such as Jet Skis.
- The Watercraft Joint Ownership endorsement provides coverage if the watercraft is owned by two or more insureds who do not reside together.
- The Watercraft Additional Insured-Lessor endorsement adds coverage for someone who leases the watercraft for a continuous period of at least six months under a written agreement.
- Increased limits are available for towing and assistance expense.
- Haul out expense coverage is available to cover up to $500 of the cost of hauling the watercraft out of the water in the event of a hurricane watch or warning issued by the National Weather Service.

A lay-up provision is also available, and premium credits can be attained if the named insured has completed a safety course qualified by the insurer or installed automatic protective devices (such as a fire sprinkler system). Exclusions are similar to those in boatowners and yacht policies.

ISO Homeowners Coverage Forms

Individuals and families have limited coverage for watercraft under an ISO Homeowners coverage form, but insurance professionals and watercraft owners should be aware of the limitations and exclusions. This coverage will not be adequate for many of the needs of boat owners.

The ISO homeowners coverage form has a $1,500 limit for property damage to the watercraft. Coverage is provided on a named-perils basis, and there is no coverage for perils of the sea. Windstorm coverage only applies when the watercraft is inside a fully enclosed building (for example, a canoe stored in a garage). Theft coverage does not apply to the boat and motor when away from the residence premises; accessories and trailers are excluded. For example, the insured's kayak would not be covered if it is stolen from the roof of his or her car while the insured is traveling on vacation.

The Homeowners 3—Special Form (HO-3) policy provides liability coverage for certain watercraft types, sizes, and lengths, such as boats that are not powered, sailboats under twenty-six feet in length, or boats powered by an outboard motor under twenty-five horsepower. There is a Watercraft endorsement (HO 24 75) that provides liability coverage for an otherwise excluded watercraft.

Personal Auto Policy

The Personal Auto Policy (PAP) does not provide physical damage or liability coverage for watercraft, motors, or watercraft-related equipment. However, physical damage loss to a boat trailer is covered if the trailer is described on the policy declarations page. Also, a boat trailer the insured owns is covered for liability whether or not it is described on the declarations page. See the exhibit "Watercraft Risk Management Techniques."

Watercraft Risk Management Techniques

Watercraft Type	Loss Exposures	Risk Control	Risk Finance (Insurance)
Small boats (canoes, kayaks, small motorboats, small sailboats)	Windstorm damage to boat Perils of the sea Theft Liability damage to other boats and persons Injury to operator and passengers in the boat (falling overboard, for example)	Boating courses Supervision of youthful operators Use of life jackets Restrictions on use of alcohol Control of wake Vessel maintenance	HO-3 (limited coverage) Watercraft Endorsement Small Boat Policy ISO Watercraft Policy Retention for property damage to the watercraft
Small personal watercraft (Jet Ski)	Liability damage to other boats and persons Injury to operator and passengers Collision damage to watercraft	Training Supervision of youthful operators Use of life jackets Avoiding alcohol before or during use	Personal watercraft endorsement Specialty policy Retention for property damage to watercraft
Larger boats and yachts (sailboats larger than twenty-six feet in length, larger motorboats)	Windstorm damage to boat Fire damage to boat Theft Perils of the sea Liability damage to other boats, property (docks, piers), and persons Injury to operator and passengers (falling overboard, burns from alcohol stoves, head injuries from sail booms) Injury to yacht crew	Boating courses Maintenance of the watercraft Automatic protective equipment Operator sobriety	Boatowners and yacht policies ISO Watercraft Policy

[DA05774]

PERSONAL UMBRELLA LIABILITY INSURANCE

Most personal umbrella policies provide not only higher limits but also broader coverage than underlying personal insurance policies.

A personal umbrella policy provides liability protection to insureds for amounts over the liability limits on existing homeowners, personal auto, and watercraft policies. Lawsuits arising from personal liability exposures can result in catastrophically high settlements that may exceed the liability limits of these existing policies. Once the liability limits under these policies are exhausted, the insured might be forced to pay a substantial amount from personal assets. Therefore, most individuals and families may benefit from having a personal umbrella policy.

Purposes of Personal Umbrella Coverage

A personal umbrella policy is designed to provide bodily injury, personal injury, and property damage liability coverage in case of a catastrophic claim, lawsuit, or judgment. Umbrella coverage provides additional liability limits over any underlying insurance policies, such as homeowners Section II—Liability Coverages, personal auto liability, and personal watercraft liability policies. A condition of umbrella coverage is that the insured must maintain certain underlying policies with specified limits. If the loss is covered by one of these underlying policies, the umbrella insurer pays only after these limits are exhausted. See the exhibit "Relationship of Personal Umbrella Policy to Typical Underlying Coverages."

The personal umbrella policy also typically provides drop-down coverage, which is broader than the underlying coverage. When the underlying insurance does not apply to a particular loss and the loss is not excluded by the umbrella coverage, the umbrella coverage "drops down" to cover the entire loss, less a self-insured retention (SIR). Usually the retention (which is similar to a deductible) is $250, but it can be as high as $10,000. The SIR applies only when the loss is not covered by an existing underlying policy.

The amount of personal umbrella coverage purchased typically ranges from $1 million to $10 million. The policy covers the named insured, resident relatives, and usually persons using (with the insured's permission) cars, motorcycles, recreational vehicles, or watercraft owned by or rented to the named insured. Also, persons younger than twenty-one who are in the care of the named insured or of a resident relative generally are covered.

Personal Umbrella Coverages

Because each insurance company has its own forms and rules, there is no single standard umbrella policy; however, most insurers' umbrella policy provisions are similar. The Insurance Services Office, Inc. (ISO) Personal Umbrella Liability Policy is a widely used form and includes a listing of definitions, the Insuring Agreement, Exclusions, and General Provisions.

Insuring Agreement

The ISO Personal Umbrella Liability Policy Insuring Agreement states that the policy covers bodily injury and property damage as well as personal injury for which an insured becomes legally liable. The definitions of these coverages are similar to those contained in other liability policies. Bodily injury is defined as bodily harm, sickness, or disease, including required care, loss of services, and death. Property damage is defined as physical injury to or

Relationship of Personal Umbrella Policy to Typical Underlying Coverages

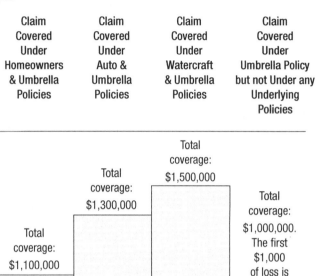

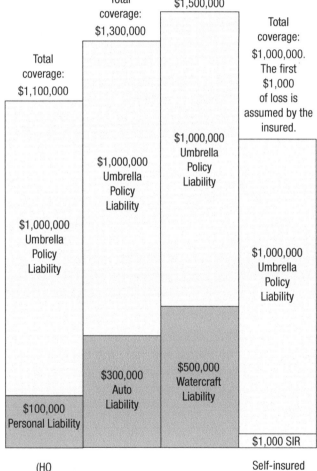

Claim Covered Under Homeowners & Umbrella Policies	Claim Covered Under Auto & Umbrella Policies	Claim Covered Under Watercraft & Umbrella Policies	Claim Covered Under Umbrella Policy but not Under any Underlying Policies

Total coverage: $1,100,000

Total coverage: $1,300,000

Total coverage: $1,500,000

Total coverage: $1,000,000. The first $1,000 of loss is assumed by the insured.

$1,000,000 Umbrella Policy Liability

$1,000,000 Umbrella Policy Liability

$1,000,000 Umbrella Policy Liability

$1,000,000 Umbrella Policy Liability

$500,000 Watercraft Liability

$300,000 Auto Liability

$100,000 Personal Liability

$1,000 SIR

(HO Section II)

Self-insured retention applies when no underlying policy applies to a given loss.

[DA00847]

destruction of tangible property and includes loss of use of the property. In addition to bodily injury and property damage, the definition of personal injury in the umbrella policy includes false arrest, false imprisonment, wrongful entry or eviction, malicious prosecution or humiliation, libel, slander, defamation of character, invasion of privacy, and assault and battery not intentionally committed or directed by a covered person. See the exhibit "Personal Umbrella Liability Policy."

Personal Umbrella Liability Policy

PERSONAL UMBRELLA LIABILITY POLICY

II. Coverages

A. Insuring Agreement

We will pay damages, in excess of the "retained limit", for:

1. "Bodily injury" or "property damage" for which an "insured" becomes legally liable due to an "occurrence" to which this insurance applies; and

2. "Personal injury" for which an "insured" becomes legally liable due to one or more offenses listed under the definition of "personal injury" to which this insurance applies.

Damages include prejudgment interest awarded against the "insured".

Copyright, ISO Properties, Inc., 1997. [DA00848]

The personal umbrella policy includes coverage for legal defense costs that are not payable by the underlying insurance policies. Defense costs include payment of attorney fees, premiums on appeal bonds, release of attachment bonds, court costs, interest on unpaid judgments, other legal costs, and loss of earnings up to a certain amount (such as $250) per day to attend court hearings.

Some states require the insurer to offer the insured the option to extend the personal umbrella to cover uninsured and underinsured motorists protection. This coverage is provided as an endorsement to the personal umbrella policy. If the insured does not want this coverage, state laws usually require that he or she reject it in writing.

Exclusions

Because personal umbrella policies provide broad coverage, certain important exclusions usually are included:

- Intentional injury—An act committed or directed by a covered person with intent to cause personal injury or property damage.
- Business property and pursuits—Liability arising out of a business activity or business property, other than claims involving an insured's use of a private passenger automobile.
- Professional liability—Rendering or failure to render professional services.
- Aircraft—All liability arising out of the ownership, maintenance, use, loading, or unloading of aircraft.
- Watercraft—Coverage for large watercraft is excluded except for the insured's liability for smaller boats that are normally covered by the underlying homeowners policy or for watercraft covered by underlying insurance.
- Recreational vehicles—Liability arising out of the ownership, maintenance, or use of recreational vehicles, such as golf carts and snowmobiles, unless there is underlying insurance.
- Transmission of any communicable diseases—Liability that results from the insured's transmission of a communicable disease.
- Directors and officers—Liability coverage for acts of directors or officers of a corporation except for officers and directors of a not-for-profit organization.
- Damage to the insured's property—Damage to property an insured owns.
- Workers compensation—Any obligation for which the insured is legally liable under a workers compensation, disability benefits, or similar law.
- Nuclear energy—Applies to insureds who are or should be insured under nuclear energy policies.

Conditions

These are among the most important conditions in the personal umbrella policy:

- The insured must maintain the underlying insurance coverages and limits shown in the declarations. If underlying coverage is not maintained, the policy will pay no more than would have been covered if the underlying insurance was in effect.
- The insured must give the insurer written notice of loss as soon as practicable.
- The umbrella policy is excess over any other insurance, whether collectible or not.
- The policy territory is worldwide.

UMBRELLA COVERAGE CASE STUDY

Individuals and families use insurance to mitigate risk of financial loss. A sound plan for personal risk management will include knowledge of what potential loss circumstances are covered by a personal umbrella policy and applicable underlying policies.

Many individuals and families typically purchase several insurance policies, such as personal auto insurance and homeowners insurance. However, they may encounter loss circumstances for which they are held liable and for which their underlying policies provide no coverage. They might also face a claim whose value exceeds the limits of the underlying policy. Such losses may be covered by an umbrella policy.

Case Facts

How does an umbrella policy, in concert with underlying coverages like personal auto and homeowners policies, respond to high-value claims?

Matt and Zoey are married and own a single-family home. They also own three cars: a new minivan driven mainly by Matt, a hybrid subcompact driven to work by Zoey, and a ten-year-old pickup truck they use mostly on weekends.

On a Saturday afternoon, Matt was driving the pickup truck to take bulky household items to donate to a charity-sponsored thrift store. In the store parking lot, Matt mistakenly stepped on the gas pedal when he meant to use the brake. He lost control of the truck and crashed into a group of customers who had just exited the store. Matt called 911 and his insurance agent immediately and complied with all other policy conditions.

No one was killed in the accident, but five persons sustained serious injuries. Matt was found to be completely liable for the $1.8 million in medical bills incurred by those injured.

Shortly after the accident, television and newspaper reporters came to Matt and Zoey's house for interviews about the incident. Zoey fielded their questions and angrily suggested that the police officer responding to the accident had advised the injured persons to exaggerate their injuries in order to extract a bigger liability award. The police officer denied having done so and sued Zoey for slander. A jury found Zoey liable and awarded $1 million to the police officer for slander.

Matt and Zoey's home is insured under a Homeowners 3—Special Form (HO-3) policy for $370,000. Their homeowners policy includes liability coverage with a $500,000 per occurrence limit and lists Zoey and Matt as named insureds.

Like the homeowners policy, their personal auto policy (PAP) carries a $500,000 per occurrence liability limit. Both Zoey and Matt are listed as named insureds.

Matt and Zoey were concerned about the risk of financial loss that could result from bodily injury, personal injury, or property damage liability in case of a catastrophic claim, lawsuit, or judgment. To address their concern, they purchased a personal umbrella policy with both Zoey and Matt listed as named insureds. Their umbrella policy provides $2 million of liability coverage, with a $500,000 deductible that applies to exposures retained under the PAP or homeowners policies. A $2,000 deductible applies to events covered by the umbrella policy but not covered by the PAP or homeowners policy.

An umbrella policy's coverage generally begins where the primary policies' coverage ends. A well-designed insurance plan will coordinate the umbrella coverage with the policy limits of the underlying primary policies. For instance, if the PAP and HO-3 policies each have $300,000 limits of liability, the umbrella policy should have a $300,000 deductible. Some umbrella policies use the term "deductible." Others (such as the ISO umbrella form) use the term "retained limit." The terms have the same meaning in umbrella insurance.

All three of Matt and Zoey's policies—PAP, HO-3, and personal umbrella—were paid up and in force at the time of the accident. See the exhibit "Case Facts."

Case Facts

Insureds	Matt and Zoey
Types of policies and coverage limits	• HO-3 $500,000 per occurrence
	• PAP $500,000 per occurrence
	• Umbrella $2 million per occurrence
Endorsements that affect this case	None
Other policy information	• Umbrella—$500,000 deductible for exposures retained under the PAP or HO-3
	• Umbrella—$2,000 for events not covered by the PAP or HO-3
Background	• The insureds have complied with the policy conditions.
	• The auto accident resulted in a $1.8 million liability loss.
	• The slander suit resulted in a $1 million liability loss.

[DA05629]

Case Analysis Tools

To determine whether Matt and Zoey's insurance policies provide coverage for the auto accident or the slander suit, the insurance or risk management professional should have copies of the policy forms and any applicable endorsements indicated on the Declarations pages of the policies. See the exhibit "Homeowners Policy Declarations."

To determine whether a policy covers a loss, many insurance professionals apply the DICE method. ("DICE" is an acronym for categories of policy provisions: declarations, insuring agreement, conditions, and exclusions.) The DICE method has four steps:

1. Review of the declarations page to determine whether it covers the person or the property at the time of the loss
2. Review of the insuring agreement to determine whether it covers the loss
3. Review of policy conditions to determine compliance
4. Review of policy exclusions to determine whether they preclude coverage of the loss

Each of these four steps is used in every case. Other categories of policy provisions should be examined. For example, endorsements and terms defined in the policy should be reviewed in relation to the declarations, insuring agreement, exclusions, and conditions.

Determination of Coverage

To determine whether the PAP, the HO-3, and/or the umbrella policy provide coverage for Matt's $1.8 million liability from the accident and for Zoey's $1 million liability from the slander suit, the insurance professional can apply the four steps of the DICE method. See the exhibit "Umbrella Policy Declarations."

Auto Accident

The first DICE step includes determination of whether the driver or vehicle is described on an insured's Declarations page and whether the accident occurred during the policy period. In this case, Matt and Zoey's PAP includes the pickup truck as a covered auto, and both Matt and Zoey are insureds under the policy. The umbrella policy Declarations page shows Matt and Zoey as insureds and notes the number of eligible automobiles. The HO-3 shows Matt and Zoey as insureds for liability coverage, but does not list any vehicles.

The second DICE step is to determine whether the events have triggered coverage under the insuring agreement of one or more of their three insurance policies. In the PAP insuring agreement, the insurer agrees to pay damages for bodily injury and property damage for which an insured is legally responsible because of an auto accident. Accidentally driving the truck into the pedestrians qualifies as an auto accident, and the resultant injuries qualify as bodily injury. See the exhibit "Part A—Liability Coverage Insuring Agreement."

Homeowners Policy Declarations

Homeowners Policy Declarations

POLICYHOLDER: **(Named Insured)**	Matt and Zoey 216 Brookside Drive Anytown, USA 40000	**POLICY NUMBER:**	296 H 578661

POLICY PERIOD: **Inception:** March 30, 20X1 **Policy period begins 12:01 A.M. standard time**
 Expiration: March 30, 20X2 **at the residence premises.**

FIRST MORTGAGEE AND MAILING ADDRESS:

Federal National Mortgage Assn.
C/O Mortgagee, Inc.
P.O. Box 5000
Businesstown, USA 55000

We will provide the insurance described in this policy in return for the premium and compliance with all applicable policy provisions.

SECTION I COVERAGES	**LIMIT**	
A—Dwelling	$ 370,000	**SECTION I DEDUCTIBLE:** $ 250
B—Other Structures	$ 37,000	**(In case of loss under Section I, we cover**
C—Personal Property	$ 185,000	**only that part of the loss over the**
D—Loss of Use	$ 111,000	**deductible amount shown above.)**

SECTION II COVERAGES	**LIMIT**	
E—Personal Liability	$ 500,000	**Each Occurrence**
F—Medical Payments to Others	$ 1,000	**Each Person**

CONSTRUCTION: Masonry Veneer **NO. FAMILIES:** One **TYPE ROOF:** Approved

YEAR BUILT: 1990 **PROTECTION CLASS:** 7 **FIRE DISTRICT:** Cook Township

NOT MORE THAN 1000 FEET FROM HYDRANT

NOT MORE THAN 5 MILES FROM FIRE DEPT.

FORMS AND ENDORSEMENTS IN POLICY: HO 00 03, HO 04 61

POLICY PREMIUM: $ 350.00 **COUNTERSIGNATURE DATE:** March 1, 20X1 **AGENT:** A.M. Abel

Umbrella Policy Declarations

COVERGOOD MUTUAL INSURANCE COMPANY
UMBRELLA POLICY DECLARATIONS
(excerpts)

Named Insured and Address
Matt and Zoey
216 Brookside Drive
Anytown, USA 40000

Policy Period
03/30/20X1 to 03/30/20X2
12:01 A.M. Standard Time

This policy covers the residence premises at the location shown above.

Umbrella Policy Limit of Liability
$2,000,000 per occurrence

Deductibles
The deductible amounts shown herein remain applicable in the event that the underlying insurer is unable to pay for any reason, such as insolvency:

Retained Exposure Type	*Deductible*
Auto Liability	$500,000 per occurrence
Personal or Homeowners Liability	$500,000 per occurrence
Watercraft Liability	$500,000 per occurrence

A $2,000 deductible will apply to any occurrence that is covered by this umbrella policy AND is not covered by any underlying insurance. The $2,000 deductible applies only if the named insured maintains the underlying insurance for the loss exposures listed below under "Eligible Loss Exposures" and has complied with the conditions of the underlying policies.

Eligible Loss Exposures
The named insured declares that, as of the effective date of this personal umbrella policy, all eligible loss exposures are listed herein:

Eligible Loss Exposure	*Number*
Automobiles	3
Residences	1
Watercraft	0

Underlying Insurance Policies
The named insured declares that, as of the effective date of this personal umbrella policy, these underlying insurance policies are in force:

Policy Type	*Insurance Company*	*Policy Number*
Personal Auto Liability	Roadworthy Risk Co.	RRC-658213
Homeowners	Covergood Mutual	CM45671

[DA05631]

Part A—Liability Coverage Insuring Agreement

PART A – LIABILITY COVERAGE

INSURING AGREEMENT

A. We will pay damages for "bodily injury" or "property damage" for which any "insured" becomes legally responsible because of an auto accident. Damages include prejudgment interest awarded against the "insured". We will settle or defend, as we consider appropriate, any claim or suit asking for these damages. In addition to our limit of liability, we will pay all defense costs we incur. Our duty to settle or defend ends when our limit of liability for this coverage has been exhausted by payment of judgments or settlements. We have no duty to defend any suit or settle any claim for "bodily injury" or "property damage" not covered under this policy.

B. "Insured" as used in this Part means:

1. You or any "family member" for the ownership, maintenance or use of any auto or "trailer".

2. Any person using "your covered auto".

3. For "your covered auto", any person or organization but only with respect to legal responsibility for acts or omissions of a person for whom coverage is afforded under this Part.

4. For any auto or "trailer", other than "your covered auto", any other person or organization but only with respect to legal responsibility for acts or omissions of you or any "family member" for whom coverage is afforded under this Part. This Provision (B.4.) applies only if the person or organization does not own or hire the auto or "trailer".

[DA05632]

In the HO-3 Section II insuring agreement, the insurer agrees to pay damages for bodily injury and property damage for which an insured is legally responsible because of a covered occurrence. The insuring agreement in the personal umbrella liability policy covers bodily injury and property damage for which an insured becomes legally liable. For the second DICE step, the auto accident appears to trigger coverage under the PAP, HO-3, and umbrella policies. See the exhibit "Personal Umbrella Liability Policy."

The third DICE step is to determine whether all policy conditions, such as timely reporting of the loss to the insurer, have been met. For the purposes of this case study, assume that they have been.

The fourth DICE step is to determine whether one or more exclusions preclude coverage that the insuring agreements have granted. Section II exclusions of the HO-3 note that liability coverage does not apply to bodily injury or property damage arising out the ownership, maintenance, or use of motor vehicles owned by the insured. Therefore, there is no coverage under the HO-3 for the auto accident.

Personal Umbrella Liability Policy

PERSONAL UMBRELLA LIABILITY POLICY

II. Coverages

A. Insuring Agreement

We will pay damages, in excess of the "retained limit", for:

1. "Bodily injury" or "property damage" for which an "insured" becomes legally liable due to an "occurrence" to which this insurance applies; and

2. "Personal injury" for which an "insured" becomes legally liable due to one or more offenses listed under the definition of "personal injury" to which this insurance applies.

Damages include prejudgment interest awarded against the "insured".

Copyright, ISO Properties, Inc., 1997. [DA00848]

Slander Lawsuit

To determine whether the PAP, the HO-3, and/or the umbrella policy provide coverage for Zoey's $1 million liability from the slander suit, the insurance professional can again apply the four steps of the DICE method.

The first DICE step includes determination of whether the party involved is described on an insured's PAP, HO-3, or umbrella Declarations page and whether the accident occurred during the policy period. In this case, Zoey is an insured under all three policies, and the incident occurred during the policy period of all three policies.

The second DICE step is to determine whether the event has triggered coverage under the insuring agreement of one or more of the three insurance policies. In the PAP insuring agreement, the insurer agrees to pay damages for bodily injury and property damage for which an insured is legally responsible because of an auto accident. Zoey's alleged slander does not qualify as an auto accident.

In the HO-3 Section II insuring agreement, the insurer agrees to pay damages for bodily injury and property damage for which an insured is legally responsible because of a covered occurrence. Importantly, the HO-3 definition of "bodily injury" does not include slander. Zoey's alleged slander does not qualify as a covered event under the HO-3.

The insuring agreement in the personal umbrella liability policy covers bodily injury and property damage as well as personal injury for which an insured becomes legally liable. Bodily injury is defined as bodily harm, sickness, or disease, including required care, loss of services (such as the inability to perform household chores after an injury), and death. Property damage is defined as physical injury to or destruction of tangible property and includes loss of use of the property. The definition of personal injury in the umbrella policy includes false arrest, false imprisonment, wrongful entry or eviction, malicious prosecution or humiliation, libel, slander, defamation of character, invasion of privacy, and assault and battery not intentionally committed or directed by a covered person. Zoey's alleged slander does qualify as personal injury under the umbrella policy.

The third DICE step is to determine whether all policy conditions, such as timely reporting of the loss to the insurer, have been met. Once again, assume that they have been.

The fourth DICE step is to determine whether one or more exclusions preclude coverage that the insuring agreements have granted. There are no umbrella exclusions that would take away the coverage for Zoey's alleged slander.

Determination of Amounts Payable

Regarding the auto accident, the $1.8 million liability exceeds Matt and Zoey's PAP liability limit of $500,000 per occurrence. The PAP will pay the full policy limits of $500,000 for this event. Because the loss amount exceeds the umbrella deductible, the personal umbrella liability policy will respond. The $500,000 deductible shown on the umbrella Declarations page (the limit payable under the PAP) will be applied, and the umbrella policy will pay $1.3 million for this occurrence. The HO-3 policy, because of the exclusion noted, will not respond to the loss from the auto accident. Because the PAP and the umbrella have covered the full $1.8 million ($500,000 by PAP and $1.3 million by the umbrella), nothing is payable by Matt.

Regarding the $1 million slander lawsuit award, the HO-3 policy provides no liability coverage because its definition of bodily injury does not include slander. The PAP provides no coverage because the insuring agreement promises to pay only for liability for which an insured becomes legally liable because of an auto accident. The personal umbrella policy will provide coverage; the $2,000 deductible applies because the event is covered by the umbrella and is not covered by the underlying PAP and HO-3 policies. Therefore, the personal umbrella policy will pay $998,000 for this occurrence. The balance of $2,000 is payable by Zoey for the slander award. See the exhibit "Relationship of a $2,000,000 Umbrella Policy to Typical Underlying Coverages."

Although the umbrella policy limit is $2 million, two claims were paid—$1.3 million and $998,000—totaling more than $2 million. The policy limits apply per occurrence; there is no limit on the number of claims that can be covered, up to $2 million each. See the exhibit "Determination of Amounts Payable."

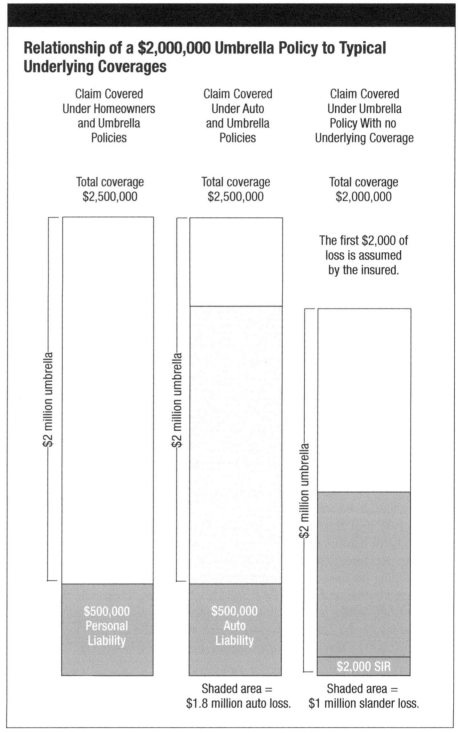

[DA05633]

Determination of Amounts Payable

Of the $1.8 million in damages resulting from the auto accident:

- Matt and Zoey's PAP will pay its policy limit of $500,000.
- Matt and Zoey's umbrella policy will pay the remaining $1.3 million.
- Matt and Zoey's HO-3 policy pays nothing.
- Matt and Zoey pay nothing.

Of the $1 million in damages resulting from the slander lawsuit:

- Matt and Zoey are responsible for the first $2,000.
- Matt and Zoey's umbrella policy will pay the remaining $998,000.
- Matt and Zoey's PAP policy pays nothing.
- Matt and Zoey's HO-3 policy pays nothing.

[DA05634]

SUMMARY

Risk management techniques for the loss exposures presented by miscellaneous vehicles include various options for insurance coverage:

- Modification of ISO homeowner or personal automobile policies with endorsements
- Specialty policies designed for specific vehicle types

Mobile homes present unique property loss exposures. The coverage needs for mobile home owners can be met through the ISO Mobilehome Endorsement to a homeowners policy, and up to five additional ISO mobilehome endorsements can be added to customize individual policies. Specialty insurers also provide independent stand-alone mobile home policies.

Insurance is an important risk management technique to transfer the financial risk of loss exposures associated with the ownership and use of the various types of watercraft. Although there is limited coverage for some types of watercraft under the HO-3 policy, more adequate coverage will usually be provided with a small boat, boatowners, yacht, or ISO Watercraft policy.

The purpose of the personal umbrella policy is to provide excess liability coverage over underlying policies, such as homeowners and personal auto policies, and to provide broader coverage than basic policies. A personal umbrella policy protects the insured against catastrophic claims, lawsuits, or judgments.

To determine how coverage applies under a personal umbrella policy and any underlying insurance, one must establish facts about the umbrella policy and underlying policies and apply the DICE method to those facts.

- Are the persons or vehicles covered under the policies, and did the event take place during the policy period?
- Is the loss event covered by the underlying policies and/or the umbrella policy?
- Have the policy conditions been met?
- Are there exclusions that may apply to deny coverage?

Answering these questions will allow determination of how much is payable by the umbrella insurer, by the underlying insurer(s), and by the insured.

10

Personal Lines Profitability and Pricing

Educational Objectives

After learning the content of this assignment, you should be able to:

▷ Explain how factors affect personal lines profitability goals for a portfolio and their effect on portfolio management.

▷ Evaluate the effectiveness of methods for increasing personal lines profitability.

▷ Explain how pricing components and relativity factors affect personal insurance profitability.

▷ Explain how insurers analyze loss data and forecast trends.

▷ Summarize factors that insurers apply to the ratemaking process, including regulatory objectives, social objectives, and investment income.

▷ Given a case study regarding a personal lines portfolio that requires a rate adjustment to restore profitability, explain how a premium and loss analysis is performed, rate relativities are determined, and the adjustment of the base rate is applied.

Personal Lines Profitability and Pricing

10

PERSONAL LINES PROFITABILITY GOALS

Profitability is essential to insurers, and various external and internal factors affect an insurer's profitability.

Underwriting goals are normally established by upper underwriting management. **Portfolio managers** must understand how the goals are established, their components, and factors that drive the goals. Such an understanding can guide individual underwriting decisions and portfolio management. The extent to which a portfolio manager contributes to the goal-setting process for production and loss ratios or negotiates goals varies by company. The factors that affect an insurer's underwriting goals include these:

- Vision and philosophy of the insurer's senior management team
- Industry trends
- Individual company trends
- Competition
- Regulatory changes
- New and retiring product lines

The financial overview exhibit depicts the various components that affect underwriting profit, which an insurer's senior management will consider when setting portfolio profitability goals. See the exhibit "Insurer's Financial Overview."

Planning and Goal Setting

Portfolio managers manage **underwriting profit** by measuring components of underwriting profit, monitoring changes in the components, comparing changes with goals, and then taking action to control the components. Managers should thoroughly understand the ratios that insurers use to measure underwriting profitability. See the exhibit "Underwriting Profitability Ratios."

For example, in the example shown in the exhibit on planning and goal setting, a portfolio manager's goal may be to increase written premium in a territory by 10 percent (understanding that expenses will increase somewhat as a cost of doing business). However, the loss ratio increases to 95 percent at the end of the second quarter because of wildfires in the territory, and this will make the combined ratio exceed 100 percent. The portfolio manager may

---

Portfolio manager

An insurer's employee responsible for achieving the premium, loss ratio, and product-mix goals for a group of insurance policies written by the insurer.

Underwriting profit

Income an insurer earns from premiums paid by policyholders minus incurred losses and underwriting expenses.

Insurer's Financial Overview

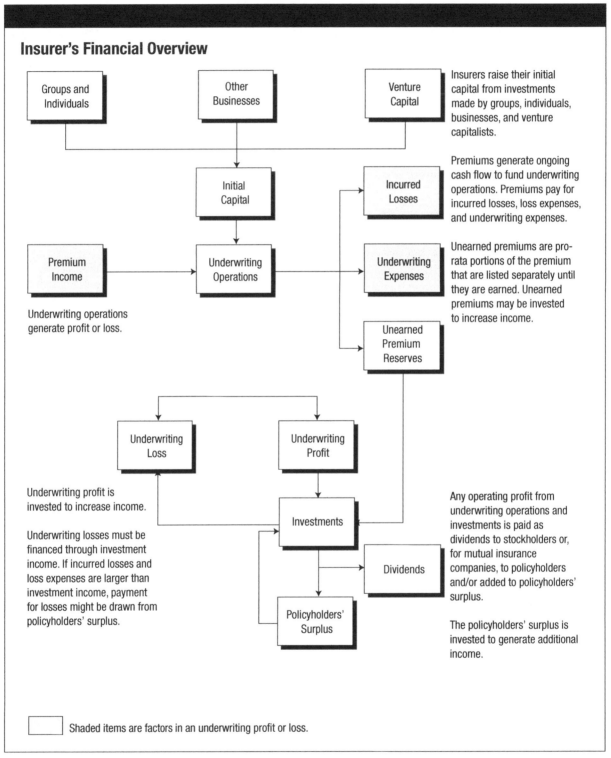

Insurers raise their initial capital from investments made by groups, individuals, businesses, and venture capitalists.

Premiums generate ongoing cash flow to fund underwriting operations. Premiums pay for incurred losses, loss expenses, and underwriting expenses.

Unearned premiums are pro-rata portions of the premium that are listed separately until they are earned. Unearned premiums may be invested to increase income.

Underwriting operations generate profit or loss.

Underwriting profit is invested to increase income.

Underwriting losses must be financed through investment income. If incurred losses and loss expenses are larger than investment income, payment for losses might be drawn from policyholders' surplus.

Any operating profit from underwriting operations and investments is paid as dividends to stockholders or, for mutual insurance companies, to policyholders and/or added to policyholders' surplus.

The policyholders' surplus is invested to generate additional income.

Shaded items are factors in an underwriting profit or loss.

[DA05783]

Underwriting Profitability Ratios

Ratio	Calculation	Comments
$\text{Loss ratio} = \dfrac{\text{Incurred losses}}{\text{Earned premiums}} \times 100$		This ratio compares incurred losses with earned premiums for a specific time period, such as a year. It illustrates what percentage of an insurer's earned income is "used up" by reserves and claim payments. For example, a loss ratio of 70 percent indicates that for every $1.00 the insurer earns in premium income, it pays $0.70 in incurred losses.
$\text{Expense ratio} = \dfrac{\text{Underwriting expenses}}{\text{Written premiums}} \times 100$		This ratio compares underwriting expenses with written premiums for a specific time period. It illustrates what percentage of an insurer's income goes to pay underwriting expenses. For example, an expense ratio of 28 percent indicates that for every $1.00 of insurance a company writes, it pays $0.28 in underwriting expenses.
Combined ratio = Loss ratio + Expense ratio		This combination of the loss and expense ratios presents a clear picture of the insurer's overall underwriting performance and compares the inflow and outflow of money from insurance operations. A combined ratio above 100 percent indicates an underwriting loss. A combined ratio below 100 percent indicates an underwriting profit.

[DA05784]

then recommend a modification to the premium growth goal in this territory to achieve profitability for the entire portfolio.

The vision and underwriting philosophy for an insurance company form the basis to determine the company's goals for each line of business. Communicating these goals to portfolio managers will help the company reach its goals in several ways:

- A clear understanding of expectations helps departments and individuals focus efforts to achieve the desired results.

- Measurement of performance against goals provides feedback and helps to identify shortfalls before they become significant.

- Coordination and communication of organizational goals help to ensure that all departments cooperate to achieve common objectives.

Goals are established during a formal, annual planning process that includes input and participation from all functional areas within a company. Insurers set goals for the following year and also create broad plans for the next three to five years.

Planners review **earned premium**, **incurred losses**, and **underwriting expenses** for the previous several years as well as the following year's projected results. The planning group also analyzes industry trends, individual company trends, and other factors affecting the insurance marketplace, while remaining mindful of the insurer's need to control expenses. Challenging yet realistic goals are then set to improve the projected performance.

Incurred losses

The losses that have occurred during a specific period, no matter when claims resulting from the losses are paid.

Earned premiums

The portion of written premiums that corresponds to coverage that has already been provided.

Underwriting expenses

Costs incurred by an insurer for operations, taxes, fees, and the acquisition of new policies.

Goals are usually described in terms of strategies and tactics. Tactics may be divided into activities and tasks. Different groups and individuals throughout the organization assume responsibility for different portions of the plan.

The planning and goal-setting exhibit illustrates how a corporate goal cascades through an organization through cross-functional cooperation. See the exhibit "Planning and Goal Setting."

Planning and Goal Setting

Goal				Example	Responsibility
Strategy				We will increase overall written premiums by 10 percent.	Sr. vice president, sales
	Tactic			Region A will increase written premiums by 8 percent.	Regional manager
		Activity		Each territory will appoint at least 15 new sales agents per quarter.	Territory managers
			Task	Each field representative will identify and recommend three new sales agents for appointment each quarter.	Marketing representatives
		Activity		Each territory will increase homeowners written premiums by 8 percent over the year.	Territory managers
			Task	Each territory will plan and implement a homeowner sales incentive contest within the first quarter.	Territory managers
			Task	Each territory will plan and deliver an "account selling" seminar for sales agents by March.	Territory managers
	Tactic			Region B will increase written premiums by 15 percent.	Regional manager
		Activity		The region will reduce automobile rates by 5 percent effective January 1 for new business and renewals.	Regional manager
			Task	Updated rates will be programmed into the system by December 15.	Information services manager
		Activity		The region will provide sales agents with training on underwriting guidelines to facilitate placing business with us.	Underwriting manager
			Task	Underwriters will spend one week each month visiting sales agents and providing training.	Underwriters
		Activity		The region will launch the new Pleasure Craft Policy in March.	Regional marketing manager
			Task	Seminars reviewing the Pleasure Craft Policy coverage, underwriting, and rating for sales agents will be conducted in each territory by February 28.	Territory managers

[DA05786]

Industry Trends

Industry trends can significantly affect an insurer's future underwriting profits by changing the insurer's competitive position relative to other insurers, by increasing or decreasing its exposure to claims, or by necessitating significant increases in its underwriting expenses.

Industry trends generally affect portfolio management by causing gradually evolving changes in written premium and expenses.

How Industry Trends Affect Goals

Economic, environmental, demographic, and general business trends affect the insurance industry and how insurers set goals.

Economic and business trends affect many areas of the insurance industry, as occurs in an economic recession. Many insurers experience investment losses or profit reductions with a consequential effect on their underwriting capacity and risk appetite. The economic downturn also has a significant impact on consumers and their demand for insurance products. There is a strong correlation between the percentage of uninsured motorists and the unemployment rate.[1] Among American motorists who maintained auto insurance coverage during the economic downturn that began in 2007, 28 percent of those surveyed reported shopping for lower rates when they would not normally have done so.[2] In setting goals, insurers need to consider whether to increase market share through price reductions, as well as the potential for increased losses.

Environmental trends are currently the subject of study and modeling throughout the industry that focus on the potential impact of weather trends on catastrophic events. Weather-related catastrophes can be devastating, not only to families and communities, but also to insurers. The costs to the insurance industry of the 2004 hurricane season exceeded $20 billion. Hurricane Katrina in 2005 cost the insurance industry more than $40 billion. Hurricane Ike in 2008 produced insured losses in excess of $10 billion. Insurers responded by withdrawing from the homeowners insurance market in coastal areas or restricting underwriting and raising prices for coverage in those areas.

There is a correlation between demographic groups and expected losses and between demographic changes and potential new insurance markets. The aging population, for example, is likely to be correlated with increases in both the frequency and severity of personal auto claims. The crash rate (based on estimated annual travel) increases in drivers age sixty-five and older, with drivers eighty-five and older having a crash rate 2.5 times as high as the average driver. The fatality rate also increases for drivers over age seventy-five.[3] Early recognition of such trends will assist insurers in setting appropriate goals. The aging population may also offer potential new insurance markets as the number of retirees grows, such as watercraft or recreational vehicle insurance.

The insurance industry is highly competitive, and there are continual changes in new products, prices, distribution systems, and technology within the industry. These are some examples of industry trends and their potential effects:

- The traditional underwriting cycle, characterized by phases of price softening followed by hardening, with which insurers evaluate competitive position and losses to determine premium and expense goals
- Introduction of new distribution systems such as the Internet, with which insurers consider technology expense along with the potential to reach new customers

Changes and trends in reinsurance also affect profitability goals for insurers. Reinsurers provide insurance coverage to insurance companies. Either the ceding company (the insurer that cedes or transfers premiums and loss exposures to the reinsurer) or the reinsurance company can change the terms and conditions of reinsurance agreements. Reinsurance capacity and pricing can either increase or decrease in response to catastrophe losses, changes in investment profit, the underwriting cycle, or other trends. Changes in a ceding company's reinsurance need to be considered when setting goals because the amount and cost of reinsurance affect the capacity of the ceding insurer for premium growth and because of the potential impact of losses on profitability.

How Industry Trends Affect Portfolio Management

Portfolio managers for insurers' personal lines portfolios need to monitor industry trends closely in order to respond effectively to them. Although some trends, such as an increase in catastrophe losses in a geographic region like the southeastern United States, might result in a major, immediate change in portfolio management such as the withdrawal from that homeowners insurance market, most changes will be more gradual.

For example, as the average age of a policyholder in an auto insurance portfolio increases, the portfolio manager may recommend incremental premium increases. Portfolio managers recommend gradual changes to written premium goals throughout the underwriting cycle.

Individual Company Trends

Improving an insurer's underwriting profitability is like piloting an ocean liner—it requires constant monitoring and small corrections to stay on course. Continual small corrections can keep a liner on course; however, correcting the direction of an ocean liner that has drifted drastically off course requires significant effort and time.

How Company Trends Affect Goals

An insurer is careful to track and monitor its portfolios' performance monthly, quarterly, and annually. This scrutiny allows the insurer's portfolio managers and senior management to identify any negative trends early and to respond quickly with small corrections. These corrections are incorporated in the organization's premium, loss, and expense goals.

These are some examples of internal trends to which an insurer will respond quickly by establishing appropriate goals:

- Slowing growth or a net decrease in policy count in a region or territory that was not part of the insurer's strategic plan
- Increasing loss ratios for a portfolio
- Increasing loss expenses for a portfolio
- Increasing underwriting expenses not matched by increasing written premiums for a portfolio

Although most changes in goals will be small and gradual in response to company trends, sometimes a significant shift in the company's vision will occur. For example, an insurer's senior management could decide to exit an entire product line or to make an acquisition as a result of the company's internal trends.

How Company Trends Affect Portfolio Management

Company trends generally affect portfolio management through small shifts in pricing or underwriting guidelines that affect written premium and losses. Exceptions occur when a company must make drastic changes to respond to a threat (such as a shift in company strategies to introduce new underwriting screening tools) or an opportunity (such as acquiring a book of business or redefining the company's target markets).

The vision and philosophy of senior management form the basis for all of the goals throughout the enterprise. Changes in senior management or the company's technology platforms can have significant impact on portfolio management. For example, a new computer system that incorrectly applies a pricing formula could have a negative affect on a portfolio's profitability as well as on customer relationships. A new senior vice president for a line of business may set aggressive growth goals that have a positive affect on a portfolio's written premium and profitability.

Competition

The insurance industry is highly competitive, and new insurers, new products and services, lower prices, and new distribution systems continually enter the insurance marketplace.

How Competition Affects Goals

The entry of new players into the marketplace influences existing insurers' goals. If the new insurers offer lower prices to establish themselves, existing insurers must decide whether to lower their prices and, if so, how to set goals to achieve profitability with the price reductions. If new players introduce new products, existing insurers will need to consider whether this will reduce their written premiums because of customers' switching to a new insurer to attain better "ease of use" or a better combined rate (for example, a customer may transfer a homeowners policy to a new insurer that also offers a specialized motor home policy). New companies may also relieve some pressure on existing insurers by expanding the number of companies providing high-risk coverage in states that mandate all insurers to participate in offering, for example, auto coverage to high-risk drivers. The new insurers could free up capacity for existing insurers, who may then increase goals for growth in written premium.

The withdrawal of companies from certain markets, such as companies withdrawing from coastal homeowners insurance markets after hurricanes, also affects an insurer's goals. The insurer will need to consider factors such as an increase in the portion of high-risk policies in setting goals after the withdrawal of significant competitors from a market.

"Ease of use" is an important issue in competition among insurers for independent agents. Changes in a competitor's computer interface that allow for easier entry of applications and access to information can influence decisions regarding placement of policies. In setting goals, an insurer needs to balance the expense of new or updated technology against the potential for additional written premium.

How Competition Affects Portfolio Management

Competition generally affects a portfolio's written premium, but aggressively targeted competition can negatively affect loss ratios over time if adverse selection results from an insurer's efforts to compete.

A competitor's products and services can create challenges for portfolio managers if the competition is meeting a need that the insurer is not. For example, a new competitor might offer a specialty policy for mobile homes in a region with a high percentage of retirees, and this new offering may attract customers to place auto coverage with the competitor, especially if there is a price reduction for multiple policies. The insurer will need to decide whether to respond by offering a similar new product with a risk of increased losses or by taking another approach—for example, increased marketing to potential customers in traditional homes or to a different demographic group.

Regulatory Changes

Insurance is a highly regulated industry, and regulatory changes can significantly affect insurers, particularly in the area of underwriting profit.

How Regulatory Changes Affect Goals

Insurance regulation changes for a variety of reasons. Regulatory changes may occur in response to requests by consumer advocates, requests by insurers, or events such as catastrophes.

Regulatory changes can significantly affect insurers' underwriting profits either positively or negatively. They can also have either a positive or a negative effect on consumers.

 Reality Check

Example of Regulatory Change

On April 1, 2008, Massachusetts introduced a managed competition system for auto insurance. This system allows auto insurers to set their own rates, with increases limited to a maximum of 10 percent. This replaced a system in which the state set the rates for auto insurance. In a survey conducted by the state's Division of Insurance, between April 2008 and April 2009, average premium per vehicle declined 8.2 percent. In this first year of managed competition, nine new companies entered the Massachusetts auto insurance market, as compared to a decline from thirty-five to nineteen companies from the early 1990s to 2008.

[DA05787]

Regulation changes affect insurer goals, from decisions about entering or exiting a market to changes in products and prices.

How Regulatory Changes Affect Portfolio Management

These are some examples of significant regulatory changes:

- Changes in the criteria that may be used for underwriting and rating risks, with potential effects on insurers' computer systems and profitability
- Changes in the way rate increases or decreases are approved and implemented, with potential impact on how quickly an insurer can make a change in response to trends and the expenses associated with the change
- Changes to the state-mandated benefits payable for some types of claims, with potential effects on a portfolio's loss ratios

- Changes to the financial stability and reporting requirements for insurers, with potential impact on an insurer's capacity for growth and expenses associated with additional reporting requirements
- Changes to regulations controlling insurers' ability to enter or withdraw from a line or territory, with effects on the portfolio manager's response to changes in loss ratios or underwriting profits

New and Retiring Product Lines

In addition to enhancing coverage on existing products, insurers offer new products in an effort to increase sales potential. For example, an insurer that writes homeowners and automobile insurance could decide to provide coverage for watercraft or mobile homes as well. An insurer can enter a new product line through acquisition of another company's book of business or by launching a new product of its own.

It is important for an insurer to plan carefully for the introduction of new product lines because it will take time to earn sufficient premium to cover the increased expenses of the acquisition or product launch and potential incurred losses. The portfolio manager needs to manage expenses as effectively as possible.

Insurers also choose to retire product lines for a variety of reasons, such as acquisition of another insurer offering a product incompatible with the purchaser's philosophy, changes in regulation, competitive forces, or vulnerability to catastrophe. Insurers usually retire product lines because they are unprofitable.

Retiring a line decreases premiums, increases expenses, and does not protect the insurer from losses until all business in the line nonrenews or cancels.

How Changing Earned Premiums Affects Goals

When a product line is retired, earned premiums diminish. As incurred losses continue and earned premiums diminish, the loss ratio increases. The insurer also continues to be exposed to the potential of large losses, and the effect of those losses becomes progressively more significant as premiums diminish. The insurer will need to modify goals to achieve profitability as the retiring line is run off. See the exhibit "Effect of Large Losses During Product Retirement."

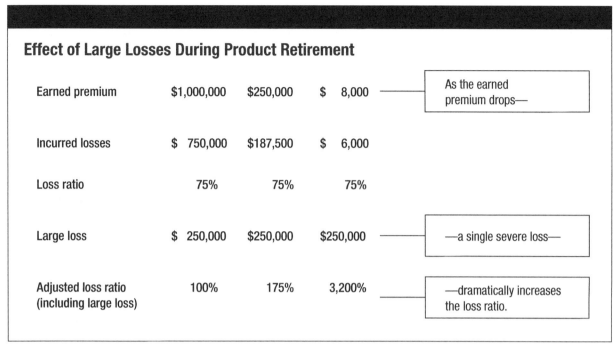

Effect of Large Losses During Product Retirement

Earned premium	$1,000,000	$250,000	$ 8,000	As the earned premium drops—
Incurred losses	$ 750,000	$187,500	$ 6,000	
Loss ratio	75%	75%	75%	
Large loss	$ 250,000	$250,000	$250,000	—a single severe loss—
Adjusted loss ratio (including large loss)	100%	175%	3,200%	—dramatically increases the loss ratio.

[DA05789]

How Changing Earned Premiums Affects Portfolio Management

Portfolio management for new and retiring product lines requires constant monitoring, with an eye toward the difference between written and earned premiums and the exaggerated nature of the loss ratios that can result:

- New product lines that have not accrued sufficient earned premium to offset losses will have exaggerated loss ratios if losses occur early in the product line's history.

- Retiring product lines that are not replaced with new sales will have decreased written premiums, directly lowering earned premiums. Additionally, insurers often lose related business in other lines by retiring a line, resulting in indirect loss of earned premium. For example, an insurer retiring from the yacht market often will lose the automobile and homeowners policies of those clients as well. Losses late in the process of policy runoff will create exaggerated loss ratios.

Using various methods, the portfolio manager can improve results during the process of retiring a product line when earned premiums decrease:

- Taking advantage of opportunities to cancel policies mid-term
- Increasing premium growth in another line when feasible

- Reallocating resources, such as transferring claim representatives and underwriters to other product lines
- Settling claims when this can be done cost effectively to reduce the loss ratio and the expense of continued claim handling

INCREASING PERSONAL LINES PROFITABILITY

Underwriting goals are established by an insurer's senior management. Although portfolio managers do not normally set these goals, they should participate in evaluating methods to increase profitability.

An insurer can improve underwriting profitability by adjusting any or all of the three primary elements that determine underwriting results:

- Premiums
- Losses
- Expenses

Increasing premiums, decreasing losses, or reducing expenses, individually or in combination, may improve a company's underwriting performance. Any change must be made with careful consideration of the interrelationship of these three elements. For example, an underwriting change to decrease losses could also decrease premiums by reducing the number of accepted policies.

Increasing Premium

The primary source of increased underwriting profit is growth. Insurers can increase premiums by increasing the number of policies through sales or acquisition of another company, increasing the average premium per policy, and raising rates. Among methods insurers use to increase sales, average premiums, and rates are these:

- Selective growth
- Growth in niche markets
- Point-of-sale marketing
- Adjusting rates and relativity factors
- Ease-of-use technology
- Improving producer/underwriter relationships

Selective Growth

Insurers manage growth carefully because it is possible to grow too quickly and to expose the company to so much risk that it becomes insolvent. Regulators monitor insurers' financial results closely to protect consumers from insurer insolvency and the resulting inability to pay claims.

One of the key financial ratios that regulators evaluate is the written premium to policyholders' surplus ratio, which compares the cushion provided by policyholders' surplus to the risk represented by written premiums. This ratio can signify an insurer's vulnerability to pricing errors, above-average losses, and declines in the values of its investments. It can also indicate an insurer's capacity to underwrite additional insurance. Ratios of greater than $3 written premium to $1 of policyholder's surplus are a cause for concern for the insurer and would generate regulatory inquiry.

If increased premiums cause losses and expenses to grow disproportionately, the strategy of premium growth will be counterproductive. Growth may be desirable in some lines but not in others.

Growth in Niche Markets

An insurer can increase premiums by targeting niche markets with risks that standard insurers may not cover, such as mobile homes, antique and art collections, or yachts. Niche markets may offer certain advantages, including these:

- Less competition
- Less price sensitivity either because of the reduced competition or the nature of the customers or both
- Ability to set underwriting standards that are more consistent with exposures
- Development of underwriting and rating expertise to increase profitability
- More effective advertising as a result of targeting a smaller, select market (for example, advertising in periodicals or on Web sites related to the niche market)
- Referrals from customers
- Recognition of the insurer as an expert in the market

Although niche markets offer potential advantages, they also present risks and uncertainties for insurers. Loss frequency and severity are less predictable than with more typical products, and pricing may be inadequate for the loss exposure. Customer and regulatory response to new specialized products is unknown. An insurer also may encounter difficulties in withdrawing from a niche market if it proves unprofitable.

Point-of-Sale Marketing

Personal insurance is marketed and distributed through a variety of channels:

- Direct to individual consumers
- Through independent insurance agents who represent multiple insurers
- Through groups and associations whose members receive value-added services, specialized coverages, or reduced premiums by purchasing insurance through the group plan

Face-to-face sales of personal insurance have been supplemented or replaced for many insurers by telephone sales through toll-free numbers and by marketing and sales over the Internet. Growth through these channels involves increased expenses for technology; however, over time, expenses may decrease as a result of improved efficiencies and an increase in premium. See the exhibit "Insurance Distribution Through Various Point-of-Sale Marketing Methods."

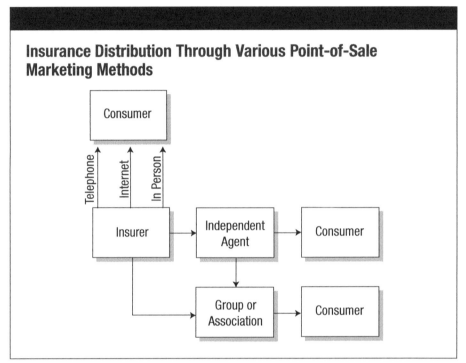

Insurance Distribution Through Various Point-of-Sale Marketing Methods

[DA05767]

Insurers can increase premium growth by using existing distribution channels more effectively and by adding distribution channels. Techniques insurers use to manage point-of-sale marketing activities include these:

- Increasing or decreasing producers in territories according to profitability
- Increasing or decreasing commission rates for product lines or portfolios to achieve improved balance in profitability
- Creating sales incentives
- Implementing or modifying direct marketing or advertising programs

Adjusting Rates and Relativity Factors

An insurer can grow by raising rates to generate additional premium per policy or by lowering rates to attract more business. Each approach has potential disadvantages. Rate increases may generate customer dissatisfaction, with a resulting loss of business in addition to possible regulatory disapproval.

Adverse selection, in which only riskier customers pay the increased rates, can result in larger losses. A decrease in rates can result in an increase to the loss ratio.

A more sophisticated approach is the assignment of actuarially determined relativity to rating variables to determine the best premium for a policy.[4] Factors such as geographical territory, age of insured, prior claims experience, credit history, and sometimes even the insured's educational level are weighted according to their relative impact on loss costs. Each factor is assigned a relativity derived from statistical analysis of the insurer's and industry data. Each prospective policy can then be evaluated by entering information for each variable into a computer system that weighs relativities and determines premium. Regulators may be more receptive to such evidence-based rate increases.[5]

Ease-of-Use Technology

Insurers must be aware of agents' preferences for easy-to-use computer interfaces for quoting and entering applications. This technology significantly influences the placement decisions of producers who represent more than one insurer.

Insurers need to weigh the expenses of changing, upgrading, or adapting their computer systems for agents' ease of use against the quantity and quality of business produced by those agents. The total cost of doing business with agents, including commissions and technology expenses, should be balanced against the premium produced.

Improving Producer/Underwriter Relationships

Insurers should recognize that, along with ease-of-use technology, the dynamics of personal interaction can influence producers to place new policies with insurers with whom they have a positive underwriting experience. Flexibility and timely underwriting decisions, as well as the availability and communication skills of underwriters, can be significant factors in agents' decisions about where to place business when they have a choice among multiple insurers.

It is important for underwriting managers to evaluate the effectiveness of their underwriters' relationships with producers and to address any conflicts.

Decreasing Losses

Decreasing the frequency or severity of losses usually requires underwriting action. An insurer will evaluate underwriting guidelines and compliance by underwriters and producers with those guidelines. The insurer will also evaluate catastrophe exposure and claim management.

Responding to Poor Loss Experience

A detailed and thorough analysis of loss exposures, paid losses, and loss reserves can provide an insurer with both the causes of poor loss experience and appropriate responses. While an insurer's loss experience can deteriorate quickly (as a result of catastrophes, for example), remedial underwriting measures can be slow to take effect. The sooner deteriorating loss experience is identified and remedial action taken, the less the insurer's profitability will be affected.

Various factors can adversely affect an insurer's loss experience, and different potential remedial actions are associated with each of these factors. See the exhibit "Factors Adversely Affecting Losses and Possible Remedial Actions."

Checking Compliance With Underwriting Guidelines

To match premiums with loss exposures, insurers develop underwriting guidelines that specify the risks they will accept and how accepted risks are to be rated. Some of these guidelines may be incorporated into insurers' computer systems that permit common variables to be updated, providing automated changes for all policy applications. Insurers that do not have adaptable computer systems, insurers that need to make an immediate change to underwriting guidelines before their computer systems can be updated (in response to an impending hurricane in a territory, for example), or insurers that consider complex risks or those outside standard underwriting guidelines may communicate changes in variables directly to underwriting staff.

If the underwriting guidelines are not applied or are applied incorrectly, the premiums an insurer collects might be insufficient to cover its loss exposures. One response to unacceptable loss ratios is to conduct an underwriting review or audit to check for compliance with underwriting guidelines.

Adjusting Underwriting Guidelines

An insurer might determine that underwriting guidelines are ineffective in matching rates to exposures. For example, an insurer that offers a discount to young drivers who have completed driver training could find that the loss experience of this group is no different from the loss experience of young drivers with no formal training, making the discount inappropriate. These unexpected outcomes occur most frequently when an insurer has entered a new line of business, but they can also result from changes in society, the regulatory environment, or demographics.

If an insurer determines that underwriting guidelines are ineffective, the insurer will make appropriate changes. Although such changes can be implemented immediately for new policies, adjustments to existing policies will not be effective until renewal. Some changes to underwriting guidelines may require regulatory approval.

Factors Adversely Affecting Losses and Possible Remedial Actions

Area	Factor	Remedial Actions and Considerations
Rating	Premiums are too low to cover loss exposures.	*Increase premiums.* Unfortunately, because premiums must be earned during the year, rate increases are slow to take effect. Also, regulatory and competitive pressures can limit an insurer's ability to increase rates.
Underwriting	Underwriting guidelines are ineffective or are not being correctly applied.	*Adjust/enforce underwriting guidelines.* This process generally involves reunderwriting the portfolio and changing the coverage or rating at each policy's renewal. Therefore, the needed adjustment requires a full year to complete, plus additional time for rating changes to be reflected in earned premium.
Policy wording	The insurer's policy language is open to broader interpretation than was intended, resulting in coverage for loss exposures that were not contemplated by the rates.	*Rewrite policy language.* Changes can strengthen the policy language. However, a complete reissue of new policies containing the new language requires a full year to implement, increased printing and mailing costs, plus additional time for the changes to be reflected in a reduction in paid losses. In addition, there is no guarantee that the new language will be free from misinterpretation or that it will receive regulatory approval.
Reserving	Loss reserves are inaccurate.	*Adjust loss reserves and train staff.* Insurers must be sure their reserves are wrong before adjusting them on a blanket basis. Manipulating reserves to achieve certain financial results is a form of fraud. Blanket reserve adjustments or changes in IBNR can be made relatively quickly. However, adjustments affect underwriting profits, policyholders' surplus, and the company's financial position. They are also subject to regulatory control. Training staff to improve the reserve setting process can be effective, but the effect on incurred losses is slow. The use of computer systems to set claim reserves can increase the accuracy of reserving.
Claim handling	Loss expenses are too high or claim representatives are inefficient or are overpaying claims.	*Train staff.* Training staff to improve claim handling skills can be effective, but the effect on incurred losses is slow, and the training itself generates additional expenses. *Effective Use of Technology.* Improving claim computer systems can increase efficiency, early recognition of changes in key loss factors, and implementation of best practices.

[DA05768]

Managing Catastrophe Exposures

Although catastrophes can be unpredictable, insurers can anticipate and minimize their exposure to them. Insurers use various methods to mitigate or manage catastrophe exposures, including these:

- Introducing policy exclusions and sublimits for loss exposures such as windstorm and earthquake

- Using reinsurance to limit the effect of catastrophe losses
- Joining risk-sharing pools with other insurers
- Increasing deductibles or introducing deductibles that are a percentage of the insured loss
- Offering lower deductibles and premium discounts to policyholders who make improvements according to safety or construction criteria
- Offsetting anticipated catastrophe losses by increasing lower-risk premium income from areas not as prone to catastrophes
- Monitoring the geographic distribution of insured risks and limiting as much as possible the concentration of policies in areas prone to catastrophe

The option of geographic redistribution must be managed carefully to avoid redlining (the practice of refusing to underwrite any risk in a particular area). Regulations usually prohibit redlining, although offsetting exposures is typically permitted, such as a one-to-ten ratio of coastal to inland property in a state's homeowners insurance portfolio.

Reunderwriting

Reunderwriting

The process of analyzing the characteristics of policies within a portfolio and the trends of those characteristics.

Reunderwriting can decrease losses through appropriate assessment of the root cause of poor loss experience and effective problem solving to improve the experience.

Changing the direction of results can be a lengthy process because policies are usually written on a twelve-month basis. Continual analysis of results after making changes to underwriting criteria is necessary to evaluate the effectiveness of reunderwriting.

Controlling Expenses

Insurers often respond to poor underwriting results by introducing expense control measures. The positive effects of controlling expenses on underwriting profits include these:

- Lowering an insurer's combined ratio
- Allowing the insurer to reduce rates, with potential for increased sales and premium volume

An additional motivation for insurers to control expenses is that regulators are more likely to approve rate adjustment requests from insurers that operate cost-effectively.

Insurers can control expenses in several ways, including these:

- Maximizing human resources
- Managing underwriting expenses
- Outsourcing underwriting activities such as application data verification services

Maximizing Human Resources

An insurer's largest underwriting expenses are those related to human resources, such as salaries, benefits, and training. Because insurance is a people-focused industry, insurers seek to maximize their human resources in several ways:

- Training employees to improve productivity and accuracy
- Using technology such as computers to improve efficiency
- Paying competitive salaries and benefits and offering career development opportunities to attract and retain good employees

Managing Underwriting Expenses

An insurer's underwriting expenses can be categorized as either fixed or variable costs. Fixed expenses include costs such as lease of premises or equipment and employee salaries and benefits. Variable underwriting expenses are those directly related to premium volume, such as commissions and premium taxes.

Methods of reducing fixed costs include these:

- Consolidation of insurer offices
- Consolidation of job functions
- Increased efficiency through the use of technology
- Increased focus on management of employees' expenses (discontinuation of company cars, for example)
- Outsourcing of services

Variable expenses can be reduced by decreasing commission rates or by increasing direct sales to consumers through efficient distribution channels such as the Internet.

Underwriting managers should carefully evaluate potential effects before making changes. Reduction in commission rates could result in a decrease in premiums. Consolidation of offices or job functions could result in the loss of experienced employees, which could, in turn, negatively affect customer relations.

Outsourcing Underwriting Activities

A method of controlling underwriting expenses is outsourcing certain functions to third-party vendors (TPVs). These vendors perform services such as property inspections and evaluations of replacement cost. It may be more cost-effective for an insurer to pay for such services from a vendor on an as-needed basis rather than have employees perform these functions.

In addition to controlling expenses, the use of TPVs may provide additional expertise to the insurer. One service that is commonly outsourced is application data verification. By checking the accuracy of the data entered on an application, a TPV may be able to provide the insurer with information not previously disclosed. Some TPVs offer data devices that can be placed in insured vehicles to monitor vehicle usage and compare it to the information provided on the applications. The expertise of the TPV may result in an increase of premiums charged as a result of improved accuracy of information.

PERSONAL LINES PRICING

Pricing is a tool that can help an insurer achieve profitability. Pure premiums and base rates are the scientific foundation on which the art of pricing, using relativity factors, is developed.

Actuaries use a variety of mathematical tools and techniques in pricing insurance products. Insurance pricing has these components:

- Pure premiums
- Base rates
- Class relativity factors

Although portfolio managers do not calculate pricing components, they should understand the actuarial recommendations they receive and be able to interpret the information and intended results in actuarial reports. Further, they should recognize situations in which relativity factors are ineffective (such as the reduction in the number of policy applications that results from new competition in a territory) and recommend changes in relativity factors when needed (such as the need for more competitive pricing for steel-framed masonry houses, which have a reduced fire-load).

Pure Premiums and Base Rates

Pure premium is charged per **exposure unit** by estimating the value of projected losses associated with the line of business based on past claim data and current trends. Because the length of coverage affects the potential for loss, exposure units are often expressed in terms of time (for example, one house insured for twelve months is one house-year). This approach allows actuaries to **factor out** varying policy inception dates and policy periods from calculations. Exposure units measure loss potential and pure premium based solely on projected value of losses and disregard other expenses and profit.

An insurer develops a **base rate** by adding a standard charge for expenses and profits to the pure premium. Base rates are expressed relative to a specific

Exposure unit

A fundamental measure of the loss exposure assumed by an insurer.

Pure premium

The average amount of money an insurer must charge per exposure unit in order to be able to cover the total anticipated losses for that line of business.

Factor out

The elimination of an element in an analysis because of its negligible effect on the calculation or because it represents an uncharacteristic event that is unlikely to recur.

Base rate

The rate (or cost) per unit of coverage required to cover the insurer's losses, expenses, and profit for a line of business.

unit of coverage, such as $1,000 of Coverage A on a homeowners policy. An insurer multiplies the base rate by the number of coverage units to derive the **base premium**.

Pooled loss cost data, adjusted to reflect **loss development** and current trends, is available to insurers from advisory organizations such as Insurance Services Office, Inc. (ISO) and the American Association of Insurance Services (AAIS). Unlike individual insurers, advisory organizations have access to industry-wide data, providing greater accuracy to insurers as they predict future **loss costs**.

Historically, advisory organizations developed actual base rates, and some insurers adopted the advisory rates. During the late 1980s, consumers and regulators became concerned that the use of advisory rates by insurers resembled price fixing. Consequently, in 1990 states began moving to a system in which advisory organizations developed and published only projected loss costs. Individual insurers were encouraged to base rates as much as possible on their own loss experience but could continue to use an advisory organization's loss costs if their own experience was insufficient to develop statistically credible rates.

Class Relativity Factors

The calculation of a base rate for an insurance class or product assumes uniformity in loss frequency and severity. In reality, however, the frequency and severity of losses and the cost of claim settlements within a portfolio can vary significantly.

For example, the potential severity of a fire loss is greater for a home located in a remote area. It may take firefighters longer to reach the site. A lack of hydrant protection may mean that water has to be transported by firefighters. Settlement costs may be higher if building materials must be brought in from a distance.

Insurers adjust pricing to respond to the different levels of risk within a portfolio in a three-step process:

1. They subdivide the line into smaller, homogeneous groups and use the process of **risk classification** to adjust rates for each group.
2. They analyze the unique loss experience for each rate class.
3. They adjust rates to reflect the relatively higher or lower loss exposure of each rate class by applying **rate relativity factors**.

Actuaries compare the loss experience of rate classes with that for the **unity classification** and then develop rate relativity factors according to the relative levels of risk.

Insurers use rate relativity factors to improve profitability by increasing prices in classes with unfavorable rates and decreasing prices in more favorably rated classes. These adjustments allow the insurer to be more competitive in the

Base premiums
The basic cost of specific insurance policies.

Loss development
The increase or decrease of incurred losses over time.

Loss costs
The portion of the rate that covers projected claim payments and loss adjusting expenses.

Risk classification
The formation of different premiums for the same coverage based on each homogeneous group's characteristics.

Rate relativity factor
A number by which a base rate may be multiplied to reflect the relatively higher or lower loss exposure of one homogeneous group compared to that of another.

Unity classification
One rate class, selected as a baseline, to which all other rate classes are compared.

preferred rate classes and improve the profitability of their portfolios. Insurers are increasingly using more risk classifications to more finely classify and price risks.

Residential Property Rate Relativities

In residential property rating, insurers classify risks according to a variety of characteristics, including these:

- Type of building construction (such as frame or masonry)
- Coverage A limits purchased
- Type of coverage purchased (such as named perils or open perils)
- Level of public coverage available (such as the distance to hydrants or the number of units between fire walls in multifamily dwellings)

Insurers develop rate relativity factors for each rate class based on industry-wide loss data, current trends, and their own past and projected loss experience. See the exhibit "Residential Property Rate Relativity Factors."

Residential Property Rate Relativity Factors

Rate Class	Relativity Factors
Construction Type	Frame Masonry Veneer Solid Masonry
Coverage A	Ranges of coverage limits Example: Below $50,000 $50,000–$99,000 $100,000–$149,000 $150,000–$199,000 $200,000 and over
Policy Form	Named perils Open perils
Public Protection	Public protection classification (PPC) based on fire-fighting factors of communities
Other Classifications	Age of roof Shape of roof (such as gable or flat) Roof covering (such as shingles or tile) Opening protection (such as storm shutters) Protective devices

[DA05790]

Analysis of claim data confirms what common sense suggests: Frame dwellings catch fire more frequently and burn more severely than do those made of brick or stone. This information helps insurers classify residential risks based on construction type. Each risk classification is assigned a rate relativity factor based on the loss experience it generates.

Insurers match rates to exposures by charging relatively more for lower Coverage A limits than for higher limits. Analysis of losses indicates that the majority of claims are relatively small and that the frequency of losses decreases with severity. Consequently, insurers may be able to increase premiums and profitability by assigning lower rate relativity factors to higher coverage limits to compete more favorably in ranges that will generate more premiums.

The broader the coverage provided by a policy, the wider the range of losses to which it will respond. Insurers analyze claim data by policy form to develop rate relativity factors that reflect the higher loss exposure associated with broader coverage.

The potential severity of any fire loss is directly related to the fire-fighting services available. ISO evaluates the fire-fighting factors of individual communities and assigns each a public protection classification (PPC) from 1 to 10. The lower the PPC, the better the fire-fighting services. This grading system is used for residential property rating by insurers in all states. Actuaries develop rate relativity factors to reflect the anticipated risk of fire losses for each PPC.

Other risk classifications for homeowners policies include the type and age of roof, the type of protection, if any, for openings such as windows and doors, the age of the dwelling, and whether any protective devices are installed in the dwelling (for example, burglar alarms or fire sprinkler systems).

Personal Auto Rate Relativity Factors

The calculation of premiums on personal automobile policies involves the use of rate relativity factors for many different risk classifications relating to the driver, the vehicle, the coverage, and the territory in which the vehicle is garaged and used. One large national insurer has millions of possible combinations of risk classification to more closely align price with risk in the auto insurance portfolio. See the exhibit "Personal Auto Rate Relativity Factors."

Just as the potential severity of a fire can depend on the location of a dwelling, an automobile's loss exposure depends on the environment in which it is garaged and operated. Throughout the United States, either insurers, regulators, or rating organizations divide each state geographically into rating territories used by all automobile insurers. The entity charged with this responsibility varies from state to state. Some states have guidelines that restrict the territory rate relativity factors for personal automobile insurance to help provide affordable rates in urban areas.

Personal Auto Rate Relativity Factors

Rate Class	Relativity Factors
Territory	Community type (urban, rural) Weather exposures
Other Classifications	Driver (age, gender, driving record) Use of vehicle (mileage) Coverage (liability limits, physical damage deductibles, collision) Vehicle type (value, age, safety rating) Protective devices (alarm, anti-theft devices, anti-lock brakes, air bags)

[DA05791]

Depending on state regulation, a variety of details relating to the driver, the vehicle, and the coverage purchased may form the basis for automobile risk classifications and rate relativity factors.

ANALYZING LOSS DATA AND FORECASTING TRENDS

Actuaries analyze data in conjunction with current trends to predict future losses and establish insurance rates.

Actuaries analyze an insurer's loss and loss expense data along with industry data and current trends to predict future losses. Actuaries also analyze loss frequency trends and loss severity trends and compare loss frequency and loss severity among groups.

Portfolio managers must understand how actuarial analyses affect the insurer's rates and what the ultimate affect will be on the insurer's business portfolio.

Loss Frequency Trends

Loss frequency

The number of losses that occur within a specified period.

Understanding the insurer's previous **loss frequency** helps actuaries forecast losses. The period on which a loss frequency is based is often described in terms of exposure units, such as losses per hundred car-years or losses per thousand house-years. This approach enables actuaries to make meaningful comparisons regarding the number of losses for a line of business, risk classification, or coverage from year to year, despite changes in the in-force policy count.

Loss frequencies are often expressed as percentages, and they are usually calculated for a particular period, such as one year. The "Components of Loss Frequency" table illustrates a hypothetical insurer's fire loss frequency for its homeowners product. The actuary would observe that the number of house-years and fire losses increase each year, therefore increasing the loss frequency. See the exhibit "Components of Loss Frequency."

Components of Loss Frequency

	Fire Losses ÷ House-Years		Loss Frequency per 100 House-Years
Year 1	401	10,000	4.01%
Year 2	487	10,500	4.64%
Year 3	529	11,000	4.80%

[DA05921]

Often, actuaries review several years' worth of loss frequency information to identify trends that enable them to project future loss experience. For example, actuaries would analyze the frequency trend in the "Components of Loss Frequency" table and observe that the insurer's fire loss frequency is trending upwards. Unless something should cause the trend to change, the actuary could project a slightly higher loss frequency during Year 4.

When analyzing loss experience, actuaries consider many factors to identify the cause of any significant change in frequency. For example, an earthquake that ruptures gas lines and downs electrical wires can cause a significant increase in an insurer's fire loss frequency for the year in which it occurs. However, the insurer may not anticipate another earthquake for twenty years; consequently, the actuary may recalculate the actual fire loss frequency for that year without the catastrophe figure, to remove its effect on any subsequent rate adjustments.

Loss Severity Trends

Loss severity trends refer to the average size losses for a rating class over time. Large losses for individual loss exposures are relatively rare in first-party personal auto and residential property insurance. Although an insurer's potential exposure can equal the limits of a policy, most claims involve much smaller amounts. To set rates commensurate with the insurer's real exposure, an actuary averages the claim payments. See the exhibit "Components of Loss Severity."

Loss severity
The amount of loss, typically measured in dollars, for a loss that has occurred.

Components of Loss Severity

	Total Paid Losses ÷ Fire Losses		Fire Loss Severity
Year 1	$1,478,040	452	$3,270
Year 2	$1,323,520	517	$2,560
Year 3	$1,360,900	439	$3,100
Year 4	$1,253,750	425	$2,950
Average severity			$2,970

[DA05922]

An actuary analyzing the "Components of Loss Severity" table would recognize that as the amounts for the total losses paid in a given year increase and the number of fires increase, the fire loss severity for the insurer's homeowner product increases. The result is an increase in the average severity. This analysis enables the actuary to identify trends and predict the cost of future losses.

A table such as the "Claim Payment Breakdown—Year 1" table enables the actuary to observe the relationship between loss severity and loss frequency. Analysis of this claim payment breakdown demonstrates that the highest frequency claims are small; therefore, loss severity is relatively low. As the loss severity (the average claim payment) increases, the frequency of losses generally declines. See the exhibit "Claim Payment Breakdown—Year 1."

Claim Payment Breakdown—Year 1

Claim Payment Range	Losses	Average Claim Payment	Total
$1 – $2,500	300	$800	$240,000
$2,501 – $5,000	76	$2,607	$198,132
$5,001 – $10,000	50	$6,850	$342,500
$10,001 – $25,000	16	$12,250	$196,000
$25,001 – $50,000	6	$31,650	$189,900
$50,001 – $100,000	3	$61,500	$184,500
$100,001 +	1	$127,008	$127,008
Totals	452		$1,478,040

[DA05923]

As with frequency, actuaries try to identify the cause of any significant variance in loss severity and may choose to exclude amounts from any event that results in misleading severity data. For example, a large loss reserve posted in a previous year is reversed in a subsequent year. This adjustment is called a **reserve takedown**. Reserve takedowns can occur, for example, when a lawsuit is settled out of court or when investigation of a claim determines that no coverage applies. A large reserve takedown reduces the incurred losses for the year in which the reserve reduction occurs and could artificially reduce loss severity for that year. As a result, actuaries may exclude the effect of reserve takedowns from their severity calculations.

Actuaries may also choose to exclude very large losses (factor out their effect), called shock losses, because they occur so rarely. Actuaries may either exclude a shock loss or cap the dollar amount of the loss to be included in severity calculations. Otherwise, severity might be overstated and rates set too high, adversely affecting the insurer's competitive position. Capping the shock loss at $100,000, for example, allows for its inclusion in severity calculations, but also recognizes the relative rarity of losses of this size.

The "Effect of Reserve Takedowns and Shock Losses on Severity" table illustrates the potential effect of reserve takedowns and shock losses on the insurer's severity calculations for Year 1. If the reserve takedown is not excluded, it would result in the artificial understatement of loss severity. The effect of including the entire shock loss would be overstated severity. See the exhibit "Effect of Reserve Takedowns and Shock Losses on Severity."

Reserve takedown

The reduction or total elimination of a previously established claim reserve.

Effect of Reserve Takedowns and Shock Losses on Severity

	Total Paid Losses ÷	Fire Losses	Fire Loss Severity
Effect of Reserve Takedown on Severity			
Year 1 results	$478,040	452	$1,058
Plus reserve takedown	$1,000,000		
Year 1 adjusted results	$1,478,040		$3,270
Effect of Shock Loss on Severity			
Year 1 results	$1,478,040	452	$3,270
Plus shock loss	$1,000,000		
Year 1 adjusted results	$2,478,040		$5,482
Effect of Capped Shock Loss on Severity			
Year 1 results	$1,478,040	452	$3,270
Plus capped shock loss	$100,000		
Year 1 adjusted results	$1,578,040		$3,491

[DA05924]

Comparing Loss Frequency and Loss Severity Among Groups

Actuaries analyze claim data by product, coverage, geographic area, risk classification, producer, branch or region, and year. They compare the frequency and severity of losses among these different groups and use the results as the basis for establishing rate relativity factors.

The "Fire Losses on Frame and Masonry Homes" table represents a hypothetical insurer's residential property fire loss experience for two different construction classes during three calendar years. The actuary would observe that as the house-years and number of losses increases, so do the total paid losses. Additionally, the actuary might observe that the total paid losses for frame homes are 59.38 percent more than those for masonry homes. See the exhibit "Fire Losses on Frame and Masonry Homes—Year End."

Fire Losses on Frame and Masonry Homes—Year End

	House-Years	Number of Losses	Total Paid Losses
Masonry Homes			
Year 1	2,000	19	$34,992
Year 2	2,500	39	$69,774
Year 3	3,000	52	$93,618
Totals	7,500	110	$198,384
Frame Homes			
Year 1	2,700	41	$66,348
Year 2	3,200	59	$110,693
Year 3	3,750	63	$156,996
Totals	9,650	163	$334,037

59.38%

[DA05925]

Frequency Analysis

Using the claim data presented, actuaries compare the incidence of fire losses for frame homes with that for masonry homes. First, they calculate the loss frequency for each construction class. Next, they compare the two frequencies and determine that the loss frequency for frame construction is 0.22 percent higher than the loss frequency for masonry construction. This difference between the two loss frequencies will form the basis for a rate relativity factor. See the exhibit "Loss Frequency Analysis."

Loss Frequency Analysis

Construction Class	Number of Losses	÷	House-Years	Frequency per 100 House-Years	
Masonry	110		7,500	1.47%	
Frame	163		9,650	1.69%	+.22%

[DA05926]

Severity Analysis

Actuaries also use severity analysis to compare two rate classes, calculating the relative severity of fire losses for masonry and frame homes and compare these loss results, determining that the loss severity for frame construction is $246 more than the loss severity for masonry construction. This difference between the two loss severities will form the basis for a rate relativity factor. See the exhibit "Loss Severity Analysis."

Loss Severity Analysis

Construction Class	Total Paid Losses	÷	Number of Losses	Severity (Paid losses/ Number of losses)	
Masonry	$198,384		110	$1,803	
Frame	$334,037		163	$2,049	+ $246

[DA05927]

RATEMAKING PRINCIPLES

Insurers use three methods of ratemaking to develop their foundation rates. Next, they apply regulatory and social objectives in conjunction with the insurer's business objectives, and they incorporate investment income requirements to establish rates.

Ratemaking is the process of incorporating the cost of losses and expenses and the need for profits into a pricing strategy. Base insurance rates are developed using one of three ratemaking methods. Additional factors are then used to adjust the rates, including competition, consumer trends, underwriting philosophy, and company strategies. The resulting rates can then be evaluated and adjusted in consideration of ratemaking objectives. See the exhibit "Ratemaking Methods."

Ratemaking Methods

Method	Source of Base Rate	Adjustments to Base Rate	Loss Expenses and Profit Included?	Applied to New Business?	Applied to Existing Business?
Judgment	Rates are based on similar risks (little or no statistical information).	The base rate is adjusted based on experience and judgment to determine the relative loss exposure of new risks.	Yes	Yes	Yes
Loss Ratio	The base rate was previously established.	The base rate is increased or reduced in response to unanticipated loss experience. The difference between the expected and actual loss ratio is divided by the expected loss ratio to determine a positive or negative percentage for rate increase or reduction. This rate is adjusted by factors for expense and profits.	Yes	No	Yes
Pure Premium	The base rate comes from insurer's loss experience or from pooled loss cost information, available through advisory organizations.	The insurer adds estimated underwriting expenses and profit factor per exposure unit.	Yes	Yes	Yes

[DA05805]

Investment income

Interest, dividends, and net capital gains received by an insurer from the insurer's financial assets, minus its investment expenses.

Two broad sets of objectives underlie rate evaluation. Regulatory objectives and social objectives influence rates as well as whether regulators approve proposed rates. Consideration of **investment income** is another broad factor in ratemaking.

Portfolio managers must have a working knowledge of all factors that influence ratemaking. With a thorough understanding of ratemaking concepts, portfolio managers can make sound recommendations for rating improvements, such as providing credits for various risk control incentives.

Regulatory Objectives

Although actuaries propose rates based on statistical analysis and projections, an insurer's flexibility in setting rates is limited by regulation. However, analysis of regulatory objectives is also required in any examination of insurance pricing.

The regulatory environment within which insurers operate provides a legal framework for ratemaking. Although regulatory systems vary by state, rates in all states must meet these specific criteria:

- They must not be inadequate.
- They must not be excessive.
- They must not be unfairly discriminatory.

Not Inadequate

Inadequacy implies that the rate charged for a particular rating class is not sufficient to cover all anticipated losses and expenses associated with that class. Incurred losses represent the largest component of insurance rates, and actuaries use them to establish pure premiums as the basis for pricing. However, pure premiums do not include underwriting expenses, nor do they anticipate the effect of investment income as an offset to underwriting expenses and losses. As a result, insurers factor in net expenses separately to establish adequate rates. Once the adequacy of a rate has been established, an acceptable profit level is factored into the final pricing.

Because incurred losses form the largest component of rates, calculation of pure premiums is the first step in determining rate adequacy. Provided that an insurer has a sufficient volume of exposure units and the loss experience to generate credible results, the insurer may use its own data as a basis for quantifying pure premiums.

In determining whether rates are adequate, most insurers consider industry results in addition to their own experience to enhance the credibility of the data and to increase confidence in those rates. However, caution is required when evaluating statewide information, as it includes losses from all insurers, some of which may have posted atypical results such as those caused by a severe windstorm season. Also, statewide information includes premium and loss data for both profitable and unprofitable insurers. Actuaries attempt to identify and factor out anomalous and unprofitable results from industry data before using it as the basis for establishing rate adequacy.

Not Excessive

Rates should not be excessive. Regulatory and competitive pressures help ensure that consumers are charged a fair price for their home and automobile insurance coverage. First, insurers are required to file rates with state insurance departments, and regulatory authorities typically prevent insurers from charging unreasonably high rates. In some states, proposed rate changes must include statistical evidence that incurred losses and expenses warrant the requested change and that the rates are not excessive. In other states, regulators may limit rate increases and restrict total rate levels regardless of an insurer's evidence of need. Finally, regulators have the authority to roll back rates if necessary.

Competitive forces ensure that rates are not excessive. Policyholders often shop for lower rates and might choose a policy with premium savings. Customers with the fewest losses might shop around in response to an insurer's significant rate increases. The insurer loses business, and its portfolio develops disproportionate numbers of poorer risks. The potential effect of such changes on an insurer's profits is sufficient to encourage most insurers to keep rates competitive.

Because of these regulatory and competitive pressures, insurers are sometimes precluded from adjusting their rates. For example, if actuarial analysis indicates that a 50 percent increase in base rate is required, it is likely that neither state regulators nor policyholders will approve. Consequently, insurers sometimes phase in indicated rate increases over a period of years.

Not Unfairly Discriminatory

Rates must not be unfairly discriminatory. Each insured should pay his or her fair share of the insurer's losses and expenses. Theoretically, this fairness would require each risk to be rated individually, based on its own unique loss and expense attributes. The volume of calculations that would be required makes such rating impractical; therefore, an insured's "fair share" is generally based on a proportional distribution of the insurer's estimated future losses and expenses, among homogeneous groups of insureds. When risks in a particular risk classification are homogeneous, rate equity is presumed.

Rating laws prohibit unfair discrimination; they do not prohibit rate discrimination. Fair and justified rate discrimination based on loss potential is encouraged and forms the basis for both the establishment of risk classifications and the development of rate relativity factors. For example, individuals with poor driving records are statistically more likely to have accidents. Therefore, reasonable discrimination in rating allows insurers to charge higher premiums for drivers with poor experience. In contrast, automobile liability rating based on gender is considered unacceptable in some states. See the exhibit "Regulatory Objectives in Ratemaking."

Regulatory Objectives in Ratemaking

Objective	Descriptions	Example
Not Inadequate	Rates are known to be sufficient to cover losses and expenses.	A rate is developed for an average middle-aged driver of a sedan that anticipates one other-than-collision loss every two years, one collision loss every five years, and all related loss expenses and costs to produce the policy.
Not Excessive	Competitive and regulatory pressures generally keep rates from being excessive. Regulators can change rating criteria, roll back rates, or refuse to approve increases if necessary.	In spite of high incidence of accidents along California highways, rates are developed that keep insurance affordable for most auto owners and that are competitive with other auto insurers in the region.
Not Unfairly Discriminatory	Rates are based on a proportional distribution of estimated future losses and expenses among homogeneous groups. Fair discrimination, based on statistically sound criteria, is encouraged.	A higher rate is developed for drivers with two accidents and four traffic violations in the past year.

[DA05806]

Social Objectives

In addition to regulatory control, social pressures are becoming influential in ratemaking, particularly for personal automobile and residential property insurance. To satisfy social objectives, insurers' rates must meet these objectives:

- They must be affordable.
- Coverage must be available.
- Insurers must provide risk control incentives.
- They must be responsive to change.
- They must provide rate stability.
- They must be responsive to controllable rating factors.

Affordable

Affordability has become a crucial social objective in determining proper rates. For example, in many cities the cost of property insurance has risen despite a decline in property values. Rates that are statistically adequate to cover the increased exposures of crime, arson, and abandonment found in inner-city areas can extend insurance premiums beyond the financial resources of many urban residents.

These strategies help ensure affordability:

- Capping insurance rates
- Spreading the risk—setting rates that transfer some costs of high-risk policyholders to the remaining policyholders
- Subsidizing rates for high-risk policyholders through sources outside the standard insurance marketplace

Available

The availability of insurance coverage is another social objective insurers consider in ratemaking, and it relates to affordability. Insurers often retire from a line, risk classification, or coverage because the rate required to offset expected losses is so high that regulators will not approve it. For example, many insurers have rejected higher-risk urban properties in favor of newer, better-protected homes in suburban communities. Consequently, residents may not be able to obtain insurance on urban properties. This could prevent them from buying homes because lenders do not offer mortgages on uninsured properties.

Catastrophes adversely affect insurance availability. For example, many companies stopped writing homeowners insurance in Atlantic coastal areas after hurricanes Hugo, Andrew, and Katrina.

Insurance regulators consider solutions to social problems of affordability and availability. One solution has been to establish risk-sharing pools in which all insurers participate. Rates are controlled, and each insurer's exposure is limited.

Provide Risk Control Incentives

Insurers can influence the behavior of policyholders by offering price incentives to control losses. Premium discounts for safe drivers or loss-free homeowners reward policyholders and encourage them to drive carefully and to maintain their homes, reducing the chance of accidental loss. Discounts for installing burglar alarms or fire extinguishers encourage insureds to use such devices that can help control loss severity. Pricing strategies that reduce the frequency and severity of losses benefit insurers through increased profits, and they benefit society by providing a safer environment in which to live, drive, and conduct business.

Responsive to Change

Another social objective in insurance pricing is to structure rates so that pricing responds quickly and effectively to changes in underlying loss exposures. Responsiveness helps ensure that rates are adequate without being excessive. For example, accident and violation surcharges on automobile policies adjust policy rates to reflect adverse prior loss experience or an increase in exposure to loss. Conversely, improvement in a community's public protection classification (PPC) can be promptly reflected in a change in a home's risk classification, resulting in reduced premiums.

Provide Rate Stability

Rate stability requires that rates do not vary dramatically from year to year. Policyholders expect some rate stability, and the affordability of insurance depends on policyholders' ability to predict or estimate their annual insurance costs.

The basic insurance concept, spread-of-risk, involves sharing potential losses among many individuals. This concept forms the basis of insurance pricing. However, spread-of-risk can also relate to time. For example, the incidence of hurricanes on the east coast of the United States can vary widely by year. If windstorm insurance rates mirrored this variation in loss exposure, policyholders could face significant annual changes in homeowners premiums. Insurers try to maintain rate stability by basing rates on loss experience over a long period of time and by tempering the statistics from years with unusually high loss experience by using long-term averages.

Responsive to Controllable Rating Factors

Some consumer advocates have proposed that insurers should be allowed to use only rating factors that insureds can control. This approach would eliminate age, gender, and location as the basis for insurance pricing. For automobile insurance, advocates propose limiting rating factors to insureds' driving records, mileage, and vehicle.

Legislators and regulators in some states have responded by modifying the basis for risk classification, for example, by rating on "years of driving experience" rather than "age." However, the costs to settle losses and to pay operating expenses are not affected by changes in rating criteria. Changes to rating criteria redistribute the cost of insurance among different customers. While that benefits those customers who receive a lower rate from such a change, those who receive a rate increase pay the difference. See the exhibit "Social Objectives in Ratemaking."

Social Objectives in Ratemaking

Objective	Description	Example
Affordability	Rates that are statistically adequate to cover some high-risk exposures are often beyond the financial resources of some policyholders.	Rate affordability strategies include rate-capping, transferring costs to lower-risk policyholders, or subsidizing the unaffordable rates.
Availability	Insurers often retire from a line, risk classification, or coverage if the rate required to offset expected losses is so high that regulators will not approve it. This objective requires developing strategies to make insurance available.	One strategy to ensure availability involves risk pooling, under which all insurers take a proportionate share of higher-risk business.
Risk Control Incentives	Insurers influence behavior of policyholders by offering price incentives to control losses. The resulting reduction in losses not only benefits insurers through increased profits, but also benefits society.	Insurers offer premium discounts to homeowners who keep and maintain security alarm systems.
Responsiveness to Change	Insurers structure rates so that pricing responds quickly and effectively to changes in underlying loss exposures. This helps insurers meet the regulatory objective that rates be adequate but not excessive.	Insurers often surcharge insureds for accidents on auto policies.
Rate Stability	Insurers try to maintain rate stability by basing rates on loss experience over long time periods and by tempering statistics generated in years with unusually high loss experience by using long-term average loss data.	To avoid excessively high rates in tornado-prone Midwestern states, insurers average loss data over a ten-year period.
Controllable Rating Factors	Consumer advocates have proposed that insurers should be allowed to use only rating factors that insureds can control. However, loss costs and expenses are not reduced by changes in rating criteria, so this approach serves to redistribute insurance costs.	Some states have responded by modifying the basis for risk classification, such as rating by "years of driving experience" (rather than age).

[DA05807]

Interest Income Considerations

The two income sources for a property-casualty insurer are its insurance operation and its investment operation. Because insurers typically collect premiums first and pay claims later, they have an advantageous cash flow.

The insurance operation writes policies, collects premiums, and pays losses. The investment operation uses the cash flow generated by the insurance operation to buy bonds, stocks, and other investments to earn an investment profit. Investment profit is derived from three sources: investment income, **realized capital gains**, and **unrealized capital gains**.

Traditionally, property-casualty insurers did not consider their investment income when setting rates, except perhaps indirectly when factoring in profits and contingencies. However, when an insurer posted an underwriting loss, investment income was often used to make up the shortfall.

Considering investment income in ratemaking has become more common. Regulators accept that insurers are entitled to earn reasonable profits and must earn reasonable profits to remain financially viable. However, the affordability of personal insurance products has become increasingly politicized and has focused regulatory attention on ratemaking practices, resulting in changes, particularly in how investment income is factored into pricing. For example, many states now require insurers to include investment income when formulating rates. However, few states require the inclusion of capital gains, and those states that do usually consider only realized capital gains.

Reflecting investment income in rates can vary based on the ratemaking method applied. See the exhibit "Variations in the Effect of Investment Income Based on Ratemaking Methods."

The effect of investment income on rates also differs among types of business because the profit earned depends partially on the duration of an investment. For example, liability claims take longer to settle than property claims; thus, the insurer has more time to earn investment income before paying claims.

Realized capital gain

The profit earned by an insurer when an asset, such as a bond or stock, is sold for more than its cost.

Unrealized capital gain

The profit not yet earned on a held asset when it exceeds its original purchase price but has not been sold.

Variations in the Effect of Investment Income Based on Ratemaking Methods

Pure Premium Method		
Pure Premium	$26.73	Pure premium can be calculated based on the insurer's own claim experience or can be developed from loss costs available from an insurance advisory organization for new lines of business.
Estimated Expenses per Exposure Unit	$9.72	For existing lines, insurers use actual data. For new lines, expenses per exposure unit may be estimated based on actual underwriting expenses for other lines the insurer currently offers.
Profit Factor	$4.05	The insurer has an initial profit goal of 10% of all base premiums. $26.73 + $9.72 = $36.45 ÷ 0.9 = $40.50 × 0.1 = $4.05)
Base Premium	$40.50	The base premiums total of the pure premiums, expenses, and profit per exposure unit.
Investment Income Method		
Pure Premium	$26.73	Based on loss costs
Estimated Expenses per Exposure Unit	$9.72	Includes such costs as salaries, benefits, premises, and computer systems
Investment Income per Exposure Unit	$4.87	Estimated income from investment divided by total number of exposure units
Adjusted Expenses per Exposure Unit	$4.85	Expenses – Investment Income ($9.72 – $4.87 = $4.85)
Profit Factor	$3.51	Insurer has an initial profit goal of 10% of all base premiums ($26.73 + $4.85 = $31.58 ÷ 0.90 = $35.09 × 0.1 = $3.51)
Base Premium	$35.09	Total pure premiums, expenses, and profit per exposure unit

[DA05808]

RATE ADJUSTMENT CASE STUDY

Portfolio managers should understand that over time, actuaries may need to adjust pricing in response to the insurer's actual results to achieve rate adequacy. Adjusting the rate of a personal lines portfolio requires performing two high-level steps: (1) premium and loss analysis and (2) application of rate relativities. The first step requires completion of several substeps, including these:

- Calculating loss costs
- Comparing the loss costs of the insurer with industry data
- Analyzing frequency and severity of losses
- Checking to see whether losses were skewed by events

The second step also requires completion of several substeps, which include these:

- Estimating what the base rate should have been
- Developing rate relativity factors from projected frequency and severity
- Applying rate relativity factors to the adequate base rate
- Applying the adjusted base rate

Case Facts

Barnley Insurance Company is a medium-sized insurer that has offered personal auto and residential property insurance for more than twenty-five years. Over the past three years, the company's traditionally profitable Tenant's Choice product, a tenant homeowners policy, has performed poorly. The deterioration in the product results has been reasonably consistent in all territories in which Barnley writes the coverage.

For each of the past three years, the portfolio has grown for the insurer's Tenant's Choice product. The average amount of coverage per policy has also increased, and the loss ratio has climbed. While the company has been able to maintain a stable expense ratio of 25 percent over the three-year period, the increasing loss ratio has resulted in an underwriting loss in each of the past three years. See the exhibit "Barnley Insurance Company—Tenant's Choice Three-Year Results."

As a result of this declining performance, Barnley's general manager requested that the actuarial team analyze the product's results and recommend pricing adjustments if required.

Case Analysis Tools

The actuaries must obtain year-end results for the last three years. Those results pertain to Barnley's and the insurance industry's losses and premium. Information about events that may have skewed the results—such as an increase or a decrease in reserves, a natural disaster, or a shock loss—must also be obtained. Finally, if the adjustment is determined to be a relatively large percentage increase, the actuaries will need to know the regulatory objectives of the state regulators, and the social objectives of policyholders and management. These objectives may limit how much of and how quickly the adjusted rate can be implemented.

Barnley Insurance Company—Tenant's Choice Three-Year Results

	Two Years Prior	Prior Year	Current Year
Exposure Units	20,000	22,000	25,000
Average Contents Limit per Risk	$15,000	$17,500	$19,000
Earned Premiums	$4,980,000	$6,391,000	$7,885,000
Written Premiums	$4,920,000	$6,301,000	$7,767,000
Incurred Losses	$3,984,000	$5,687,990	$7,648,450
Number of Losses	3,200	4,180	5,250
Underwriting Expenses	$1,245,000	$1,597,750	$1,971,250
Loss Ratio	80%	89%	97%
Expense Ratio	25%	25%	25%
Combined Ratio	105%	114%	122%
Current Base Rate	$16.60	$16.60	$16.60

[DA05829]

Premium and Loss Analysis

The primary purpose of premium and loss analysis is analyzing the product's results. The analysis requires four substeps. The first substep is calculating loss costs.

Calculating Loss Costs

The actuarial staff began by calculating the average loss costs for the product over the past three years. See the exhibit "Calculation of Tenant's Choice Loss Costs."

Calculation of Tenant's Choice Loss Costs

Year	Incurred Losses	÷ Exposure Units	= Loss Costs
Two years prior	$3,984,000	20,000	$199
Prior year	$5,687,990	22,000	$259
Current year	$7,648,450	25,000	$306
Totals	$17,320,440	67,000	$259

[DA 05831]

Comparing the Loss Costs of the Insurer With Industry Data

Once Barnley's loss costs had been calculated for the period, actuaries performed the second substep, which involved comparing the company's own results in each year with pooled industry data for the territories in which Barnley writes tenants insurance. The pooled data were available through an insurance advisory organization. See the exhibit "Barnley's Loss Costs Compared With Industry Data."

Barnley's Loss Costs Compared With Industry Data

Year	Barnley's Loss Costs	Pooled Loss Costs	Relative Performance
Two years prior	$199	$207	Barnley's loss cost is 96% of pooled loss costs.
Prior year	$259	$251	Barnley's loss cost is 103% of pooled loss costs.
Current year	$306	$315	Barnley's loss cost is 97% of pooled loss costs.

[DA05832]

Because Barnley's own loss costs tracked reasonably closely with the pooled industry data, Barnley's results were seen as credible. As a result, the actuaries' confidence in the company's own data increased.

Analyzing Frequency and Severity of Losses

After reviewing loss costs, actuaries completed the third substep: a frequency and severity analysis of the Tenant's Choice product results.

The actuaries noted that both the loss frequency and loss severity increased each year for the last two years. These calculations are necessary to know whether the increase in incurred losses from year to year is caused by increased exposure units or loss frequency and loss severity.

Checking to See Whether Losses Were Skewed by Events

In the fourth substep, the actuarial team checked to see whether these results might have been skewed by an event such as an increase or a decrease in reserves, a natural disaster, or a shock loss. They confirmed that no such event had occurred and that the frequency and severity data were accurate and credible.

Application of Rate Relativities

The application of rate relativities requires that one homogeneous group be selected as the unity classification and all other risk classifications be priced relative to it. As a result, it is essential that the base rate for the unity classification be adequate. If the base rate for the unity classification is inadequate, any other rates developed from it will also be inadequate.

Barnley knew that its current rates for its Tenant's Choice product were not adequate. If actuaries simply calculated how much greater losses will be next year and then increased current rates by that percentage, the Tenant's Choice rates would continue to be inadequate. Therefore, the actuaries applied rate relativities, which requires four substeps. The first substep involves estimating what the base rate should have been in the current year.

Estimating What the Base Rate Should Have Been

The actuaries estimated what the current year's rates should have been, using the loss cost method and basing calculations on the current year's data. See the exhibit "Calculating an Adequate Base Rate Using Loss Costs."

Developing Rate Relativity Factors From Projected Frequency and Severity

For the second substep, the actuaries used the next year's projected frequency and severity to develop rate relativity factors that reflect the company's anticipated results for the following year. See the exhibit "Developing Rate Relativity Factors From Projected Frequency and Severity."

Applying Rate Relativity Factors to the Adequate Base Rate

For the third substep, the actuaries applied the relativity factors to the rates developed in the first substep, which they knew were adequate, instead of the actual rates, which they knew were inadequate. See the exhibit "Adjusting Adequate Base Rate."

Applying the Adjusted Base Rate

Based on these calculations, the adjusted base rate for the following years was $23.60. However, this posed a problem in that the current rate was only $16.10. Correcting the current rate would require a 47 percent increase. State regulators would be unlikely to approve such an increase, and policyholders would not accept such a significant change in their premiums.

After discussions with the underwriting manager, the sales manager, and the chief actuary, Barnley's senior management ultimately decided to phase in the required rate adjustment over five years. This gradual adjustment would result in further underwriting losses until the rate reached an adequate level,

Calculating an Adequate Base Rate Using Loss Costs

	Value	Explanation
Exposure Unit	25,000	
Incurred Losses	$7,648,450	
Loss Cost	$306	Incurred losses ÷ Exposure units $7,648,450 ÷ 25,000 = $306 Loss cost = Pure premium
Total Expenses	$1,971,250	
Total Units of Coverage	475,000	The standard unit of coverage for tenants insurance is $1,000 of Coverage C. (Average Coverage C limit × Exposure units) ÷ $1,000 ($19,000 × 25,000) ÷ $1,000 = 475,000 coverage units
Rate Component for Losses	$16.10	The amount Barnley needs to charge per unit of coverage in order to pay losses. Incurred losses ÷ Units of coverage $7,645,450 ÷ 475,000 = $16.10
Rate Component for Expenses	$4.15	The amount Barnley needs to charge per unit of coverage in order to pay expenses. Expenses ÷ Units of coverage $1,971,250 ÷ 475,000 = $4.15
Rate Subtotal	$20.25	Component for losses + Component for expenses $16.10 + $4.15 = $20.25
Rate Component for Profit	$1.01	Barnley's goal is to make a 5 percent underwriting profit. $20.25 × 1.05 = $21.26
Adequate Base Rate	$21.26	Incurred loss + Expenses + Profits

[DA05917]

Developing Rate Relativity Factors From Projected Frequency and Severity

Year	Change in Loss Frequency	Change in Loss Severity
Two years prior		
Prior year	3% increase (19% − 16%)	9% increase ($1,361/$1,245%)
Current year	2% increase (21% − 19%)	7% increase ($1,457/$1,361%)
Average percent increase	2.5% increase	8% increase
Projection	2.5% increase	8% increase
Rate relativity factor	1.025	1.08

[DA05918]

Adjusting Adequate Base Rate

Frequency Rate Relativity Factor	Severity Rate Relativity Factor	Adjusted Base Rate
1.025	1.08	$23.60
		($21.32 × 1.025) = $21.85
		($21.85 × 1.08) = $23.60

[DA05919]

but company executives believed that Barnley's regulatory, social, and competitive obligations would be better served by this approach. See the exhibit "Suggested Correct Answers."

Suggested Correct Answers

Year	Loss Costs	Relative Performance	Loss Frequency	Loss Severity	Adequate Base Rate	Frequency Rate Relativity Factor	Severity Rate Relativity Factor	Adjusted Base Rate
Two Years Prior	$199	96% of pooled loss costs	16%	$1,245				
Prior Year	$259	103% of pooled loss costs	19%	$1,361				
Current Year	$306	97% of pooled loss costs	21%	$1,457	$21.32			
Following Year						1.025	1.08	$23.60

[DA05920]

SUMMARY

Portfolio managers must be aware of the trends affecting goals for personal lines of insurance in order to recommend effective actions to reach the insurer's profitability goals.

Insurers can improve underwriting profitability by taking these actions:

- Increasing premiums
- Decreasing losses
- Reducing expenses

Premiums, losses, and expenses are interrelated. Any method designed to improve profitability should be carefully evaluated to determine its potential effects.

The use of actuarially calculated rate relativity factors allows insurers to develop prices for personal lines policies that accurately reflect the loss exposures for risk classifications. The development of appropriate price components significantly affects an insurer's profitability.

Actuaries analyze an insurer's loss and loss expense data along with industry data and current trends to predict future losses. Portfolio managers must understand how loss frequency and severity trends affect the insurer's rates, how loss frequency and severity among various groups relate to rate making, and the ultimate affect on the insurer's business portfolio.

Numerous factors influence policy pricing, including competition, consumer trends, underwriting philosophy, and company strategies. Two broad objectives, regulatory objectives and social objectives, influence rates and determine whether the rates are approved by state regulators. Consideration of investment income is another broad factor in ratemaking. Portfolio managers must have a working knowledge of all factors that influence ratemaking.

Portfolio managers should understand that over time, actuaries may need to adjust pricing in response to the insurer's actual results to achieve rate adequacy. Actuaries adjust pricing based on predictions of future losses. To predict future losses, actuaries review the insurer's frequency and severity data and the industry's loss costs. They look for trends and apply rate relativity factors to determine the adjusted base rate needed to achieve rate adequacy.

ASSIGNMENT NOTES

1. Insurance Research Council, "Uninsured Motorists" news release (Malvern, Pa.: Insurance Research Council), January 21, 2009.

2. Insurance Research Council, "In Response to Economic Downturn Most Consumers Maintain Essential Insurance Coverages" news release (Malvern, Pa.: Insurance Research Council), April 28, 2009.

3. Ezio C. Cerrelli, "Crash Data and Rates for Age-Sex Groups of Drivers 1996," United States Department of Transportation, National Highway Traffic Safety Administration, January 1998.

4. Geoff Werner, FCAS, MAAA, and Claudine Modlin, FCAS, MAAA, "Basic Ratemaking," Casualty Actuarial Society, January 2010,www.casact.com/pubs/ (accessed March 15, 2010).

5.   Massachusetts Division of Insurance, "2008–11 Regulatory Review Standards Applicable to Private Passenger Motor Vehicle Insurance Rate Filings in the Voluntary Market for Rates Effective April 1, 2009 through March 31, 2010,"www.mass.gov (accessed March 16, 2010).

11

Personal Lines Portfolio Management

Educational Objectives

After learning the content of this assignment, you should be able to:

▷ Apply analysis tools and approaches used in personal lines portfolio management to determine the root cause of results that do not meet goals.

▷ Explain how changes in key indicators and the risk profile for a portfolio are analyzed and corrected.

▷ Given a case regarding a personal lines portfolio that is not meeting its loss ratio goals, apply the reunderwriting process to bring the portfolio within goals.

▷ Evaluate methods of improving portfolio management.

▷ Given a case study regarding a personal lines portfolio that is not meeting its goals, formulate actions that will improve underwriting profitability.

Personal Lines Portfolio Management

11

PORTFOLIO MANAGEMENT ANALYSIS TOOLS AND APPROACHES

When portfolios of insurance policies are not meeting their policy count and profitability goals, insurance companies analyze data to determine why and make appropriate changes in products, underwriting standards, or pricing. Several available tools and approaches help portfolio managers uncover the causes of discrepancies between performance and goals in a portfolio of personal lines policies so that corrective actions can be formulated.

Most organizations have encountered the problem of a business or product not meeting its performance goals and have developed a number of tools and techniques to uncover causes of underperformance. If the root cause of a problem cannot be determined with a high degree of certainly, multiple corrective actions might be initiated simultaneously to remedy the problem, but with reduced chances of success.

Identifying and evaluating the root cause(s) of a portfolio performance problem is a major responsibility of an insurance company portfolio manager. When policy-count or profitability goals are not being met, a portfolio manager will take these steps:

- Identify potential causes of the problem
- Analyze data to confirm the cause of the problem
- Identify and recommend changes in product, underwriting, or pricing to assist in meeting the policy count or profitability goals

As portfolio managers evaluate a portfolio, they use these tools and approaches:

- Make assumptions and work with imperfect data
- Apply **root cause analysis (RCA)** tools and approaches
- Apply **reunderwriting** tools and approaches to the portfolio

Making Assumptions and Working With Imperfect Data

In evaluating portfolios, portfolio managers examine a variety of performance indicators, such as loss ratio, loss frequency, loss severity, low new-business

Root cause analysis (RCA)
A step-by-step evaluation method to identify the root cause of an undesirable outcome and the actions that can be taken to prevent its recurrence.

Reunderwriting
The process of evaluating the policies within a portfolio against their goals, identifying causes of underperformance, and implementing corrective actions.

count, policies in force (PIF), mix of business, and portfolio profile. These indicators are analyzed in addition to the profitability goals. As portfolio managers evaluate these indicators to uncover differences in performance, they make assumptions and work with imperfect data. Recognizing that they are working under these conditions, portfolio managers strive to sharpen their questions and data analysis to increase the validity of their analysis. For example, the data in an insurer's risk profile of one of its homeowners territories may generate some assumptions and data concerns on the part of the portfolio manager. See the exhibit "Homeowners Risk Profile Indicators."

Homeowners Risk Profile Indicators

Risk Profile Indicators
Insurer's Risk Profile for Its Northwest Homeowners Territory
(Averages)

Year	Age of Dwelling (in years)	Age of Policy (in years)	Percentage with Wood Shingles	Percentage in Protection Class 10
2004	10	5	9	2
2005	10	5	10	2
2006	11	4	11	3
2007	12	5	12	4
2008	13	6	14	5
2009	14	6	15	5

[DA05779]

The portfolio manager may assume from these data that the average age of homes is increasing and the average age of policies is increasing and that, as a result, more policies are being retained, but that fewer new policies are being written on new homes. The portfolio manager might also conclude that loss exposures are increasing overall because of the increasing percentage of homes with wood shingles and the increasing percentage of homes in Protection Class 10, which are homes without fire protection because of their isolated location. However, this assumption does not take into account whether the wood-shingle roofs have been treated with fire retardant chemicals, whether local codes require such treatment, and whether local municipalities enforce the requirements. As the portfolio manager identifies such assumptions and questions, he or she must gather additional information to support or disprove them.

To test the assumption that loss exposures are increasing, the portfolio manager would want to know whether the homes in the portfolio have wood roofs that have been chemically treated to resist fire. That information may not be available for some or all of the homes, depending on if and when the insurer started asking that question as part of the application process. If the insurer does not include that question in the policy application, then no data is available. If the insurer added that question to the policy application two years ago, data would be available for only part of the portfolio. Working with assumptions and imperfect data means that portfolio managers work with a degree of uncertainty when evaluating the causes of problems of portfolio performance. They must use as many tools and approaches as practical to strengthen the validity of their analyses and recommended actions.

Root Cause Analysis Tools and Approaches

Portfolio managers commonly use three tools or approaches to ask questions and identify root causes:

- "Five Whys"
- Root cause analysis (RCA)
- **Common cause analysis (CCA)**

The term "root cause" implies that a problem has one or more less visible underlying causes beyond the immediately visible cause. As problems become more complex or complicated, different approaches, including techniques and tools not discussed here, may be used to identify the root cause or causes of a problem.

Five Whys

Five Whys is a very basic approach to identifying root causes by repeatedly asking the question "Why?" The use of the number five indicates that one may have to ask "Why?" many times to get to the root of the problem. There is no magic in the number five. Sometimes a root cause is uncovered in fewer than five whys; sometimes more than five. More importantly, the number signifies that asking "Why" just once is not enough. The steps are straightforward:[1]

1. Write down the problem, describing it completely so those considering it can have a common understanding

2. Ask why the problem happens and write down the answer directly under the problem described

3. If the written answer doesn't explain the root cause of the problem, ask why again and write that answer

4. Repeat Step 3 until satisfied that the cause has been identified

The Five Whys technique can be helpful in portfolio management when a cause is not obvious, a new cause is emerging, or a cause is hidden within certain territories or categories of risk. See the exhibit "Five Whys."

Common cause analysis (CCA)

An analysis of root cause analyses for a given period to identify themes and trends in an organization's operations that should be addressed strategically.

Five Whys

Problem: An unusually high number of auto insurance policyholders in a geographic territory are not renewing their policies.

1. *Why are policyholders not renewing?*

Because they had to wait two weeks for action on an auto claim because the claim adjuster staff had to handle a higher than usual number of claims due to multiple hail storms in a one-month period.

2. *Why didn't the claim adjuster staff request additional adjuster help from adjacent territories to reduce the waiting time?*

They did, but adjacent available staff were in short supply and could not provide any help.

3. *Why were adjuster staff in short supply?*

Because the adjacent territory staff had been assigned to special duty in a more distant territory to respond to a serious and widespread catastrophe.

4. *Why weren't other claim support personnel quickly trained to handle simple auto claims and assigned to such claims?*

Because no training material had been prepared.

5. *Why was there no prepared training?*

Because no one had foreseen the need for or the possibility of using claim support personnel in a limited role.

[DA05777]

Root Cause Analysis

Some approaches to causation analysis are more detailed than the Five Whys approach. Greater detail is needed when root causes are multiple and have far-reaching implications for an organization and when, as a result, it is important to look beyond the visible cause. RCA helps determine what happened, how it happened, and why it happened. If an RCA is not performed, and only the visible causes are addressed, the underlying causes may continue to produce similar problems.

RCA typically follows these steps:[2]

1. Clearly define the undesired outcome
2. Gather data, including a list of all potential causes
3. Continue asking "Why" to identify root causes
4. Check logic and eliminate items that are not causes
5. Generate solutions that address the visible causes and root causes

From the third step, RCA looks very much like the Five Whys approach, continuing to ask why until a thorough understanding of the cause or causes of a problem are uncovered. However, RCA uses a number of more elaborate tools and techniques to conduct its analysis. The more detailed analysis approach of RCA is appropriate for major events that result not from a single cause but from a complex set of conditions that have evolved over time and that involve multiple work groups, tasks, systems, or components. Here are three of the more elaborate tools used as part of RCA:

- **Event and causal factor chart**
- **Change analysis**
- **Barrier analysis**

An event and causal factor chart assists the analyst in understanding the sequence of events and causes that have led to a problem situation. Sometimes this graphic depiction is done vertically and is called an event and causal tree. In either case, the objective is to graphically depict the sequence of events and facts in chronological order. This charting is most helpful in complex and complicated situations because their visual representation conveys information more effectively than a narrative description. The chart or tree offers several benefits:

- Shows the sequence of events from beginning to end
- Stimulates identification of additional information as it is being developed
- Incorporates other data and information
- Contributes to objectivity

These flow charts are usually drawn using text within symbols to signify certain types of events or factors; for example, a circle is the terminal event, a rectangle is a preceding event, and an oval is a condition. Arrows connect events and conditions. See the exhibit "Event and Causal Flowchart."

Event and causal factor chart

A horizontal flowchart that shows the chronological sequence of events and facts leading to a problem situation.

Change analysis

A systematic process used to analyze a single event, focusing on conditions or elements that changed and became causal factors.

Barrier analysis

A methodical process used to identify causal factors stemming from physical, administrative, and procedural barriers or controls that should have prevented an event from happening.

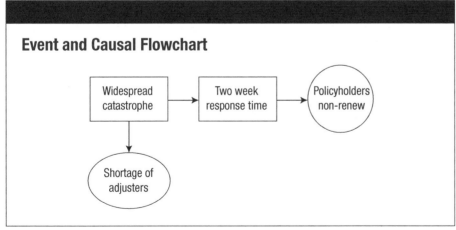

Event and Causal Flowchart

[DA05780]

A change analysis is an RCA approach that compares two similar occurrences, one with the problem occurring and the other without it occurring. The objective of the comparison is to identify the similarities and differences between the two occurrences; identification of differences may reveal factors that caused or contributed to the problem. For example, a change analysis would be effective in examining the cause of a failure of a product in one territory with the success of the product in another territory. A change analysis involves these steps:

1. Describe in writing the problem situation, including timing, personnel, equipment, procedures, physical surroundings, and event severity.
2. Describe a similar event in which the problem did not occur. To the extent possible, choose a situation in which the circumstances described in Step 1 were the same.
3. Compare the two situations, and note any differences regardless of how slight they might be.
4. Group the differences to the extent possible according to the items in Step 1.
5. Analyze the differences to identify their effects on the problem situation.
6. Add contributing differences to causal factors (in an event and causal chart or tree) being considered in the overall analysis.

The objective of a barrier analysis, another RCA approach, is to identify whether a barrier to an event was in place, whether it functioned as intended, and if it did not, why it failed to perform as intended. In effect, a barrier analysis is an RCA of the existence of a barrier and of the failure of a barrier to perform its intended function. For example, a barrier analysis would be effective in helping explain why underwriting guidelines failed to prevent unacceptable applications from being written.

A barrier analysis asks a number of different questions depending on the situation under evaluation. A portfolio manager might begin a barrier analysis with these questions; other questions would be generated as these are answered:

- Did barriers exist between a condition and an event?
- If they existed, did they perform their function? Why or why not?
- Was the barrier design inadequate? Why?
- What design changes in the barrier could have prevented the event?
- Were the barriers maintained?
- Could the event that occurred have been foreseen? Why?
- Would it be practical to develop steps to reduce the risk of the event's occurring?

Common Cause Analysis

Regardless of the tools used, RCA is directed at identifying the underlying causes of the specific events or performance failures under study. An organization may conduct a number of root cause analyses over time, and those individual analyses, if analyzed together, may uncover trends and themes that an organization should address.

To uncover trends and themes, organizations can conduct a CCA by reviewing all root cause analyses done within a specified period. The action plans resulting from the root cause analyses are reviewed and grouped according to identified themes or issues. The themes are typically rated by scoring the factors of severity, occurrence, and detectability on a scale of 1 to 10 and multiplying the three scores to attain an overall score. Themes with the highest scores or scores above a threshold number are brought to the attention of senior management, which is responsible for addressing the themes in the organization's strategic planning for the coming year.

For example, an insurer may require that a formal team conduct each RCA and enter its findings into a root cause database. After one year, the company analyzes the root cause analyses and learns that a significant number of the action plans implicate its single-location call center operation as a cause of problems. The call center operations are subject to weather, equipment, and staffing problems. With this information, the insurer may decide to organize its call center at two or more locations, provide improved hardware and software systems, and improve staffing and training patterns.

An organization can use CCA in a less structured manner than that just described. Portfolio managers might keep their own records of the knowledge gained from prior RCAs to consult when other problems arise. However, more structured approaches lead to more effective organizational strategic planning.

Reunderwriting Tools and Approaches

Reunderwriting is the specialized process of identifying root causes of portfolio underperformance and taking corrective action. A general approach used to analyze why loss results are not meeting goals, reunderwriting involves all the activities of analysis, identification, and correction of loss-related variances in a portfolio. As portfolio managers review data of policy counts and profitability goals, they note variances between performance and goals and ask key questions that help the insurers address the problems.

Analyzing the portfolio requires analyzing data from individual policies. If all the data from policy applications have been captured in a database, the portfolio manager can generate various reports to analyze various aspects of the portfolio. When not all policy application data have been entered into a database, the portfolio manager may have collected data entered into a spreadsheet or into database software on a personal computer. If the required analysis is based on a large number of policies, the portfolio manager may choose to work with a random sampling of 50 to 100 files, rather than the entire set of files, to determine whether a pattern can be identified.

For example, the portfolio manager for an insurer's homeowner portfolio may analyze the six-months' results to evaluate the losses against the goals. See the exhibit "Six-Months' Results for Insurer's Homeowner Portfolio: Loss Results."

Six-Months' Results for Insurer's Homeowner Portfolio: Loss Results

	Incurred (000s)	Percentage of Goal	Loss Count	Percentage of Goal	Average Loss
Annual goals (Monthly goals are an even distribution of annual goals throughout the year.)					
	$4,300		3,909		$1,100
YTD Results					
Jan.	$394	110%	358	110%	$1,100
Feb.	$781	109%	710	109%	$1,100
March	$1,161	108%	1,143	117%	$1,015
Apr.	$1,56	109%	1,642	126%	$952
May	$1,989	111%	2,248	138%	$885
June	$2,430	113%	2,834	145%	$857

[DA 05781]

In reviewing the data, the portfolio manager notes incurred losses through-out the six months are 13 percent above the year-to-date (YTD) goals, and the number of losses is 45 percent above the YTD goals. On the other hand, the average loss is decreasing rather than remaining stable or increasing. The portfolio manager might therefore interpret the problem as a loss frequency problem, rather than a loss severity problem. However, these data do not provide any insight into the reason for the increase in loss frequency. To look for possible causes of the increase in loss frequency, the portfolio manager will have to order a report on all the claims filed in this period and examine such elements as type of loss, cause of loss, and territory.

Investigations Based on Questions

In applying the reunderwriting process, portfolio managers draw on an accumulation of experience in the types of policies their companies write, including cause analysis knowledge they have acquired in prior portfolio analyses in similar lines of business. As portfolio managers analyze and iden-tify causes of loss-related variances, they draw upon this accumulation of knowledge to determine what questions to ask to initiate their analysis, what data to examine, and once the problem is identified, what corrective actions are needed and are most likely to be effective. See the exhibit "Sample Investigation Questions for a Homeowner Portfolio."

Sample Investigation Questions for a Homeowner Portfolio

Question	Data to Examine
Are the losses isolated to a few territories?	Extract loss data for the isolated territories.
Are the losses isolated to specific causes of loss?	Extract loss data for causes of loss.
Can the losses be categorized as preventable or non-preventable?	Review claim files regarding aspects of losses that were preventable or that were the result of carelessness, maintenance issues, or economic pressures.
Was the loss exposure that caused the loss known at the time of application?	Review claims advice reports or compare applications to claim files.

[DA05782]

Fix-It-Twice Approach

Analysis tools and approaches frequently reveal both visible causes and underlying root causes. Given two levels of causation, sometimes it is important to fix a problem twice: first at the visible level, and second at the underlying, root cause level. This fix-it-twice approach can be useful in reunderwriting when there is an immediately recognizable problem, but no readily apparent root cause. For example, auto policies in one territory are suddenly experiencing excessive liability losses, but the cause is not apparent. To reduce losses as quickly as possible, the insurer may stop writing policies (if allowed by state regulation) or tighten underwriting scrutiny of auto insurance applications. This immediate fix may decrease the losses while the portfolio manager performs a more exhaustive investigation to uncover the underlying cause and identify and implement the appropriate action plan.

PORTFOLIO KEY INDICATOR ANALYSIS

A personal insurance portfolio that is losing its policies in force, failing to gain new policies, or deteriorating in policy retention could be failing to compete in the marketplace on product, price, or service. Therefore, insurers monitor key indicators of their portfolios of policies to determine whether products, underwriting practices, or pricing need to be changed.

The key indicators of an insurer's success are its ability to attract and retain policyholders and to increase the overall size of its portfolio. A portfolio of sufficient size can be priced and managed to achieve the insurer's profitability goals. A portfolio manager analyzes key portfolio indicators and the portfolio's risk profile to determine what changes in the portfolio, if any, are taking place and require corrective action. An effective portfolio manager must know several things:

- How to identify and analyze key indicators
- What elements of the risk profile to monitor
- Possible corrective actions and their limitations

Experienced portfolio managers begin their analysis by looking at high-level key indicators. Then they move their analysis to a more detailed level. They use a risk profile based on characteristics of policies and loss exposures that they have determined are useful for monitoring potential problem spots. The risk profile also allows them to examine relationships between portfolio characteristics that they suspect may affect portfolio performance.

Key Policy Indicators

Policies in force (PIF) is the number of policies that are effective at any point in time. PIF is measured monthly, quarterly, and annually. During the year, the actual PIF counts are often compared to the annual PIF goals to assess the growth or decrease in portfolio size.

For example, the portfolio manager compares the insurer's annual goals with the actual count data for the years 2004 through 2010 and tentatively concludes that the portfolio is showing a long-term increase that parallels the projected growth goal. When the data are displayed in a graph, however, the portfolio manager notes a spike in the actual results. The portfolio manager then wants to determine whether this larger-than-anticipated increase reflects a product change or some other change in marketplace dynamics that represents either a threat or an opportunity. In this instance, the portfolio manager learns that the sudden growth in 2006 reflects the withdrawal of another insurer from a state because of unacceptable losses. By tightening underwriting guidelines in subsequent years, the insurer might be able to restrict the addition of new policies with unacceptable loss exposures. See the exhibit "Policies in Force Key Indicator."

The new policy count, also known as the new business count, is the number of new policies written during a period of time, such as one quarter or one year. Comparisons of portfolios or segments within portfolios are helpful to show where growth is occurring. Often a portfolio manager will display the data in a chart and a bar graph to more effectively view trends and differences in performance. For example, when the portfolio manager reviews the insurer's new policy count data for an entire portfolio, the new policy count appears to be growing steadily. However, when the data are broken down by territory in a subsequent chart and bar graph, a different picture of the growth is revealed. Territory I's new policy count is relatively stable, Territory II's new policy count is increasing markedly, and Territory III's new policy count is decreasing. See the exhibit "New Policy Count Key Indicator."

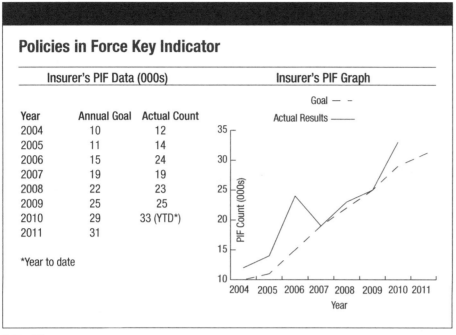

Policies in Force Key Indicator

Insurer's PIF Data (000s)

Year	Annual Goal	Actual Count
2004	10	12
2005	11	14
2006	15	24
2007	19	19
2008	22	23
2009	25	25
2010	29	33 (YTD*)
2011	31	

*Year to date

[DA05760]

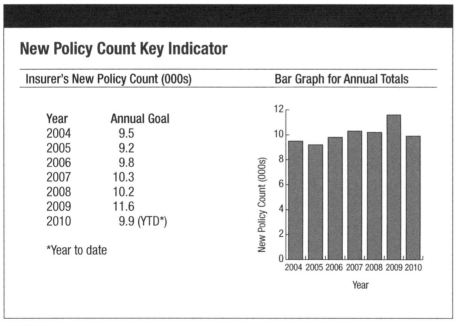

New Policy Count Key Indicator

Insurer's New Policy Count (000s)

Year	Annual Goal
2004	9.5
2005	9.2
2006	9.8
2007	10.3
2008	10.2
2009	11.6
2010	9.9 (YTD*)

*Year to date

[DA05761]

With the new understanding that territory growth differs, the portfolio manager will analyze other subsets or characteristics of the portfolio to determine what changes are taking place, why they are taking place, and what changes might need to be made to either take advantage of an opportunity or blunt the effects of an underwriting threat or set of loss exposures. For example, if these key indicator data reflect a portfolio of personal automobile policies, the portfolio manager might examine the classification of drivers and vehicle uses that the insurer is accepting on new policies. If an unusually high number of drivers are using their vehicles in their businesses, the portfolio manager would conduct additional investigations to determine why. The additional investigations could involve any of an array of market information: data gathering from underwriters, front line field people, producers, or researching demographic and economic trends. See the exhibit "New Policy Count Key Indicator by Territory."

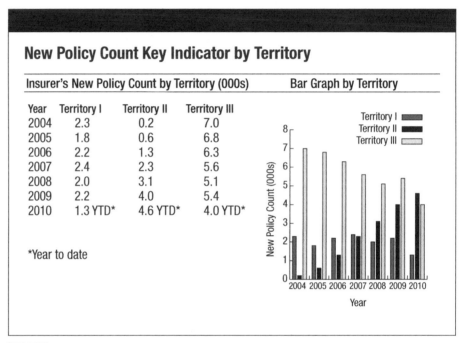

New Policy Count Key Indicator by Territory

Insurer's New Policy Count by Territory (000s)

Year	Territory I	Territory II	Territory III
2004	2.3	0.2	7.0
2005	1.8	0.6	6.8
2006	2.2	1.3	6.3
2007	2.4	2.3	5.6
2008	2.0	3.1	5.1
2009	2.2	4.0	5.4
2010	1.3 YTD*	4.6 YTD*	4.0 YTD*

*Year to date

[DA05762]

Policy retention is usually measured as the percentage of policies that are renewed. It is most frequently measured on an annual basis. Insurers want to retain their current profitable business for several reasons:

- Current policyholders have a known history with the insurance company.
- Additional expense is not required to attract them to place their coverage with the insurer.
- Current policyholders represent a continuous stream of renewal premiums.
- They represent product cross-selling opportunities.
- They are a potential source of customer referrals.

Because demographics, overall consumer attitudes, and property values can change the nature of loss exposures and insurance needs, a portfolio manager can find it useful to compare policy retention rates to industry retention rates.

If a portfolio manager determines that the company retention rates are significantly higher or lower than industry rates, there may be problems to identify and changes to make.

For example, a portfolio manager may examine homeowner policy retention data for a six-state area. Viewed in isolation, the data reveal that the insurer's retention percentage has dropped slightly over the last several years. However, when the data are compared to industry results for the same period, the results have a different meaning. The insurer is actually retaining more homeowners policies than the industry average for the last several years shown. Nonetheless, the portfolio manager will want to examine additional questions to better understand the retention of this portfolio:

- Is the industry's average retention for the homeowners policies the same as the average for the six states in this portfolio?
- What is the insurer's retention rate for each state in the portfolio, and how does that compare to the state averages for the industry?
- Should the company monitor any other retention rates, such as retention by Coverage A limit? These data would indicate whether the company is losing homeowners policies for higher- or lower-valued homes.

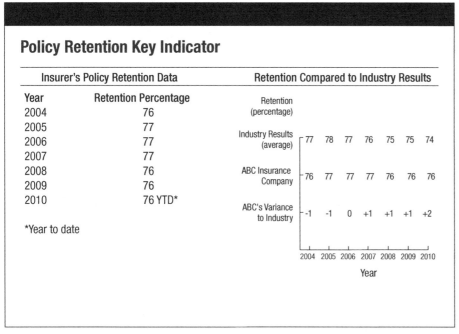

[DA05763]

Risk Profile Analysis

A risk profile analysis is a careful examination of key policy characteristics at specific times or for specific time periods undertaken to uncover relationships between policy characteristics or factors that may affect portfolio performance. The current capabilities of data collection, database technology, and statistical software enable portfolio managers to develop and use customized risk profiles for any given portfolio or subset of insurance policies. The data captured, displayed, and analyzed in a risk profile depend on the type of policies in a portfolio, the extent of the insurer's database, and the particular concerns of the portfolio manager.

Risk profiles may be done monthly, quarterly, or annually and may be compared to goals or benchmarks established by the insurer, depending on the desires of the analyst. By comparing risk profiles over a period of time, a portfolio manager can better understand changes in the portfolio and analyze the importance of those changes. Changes in risk profiles can occur because of consumer trends, changes in competitors' products and services, unmet needs of the customer or producer, or conflicts between the underwriter and the producer.

For example, a portfolio manager might evaluate selected risk profile characteristics for a homeowners portfolio for a specific territory. After reviewing the data, the portfolio manager reaches these conclusions:

- Coverage A had been increasing slowly; however, it has not increased in the last three years.

- The average age of homes is increasing, as is the average age of policies. These figures could mean that more policies are being retained and/or that fewer new policies are being written on new homes.

- The percentage of homes with wood shingles and the percentage of homes in Protection Class 10 (homes without fire protection because of isolated location) are increasing. Houses in isolated and heavily forested areas are at high risk of losses from forest fires. The loss exposure can be compounded when houses have wood shingle roofs that have not been properly treated with fire-retardant chemicals. For this portfolio, the Class 10 and wood shingle roofs percentages are increasing, indicating a possible overall increase in loss exposures.

After identifying tentative conclusions, the portfolio manager will conduct additional risk profile analyses on characteristics that will shed further light on the possible increase in loss exposures or other portfolio measures. Examining the relationship between two or more characteristics will help the portfolio manager evaluate the extent of a loss exposure increase and thus the need for pricing or underwriting adjustments to handle potentially higher losses. For example, the portfolio manager may conduct a further analysis of the homes with wood shingle roofs to learn what percentage of wood shingle homes are not in Protection Class 10, but rather are located in townships with enforced codes that require wood shingles to be treated with fire-retardant chemicals. Assessing how home or policy characteristics interplay assists the portfolio manager in determining whether an increase in loss exposure exists and whether pricing adjustments or underwriting adjustments are necessary to pay for losses or prevent losses. See the exhibit "Selected Risk Profile Indicators."

Selected Risk Profile Indicators

Insurer's Selected Risk Profile for Northwest Homeowners Territory

Year	Coverage A Amount	Age of Dwelling (in years)	Age of Policy (in years)	Percentage With Wood Shingles	Percentage in Protection Class 10
2004	250,000	10	5	9	1
2005	251,000	11	5	9	2
2006	253,000	11	5	10	2
2007	255,000	10	4	11	3
2008	257,000	11	5	12	4
2009	256,000	12	6	14	5
2010	256,000	13	6	15	6

[DA05764]

As another illustration of the need to analyze combined indicators, a portfolio manager examining personal auto policies might want to examine the percentage of drivers under age twenty and the percentage of drivers who commute to work by personal auto. An increased percentage in these two indicators—that is, a higher percentage of drivers under age twenty who commute by car to work—might indicate a significant negative trend that could require correction.

Possible Corrective Actions and Their Limitations

Once a portfolio manager has analyzed key indicators and policy characteristics to determine why a portfolio is not achieving its goals, the insurer must take corrective actions to facilitate the portfolio's achieving its goals. The insurer can choose from a range of corrective actions to address product, underwriting, service, or automation problems identified in the portfolio.

Product Changes

If an insurance policy does not meet customers' needs, or if customers are attracted to the coverage offered by another insurance company, an insurer can change the policy language, create additional endorsements to meet specific needs, or package coverages to meet customers' particular requirements. Each of these possible changes presents additional issues to consider within the personal insurance market.

When insurers change insurance contracts to retain or attract customers, they must consider several potential effects of altering contract language:

- Will a change in contract language introduce loss exposures that the insurer had not anticipated? Standard policy language has been examined and defined over many years. New language can generate coverage ambiguities that the insurer had not anticipated, resulting in payment of claims that were unanticipated when pricing the policy. Thus, an increase in both loss frequency and loss severity may occur.

- Will regulators understand how the products are priced? New policy changes could include exposures and coverages that are difficult to assess, making it challenging for regulators to understand and approve pricing.

- Could the change alter the statistical basis for the policy pricing? When personal insurance policy coverage has been consistent for years, the statistical credibility of premium and loss information is valuable in identifying trends and pricing coverages. Changes in losses and premiums may cause concern about the credibility of the data underlying pricing.

Insurers can respond to emerging customer needs by offering endorsements that extend current coverage or offer new coverages. For example, an insurer notes the growing number of people residing in assisting living facilities. It decides to offer three endorsements to its tenant homeowners policies to (1) provide golf cart liability and property coverage, (2) extend property coverage to include service animals such as seeing eye dogs, and (3) expand the limits of coverage for cash. An endorsement has the benefit of adding coverage while leaving the basic contract language and pricing unchanged. Of course, the insurer must still address the issues of justifying the pricing of the added coverage and of wording the language in the endorsement to guard against providing coverage that was not intended.

To meet specific customer needs or provide attractive pricing, insurers may offer a package of coverages that combine homeowners and personal auto policies with other coverages such as personal umbrella coverage, personal articles floaters, or watercraft coverage. This package might combine the coverages with one liability limit for all exposures, or it might be a collection of standard contracts and coverage limits combined in a single policy jacket with a discounted premium. A package is attractive to the customer for the ease of billing and reduced gaps in coverage. It assists the insurer in retaining policyholders because they are less likely to place one of their primary policies, such as automobile or homeowners, with another insurer if they must replace all of their previously packaged coverages.

When insurers package coverages, they must be alert to potential problems with state regulations. If a state has compulsory automobile insurance programs, an assigned risk program, or a reinsurance facility, will the automobile portion of the package policy be subject to regulatory requirements that affect individually written automobile policies? Will the insurer be allowed to have different underwriting guidelines for the automobile portion of the package policy and for the individually written automobile policies? The answers to these questions can affect the insurer's ability to select accounts that meet the underwriting guidelines for the range of exposures covered in the package.

Underwriting Changes

If insurance policies do not sell successfully because the underwriting criteria are too restrictive, or if unanticipated loss exposures are being accepted on new insurance policies, an insurer can change its underwriting guidelines. More restrictive guidelines can be used to screen new submissions or to reunderwrite the existing portfolio of policies. Changing the underwriting criteria might require filing the changes with the state insurance department, if the state requires such notice. In addition, producers must be notified of the underwriting changes so they can modify the types of risks submitted.

Service Changes

If services offered by an insurer do not meet customer needs or if customers are attracted to unique services offered by another insurance company, the insurer can modify its services to retain or attract customers. Service modifications do not involve the issues that product changes might involve. However, they will most likely involve expenses for implementation and maintenance. The insurer must decide whether the additional expenses can be justified by the benefits derived from the policies retained or written. Some of the services that insurers can offer to attract personal insurance customers include these:

- A variety of payment plans
- Premium payments through automatic fund transfers or credit cards
- Access to customer service and claim representatives twenty-four hours a day
- Drive-in claim services
- Telephone claim handling
- Telephone and Internet quoting services
- Internet access to customer service

Automation Changes

Providing insurance to the public involves a constant exchange of information between insurers and their distribution systems, regardless of whether the insurer uses the independent agency and brokerage system, the exclusive agency system, or the direct writer system. It is imperative that data be exchanged accurately and consistently. As consumers have become more accustomed to Internet-based business transactions, their expectations for fast, efficient, effective agency-company interfaces have grown. Agents and brokers insist that insurers provide both batch systems, in which transactions are processed at predetermined intervals, and real-time, immediate processing solutions for their marketing and sales needs so that they can be competitive in the marketplace. Agents, brokers, and insurers benefit from effective electronic interfaces through more accurate and consistent data, the automatic application of underwriting criteria to submissions, automatic premium quoting, and policy approval.

Agencies and brokerages may use an agency management system provided by a generic insurance industry software provider or a proprietary agency management system provided by an insurer. Organizations such as ACORD and IVANS have been instrumental in streamlining the agency-company interface through common standards and software solutions. Electronic data gathering and analysis have enabled the personal insurance industry to gather enormous amounts of data on loss exposures and losses incurred and analyze them in order to formulate underwriting criteria and pricing models and apply them uniformly to application submissions.

The ease of use of the automated interface between insurer and producer creates a significant competitive advantage for insurers who facilitate processes for independent agents. Independent agents choose to place more business with insurers who make entry of information into an automated system easier. One way for an insurer to elevate new policy count and policies in force is to improve the insurer-producer interface. However, one disadvantage of automated systems is the development cost. A second disadvantage is the greater amount of customer or policyholder data producers must enter into the interface. When selecting the insurer with which they will place their applications, producers prefer insurers that require the least amount of data entry by the producer.

PORTFOLIO REUNDERWRITING CASE STUDY

The ability to apply the reunderwriting process to bring a portfolio within its goals is a critical skill for the portfolio manager, and this case study introduces application of that process.

Reunderwriting corrects variations from goals in an insurer's portfolio results. An insurer's portfolio manager monitors the results during a calendar year because discrepancies in loss results can jeopardize the insurer's ability to reach its profitability goals for that year. The insurer often must take action to identify the cause of the losses and to reduce or eliminate future losses from similar causes. See the exhibit "The Purpose of Portfolio Reunderwriting."

In this case, the portfolio manager for AmberRock Insurance Company notes that, although the company's premiums are roughly on target, policies are growing faster than the annual goal. Additionally, even though new policies meet underwriting guidelines, the losses incurred are far above those predicted. Therefore, the portfolio manager must take action by using the reunderwriting process. See the exhibit "When to Initiate Reunderwriting."

The Purpose of Portfolio Reunderwriting

Reunderwriting involves managing the profitability of a personal insurance portfolio by examining losses. Although premium pricing can compensate for greater losses than expected, an insurer might price its products higher than those of competitors, resulting in a written premium loss and compounding corrective actions the insurer must take to regain profitability. Rather than addressing this problem through pricing, a portfolio manager can determine the root causes for variances from goals, taking steps to prevent a future pattern of similar losses, through the reunderwriting process:

- The reunderwriting process might address written premium variances, such as through examination of new policy growth exceeding expectations.

- Reunderwriting can identify loss exposures or hazards before a problem reveals its existence as a variance, as when an insurer assumes a portfolio from another insurer or suspects an increase in loss exposure because of changes in the physical, social, or legal environment.

The more quickly reunderwriting process steps are implemented after identification of a portfolio's variance from goals, the better the chances of correcting problems and improving results.

[DA05809]

AmberRock Case Facts

"Six-Month Results for AmberRock's Homeowners Portfolio" displays the results for a portfolio of homeowners policies written by the AmberRock Insurance Company. This report includes annual goals for premiums, policy counts, and losses. Goals for the year appear with monthly results. The percent of goal shown is a comparison of the results that should have been experienced year-to-date (YTD) and the actual results experienced. Additionally, expenses and overall combined ratios might be displayed. Such reports are usually generated and reviewed monthly. See the exhibit "Six-Month Results for AmberRock's Homeowners Portfolio."

AmberRock's homeowners policy results appear for the first six months of the year, along with the goals and the percent of the goals achieved. A portfolio manager will review this report for trends, will compare results to the plan, and will begin an examination for any results that are unlikely to reach the annual goals established if they follow the current trends.

Based on the reported information, premiums are roughly on target, the policies in force (PIF) and the new policy count are growing faster than the established annual goal, and the notation indicates that the growth has been examined and that the new policies meet underwriting guidelines.

However, the report also indicates that the losses incurred are far above those predicted. If these trends are allowed to continue, the loss ratio likely will continue to deteriorate, and the portfolio will be unprofitable. For AmberRock to meet the annual goals, the portfolio manager must take action, often making assumptions and working with imperfect data.

When to Initiate Reunderwriting

Reports and Reviews	Considerations
Variations in Monthly Reports	The portfolio manager might modify reports received and the questions they ask to determine trends. A large catastrophe loss can change the results for the entire year, masking other problems within a portfolio. The portfolio manager might ask, "What is occurring that we cannot observe because the catastrophe losses have substantially changed the results?"
Quarterly Reports	If loss-related problems are identified at the end of the first quarter, most negative trends can be improved, if not corrected, by year-end. At the end of the second quarter, some corrections can still improve the results by the end of the year. At the end of the third quarter, drastic measures might be necessary to improve that year's results.
Underwriting Audits	Underwriting audits determine whether the applications selected by underwriters meet the underwriting guidelines and provide feedback to an underwriter and information regarding changes in activity that might help improve the decision-making process. The portfolio manager might reunderwrite the portfolio or portions of the portfolio to determine whether the trends identified continue through all of the policies written.
New Business Reviews	The portfolio manager might sense a pattern emerging in the new policies that does not allow for a geographic spread of risk and that includes risks that meet only the minimum underwriting requirements. If so, he or she might reunderwrite those policies accepted in the previous twelve months to determine whether a problem exists.
Loss Reviews	The occurrence of a series of losses or a trend in losses is a common reason for the portfolio manager to reunderwrite a portfolio. A portfolio manager will recognize the need to act quickly to change the trend and to improve the profitability of the portfolio, identifying the cause before initiating corrective action.
Special Event Reviews	An insurer considering acquiring a portfolio will review the risk profile of the portfolio and compare it to (1) the profile that it would consider ideal, (2) the underwriting guidelines established for the portfolio to identify compliance with guidelines, and (3) the rates applied to the portfolio. The insurer will determine what effort will be required, if any, to improve the portfolio's profitability. If reunderwriting is required, the insurer will consider the cost involved, as well as the drop in written premiums for the policies that might be nonrenewed.

[DA05810]

Six-Month Results for AmberRock's Homeowners Portfolio

	Premiums			Policies			Losses			
	Written percent of goal (000s)	Earned percent of goal (000s)	PIF	New policies	Retention	Incurred percent of goal (000s)	Loss count percent of goal		Average loss	Loss ratio
Annual Goals (Monthly goals are an even distribution of annual goals throughout the year.)										
	$7,000		$6,650		16,471	3,294	80%	$4,300		3909	$1,100	65%
YTD Results										
Jan.	$ 583	100%	$ 554	100%	15,976	275	80%	$ 394	110%	358	110%	$1,100	71%
Feb.	$1,167	100%	$1,086	98%	16,059	1,043	81%	$ 781	109%	710	109%	$1,100	72%
Mar.	$1,715	98%	$1,613	97%	16,108	1,290	80%	$1,161	108%	1,143	117%	$1,015	72%
Apr.	$2,263	97%	$2,150	97%	16,388	1,675	81%	$1,562	109%	1,642	126%	$ 952	73%
May	$2,858	98%	$2,715	98%	16,553	2,059	81%	$1,989	111%	2,248	138%	$ 885	73%
June	$3,465	99%	$3,292	99%	17,294	2,471	81%	$2,430	113%	2,834	145%	$ 857	74%

Written and earned premiums are roughly on target for YTD results compared to the annual goals. The earned premium is about 95% of written premium because this is a line of business that is growing.	Retention is on target YTD. However, at six months, the new policy count has reached 75% of the annual goal. These new policies have been reviewed and are determined to meet underwriting guidelines.	Through six months, incurred losses are 13 percent above the YTD goals, and the number of losses is 45 percent above the YTD goals. The result is a loss ratio that is substantially above goal and increasing.

[DA05811]

Case Analysis Tools and Information

A basic tenet of portfolio management is that deteriorating results caused by a loss frequency problem indicate faulty policy selection, while a loss severity problem indicates pricing inadequacy. As a result, AmberRock's portfolio manager decides to examine the losses that have occurred in the last six months and the associated loss exposures that are causing these losses. If the portfolio manager can find a pattern in the losses that have occurred, it may be possible to identify the associated loss exposures or hazards and to take action.

In the analysis and problem identification phases of application of the reunderwriting process to AmberRock's situation, the portfolio manager will use one or more analysis tools to determine the root causes(s) of the loss ratio deterioration. See the exhibit "Portfolio Management Analysis and Approach Summary."

Underlying the reunderwriting process is the portfolio manager's understanding of profitability ratios. By understanding the components of the ratios, the portfolio manager can analyze the components of those ratios. See the exhibit "Underwriting Profitability Ratios."

Portfolio Management Analysis and Approach Summary

- "Five Whys"—This process repeatedly asks the question "Why?" (with no magic in the number five) and helps when a cause is not obvious or is hidden within territories or risk categories, or when a new cause is emerging.

- Root cause analysis (RCA)—RCA helps determine what happened that caused the problem, how, and why. RCA's detailed analysis is appropriate for major events that usually do not result from a single cause, but from a complex set of conditions developing over time and involving multiple work groups, processes, and tasks. RCA employs an event and causal factor chart, as well as change and barrier analyses.

- Common cause analysis (CCA)—CCA involves reviewing all root cause analyses done within a specified period of time, reviewing action plans resulting from them, and grouping them according to identified themes or issues. The themes are rated using a scoring system that rates factors of loss severity, occurrence, and detectability, and the most highly scored themes are used to address the goals in strategic organizational plans.

- Investigations based on questions—Portfolio managers often draw on an accumulation of experience in prior portfolio analyses in the form of questions to initiate an analysis of new problems.

[DA05812]

Underwriting Profitability Ratios

Ratio	Calculation	Comments
Loss ratio = $\dfrac{\text{Incurred losses}}{\text{Earned premiums}} \times 100$		This ratio compares incurred losses with earned premiums for a specific time period, such as a year. It illustrates what percentage of an insurer's earned income is "used up" by reserves and claim payments. For example, a loss ratio of 70 percent indicates that for every $1.00 the insurer earns in premium income, it pays $0.70 in incurred losses.
Expense ratio = $\dfrac{\text{Underwriting expenses}}{\text{Written premiums}} \times 100$		This ratio compares underwriting expenses with written premiums for a specific time period. It illustrates what percentage of an insurer's income goes to pay underwriting expenses. For example, an expense ratio of 28 percent indicates that for every $1.00 of insurance a company writes, it pays $0.28 in underwriting expenses.
Combined ratio = Loss ratio + Expense ratio		This combination of the loss and expense ratios presents a clear picture of the insurer's overall underwriting performance and compares the inflow and outflow of money from insurance operations. A combined ratio above 100 percent indicates an underwriting loss. A combined ratio below 100 percent indicates an underwriting profit.

[DA05784]

Steps in the Reunderwriting Process

The reunderwriting process involves six steps, which address process questions:

- Analyzing the portfolio—What is causing the increase in losses?

- Identifying and distinguishing the problems—What underlying causes might affect the entire portfolio?

- Formulating possible corrective actions—What are possible actions that might address the cause of the losses and correct the problem?

- Selecting corrective actions—Of the various possible ways of addressing the cause of the losses, which is the best action?

- Implementing corrective actions—How will the effectiveness of these actions be determined?

- Monitoring the portfolio—How should the chosen action be implemented?

Analyzing the Portfolio

The portfolio manager works with a significant amount of data in the AmberRock case, choosing tools to determine the root cause of the problem and employing the most appropriate ones. The portfolio manager has decided to apply the Five Whys analysis to this problem. The first question is, "Why is the loss ratio suddenly deteriorating?"

To analyze the portfolio to identify a problem, the portfolio manager must organize the data to identify patterns. The level of quality and the degree of relevance of the data captured for individual policies in the portfolio, and the access staff members have to those data, affect the quality and the relevance of the overall data organization process.

The portfolio manager usually receives standard reports showing results at the end of each month, such as a "Causes of Loss" summary. See the exhibit "Causes of Loss and Territory Summary."

From this standard report, the portfolio manager recognizes a concentration of loss activity by cause of loss. The second "why" question that the portfolio manager asks is, "Why are these concentrations of losses occurring?" To narrow the search, this report is expanded to show the territories in which the losses are occurring. Losses are concentrated in Territories 29, 30, and 31.

The portfolio manager then asks the third "why" question: "Why are these concentrations of losses occurring in these territories?" By examining a representative sample of the claim files, the manager can identify similar characteristics, as shown in "Results of Claim Review for Sample Claims in Territories 29—31." The sample shows a high percentage of loss occurrences that could have been prevented by the insured or that involved insureds under economic pressures. See the exhibit "AmberRock Homeowners Portfolio: Results of Claim Review for Sample Claims in Territories 29–31."

Causes of Loss and Territory Summary

Summary of All Homeowners Claims Reported
January 1 Through June 30 of Current Year

CAUSE OF LOSS			TERRITORY	
Code	Description	Percentage of Losses	Territory Code	Percentage of Losses
01	Windstorm	2.2	24	5.3
02	Hail	0.1	25	7.6
03	Earthquake	0.0	26	4.5
04	Fire—forest/wild fire	0.0	27	3.2
05	Fire—arson	5.0	29	15.4
06	Fire—other	12.3	30	27.3
07	Theft	39.4	31	14.9
08	Vandalism	4.7	32	4.7
09	Liability	5.2	33	7.2
10	Medical payments	4.0	34	3.9
11	Other property loss	27.1	35	3.7
	Total	100.0	36	2.3
			Total	100.0

[DA05813]

Based on these results, the portfolio manager asks the fourth "why" question: "Why are these losses that seem to be related to economic hardships occurring in a few territories?" A review of the territory map shows that these areas are adjacent. Phone calls to producers in these territories reveal that a major employer in the area closed about a year ago.

Identifying and Distinguishing Problems

A deterioration of loss results can result from an increase in losses covering several states and can arise from multiple causes. Even after an analysis has been completed, the underlying problem and the size of the problem can be difficult to identify with certainty. The fifth "why" question the portfolio manager will ask is, "Why has the closing of an employer caused an increase in losses?"

Assuming that the analysis of the AmberRock homeowners portfolio losses is correct, the sudden economic decline in a community can result from the loss of one or more large employers in an area that has no other industry to bring employment and economic stability to the community. Often, this situation

AmberRock Homeowners Portfolio: Results of Claim Review for Sample Claims in Territories 29–31

Characteristics	Percentage of "Yes" Occurrences
The loss could have been prevented by the insured.	55%
The insured was careless, and carelessness was a factor in the claim.	10%
Poor maintenance contributed to the loss.	38%
Additional living expenses were paid in the claim.	12%
Economic pressures were found in the policyholders' comments.	78%
Other	
Policyholder was unemployed at the time of the loss.	59%
Claim has not been paid. File is marked for investigation for arson, fraud, or suspected policyholder involvement.	17%
Maintenance issues did not contribute to the loss; however, photographs reflect maintenance problems or morale issues.	48%

[DA05815]

occurs when other possible employers are too far away for property owners to commute to new jobs while retaining their property. The price of real estate drops as property owners attempt to relocate. Property owners are unable or unwilling to maintain their property when the future is so uncertain. When the market value of property drops too far below mortgage obligations for owners to absorb the losses, some property owners might resort to drastic measures, such as insurance fraud, to eliminate the financial burden that the property creates.

An increase in theft losses is another indication of a community with economic problems. Some individuals might break into homes to obtain property that can be converted to cash, and property owners might feel justified in exaggerating the extent of theft losses. Vacant homes, abandoned or waiting for sale, can become targets for thieves and vandals. AmberRock's staff members must identify the magnitude of the problem and the extent to which the portfolio might continue to decline.

If AmberRock uses insurance scores as an underwriting tool, a review of all the insurance scores for all policyholders submitting fire, theft, or other property loss claims in territories 29, 30, and 31 would be useful. If the percentage of unacceptable insurance scores is significantly higher for those territories than the average number of unacceptable insurance scores identified for new applicants or for renewals, the extent of the problem can be identified by ordering insurance score reports for the entire portfolio or for policies in selected territories. If AmberRock does not use insurance scores, property inspections in the selected territories can help identify vacant houses or maintenance problems that might lead to further losses.

Formulating Possible Corrective Actions

Correcting AmberRock's problem of losses that exceed expectations begins with identifying all the possible corrective actions that the portfolio manager might apply. Some corrective actions might appear obvious considering the circumstances. However, restrictions in the policy language or state regulations can limit an insurer's ability to cancel or nonrenew personal insurance policies. The possible corrective actions here are listed in order of complexity, from simple solutions that affect only some policies to complex solutions that affect all of the policies in the portfolio. See the exhibit "Complications in Selecting Corrective Actions."

Complications in Selecting Corrective Actions

The urgent need for correcting a loss problem is compounded by the long time frame required to complete a corrective action. Any plans for nonrenewals or coverage modifications require time for the insurer's decision makers to reach an agreement and for any state filing regarding coverage modifications, as well as a full year to implement the corrective action as the policies nonrenew. A portfolio manager must ensure that any action selected is actually the best choice. He or she might perform the following additional research to ensure the best possible selection:

- Review the claim reserves for the portfolio to determine whether any outstanding reserves might affect the incurred losses. Also review the ratio of claim reserves to claim settlements to determine whether any redundancy has occurred in the past that might also be reflected in the current incurred losses.

- Check for other patterns of losses within the portfolio by comparing loss results by producer, territory, property value, driver age, or any other major characteristic of the policies in the portfolio.

Some corrective actions might not be permitted by state regulation, might not match the insurer's mission statement or strategies, or might have consequences that are too severe for them to be considered feasible.

[DA05816]

Selecting Corrective Actions

The portfolio manager has several corrective actions from which to choose for AmberRock. See the exhibit "Identifying Possible Corrective Actions."

Identifying Possible Corrective Actions

Possible Corrective Action	Cautions	Consequences
Nonrenew all policies with identified loss exposure	Insurer will continue to experience losses until entire annual cycle of unacceptable policies has been nonrenewed.	Action eliminates moral and morale hazards, corrects problem.
Modify coverages	Insurer must clearly communicate to policyholders or risk customer relations problems.	If modifications are not clearly communicated, policyholders might deny having been notified.
Modify coverage limits to match property values	Increasing rates might not resolve underlying problems of insuring property to appropriate value.	Action reflects more realistic values.
Modify risk profile of overall portfolio	Underwriting guidelines have latitude, which must be reflected in this modification.	Action reflects a preferred portfolio.
Modify underwriting guidelines	Filing with state regulators might be necessary.	Action applies only to some policies.
Modify pricing through tiered rates	Action can result in competitive disadvantage.	Action results in more appropriate rates.
Discontinue portfolio	Most drastic action.	Action eliminates problem entirely.

[DA05817]

Possible corrective actions can include multiple approaches.

AmberRock's portfolio manager decides to take a "fix-it-twice" corrective approach:

1. Nonrenew all policies with insurance scores that were not acceptable.
2. Modify the underwriting guidelines to raise the insurance score threshold.

Implementing Corrective Actions

After selecting one or more corrective actions to address the problems identified, the portfolio manager puts the processes in place that will ensure consistent implementation. If criteria are established for the nonrenewal of some policies, activity must take place far enough in advance of the current policy expirations to select the policies; order any necessary external reports; review the reports; and issue notices to policyholders, mortgagees, and lienholders.

The length of time required for issuing a nonrenewal notice before the expiration of a policy is established in each policy contract. However, 30 days' notice is a standard requirement. Insurers often work 90 to 120 days in advance of the policy expiration dates to ensure that all policies that need to be discontinued are properly processed. Policies that are not processed in time to issue adequate notice must be renewed for another policy term.

The portfolio manager must expedite actions that require state filings for rate changes, underwriting changes, or the development of coverage tiers. Any delay can result in additional losses that further deteriorate portfolio profitability. Actions that involve increasing the Coverage A limit to create a more precise match with the values of the dwellings might require a review of all policies within a portfolio. AmberRock might obtain external reports and use vendors who specialize in calculating insurance to value to develop recommendations. They can then recommend that policyholders increase the coverage value in the middle of the policy term or at the next renewal. Such an extensive project will generate additional expenses. However, the projected increase in premiums can justify the associated expenses.

Monitoring the Portfolio

AmberRock's reunderwriting process began with problems identified as the portfolio manager monitored the results of a portfolio compared to the goals established, and the cycle begins again with monitoring the results to determine whether the actions taken have corrected the problems.

Changing the direction of the results in a portfolio is a lengthy process. If policies are written on a twelve-month basis, twelve months must pass before a corrective action involving the nonrenewal of policies can be completed. Twenty-four months may pass from the time a problem is identified, corrective actions are selected, and the corrective actions are applied to the entire portfolio.

The portfolio manager must carefully evaluate the success of the actions. Another spike in losses could result from storms or winter-related losses that are unrelated to the original problem identified. To determine the relative success of an action, the portfolio manager must monitor the same type of losses originating from similar loss exposures or hazards to detect any reduction in loss frequency.

Using the Five Whys to determine why homeowners policy losses incurred are far higher than expected, AmberRock's portfolio manager finds that losses are highest in three adjacent territories because of a major employer's closing. The portfolio manager then chooses a fix-it-twice approach as corrective action: (1) nonrenew all policies with insurance scores that were not acceptable and (2) modify the underwriting guidelines to raise the insurance score threshold. The portfolio manager must then implement these corrective actions and monitor portfolio performance. See the exhibit "AmberRock Case Resolution."

AmberRock Case Resolution

Reunderwriting Process Step	Corrective Action for AmberRock
Analyzing the portfolio—What is causing the increase in losses?	The portfolio manager applied the "Five Whys" approach, finding economic hardships in three adjacent territories resulting from a major employer closing business.
Identifying and distinguishing the problems—What underlying causes might affect the entire portfolio?	The portfolio manager continued to identify the size of the problem and the extent to which the portfolio might continue to decline.
Formulating possible corrective actions—What are possible actions that might address the cause of the losses and correct the problem?	Possible corrective actions range from simple to complex, including these two possibilities: (1) Review the claim reserves for the portfolio to determine whether any outstanding reserves might affect the incurred losses, and review the ratio of claim reserves to claim settlements to determine whether redundancy has occurred in the past that incurred losses might also reflect. (2) Check for other patterns of losses within the portfolio by comparing loss results by producer, territory, property value, or any other major characteristic of the policies in the portfolio.
Selecting corrective actions—Of the various possible ways of addressing the cause of the losses, which is the best action?	From among several options, AmberRock's portfolio manager decided to take a fix-it-twice approach: (1) Nonrenew all policies with insurance scores that were not acceptable, and (2) Modify the underwriting guidelines to raise the credit score threshold.
Implementing corrective actions—How will the effectiveness of these actions be determined?	The length of time required for issuing a nonrenewal notice before the expiration of a policy is established in each policy contract; however, thirty days' notice is a standard requirement. Actions requiring state filings for rate changes, underwriting changes, or the development of tiers must be expedited. AmberRock might obtain external reports and use vendors who specialize in calculating insurance to value to develop recommendations and then recommend that policyholders increase the coverage value in the middle of the policy term or at the next renewal.
Monitoring the portfolio—How should the chosen action be implemented?	To determine the relative success of an action, the portfolio manager must monitor the same type of losses originating from similar loss exposures or hazards to detect any reduction in loss frequency.

[DA05818]

EVALUATING PORTFOLIO MANAGEMENT METHODS

A portfolio manager's ability to improve the profitability of a book of business can be improved through a variety of portfolio management methods.

Portfolio managers use various tools and approaches to determine the root cause of portfolio results that do not meet an organization's goals. Then, an analysis of key indicators can aid portfolio managers in determining which corrective actions to take. In support of these objectives, an organization should be continually evaluating the methods it uses to improve its portfolio management.

Evaluating portfolio management methods requires an understanding of these approaches:

- Credit-related underwriting and pricing
- Modeling
- Outsourcing data collection
- Increasing data collection needs

Credit-Related Underwriting and Pricing

Credit scoring

A decision-making tool that uses credit report information to develop a predictive score on the creditworthiness of an applicant for additional credit.

Credit scoring is generally based on an individual's overall credit history, which is determined by use of credit, number of late payments made to creditors, payment history, length of time the account has been active, and other similar factors. Individuals with good payment histories and few late payments have higher credit scores. Lower credit scores are assigned to individuals who have poor payment histories, accounts that are in collection, or have had a previous bankruptcy. Credit scores generally range from a low of 300 to a high of 850. A variety of credit score models exist. However, the manner in which they are calculated is generally proprietary.

Credit scores have traditionally been used by the financial industry to determine customers' eligibility for consumer credit, such as loans or credit cards. More recently, these scores have been used by insurers as the basis for credit-based insurance scores, which are often referred to as Insurance Bureau Scores (IBS). Insurers use such scores as part of the underwriting selection and pricing process when reviewing applications for coverage.

Insurance risk score models enable insurers to establish a correlation between credit or "insurance scores"and personal claim potential. Based on this correlation, most insurers have begun using credit-based insurance scores in the selection of personal lines insureds, the pricing of personal lines policies, or for both selection and policy pricing, subject to any applicable state guidelines or restrictions on use. See the exhibit "Credit Scores and Loss Potential."

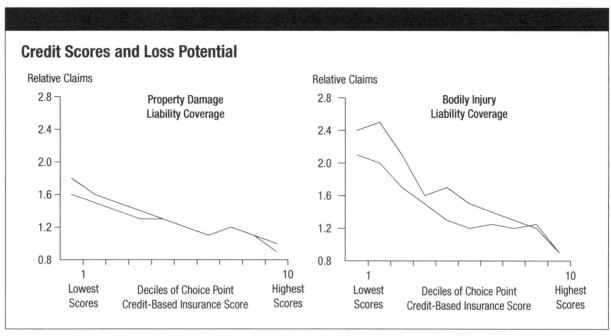

Credit Scores and Loss Potential

Credit-Based Insurance Scores: Impacts on Consumers of Automobile Insurance, A Report to Congress by the Federal Trade Commission, July 2007, p. 127
[DA05825]

Insurers may use applicants' credit scores to determine that they have a higher-than-average loss potential and decline to provide insurance coverage for them. Credit-based insurance scores are also used to determine rating classifications that result in a higher premium for customers who have higher loss potentials. Insurers can also use credit scores to make adjustments in existing rate classifications to more appropriately reflect the expected loss potential of their customers.

The use of credit-based insurance scores provides several advantages for insurers. Because numerous statistical studies have established the correlation between credit scores and loss potential, credit-based insurance scores allow insurers to improve rating methodologies and develop premiums that are commensurate with expected loss levels. Also, insurers can use credit-based insurance scores to target existing customers who have lower loss potential to improve account retention and overall profitability.

The disadvantages to insurers in using credit-based insurance scores include their complexity, which makes them difficult for consumers and regulators to understand.[3] Also, regulators in some jurisdictions prohibit or restrict the use of credit scores in either the underwriting or pricing of insurance policies.

Modeling

The ability to use models has become more important as insurers have shifted their emphasis from individual account underwriting to management of a portfolio of personal lines accounts. Insurers collect large amounts of data and

Modeling

In data analysis, a system of calculating known outcomes based on current data and then applying these calculations to new data to predict future outcomes.

use data warehousing to store it. The key to effective **modeling** is to extract this information so that it can be evaluated to uncover patterns or recurring results in such areas as claims and loss reserve analysis, sales trends, and customer profitability. This process is often referred to as data mining. Data developed from current customers and past experience are used to build predictive models and catastrophe models.

Modeling allows portfolio managers to use technology to improve the underwriting process. Various types of hypothetical models are used to project future loss levels, the frequency or severity of catastrophes, required pricing, and other underwriting variables. Such hypothetical models can be used to determine changes required on a portfolio of existing business or to determine eligibility and pricing for new business. For example, a portfolio manager can review a book of homeowners business in a particular state and project year-end losses based on the current underwriting guidelines. Additional models can then be employed to determine the effect of proposed changes in guidelines to determine if profitability can be improved. Based on this review, appropriate modifications in guidelines can be introduced.

Business rules engines are used to automate the underwriting decision-making process and to improve the overall consistency of underwriting decisions. Automating underwriting selection improves an insurer's efficiency and permits underwriters to concentrate on applicants who do not meet the guidelines established within the business rules engine.

Predictive Models

Predictive models are used to analyze a book of business to determine future losses and profitability. Portfolio managers can examine specific variables related to the book of business and use models to configure combinations of variables to generate scores and project future results. For a book of personal auto policies, variables could consist of characteristics such as type and use of vehicles, miles driven, age of drivers, and rating territory. The variables for homeowners policies could include construction type, age, public protection class, and cause of loss. This analysis can uncover potential problems in an existing book of business and allow the portfolio manager to recommend adjustments in guidelines.

Predictive modeling

A process in which historical data based on behaviors and events are blended with multiple variables and used to construct models of anticipated future outcomes.

Predictive modeling can also be used to determine eligibility requirements for prospective customers to assist in building a profitable book of business in the future. Predictive models can also be used to assist marketing in segmenting prospective customers and in niche marketing initiatives. The marketing and underwriting departments can work together to establish effective pricing levels for target segments and increase the number of policies written.

Price optimization models use predictive methods to determine appropriate pricing based on customer data and the insurer's profitability goals. Insurers can use models to select more profitable business, reduce marketing expenses, and reduce the number of applications that are declined. Effective targeting of market segments through modeling can also improve relationships with producers and with customers.

Using specific variables within a predictive model can also assist portfolio managers with determining when additional underwriting information, such as financial information or motor vehicle records, should be requested. This can reduce administrative expenses and eliminate the need to obtain additional information when it would be of limited value in managing the overall book of business.

There are some disadvantages in using predictive modeling, mostly related to the technological aspects of the models. It is important that insurers integrate the use of models consistently within their business units and ensure that all users are properly trained in the features of the model. Unless users have a thorough understanding of the capability of the models and supporting software, they will be unable to maximize the use of these programs. As with any software program, improper or inaccurate inputs will provide less than satisfactory output, resulting in flawed decisions.

Catastrophe Modeling

Catastrophe models are used to simulate events, such as hurricanes or earthquakes, to measure expected future losses based on the insurer's book of business. Catastrophe models for a personal lines book of business incorporate these elements:

Catastrophe model
A type of computer program that estimates losses from future potential catastrophic events.

- Geographic location
- Type of catastrophe
- Exposure information
- Replacement cost estimates

Depending on the portfolio manager's preference, the geographic location may be isolated by the city, county, ZIP code, or other descriptor. Separate models are used to simulate the effects of each type of event based on the causes of loss covered under the book of business. This model component is sometimes referred to as the science component. Exposure information, or the engineering component of the model, includes specific data on building construction, coverages provided, number of stories, and other similar factors. Another important data element is the current replacement values of all structures included in the portfolio being analyzed—generally all of the current in-force policies, or the insurance component. If property values are not accurate, then projected loss values for each type of catastrophe will also be inaccurate.

The output from catastrophe models provides the portfolio manager and senior management an estimate of average annual loss potential and/or probable maximum loss amounts for natural catastrophic events in the insurer's book of business. Based on this estimate, decisions are made regarding the management of these exposures. These decisions include underwriting guidelines, policy language, mitigation techniques, and reinsurance needs. See the exhibit "Catastrophe Modeling."

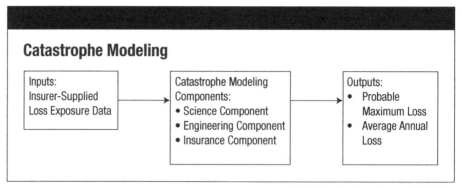

[DA05821]

Catastrophe modeling provides valuable loss projection data to insurers for claims arising from natural perils covered under their policies. As with other types of models, it is important that the portfolio manager know the parameters of the model and that accurate data is used. Insurers may develop their own models or use external models. If external models are used, it is important for portfolio managers to understand their underlying assumptions. Also, external models may present compatibility problems between the insurer's data and the model's input requirements. Complying with these requirements may result in increased expenses for the insurer.

Because catastrophe models are used as part of an insurer's ratemaking process, another potential downside is regulatory constraints that could apply to the use of modeling. Regulators may require information regarding the methodology or components of the catastrophe model. Because much of this information is proprietary, model developers are hesitant to share details with external parties, including regulators.

Outsourcing Data Collection

Insurers collect large amounts of data for use in portfolio management and in models. For existing policies, data such as loss information and premiums are internal to the company. Other information is available from external sources. Using third party vendors (TPVs) provides insurers with the advantage of gathering more data and the potential for lowering expenses. Portfolio managers must continually evaluate the expenses related to outsourcing data collection to ensure that the costs do not outweigh the benefits gained by the insurer. This involves comparing these costs to the value outsourcing contributes toward improving decisions that reduce overall loss frequency and severity. Information and services provided by external sources can include these:

- Information verification
- Subject matter experts
- External reports

Information Verification

Verification of information provided by customers on insurance applications is an important function for insurers. If application information is inaccurate, then the selection and pricing decisions based on the information will also be incorrect and could result in poor underwriting results. Some insurers use internal staff to verify application information with producers or directly with the customer using mailed surveys or telephone inquiries.

Other insurers have found it more cost effective to outsource information verification to TPVs. These vendors have developed methods of phrasing questions in a manner that allows them to uncover missed rating information or to verify the accuracy of information on an application. The insurer can then make corrections to the rating to generate an adequate premium for actual loss exposures.

Subject Matter Experts

In highly specialized lines of business, insurers may depend on external subject matter experts (SMEs) to provide input on pricing and selection of insureds. This use of external expertise provides cost savings for the insurers and eliminates the need to incur salary expenses related to a full-time employee.

For example, personal lines underwriters may seek assistance from an SME when reviewing an application for a restored wooden-hull sailboat. While the underwriter may have substantial experience in writing personal watercraft coverage, this type of vessel has unique characteristics. In order to accurately assess the loss exposure and establish an appropriate price, the underwriter can rely on the assistance of an external SME with expertise in this area.

External Reports

Insurers rely on an extensive amount of external information to effectively manage their books of business. External reports include motor vehicle records (MVRs), which list accidents and traffic violations for insured drivers. Many companies subscribe to centralized external claim databases that enable them to submit and receive loss data on current and new customers.

For homeowners or dwelling policies, the insurer may order an inspection of the property. Because of the cost of such inspections, reports are usually ordered only for high-valued or unique properties, such as log cabins or pre-manufactured homes. Rather than incurring the expense of a full inspection of the property, insurers may instead use photographs of the property, which are often provided by the producer. Inspections and photographs can be obtained either during the selection process or after the application has been accepted and a policy has been issued.

Increasing Data Collection

As insurers increase their use of models for personal lines insurance and move from individual account underwriting to portfolio management, the need for data grows. In order for models to operate efficiently to improve selection and increase profitability, a sufficient amount of information is required. Without an appropriate level of information, especially in these areas, insurers cannot operate effectively and make informed decisions:

* Predictive variable information
* Rating variable information
* Underwriting exception tracking

Predictive Variable Information

As predictive models become more sophisticated, the types and amount of information gathered for them increases. As portfolio managers complete their evaluation of underwriting results, they can refine the variables that are used within the models.

For example, if a portfolio manager identifies emerging trends involving windstorm losses within a book of business, he or she may examine specific property-related variables. This examination could result in addition of variables related to the type, condition, and age of roofs to predictive models. Portfolio managers could then use roof data to develop underwriting guidelines, such as requiring actual cash value rather than replacement cost coverage for homes with roofs over a certain age or requiring separate wind deductibles. The portfolio manager could also combine rating variables, such as geographic location, roof age, and credit score to better predict expected amounts for windstorm losses.

A similar approach could be used to identify loss trends related to brush or wild fires. Variables related to geographic location and history of past fires could be added to the predictive model to segregate homes that are susceptible to this type of occurrence.

Portfolio managers may also identify trends related to the size of the homes being insured and add property-related variables for total square footage to predictive models. Such a change could allow the insurer to determine if there is a difference in loss levels for smaller homes as compared to larger homes. Portfolio managers could also increase the use of people-related variables, such as additional variables regarding driver age, to refine personal auto underwriting guidelines for youthful drivers.

Rating Variable Information

As predictive variables are changed or added to models, the portfolio manager will not only change underwriting guidelines, but will also adjust rating structures.

For example, data for roof type, age, and condition could also be used to refine pricing based on the age or condition of roofs to improve profitability by lowering loss frequency and severity. This would be accomplished by charging a higher premium for homes with older roofs and a greater loss potential from windstorms. If predictive models indicated that loss frequency was greater for larger homes, the portfolio manager would adjust pricing structures to reflect this higher loss potential.

Underwriting Exception Tracking

Personal lines underwriting has grown increasingly automated. However, not every application or policy can be reviewed using business rules engine technology. A certain percentage of customers will always fall outside the established parameters of automated guidelines. Such customers are referred to underwriters for individual review and consideration. Underwriters have varying levels of authority to grant exceptions and write coverage for customers who do not exactly match established guidelines. A less-experienced underwriter may be required to refer exceptions to a manager, while a senior underwriter may have the authority to make the final decision.

It is critical for insurers to establish a system for tracking all exceptions and capturing details on which guidelines triggered the exception as well as justification for accepting the application. The policy must then be tracked to determine future economic results. Some of these exceptions may be an indication of an emerging trend, such as the use of green technology in automobiles or eco-friendly building materials in homes. The early adopters of such building methods will establish future underwriting guidelines and pricing structures, which will be included in future predictive models. Alternatively, poor results for other types of exceptions may lead to changes in underwriting guidelines that make future applications ineligible for coverage.

PERSONAL LINES PORTFOLIO MANAGEMENT/ UNDERWRITING PROFITABILITY CASE STUDY

When its profitability goals are not being met, an insurer must formulate actions to identify and correct problems.

Portfolio managers are responsible for working with senior management to make recommendations for improving the profitability of an underperforming book of business. These recommendations are based on conclusions drawn from a review of information in periodic reports and from other sources that provide the details required to diagnose the underlying causes of the problem.

Case Facts

At the end of Year 1, Homesaver General Insurance Company, a hypothetical insurer writing only personal auto and homeowners policies, posted a

$13 million underwriting loss. Concerned about this poor performance, the insurer's management team examined these results and identified the personal auto insurance portfolio as the source. See the exhibit "Homesaver General Company Year-End Results."

Homesaver General Company Year-End Results

Overall	Year 1
Written premiums	$119 million
Earned premiums	$113 million
Incurred losses	$92 million
Underwriting expenses	$34 million
Underwriting profit	($13 million)
Loss ratio	81%
Expense ratio	28.5%
Combined ratio	109.5%

Personal Auto

Written premiums	$83 million
Earned premiums	$80 million
Incurred losses	$72 million
Underwriting expenses	$24 million
Underwriting profit	($16 million)
Loss ratio	90%
Expense ratio	29%
Combined ratio	119%

Homeowners

Written premiums	$36 million
Earned premiums	$33 million
Incurred losses	$20 million
Underwriting expenses	$10 million
Underwriting profit	$3 million
Loss ratio	61%
Expense ratio	28%
Combined ratio	89%

*Numbers in parentheses indicate losses.

[DA05901]

Case Analysis Tools

When reviewing the personal auto portfolio to improve profitability, Homesaver will examine these three primary determinants of underwriting results:

- Increasing premiums
- Decreasing losses
- Reducing expenses

Homesaver will also use portfolio management analysis tools such as making assumptions and working with imperfect data, root cause analysis, and reunderwriting. The reunderwriting process follows steps to analyze the portfolio to identify problems, formulate potential corrective actions, and to select the most appropriate solution. See the exhibit "Steps in the Reunderwriting Process."

Steps in the Reunderwriting Process

1. Analyzing the portfolio—What is causing the increase in losses?

2. Identifying and distinguishing the problems—What underlying causes might affect the entire portfolio?

3. Formulating possible corrective actions—What are possible actions that might address the cause of the losses and correct the problem?

4. Selecting corrective actions—Of the various possible ways of addressing the cause of the losses, which is the best action?

5. Implementing corrective actions—How will the effectiveness of these actions be determined?

6. Monitoring the portfolio—How should the chosen actions be implemented?

[DA05834]

Additionally, portfolio management methods such as modeling, outsourcing data collection, and increasing data collection may prove useful in examining the personal auto portfolio to improve profitability.

Case Analysis Steps

Homesaver will follow these steps to formulate actions to improve its portfolio:

1. Examine results compared to goals
2. Examine trends in results
3. Formulate actions
4. Implement actions
5. Monitor results

Examine Results Compared to Goals

Almost 70 percent of Homesaver's written premium was generated by the sale of personal auto insurance. However, the auto portfolio showed a loss ratio of 90 percent and a combined ratio of 119 percent. The results in the home-owners portfolio were much better—a combined ratio of 89 percent and an underwriting profit of $3 million. The comparatively small size of the home-owners portfolio, however, meant that this excellent performance had little effect on the insurer's overall results. Homesaver determined that concentrating on the auto portfolio's associated premiums, losses, and expenses would have the most immediate effect on improving the company's profitability. At the same time, the insurer will examine its small but profitable homeowners book of business, which will further contribute to improved profitability.

Homesaver's competitive position in the marketplace makes a rate increase across its entire book of business difficult. The insurer charges higher premiums than many of its competitors, and the vice president of marketing is concerned that a rate increase would undermine its ability to meet growth targets and retain existing business.

Review of the insurer's incurred losses from the auto portfolio showed that reserving was adequate and that claim representatives were working very efficiently to minimize loss expenses. The severity of the paid losses was one cause of the high loss ratio, and further analysis indicated a frequency problem. Policyholders were making significantly more low-value claims than projected, and the rates the insurer was charging were insufficient to cover the losses. The insurer should examine these areas further to determine treatment using portfolio management methods such as reunderwriting or predictive modeling.

The insurer has already undertaken extensive internal expense reduction methods. An external expense area to consider is the commissions Homesaver pays to its producers. The insurer distributes its products through the independent agency system. Many of these producers have long-term, loyal relationships with the insurer and continue to support it despite its uncompetitive rates. As a result, the insurer has been reluctant to follow an industry trend toward lower commissions and had not adopted the 5 percent reduction that many other insurers implemented.

Based on this examination of results compared to goals, Homesaver decides to focus primarily on making adjustments in the loss and expenses areas to improve its profitability.

Examine Trends in Results

The next step is to more closely examine the personal auto portfolio to reveal any trends in the results. The purpose of this review is to identify areas that may have improved as well as those that have deteriorated. This review forms the basis for recommendations of needed adjustments to accomplish a reduction in loss levels and in expenses.

Portfolio managers begin this process by reviewing the performance indicators provided to make assumptions and work with imperfect data. This initial review begins to clarify some of the sources of the loss frequency and severity problems. Many of these losses are occurring in suburban areas that are close to major cities. Reunderwriting the individual policies in the affected book of personal auto business will allow the portfolio managers to look more closely at this loss problem. Root cause analysis (RCA) will also be used to eliminate possible causes of the frequency and severity problem and more clearly identify the actual reason for the increased undesirable loss ratio for this book of business.

The result of this review indicates that the root cause of the loss problem involves individuals who routinely use their autos to commute from the suburbs to the city. The personal auto policy application does not gather specific information about vehicle usage, resulting in inaccurate premiums for these customers. Although adjusting premiums was not originally a focus of this review, portfolio managers will need to work with actuaries to adjust rate relativity factors for these territories and to redefine Homesaver's personal auto rate tiers and classifications. Such adjustments are necessary so that premiums will accurately reflect the actual loss potential of these customers.

The reunderwriting process also reveals several books of personal auto policies in which application information has not been updated in over five years. Further reunderwriting will be required on individual policies to update application information and develop potential root causes of loss frequency for these personal auto policies.

Portfolio managers will use these results to recommend corrective actions to senior management, including nonrenewing policies, modifying coverage, modifying underwriting guidelines, or modifying pricing through tiered rates. When formulating recommendations, portfolio managers will use predictive models to analyze both the personal auto and homeowners books of business and use various combinations of these corrective actions to project future results.

Formulate Actions

Based on the input from the portfolio managers and after discussions and negotiation among all business units within the organization, as well as with many of its long-term agents, Homesaver establishes a strategic goal and tactical plans to support that goal.

The goal of the overall strategy is to reduce Homesaver's combined ratio. Tactical plans to support this strategic goal focus on reducing the auto loss ratio, changing the product mix by increasing the number of homeowners policies written, and reducing the overall expense ratio. See the exhibit "Homesaver's Strategy, Tactics, and Activities."

Homesaver's Strategy, Tactics, and Activities

Strategy   We will reduce the combined ratio to 103 percent.

    Tactic   Reduce the automobile loss ratio to 75 percent.

        Activity   Recalculate rate relativity factors for personal auto policies

        Activity   Identify and reunderwrite all policies with more than 3 losses in the past 5 years.

        Activity   Increase physical damage deductibles on 60 percent of all automobile policies.

    Tactic   Improve the ratio of automobile to homeowners policies in force by increasing homeowners written premiums by 10 percent.

        Activity   Launch a homeowners sales incentive program.

        Activity   Decrease homeowners rates by 10 percent.

    Tactic   Reduce the overall expense ratio to 25 percent.

        Activity   Reduce commission rates paid to producers by 3 percent.

[DA05904]

Implement Actions

During Year 2, the management and staff at Homesaver work together to achieve their goals. Each month, reports are circulated to all staff comparing the insurer's performance to its goals. This information helps focus the organization and ensures that all levels and departments work cooperatively.

The rate adjustment process and reunderwriting of the auto portfolio requires more staff and causes some initial increases in expenses. Based on the reunderwriting activities, a total of $2.2 million in written auto premiums is nonrenewed at the election of the insurer. Additionally, personal auto policy sales are very slow because of Homesaver's noncompetitive rates and rate increases applied to some policies to correct the rate relativity problem. The insurer, however, remains confident that correcting the identified rate relatively problem will provide improved results over the longer term. The insurer loses an additional $500,000 in written premiums when some policyholders choose to replace their coverage with more competitive insurers.

The increased deductibles are also responsible for a slight reduction in written premium. However, Homesaver's marketing department designs a program to inform policyholders that deductible increases have resulted in policy credits and provided them an opportunity to save money on premiums. This program is successful, and the insurer loses very few customers as a result of the deductible change.

Monitor Results

The combined effect of increasing rates in some territories, nonrenewing loss-prone drivers, and increasing deductibles has a positive effect on the insurer's claim frequency, and the overall loss ratio drops to 71 percent. Although some premiums increase because of the rate adjustments, the actions taken in the auto portfolio result in a net reduction in total written premiums of $3 million over the year. In contrast, the sales incentive for producers and the rate decrease in the homeowners line result in significant growth, and the insurer meets its target of increasing homeowners written premiums by 10 percent.

Reducing the sales commission rate by 3 percent results in savings as well; although Homesaver's producers are not enthusiastic about the decrease. In an effort to support its loyal producers, the insurer increases its front-line underwriting authority. This change makes writing business with the Homesaver faster and easier for producers and allows them to provide better service to its customers. Increasing producers' underwriting authority also reduces some of the underwriting expenses incurred by the insurer. The combined result of these changes is an overall drop of 3.5 percent in Homesaver's expense ratio.

At the end of Year 2, the management and staff of Homesaver General have managed to exceed its goals and to show a small underwriting profit. See the exhibit "Homesaver General Company Year-End Results."

Homesaver General Company Year-End Results

Overall	Year 1	Year 2
Written premiums	$119 million	$119 million
Earned premiums	$113 million	$114 million
Incurred losses	$92 million	$81 million
Underwriting expenses	$34 million	$29.7 million
Underwriting profit	($13 million)	$3.3 million
Loss ratio	81%	71%
Expense ratio	28.5%	25%
Combined ratio	109.5%	96%
Personal Auto		
Written premiums	$83 million	$80 million
Earned premiums	$80 million	$78 million
Incurred losses	$72 million	$59 million
Underwriting expenses	$24 million	$20 million
Underwriting profit	($16 million)	($1 million)
Loss ratio	90%	75.6%
Expense ratio	29%	25%
Combined ratio	119%	100.6%
Homeowners		
Written premiums	$36 million	$39 million
Earned premiums	$33 million	$36 million
Incurred losses	$20 million	$22 million
Underwriting expenses	$10 million	$9.7 million
Underwriting profit	$3 million	$4.3 million
Loss ratio	61%	61%
Expense ratio	28%	25%
Combined ratio	89%	86%

*Numbers in parentheses indicate losses.

[DA05905]

Case Resolution

Case Analysis Steps	Conclusion
Examine results compared to goals	A comparison of results to goals indicates that Homesaver's overall combined ratio is unprofitable. The primary driver of this poor combined ratio is the insurer's poorly performing personal auto portfolio.
	Homesaver decides to focus primarily on making adjustments in the loss and expenses areas to improve its profitability.
Examine trends in results	Using RCA and reunderwriting, these were identified as potential areas of improvement:
	• Rate relativity problem for suburban drivers commuting to the city
	• Policies with application information that has not been updated in over five years
Formulate actions	An overall strategy was developed to reduce the combined ratio to 103 percent.
	These activities are planned to meet this goal:
	• Recalculate rate relativity factors for personal auto policies
	• Identify and reunderwrite all policies with more than three losses in the past five years
	• Increase physical damage deductibles on 60 percent of all auto policies
	• Launch a homeowners sales incentive program
	• Decrease homeowners rates by 10 percent
	• Reduce producer commission rates by 3 percent
Implement actions	Actions were implemented during Year 2 that yielded these results:
	• A $2.2 million reduction in auto written premiums due to reunderwriting activities
	• A $500,000 reduction in auto written premiums due to rate increases
	• Slight reduction in overall written premiums due to producer commission reduction
Monitor results	Year 2 results indicated an improvement in profitability:
	• Overall loss ratio dropped to 71 percent.
	• Overall expense ratio was reduced by 3.5 percent to 25 percent.
	• Overall combined ratio exceeded expectations at 96 percent.
	• Small underwriting profit earned.
	• Personal Auto combined ratio—100.6 percent (15 percent improvement).
	• Homeowners combined ratio—86 percent (3 percent improvement).

SUMMARY

Portfolio managers evaluate a portfolio's performance by analyzing results compared to profitability goals. When a portfolio is not meeting goals, the portfolio manager then applies analysis tools and approaches to identify root causes and correct the problems.

In carrying out the reunderwriting process, the portfolio manager uses various root cause analysis tools and techniques and the accumulated knowledge of other experiences of analyzing other portfolios, lines of insurance, and corrective actions taken.

A portfolio manager analyzes key portfolio indicators and policy characteristics to determine why a portfolio is losing policies in force, failing to gain new policies, or failing to retain current policyholders. Understanding the causes underlying the changes in these performance indicators or other key policy characteristics assists the portfolio manager in recommending possible corrective actions and in evaluating the considerations involved in implementing them.

Reunderwriting, as in AmberRock's case, describes a systematic process that a portfolio manager can use to identify a portfolio's variations in results compared to goals and then take corrective actions to improve results. It involves these steps: analyzing the portfolio, identifying and distinguishing the problems, formulating possible corrective actions, selecting corrective actions, implementing corrective actions, and monitoring the portfolio.

Personal lines portfolio managers must be aware of emerging trends that will affect their company's book of business. This requires researching the methods available for evaluating the portfolio to improve efficiency and profitability.

Insurers establish profitability goals and periodically monitor the performance of the key components of profitability. There are several options available to improve profitability when targets are not being met.

ASSIGNMENT NOTES

1. iSixSigma, "Determine the Root Cause: 5 Whys," www.isixsigma.com//library/content/c0206109.asp (accessed February 25, 2010).
2. "Root and Common Cause Analysis and Corrective Action," Department of Energy, May 31, 2006, www.hanford.gov/orp/upload_files/TFC-ESHQ-O_ADM-C11.pdf (accessed February 25, 2010).
3. American Academy of Actuaries, "The Use of Credit History for Personal Lines of Insurance; Report to the National Association of Insurance Commissioners" (Washington, DC: American Academy of Actuaries, 2002), p. 12.

Index

Page numbers in boldface refer to pages where the word or phrase is defined.